Emotion Regulation in Couples and Families

Emotion Regulation in Couples and Families

Pathways to Dysfunction and Health

EDITED BY

Douglas K. Snyder, Jeffry A. Simpson, and Jan N. Hughes

AMERICAN PSYCHOLOGICAL ASSOCIATION

Washington, DC

Published by
American Psychological Association
750 First Street, NE
Washington, DC 20002
www.apa.org

To order
APA Order Department
P.O. Box 92984
Washington, DC 20090-2984
Tel: (800) 374-2721; Direct: (202) 336-5510
Fax: (202) 336-5502; TDD/TTY: (202) 336-6123
Online: www.apa.org/books/
E-mail: order@apa.org

In the U.K., Europe, Africa, and the Middle East, copies may be ordered from
American Psychological Association
3 Henrietta Street
Covent Garden, London
WC2E 8LU England

Typeset in Goudy by Stephen McDougal, Mechanicsville, MD

Printer: United Book Press, Inc., Baltimore, MD
Cover Designer: Minker Design, Bethesda, MD
Technical/Production Editor: Genevieve Gill

The opinions and statements published are the responsibility of the authors, and such opinions and statements do not necessarily represent the policies of the American Psychological Association.

Library of Congress Cataloging-in-Publication Data

Emotion regulation in couples and families : pathways to dysfunction and health / edited by Douglas K. Snyder, Jeffry A. Simpson, Jan N. Hughes.— 1st ed.
    p. cm.
Includes bibliographical references and indexes.
ISBN 1-59147-394-2
1. Emotions. 2. Emotions—Social aspects. 3. Interpersonal relations. I. Snyder, Douglas K. II. Simpson, Jeffry A. III. Hughes, Jan N., 1949–

BF531.E4955 2006
152.4—dc22   2005031777

British Library Cataloguing-in-Publication Data
A CIP record is available from the British Library.

Printed in the United States of America
First Edition

To my wife, Linda, and to Christopher, Eric, Natalie, and Jason,
for your love and support.
—*Douglas K. Snyder*

To Cindy, Chris, and Natalie, for your support and
the many good times that we have shared.
—*Jeffry A. Simpson*

To Mrs. Harding, my kindergarten teacher, for a good start.
—*Jan N. Hughes*

CONTENTS

ABOUT THE EDITORS

Douglas K. Snyder, PhD, is a professor and the director of clinical psychology training at Texas A&M University. He received the American Psychological Association's 2005 award for Distinguished Contributions to Family Psychology for his work on empirical approaches to assessment and interventions with distressed couples. He is the author of the widely used *Marital Satisfaction Inventory* and is coeditor of *Treating Difficult Couples*. He received the American Association for Marriage and Family Therapy's 1992 Outstanding Research Award for his 4-year follow-up study comparing behavioral and insight-oriented approaches to couple therapy, funded by the National Institute of Mental Health. Dr. Snyder is a fellow of the American Psychological Association and has served as associate editor for the *Journal of Consulting and Clinical Psychology* and the *Journal of Family Psychology*.

Jeffry A. Simpson, PhD, is a professor of psychology at the University of Minnesota, Twin Cities Campus. His primary research interests center on adult attachment processes, models of human mating, idealization processes in relationships, the management of empathic accuracy in relationships, and social influence strategies. He is a fellow of the American Psychological Association and the American Psychological Society. From 1998 to 2001, he served as editor of the journal *Personal Relationships* and currently serves as an associate editor for the *Journal of Personality and Social Psychology: Interpersonal Relations and Group Processes*. In addition, he has served on grant panels at the National Science Foundation and the National Institute of Mental Health. His various programs of research on close relationships have been funded by grants from the National Science Foundation, the National Institute of Mental Health, and the Marsden Foundation in New Zealand.

Jan N. Hughes, PhD, is a professor of educational psychology at Texas A&M University. She is a distinguished research fellow in the College of Education and Human Development, and her primary research interests center on the development and treatment of childhood aggression, teacher–student relationships as developmental resources, the development of social and emotional competencies, and peer relationships. The National Institute of Child Health and Human Development, the National Institute on Drug Abuse, and the U.S. Department of Education have funded her research. She serves on the editorial boards of the *Journal of Clinical Child and Adolescent Psychology* and the *Journal of School Psychology*. A fellow of the American Psychological Association, she has served in numerous leadership roles including president of the division of School Psychology.

CONTRIBUTORS

William F. Arsenio, PhD, Ferkauf Graduate School of Psychology, Yeshiva University, New York

Lisa Feldman Barrett, PhD, Department of Psychology, Boston College, Boston, MA

Marc Brackett, PhD, Department of Psychology, Yale University, New Haven, CT

Mina Cladis, PhD, Department of Psychology, Vassar College, Poughkeepsie, NY

M. Lynne Cooper, PhD, Department of Psychological Sciences, University of Missouri, Columbia

E. Mark Cummings, PhD, Department of Psychology, University of Notre Dame, IN

Nancy Eisenberg, PhD, Department of Psychology, Arizona State University, Tempe

Barbara H. Fiese, PhD, Department of Psychology, Syracuse University, Syracuse, NY

Mindy E. Flanagan, PhD, Roudebush Veterans Administration Medical Center, Indianapolis, IN

Alan E. Fruzzetti, PhD, Department of Psychology, University of Nevada, Reno

Rhonda N. Goldman, PhD, School of Professional Psychology, Argosy University, Schaumburg, IL; The Family Institute at Northwestern University, Chicago, IL

Leslie S. Greenberg, PhD, Department of Psychology, York University, Toronto, Ontario, Canada

Daisy Grewal, MS, Department of Psychology, Yale University, New Haven, CT

James J. Gross, PhD, Department of Psychology, Stanford University, Stanford, CA

Neta Horesh, PhD, Department of Psychology, Bar-Ilan University, Ramat-Gan, Israel

Jan N. Hughes, PhD, Department of Educational Psychology, Texas A&M University, College Station

Katherine M. Iverson, MA, Department of Psychology, University of Nevada, Reno

Oliver P. John, PhD, Department of Psychology, University of California, Berkeley

Francis J. Keefe, PhD, Department of Psychiatry and Behavioral Sciences and Psychology: Social and Health Sciences, Duke University Medical Center and Duke University, Durham, NC

Peggy S. Keller, MA, Department of Psychology, University of Notre Dame, Notre Dame, IN

Jeffrey Labban, BA, Department of Psychiatry and Behavioral Sciences, Duke University Medical Center, Durham, NC

Melinda S. Leidy, MA, Department of Psychology, University of California, Riverside

David J. McDowell, PhD, Department of Clinical and Social Psychology, University of Rochester, Rochester, NY

Lada Micheas, MS, Department of Psychological Sciences, University of Missouri, Columbia

Mario Mikulincer, PhD, Department of Psychology, Bar-Ilan University, Ramat-Gan, Israel

Ross D. Parke, PhD, Department of Psychology, University of California, Riverside

Paula R. Pietromonaco, PhD, Department of Psychology, University of Massachusetts, Amherst

Laura S. Porter, PhD, Department of Psychiatry and Behavioral Sciences, Duke University Medical Center, Durham, NC

Sally I. Powers, EdD, Department of Psychology, University of Massachusetts, Amherst

Jane M. Richards, PhD, Department of Psychology, University of Texas, Austin

Peter Salovey, PhD, Department of Psychology, Yale University, New Haven, CT

Phillip R. Shaver, PhD, Department of Psychology, University of California, Davis

Jeffry A. Simpson, PhD, Department of Psychology, University of Minnesota, Minneapolis

Douglas K. Snyder, PhD, Department of Psychology, Texas A&M University, College Station

Amelia E. Talley, MA, Department of Psychological Sciences, University of Missouri, Columbia

Carlos Valiente, PhD, Department of Family and Human Development, Arizona State University, Tempe

Emotion Regulation in Couples and Families

INTRODUCTION: CROSS-DISCIPLINARY APPROACHES TO EMOTION REGULATION

JEFFRY A. SIMPSON, JAN N. HUGHES, AND DOUGLAS K. SNYDER

In recent years, there has been growing interest in emotion regulation processes within different areas of psychology. This interest has been sparked both by the development of new theoretical models of emotion regulation processes and by the growing realization that poor or inappropriate regulation of emotions often constitutes a core component of common individual and interpersonal problems. Indeed, the ability to effectively control and manage emotions during social interactions—especially interpersonally caustic negative emotions—may assume a pivotal role in keeping individuals and their significant relationships happy and functioning well. New theoretical approaches to understanding emotion regulation (e.g., chaps. 2 and 3, this volume) and new process models outlining exactly how emotions might be regulated (e.g., chap. 1, this volume) have begun to illuminate when, how, and why people succeed or fail to regulate certain emotions in social contexts. This theoretical work is also beginning to identify some of the important processes, both intrapersonal and interpersonal, that may be associated with successful versus unsuccessful emotion regulation. For example, more emotionally intelligent individuals, who are particularly skilled at controlling and managing negative emotions, tend to be better adjusted on many different dimensions than those who are less emotionally intelligent. In addition, more emotionally intelligent, well-regulated people are often more likely to be involved in happier and better-functioning relationships, including romantic and family-based ones.

From an applied standpoint, a deeper understanding of how emotion regulation processes operate in both community and clinical populations could eventually help practitioners to more effectively treat a wide range of interpersonal problems and disorders, many of which may originate, at least in part, from poor or deficient emotion regulation. As several chapters in this volume highlight, delineating how various emotion regulation processes and psychological mechanisms vary across community and clinical populations may shed important light on some of the conditions that initiate, sustain, or potentially ameliorate several comorbid interpersonal disorders.

When we convened the Texas A&M University Conference on Emotion Regulation in Couples and Families in February 2004, on which this volume is based, our overarching goal was to bring together some of the top international scholars who were conducting important, cutting-edge research on emotion regulation in different fields of psychology. We anticipated that these individuals would (a) openly propose and discuss how the construct of emotion regulation should be optimally conceptualized, defined, and measured; (b) share and critique the major theories, ideas, and knowledge on important emotion regulation processes and outcomes in their respective fields; and (c) begin to develop some cross-disciplinary theories, models, hypotheses, or new ways of thinking about emotion regulation that would facilitate cross-disciplinary work among different fields in psychology (e.g., clinical, developmental, educational, family studies, social–personality, and quantitative–methodological). This book is the legacy of that successful conference.

The inability to regulate emotions can increase an individual's risk for problems in many social, interpersonal, academic, work-related, and health domains. This book covers a wide range of important theoretical, conceptual, and methodological issues that are critical to understanding both normal and adaptive emotion regulation processes as well as more dysfunctional ones. In particular, the chapters in the book present empirical findings relevant to emotion regulation processes both within and between individuals involved in different types of relationships across the life span. The chapters also contain myriad insights and implications for clinical intervention, public policy, and directions for future research. Because the chapter contributors hail from different academic disciplines and have diverse theoretical perspectives regarding the role that emotion regulation processes might play in both healthy and dysfunctional outcomes, the book should be relevant to a broad range of people who share an interest in emotion regulation, including clinical and counseling psychologists, developmental psychologists, social and personality psychologists, and communication and family studies scholars, to name a few. In addition to focusing on recent research findings, the book also highlights therapeutic and public policy issues. Thus, it should also be quite useful to practitioners who are working with children, adolescents, adults, couples, and families, especially those who struggle with emotion regulation difficulties.

CONCEPTUAL AND THEORETICAL ISSUES

Because intense research interest in emotion regulation is a recent phenomenon and emotion regulation has broad relevance to many domains of human functioning across the life span (including emotional and physical health, learning, work, and social relationships), it is not surprising that a consensus definition of emotion regulation has not yet emerged. Whereas some researchers decry the lack of theoretical consensus and operational definitions (Cole, Martin, & Dennis, 2004), at this point in the development of the science of emotion regulation, a degree of pluralism in theoretical conceptualizations, definitions, and measures prevents the premature narrowing of research foci and methods.

The authors in this volume agree on much concerning the construct of emotion regulation yet also differ in important ways. Whether explicitly or implicitly, they agree that the construct of emotion regulation includes conscious and unconscious, voluntary and less-than-voluntary, physiological, behavioral, and cognitive processes that permit individuals to "influence which emotions they have, when they have them, and how these emotions are experienced and expressed" (chap. 1, p. 14). Furthermore, emotion regulation is viewed as functionally adaptive in that it facilitates attainment of one's goals. As a corollary, emotion regulation, which is adaptive, is distinguished from emotion control, which can be adaptive (e.g., when suppressing a display of anger toward one's boss) or maladaptive (e.g., in the case of an inhibited boy who suppresses his expression of both positive and negative emotions, resulting in poor peer relationships and restricted exploration of his environment). In addition, regulation can involve the initiation, maintenance, and expression of positive emotions as well as the avoidance, minimization, and masking of negative ones. Generally, the authors accept Gross and colleagues' distinction in chapter 1 between antecedent-focused emotion regulation, which involves regulatory processes that precede and anticipate an emotional reaction, and response-focused regulation, which occurs in response to an activated emotion. The authors also concur that emotion regulation is only one aspect of "an interrelated family or cluster of abilities that work together" (chap. 7, p. 145) to achieve interpersonal and intrapersonal goals.

Despite these areas of general consensus, the authors' conceptualizations of emotion regulation diverge explicitly or implicitly in important ways that reflect points of disagreement discussed in recent literature (e.g., Bridges, Denham, & Ganiban, 2004; Campos, Frankel, & Camras, 2004; Cole et al., 2004). For example, how much "voluntariness" over some activity is required for it to be considered emotion regulation? Grewal, Brackett, and Salovey's definition of emotion regulation (chap. 2) emphasizes conscious and voluntary aspects (i.e., "the ability to monitor and label one's own feelings effectively and self-efficacy about the ability to modify these feelings, as well as the knowledge and motivation to use effective strategies to alter emotions," p. 41). Mikulincer, Shaver, and Horesh (chap. 4), however, view emotion regulation as an aspect of an individual's attachment system that operates predominantly outside of conscious awareness and influences individuals' emotional reactions to threats to their security. Valiente and Eisenberg (chap. 6) engage the "voluntariness" issue head on, distinguishing between reactive control, which is considered an aspect of temperament evident in early infancy, and effortful control, which is more voluntary, emerges toward the end of the first year of life, is more influenced by socialization experiences, and becomes increasingly important with age in contributing to individual differences in coping with emotions.

In addition, the authors also differ in their relative focus on discrete emotional, cognitive, or physiological responses to emotionally arousing situations versus organized patterns of responding. The field appears to be moving more to configurations of emotion expression and regulation (see chaps. 8 and 13). As the field moves in this direction, it will be important to differentiate between processes associated with the initial arousal of emotions (e.g., individual differences in general emotional reactivity) and those associated with emotion regulation processes per se (see chap. 1). To date, insufficient attention has been focused on questions of whether or how emotion regulation processes might be influenced by stable individual differences in the tendency to initially experience stronger versus weaker emotional reactions in response to specific stimuli. Effective emotion regulation may, for instance, be more difficult to achieve for individuals who habitually experience strong emotional reactions to certain stimuli or events.

Given the lack of consistency in operational definitions of emotion regulation, it is important that researchers clearly link their measurements of emotion regulation to theoretical conceptualizations, a goal that is met to varying degrees by the authors in this volume. For example, Valiente and Eisenberg (chap. 6) achieve this when they distinguish between two aspects of emotion regulation that differ in voluntariness. Cummings and Keller (chap. 8) accomplish this by studying emotion regulation in one context (marital conflict) and interpreting their findings within the broader framework of the emotional security hypothesis, which has strong empirical and theoretical support. Gross and his colleagues (chap. 1) classify emotion regulation strategies in terms of when they have their primary impact on the emotion-generation process. Adopting an attachment framework, Pietromonaco and her colleagues (chap. 3) distinguish between two affect-based processes that underlie working models of attachment: affect reactivity and affect regulation.

The emotion regulation area will benefit from continued efforts to define and operationalize key constructs. For example, when does another person's attempt to modify an individual's emotions constitute emotion regulation? Do strategies initiated by or perhaps imposed on another individual constitute emotion regulation, such as a parent reminding her daughter that her unkind remark to another child resulted in the other child feeling sad (an example of an intrapersonal attempt to up-regulate empathy)? Does the common inference of "poor emotion regulation" when individuals display problematic or disruptive behavior overextend the construct, limiting its usefulness? Rejecting this concern, Cooper, Flanagan, Talley, and Micheas (chap. 9) assert that adolescent risk-taking behavior (e.g., alcohol abuse and aspects of sexual behavior) reflects an effort to regulate the quality of both positive and negative emotional experience. In a similar way, Arsenio (chap. 5) proposes a phenomenon of "happy victimization" as an indicator of poor emotion regulation, arguing that such victimizing behavior reflects either a failure to experience empathy that inhibits aggression or a moral or emotional deficit.

By bringing together in one volume scholars from diverse fields, one gains an appreciation of the wide range of conceptualizations, definitions, and measures of emotion regulation that exist across different contexts, ages, and purposes, ranging from understanding the origins of individual differences in emotion regulation to teaching one member of a couple how to relieve chronic pain experienced by his or her partner. We hope that the opportunity this volume provides to understand how different disciplines are approaching common issues in emotion regulation will lead to refined conceptualizations and measures that will be valuable both from scientific and clinical perspectives.

EMOTION REGULATION IN THE CONTEXT OF FAMILIES AND CLOSE RELATIONSHIPS

Attention to the role of parenting in the socialization of children's emotional competencies has a long history in child development. The authors in this volume contribute to this rich tradition by delineating how both specific parenting practices (see chaps. 6 and 7) and repetitive patterns of family interaction (chaps. 8 and 13) are associated with children's abilities to manage their emotions. Scholars from diverse backgrounds present converging evidence that secure mental representations of parent–child and family interactions may be responsible for some of the connections between family interactions and children's emotion regulation. The authors in this volume also "raise the bar" for research on how parenting socialization affects emotions, from studies demonstrating bivariate associations among various parenting behaviors and children's emotion-related skills to longitudinal studies testing causal pathways. Such designs are contributing greatly to our knowledge and understanding of how children's emotion regulatory skills and abilities both mediate and moderate the effects of parenting on children's social competence. These studies also permit the testing of bidirectional causal pathways between child and parent behaviors. Moreover, several research findings reported in these chapters highlight the fact that parenting and emotion regulation occur within a cultural context, and that links between parent emotion-related socialization behaviors and children's social competencies often differ across cultures.

Chapters in this volume also address the importance of emotion regulation in close relationships. As several chapters highlight, poor or inadequate emotion regulation at the intrapersonal level (i.e., within individuals) or the interpersonal level (i.e., between relationship partners) might be one of the primary grounds for relationship dissatisfaction and dissolution (see chaps. 2–4 and 11–12). Much more is currently known about how emotions are regulated intrapersonally (within individuals) than interpersonally (between individuals). Investigators are only beginning to propose and test dyadic models specifying how the emotion regulation abilities, skills, and styles of each relationship partner are related to important relationship outcomes experienced by one or both partners (e.g., perceptions of commitment, trust, satisfaction, or relationship longevity). Recent models derived from attachment theory, for example, suggest that having securely attached partners who regulate their emotions in a constructive, problem-focused manner may buffer even insecurely attached individuals from a host of negative interpersonal outcomes (see chap. 4). Nevertheless, our knowledge and understanding of when, how, and why certain individuals are proficient at managing their emotions in the service of calming and soothing their distressed partners whereas others are not remain surprisingly limited.

CLINICAL IMPLICATIONS

Because poor emotion regulation is linked with impaired social, emotional, and physical health across the life span, it is important to develop, test, and disseminate interventions to improve individuals' abilities to manage their emotions. The authors in this volume offer considerable guidance toward this effort. As Cummings and Keller (chap. 8) and others suggest, emotion-relevant socialization behaviors constitute organized patterns of responding that both affect and are affected by relationship schemas and representations. Thus, parent-focused interventions that extend beyond managing children's behavior to creating relationships characterized by warmth, acceptance, and mutuality are likely to pay larger dividends in terms of improving long-term child outcomes. Mikulincer et al. (chap. 4) report findings suggesting that interventions that help people to access secure mental representations in times of stress will increase their resiliency. The authors in the third section of the volume report promising outcomes from emotion-focused couples and family intervention research. For example, Keefe, Porter, and Labban (chap. 10) present evidence that supports their intervention targeting partner-assisted pain coping skills, which focuses on helping both patients experiencing persistent pain and their partners regulate emotional processes. Their intervention protocol involves training in both up-regulating positive emotions as well as down-regulating negative ones. Fruzzetti and Iverson (chap. 12) focus on a number of intrapersonal and interpersonal emotion regulation skills important to couple and family functioning, particularly as these relate to more serious emotional difficulties or psychopathology. Goldman and Greenberg's attention in chapter 11 to both process and outcome variables in intervention research ensures the continued refinement of emotion-focused treatments for distressed couples. Moving to a "whole family" approach, Fiese (chap. 13) reports findings indicating that interventions that help families establish or maintain family routines may enable families to better meet the demands of providing medical care to asthmatic children.

PLAN OF THE BOOK

The book is organized into four major parts. The chapters in Part I focus on cutting-edge theoretical and conceptual issues that are associated with emotion regulation processes. Each chapter adopts a slightly different theoretical stance toward understanding and explaining how individual differences and normative aspects of emotion regulation are likely to operate, both within individuals and between relationship partners. In chapter 1, for example, Gross, Richards, and John provide an overview of a newly developed emotion regulation process model that specifies when and how positive and negative emotions might be regulated, from before a discrete emotion is experienced (antecedent-focused strategies) to well after it has been felt (response-focused strategies). In the second chapter, Grewal, Brackett, and Salovey showcase recent theoretical and empirical work on emotional intelligence, a higher-level construct that subsumes emotion regulation processes. In chapter 3, Pietromonaco, Feldman Barrett, and Powers adopt an attachment theory perspective toward understanding and explaining emotion regulation processes.

Chapters in Part II of the book explicate some of the basic empirical linkages of family interactions and their mental representations with biological predispositions and individual differences in emotions and emotion regulation. In chapter 4, Mikulincer, Shaver, and Horesh present empirical evidence that indicates the way in which attachment processes are associated with individuals' responses to traumatic events and posttraumatic adjustment. Arsenio, in chapter 5, discusses how the lack of a mutually reciprocal, cooperative parent–child relationship may contribute to the phenomenon of "happy victimization." Valiente and Eisenberg (chap. 6) and Parke, McDowell, Cladis, and Leidy (chap. 7) present findings on connections between parenting and children's emotional development. Rather than focusing on the discrete strategies that parents use to influence their children's emotion regulatory abilities, Cummings and Keller (chap. 8) move to the representational level and test predictions from the emotional security hypothesis. In chapter 9, Cooper, Flanagan, Talley, and Micheas propose that risk-taking behaviors result from efforts to regulate the quality of both positive and negative emotional experiences.

The chapters in Part III center on how different aspects of individual and relationship functioning can be targeted by different clinical treatments and the specific mediating mechanisms that may underlie different interventions. Keefe, Porter, and Labban (chap. 10) discuss the role of emotion regulation processes within a broader biopsychosocial model, focusing on the experience and management of chronic pain. Goldman and Greenberg (chap. 11) examine basic processes of emotional expressiveness and responsiveness, including the ways in which expressiveness and responsiveness relate to couple intimacy and distress. Fruzzetti and Iverson (chap. 12) accentuate the importance of understanding and intervening in emotion regulation processes in couples and families, particularly when one member struggles with dysregulated emotions. In chapter 13, Fiese moves beyond a dyadic emphasis by adopting a "whole family" approach to examining emotion regulation in family routines and rituals.

In Part IV of the book, we (the editors) explicate implications of previous chapters for couple- and family-based research and intervention. In doing so, we offer several observations and recommendations regarding the most critical conceptual, methodological, and application issues that emotion regulation researchers will need to address and resolve in the future.

REFERENCES

Bridges, L. J., Denham, S. A., & Ganiban, J. M. (2004). Definitional issues in emotion regulation research. *Child Development, 75,* 340–345.

Campos, J. J., Frankel, C. B., & Camras, L. (2004). On the nature of emotion regulation. *Child Development, 75,* 377–394.

Cole, P. N., Martin, S. E., & Dennis, T. A. (2004). Emotion regulation as a scientific construct: Methodological challenges and directions for child development research. *Child Development, 75,* 317–333.

I

EMOTION REGULATION: THEORETICAL PERSPECTIVES

1

EMOTION REGULATION IN EVERYDAY LIFE

JAMES J. GROSS, JANE M. RICHARDS, AND OLIVER P. JOHN

Sometimes, our emotions lead us to do the oddest things. Grown men pull over so they can brawl over which driver is the bigger idiot. Parents lose their cool and bark hateful things at their children that they later regret. Adolescents who were best friends before a jealous spat vow never to speak again. And children throw tantrums as if on cue at the supermarket candy display.

Moments such as these are reminders of the fundamental role that emotion regulation plays in civilized life. Emotions can be helpful, providing crucial information about the state of one's interactions with the world (Clore, 1994) or speeding one's responses in life-threatening situations (Frijda, 1986). However, people frequently experience strong emotions that need to be managed if they are to keep their appointments, careers, and friendships. Indeed, successful emotion regulation is a prerequisite for adaptive functioning. To get along with others, one must be able to regulate which emotions one has and how one experiences and expresses these emotions.

Over the past 2 decades, emotion regulation has become the focus of intense research activity in both child (e.g., Thompson, 1991) and adult (e.g., Gross, 1998) literatures, as demonstrated by the chapters in this volume. What is not yet clear, however, is (a) how to best conceptualize the potentially overwhelming array of emotion regulatory processes, and (b) how people actually regulate their emotions in everyday life. In this chapter, we first discuss how we are using the slippery terms "emotion" and "emotion regulation." Next, we present a process model of emotion regulation and review experimental and individual-difference data relevant to two important forms of emotion regulation. Then, we examine the question of how people regulate their emotions in everyday life, presenting new data from studies that represent three major empirical approaches to this issue. We conclude by considering what these findings might tell us about the larger issues related to emotion regulation as it occurs in everyday life.

CONCEPTUAL, THEORETICAL, AND METHODOLOGICAL ISSUES

Our starting point is a conception of emotion that is shared with a number of prior theorists (e.g., Ekman, 1972; Frijda, 1986). According to this conception, the emotion-generative process begins when an external or internal event signals to the individual that something important may be at stake. When attended to and evaluated in certain ways, these emotion cues trigger a coordinated set of response tendencies that involve experiential, behavioral, and central and peripheral physiological systems. Once these emotion response tendencies arise, they may be modulated in various ways, thereby shaping the individual's observable responses.

Emotion regulation refers to attempts individuals make to influence which emotions they have, when they have them, and how these emotions are experienced and expressed. Such efforts may be relatively automatic or controlled, conscious or unconscious. It has also been asserted (but not empirically demonstrated) that emotion regulation may involve the up- or down-regulation of various aspects of negative or positive emotions (Parrott, 1993). Thus conceived, emotion regulation is one of several forms of affect regulation, all of which involve attempts to alter some aspect of the interplay between the individual and the environment that is coded by the individual in a valenced (good or bad) manner. Emotion regulation may be distinguished from three other forms of affect regulation: coping, mood regulation, and psychological defenses (for a more detailed exposition of these differences, see Gross, 1998).

Coping refers to the organism's efforts to manage its relations with an environment that taxes its ability to respond (Lazarus & Folkman, 1984). Coping and emotion regulation overlap, but coping includes nonemotional actions taken to achieve nonemotional goals (e.g., studying hard to pass an important exam), whereas emotion regulation is concerned with emotions in whatever context they may arise. *Mood regulation* refers to attempts to alter a second important class of affective responses, which, compared with emotions, are typically of longer duration and lesser intensity and are less likely to involve responses to specific "objects" (Parkinson, Totterdell, Briner, & Reynolds, 1996). Thus, the focus in mood regulation research is typically the activities people engage in to reduce negative mood states (e.g., running, sleeping well). A third type of affect regulation is *psychological defense*, long a focus of psychodynamic theorizing and research. As with coping, the domain of psychological defenses overlaps with the domain of emotion regulation, but defenses typically refer to relatively stable characteristics of an individual that operate outside of awareness to decrease the subjective experience of anxiety and other negative affect. Studies of emotion regulation, by contrast, have as their focus the full range of emotions and consider both stable individual differences and the basic processes that operate across individuals.

A PROCESS MODEL OF EMOTION REGULATION

If emotions are seen as involving a coordinated set of responses that arise during an organism–environment interaction, emotion regulation strategies may be differentiated along the timeline of the unfolding emotional responses (Gross, 1998, 1999, 2001; John & Gross, 2004). That is, emotion regulation strategies may be distinguished in terms of when they have their primary impact on the emotion-generative process. We have proposed a process model of emotion regulation that embodies this approach, shown in Figure 1.1.

At the broadest level, this model distinguishes between *antecedent-focused* and *response-focused* emotion regulation strategies. Antecedent-focused strategies refer to things one does before the emotion response tendencies have become fully activated and have changed one's behavior and one's peripheral physiological responding. The goal of such antecedent-focused strategies is the modification of future emotional responses. For example, on hearing a noxious comment from an acquaintance, one might cognitively reevaluate the comment (e.g., as a sign of insecurity) and thereby alter the entire emotion trajectory, feeling pity for the acquaintance rather than anger. By contrast, response-focused strategies refer to things one does once an emotion is already underway, after the response tendencies have already been generated. The focus of such response-focused strategies is the management of existing emotions. For example, one might try to appear unfazed by a noxious comment despite underlying feelings of anger.

As shown in Figure 1.1, five families of more specific strategies can be located along the timeline of the emotion process (Gross, 1998, 2001). *Situation selection*, denoted in Figure 1.1 by the solid line toward one situation (S1) rather than another (S2), refers to approaching or avoiding certain people, places, or activities so as to regulate emotion. Once a situation is

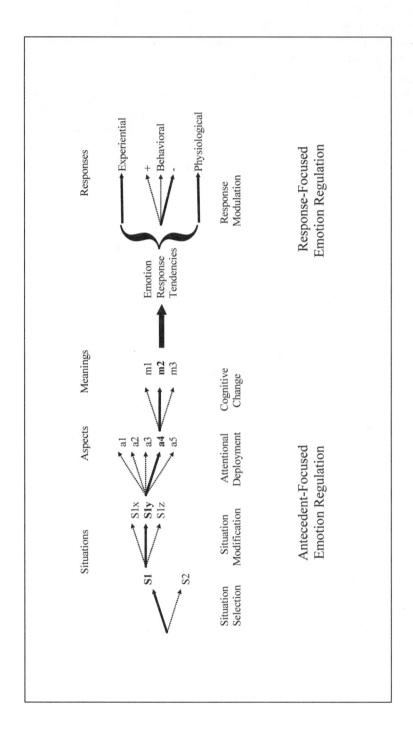

Figure 1.1. A process model of emotion regulation. From "Emotion Regulation in Adulthood: Timing Is Everything," by J. J. Gross, 2001, *Current Directions in Psychological Science, 10,* p. 215. Copyright 2001 by Blackwell Publishing, Ltd. Adapted with permission.

selected (e.g., S1), *situation modification* acts on it so as to modify its emotional impact, creating different situations (S1x, S1y, or S1z in the figure). Third, situations have many different aspects (e.g., a1, a2), and *attentional deployment* can be used to pick which aspects to focus on. Once one is focused on a particular aspect of the situation, *cognitive change* constructs one of the many possible meanings (e.g., m1, m2, m3) that may be attached to that aspect. Finally, *response modulation* refers to attempts to influence emotion response tendencies once they already have been elicited. Response modulation is illustrated in Figure 1.1 by decreasing (–) rather than increasing (+) expressive behavior but may also involve altering experience or physiology.

TWO SPECIFIC STRATEGIES: COGNITIVE REAPPRAISAL AND EXPRESSIVE SUPPRESSION

Rather than studying all types of emotion regulation at once, our research strategy has been to focus on a smaller number of well-defined strategies. We considered three factors when selecting which strategies to study: (a) strategies should be used commonly in everyday life; (b) strategies should lend themselves to both experimental manipulation and individual-difference analyses; and (c) because the distinction between antecedent-focused and response-focused strategies is so central to our model, we wanted to include one exemplar of each in our studies. Two specific strategies met these criteria: cognitive reappraisal and expressive suppression.

Cognitive reappraisal is a form of cognitive change that involves construing a potentially emotion-eliciting situation in a way that changes its emotional impact. This form of emotion regulation was the subject of early work by Lazarus and colleagues, who showed that leading participants to view a potentially upsetting surgical procedure in more analytical and detached terms decreased their subjective and physiological responses (Lazarus & Alfert, 1964). Cognitive reappraisal also was implicated in Mischel's early work on delay of gratification, which showed that leading children to think about food treats in ways that made them more abstract (e.g., putting a mental "picture frame" around a cookie) decreased children's impulse to eat the cookie, allowing them to obtain a preferred but delayed reward (Mischel & Moore, 1973).

Expressive suppression is a form of response modulation that involves inhibiting ongoing emotion-expressive behavior (Gross & Levenson, 1993). It has been observed repeatedly that outwardly inexpressive individuals are often more physiologically responsive than their more expressive counterparts (e.g., Jones, 1950). Along similar lines, behavioral inhibition associated with interpersonal deception leads to heightened physiological responses (DePaulo, Kashy, Kirkendol, Wyer, & Epstein, 1996). Until recently, however, few studies have experimentally manipulated expressive suppression and observed how suppression actually affects the components of the unfolding emotional response.

AFFECTIVE, COGNITIVE, AND SOCIAL CONSEQUENCES OF REAPPRAISAL AND SUPPRESSION

Because reappraisal occurs early in the emotion-generative process, we hypothesized that it should be able to modify the entire emotional sequence before emotion response tendencies have been fully generated. This suggests that reappraisal may lead to reductions in negative emotion experience and expression, require relatively few additional cognitive resources to implement, and produce interpersonal behavior that is appropriately focused on the interaction partner and is perceived by such partners as emotionally engaging and responsive. Suppression, by contrast, comes relatively late in the emotion-generative process and primarily modifies the behavioral aspect of the emotion response tendencies, without reducing the experience of negative emotion. Because suppression comes late in the emotion-generative process, it requires the individual to effortfully manage emotion response tendencies as they continually arise. These repeated efforts should consume cognitive resources that could otherwise be used for optimal performance in the social contexts in which the emotions arise. Moreover, suppression may create a sense of discrepancy between inner experience and outer expression, leading to feelings of inauthenticity and impeding the development of emotionally close relationships.

In a series of experimental and individual-difference studies, we have tested these hypotheses regarding the affective, cognitive, and social consequences of reappraisal and suppression (for a review of these studies, see Gross, 2002; Gross & John, 2003; John & Gross, 2004). Across experiments, we have found that reappraisal effectively decreases emotion experience and expressive behavior in negative-emotion-eliciting contexts, and it does so without appreciable cognitive, physiological, or interpersonal costs. In individual-difference studies, we have found evidence that individuals who make more frequent use of reappraisal show enhanced functioning in the domains of emotion and interpersonal functioning, without any detectable cognitive or social costs.

Suppression, by contrast, is effective in down-regulating expressive behavior but fails to provide subjective relief in the context of negative emotions. Moreover, suppression has substantial physiological and cognitive costs. Specifically, experiments show that suppression leads to increased sympathetic activation of the cardiovascular system, worse memory for social information such as names or facts about individuals seen on slides (Richards & Gross, 2000), and social interactions that are less satisfying for both suppressors and their interaction partners (Butler et al., 2003). Over the longer term, individuals who make more frequent use of suppression show worse functioning in emotional, interpersonal, and well-being domains. In addition, suppressors show worse memory for conversations, as well as for emotion-eliciting events previously described in a daily diary.

EMPIRICAL FOUNDATIONS: EMOTION REGULATION IN EVERYDAY LIFE

These studies demonstrate the divergent impact of differing forms of emotion regulation such as reappraisal and suppression. Now what is needed is a broader understanding of when and how individuals actually regulate their emotions in everyday life. A number of pressing questions need to be addressed. First, which emotions are actually the target of regulation? Intuitively, negative emotions such as anger seem likely candidates. Parrott (1993) has suggested that positive emotions also are regulated, although the evidence for this proposition is not yet in. Second, given that emotions have many aspects (e.g., behavioral, experiential, physiological), which aspects are typically targeted? Hedonic accounts suggest that people generally want to feel good, not bad. These accounts suggest that people want to change the inner experience of emotion. Ekman's (1972) notion of "display rules" highlights another important target for regulation, namely expressive behavior. Third, what strategies are actually used to regulate emotion in everyday life? We have focused on two particular forms of regulation, but we do not yet know how frequently these and related strategies are used in everyday life. To illustrate how such questions might be addressed, we describe recent work that represents three complementary approaches to studying emotion regulation.

Approach 1: The Semistructured Interview

One approach to studying emotion regulation is to ask people about their emotion regulatory efforts. To illustrate this approach, we present a study based on semistructured interviews in which young adults described a time in the past 2 weeks when they regulated their emotions. This approach is attractive for several reasons. First, although emotion regulation includes nonconscious aspects, its conscious aspects are salient and important (Gross, 1999), and an interview format provides insight into people's regulatory goals and activities. Second, using a relatively recent time frame makes it possible to capture events while they are still fresh. Third, a semistructured interview format permits participants to describe events in their own words but also makes it possible to cover roughly the same ground with each participant. Our questions were as follows:

1. Would each participant recall an emotion regulatory episode?
2. If so, which emotions would be selected for regulation?
3. Which aspects of these emotions would be targeted, and would participants be trying to up- or down-regulate?
4. Which emotion regulation strategies would be used?
5. Would these emotion regulatory efforts vary by social context?

To answer these questions, we interviewed 91 participants (70 women), using the following prompt:

> I would like you to think of a time in the past week or two when you tried to alter your emotions. Go ahead and take a few moments to think of a time when you tried to alter your emotions. When you're ready, I'd like you to describe this time to me in as much detail as you can.

Participants were videotaped as they described the episode in their own words. Interviews typically lasted about 15 minutes. Prompts were used as needed to ensure that our core questions were answered.

Transcripts of the interviews were coded independently by two trained raters. Coding categories included (a) the primary target emotion (e.g., anger, amusement); (b) the response system primarily targeted (e.g., behavioral, experiential, physiological) and the direction of regulation (up- or down-regulation); and (c) the strategy used. In addition, coders rated the social context (social or nonsocial), and, for social emotion regulation episodes, coders indicated who was with the participant (e.g., stranger, friend). Target emotions were subsequently coded independently by the first two authors. In a first step, the 35 target emotions collectively generated by the participants were combined into 24 distinct emotions by combining highly overlapping terms (e.g., anger included "mad," "irritated," and "angry"). In a second step, emotions were coded as negatively valenced, positively valenced, or neither.

Our first question was whether participants would be able to describe recent emotion regulation episodes. Indeed, we found that all of our 91 participants were able to describe a time in the past 2 weeks when they had tried to regulate their emotions.

Regulation Episodes and Target Emotions

The episodes described by participants varied substantially. Some participants described episodes in which they changed their thinking to decrease negative emotion:

> Yesterday I was life guarding . . . and . . . I fell into the pool wearing all my clothes . . . [I] could've gotten really mad but I just decided to laugh it off . . . I suppose [I] altered my anger into amusement. [I was trying to change] my response to the situation. Changing my outlook on what happened throughout the day when I could've been angry about everything. But I

decided to laugh about it—just kind of blow it off. So basically I thought about it and put it in perspective.

Other participants described episodes involving positive emotions. For example, one participant concentrated his efforts on changing his expressive behavior:

We had a paper that was given back in my class and my roommate actually is in that class also. And we got very conflicting grades. He got a very bad grade, and I got a very good grade. . . I didn't work very hard on this paper, so . . . I was surprised. My roommate actually did some work and didn't get a good grade, so he was very, very down about it. So I kind of had to cover my emotions. Instead of acting happy and surprised, I . . . had to kind of cover up—I was very happy inside, but at the same time, I didn't want to show up my roommate because he's my friend too. So I kind of put on my depressed face and you know, my academic sad face and said, "Oh well, I didn't do well either." I guess I was trying to [change] my expressions on my face more than anything.

Across the 91 respondents' regulation episodes, 24 types of emotion were represented. The three most common were anger (23%), sadness (22%), and anxiety (10%). Together, these accounted for more than half of the emotion regulation episodes. The majority of the episodes described concerned negative emotions (81%). However, as predicted by Parrott (1993), there were also instances of regulating positive emotions (9%), including three instances of regulating happiness, two instances each of regulating romantic attraction and excitement, and one of regulating interest, as well as a number of episodes involving the regulation of less clearly valenced emotional states (10%), with two instances each of regulating surprise, tiredness, and apathy, as well as one instance each of boredom, confusion, and shock.

Emotion Response Systems and the Direction of Regulation

Emotions involve changes across multiple systems, including behavioral, experiential, and physiological response systems (Lang, Greenwald, Bradley, & Hamm, 1993). It is not clear, however, which aspects of the emotional response people typically regulate. Our findings show that regulation efforts focused almost equally on expressive behavior and subjective experience. Forty-eight percent of episodes involved changes to expressive behavior (37% involved nonverbal behavior alone, 1% involved verbal behavior alone, and 10% involved changes to both nonverbal and verbal behavior). Fifty-three percent of episodes involved changes to subjective experience. Only 2% of episodes involved changes to physiological responses. These percentages total more than 100% because some episodes involved changes to more than one response system. In terms of the direction of change, all but one instance of emotion regulation (which involved behavioral regulation) primarily involved emotion down-regulation.

Emotion Regulation Strategies

Our process model of emotion regulation (Figure 1.1) suggests that emotion regulatory processes can be categorized on the basis of when a given emotion regulation strategy has its primary impact on the emotion-generative process (Gross, 2001). Within the broader rubric of antecedent-focused and response-focused emotion regulation we have argued that five more specific families of emotion regulation strategies may be discerned.

How frequently are these five emotion regulation strategies used in everyday life? We found that whereas situation selection and situation modification were rare, each represented by only one exemplar, the other three types of regulation were much more common. Attention deployment was used in 39% of episodes. Cognitive change was used in 33% of episodes, and a full 83% of these involved cognitive reappraisal (25/30), including the first example given earlier. Finally, response modulation was used in 53% of episodes, and 40% of these (19/48) involved expressive suppression, including the second example given earlier. Although situation selection and modification may be less prototypic, or may occur outside of awareness, these findings nonetheless provide strong evidence for the common use of three major families of emotion regulation strategies (attentional deployment, cognitive change, response modulation) in everyday life.

Social Context

Emotion researchers have long emphasized the social embeddedness of emotional responding (Scherer, Summerfield, & Wallbott, 1983). Consistent with this view, we found that 98% of the emotion regulation episodes took place in the presence of other people, and in only 2% of episodes were the respondents clearly alone. Furthermore, episodes that occurred in a social context appeared to follow a "closeness gradient." Regulation episodes that were described by participants in the interviews most commonly involved friends (19%), romantic interests (14%), roommates (11%), or family members (10%), and were least likely to involve mere acquaintances (3%) or disliked others (2%).

Approach 2: The Survey

The interview data derived from our first approach suggest that emotion regulation in everyday life predominantly involves negative emotions (e.g., anger, anxiety, sadness), whose behavioral and experiential aspects participants try to down-regulate. However, there were also instances of the up-regulation of emotion and the regulation of positive emotion. The richness of the emotion regulation episodes captured by these interviews suggests the need to cast a very broad net indeed when examining emotion regulation in everyday life, even when one focuses—as we have done here—primarily on consciously accessible emotion regulation processes.

One limitation of our interview-based approach, however, is that we did not standardize the emotions we asked participants to consider when selecting their emotion regulation episode. A second limitation is that we cannot be sure how representative these episodes are, given that our strategy was to ask participants to describe the most salient episode of emotion regulation during the past 2 weeks. A third limitation of the interview-based approach is that it typically limits samples to relatively small sizes. Because conducting, transcribing, and coding interviews is terribly time-consuming, interview-based studies often use such small samples that robust tests of group differences (e.g., sex, ethnicity) are not possible.

To address these issues, we next used survey methods to present a standardized set of potential targets of emotion regulation to 500 undergraduates (305 women) in a mixed-ethnic sample (4% African American, 35% Asian American, 39% Caucasian, 13% Latino, and 9% other). We asked participants to describe not a single emotion regulation episode, but rather if and how they generally regulate the experience and expression of 15 discrete emotions in everyday life. Finally, we examined the role played by sex, ethnicity, and social context.

To assess frequency of emotion regulation, we asked participants how frequently they regulated their emotions each week: "At times, people try to alter their emotions by influencing which emotions they have, when they have them, or how these emotions are experienced or expressed. How often do you try to alter your emotions (number of times per week)?"

To examine the role of social context, we asked participants how frequently they regulated emotion in each of four types of social contexts: "With people I don't know," "With friends," "With family," and "When I'm by myself," rated on a scale where 1 = *Not at all*, 2 = *A little bit*, 3 = *Sometimes*, 4 = *Most of the time*, and 5 = *All of the time*.

To determine the valence of the emotion being regulated, we asked participants whether they tried to regulate positive or negative emotions more frequently. Specifically, we asked: "Which do you try to alter more often, positive or negative emotions?"

Given our interest in the use of reappraisal and suppression, we asked participants how much they used these strategies in the past 2 weeks on a scale where 1 = *Not at all* and 7 = *A great deal*. The following definitions were offered: *Reappraisal* is

> when you try to think about a situation differently to change your emotions. An example of reappraising is recalling that air travel is statistically safer than driving to reduce your anxiety about being on an airplane. Another example is thinking that a friend's weak compliment is probably the nicest thing he's ever said to anyone.

Suppression is

> when you try *not* to show on the outside an emotion you feel on the inside. An example . . . is biting your tongue and not letting your feelings show

when someone insults you. Another example is concealing your happiness with a "poker face" after being dealt an unbeatable hand of cards.

For both reappraisal and suppression, separate ratings were made for "negative emotions" and "positive emotions."

We also wished to learn about the specific emotions that were being regulated and which of the components (*experience* and *expression*) of each emotion was targeted for regulation. We did this by asking: "To what extent do you generally try to alter the experience of the following emotions?" This was followed by a list of the 15 emotions. Then participants were asked "To what extent do you generally try to alter the expression of the following emotions?" This was followed by the same 15 emotions presented in a different order. Both the regulate-experience and regulate-expression items were rated on 7-point scales (0 = *Not at all* to 6 = *A great deal*). We focused on these two aspects of emotional responding (experience and expression) because our first approach had previously shown that these two components were overwhelmingly favored as targets for emotion regulation.

Frequency of Emotion Regulation

How frequently did participants report regulating their emotions? The mean frequency of emotion regulation was 6.6 times per week, that is, almost once a day. However, there was considerable variability in responses, as reflected in a standard deviation of 12.5, and a range of 0 to 100. Nonetheless, most participants reported at least some use of emotion regulation; only 4% of participants reported that they did not regulate their emotions at all (regulation of 0 times per week). Given this substantial variability, we also computed measures of central tendency less sensitive to outliers, including the 5% trimmed mean (4.6 times per week) and the median (3.5 per week).

Social Context for Regulating Emotion

We found that the frequency of emotion regulation varied by context, with frequency ratings of 3.1 for strangers, 2.5 for friends, 2.3 for family, and 1.7 for alone. One noteworthy finding is that these survey data indicated that emotion regulation was more frequent with strangers than with better-known partners. This finding is at odds with the "closeness gradient" described in the interview approach, which found that emotion regulation episodes were more likely to be reported in the context of close relationships than in more distant relationships. One possible explanation for this discrepancy is that emotions may be more frequent and intense in close than in distant relationships, leading to a larger absolute number of effortful and salient regulation episodes in close than distant relationships (interview approach). However, when expressed as a fraction of the total number of emotions experienced, as in the survey approach, emotion regulation may be more likely to occur in distant than in close relationships.

Valence of the Emotion Being Regulated

We expected participants to regulate negative emotions more frequently than positive emotions. Indeed, 84% of participants said they tried to alter negative emotions more frequently than positive emotions, and only 16% indicated greater regulation of positive emotions.

Use of Reappraisal and Suppression

Both reappraisal and suppression were used quite frequently, with mean ratings of 3.8 for each. Consistent with participants' general reports of greater regulation of negative than positive emotions, negative regulation was more frequent than positive regulation for both reappraisal (M negative reappraisal = 4.2, M positive = 3.3) and for suppression (M negative suppression = 4.6, M positive = 3.0).

Specific Emotions Being Regulated, Separately for Experience and Expression

Participants indicated the extent to which they regulated the experience and expression of 15 specific emotions. Table 1.1 shows the mean ratings of control of experience and Table 1.2 shows the means for expression. The most striking finding was the difference between negative and positive emotions: Even the most-regulated positive emotion (pride) was regulated to a lesser extent than the least-regulated negative emotion (disgust). A second finding is that the survey approach replicated the results of the interview approach for the specific emotions most often targeted for regulation. The top five regulated emotions were sadness, anger, embarrassment, anxiety, and fear. Among the positive emotions, the two most regulated were pride and love. A third noteworthy finding is how closely ratings of regulating emotion experience and emotion expression traveled together. Mean levels of control of experience and control of expression differed in only 2 of 15 instances, with expressive behavior being regulated more tightly than experience in each case.

Group Differences: Sex and Ethnicity

Sex and ethnicity are both factors that have been associated with differences in emotional responding in prior research (Gross & John, 2003). To examine the impact of ethnicity on emotion regulation, we selected the two largest ethnic groups (Asian American and European American) and revisited each of the aspects of emotion regulation described in the previous section.

We found no effect of sex or ethnicity for overall frequency of emotion regulation. With respect to the social context for regulating emotion, we found that with strangers, Asian Americans (M = 3.0, SD = 1.4) reported levels of emotion regulation similar to those reported by European Americans (M = 3.2, SD = 1.1). For the other three social contexts, however, Asian

TABLE 1.1
Approach 2: Mean Control of Emotion Experience (Standard Deviation) by Sex and by Ethnicity

Emotion	Sex		Ethnicity		
	Male	Female	Asian American	European American	All participants
Positive					
Pride	2.34 (1.81)	2.46 (1.64)	2.60 (1.64)	2.32 (1.64)	2.42 (1.71)
Love	2.45 (1.93)	2.35 (1.96)	2.72^c (2.04)	2.31^d (1.93)	2.39 (1.94)
Interest	2.35 (1.79)	2.04 (1.73)	2.54^c (1.77)	1.83^d (1.70)	2.16 (1.76)
Joy	2.20 (1.78)	1.87 (1.75)	2.37^c (1.80)	1.61^d (1.61)	2.00 (1.77)
Surprise	1.99 (1.64)	1.86 (1.68)	2.32^c (1.76)	1.68^d (1.56)	1.91 (1.66)
Amusement	2.15^a (1.88)	1.70^b (1.65)	2.17^c (1.73)	1.75^d (1.83)	1.88 (1.78)
Mean	2.25 (1.39)	2.04 (1.29)	2.45^c (1.38)	1.85^d (1.23)	2.12 (1.33)
Negative					
Sadness	3.22 (1.71)	3.51 (1.63)	3.29 (1.69)	3.45 (1.62)	3.40 (1.67)
Anger	3.12 (1.65)	3.40 (1.53)	3.40 (1.53)	3.23 (1.50)	3.29 (1.58)
Embarrassment	3.07 (1.75)	3.31 (1.67)	3.13 (1.71)	3.27 (1.70)	3.21 (1.71)
Anxiety	3.03 (1.60)	3.16 (1.52)	2.95 (1.47)	3.17 (1.61)	3.11 (1.55)
Fear	2.88 (1.75)	3.22 (1.66)	2.96 (1.68)	3.07 (1.66)	3.09 (1.70)
Shame	2.96 (1.72)	3.01 (1.77)	3.08 (1.70)	2.87 (1.74)	2.99 (1.75)
Contempt	2.68 (1.62)	3.01 (1.74)	2.79 (1.61)	2.91 (1.73)	2.88 (1.70)
Guilt	2.80 (1.81)	2.83 (1.83)	2.88 (1.76)	2.90 (1.78)	2.82 (1.82)
Disgust	2.67 (1.71)	2.79 (1.67)	2.81 (1.59)	2.76 (1.62)	2.74 (1.68)
Mean	2.93 (1.23)	3.14 (1.17)	3.03 (1.19)	3.07 (1.10)	3.06 (1.20)

Note. Different superscripts denote significant differences (*a* vs. *b* = sex difference; *c* vs. *d* = ethnic difference).

TABLE 1.2
Approach 2: Mean Control of Emotion Expression (Standard Deviation) by Sex and by Ethnicity

Emotion	Sex		Ethnicity		All participants
	Male	Female	Asian American	European American	
Positive					
Pride	2.59 (1.83)	2.77 (1.81)	2.77 (1.74)	2.66 (1.81)	2.70 (1.82)
Love	2.73 (1.97)	2.37 (1.96)	3.02[c] (2.04)	1.92[d] (1.74)	2.51 (1.97)
Interest	2.38 (1.79)	2.04 (1.74)	2.57[c] (1.85)	1.89[d] (1.64)	2.18 (1.76)
Joy	2.29 (1.83)	1.90 (1.83)	2.48[c] (1.85)	1.60[d] (1.63)	2.05 (1.84)
Surprise	2.18 (1.64)	1.94 (1.67)	2.44[c] (1.76)	1.76[d] (1.50)	2.03 (1.66)
Amusement	2.11[a] (1.77)	1.71[b] (1.60)	2.14[c] (1.72)	1.68[d] (1.69)	1.87 (1.68)
Mean	2.38[a] (1.40)	2.12[b] (1.27)	2.57[c] (1.37)	1.92[d] (1.20)	2.22 (1.33)
Negative					
Sadness	3.21[a] (1.72)	3.55[b] (1.48)	3.36 (1.60)	3.33 (1.63)	3.42 (1.59)
Anger	3.12[a] (1.76)	3.57[b] (1.65)	3.32 (1.64)	3.45 (1.69)	3.39 (1.70)
Embarrassment	3.18 (1.82)	3.38 (1.67)	3.16 (1.74)	3.41 (1.73)	3.30 (1.73)
Fear	3.14 (1.83)	3.25 (1.67)	3.11 (1.75)	3.21 (1.68)	3.21 (1.74)
Anxiety	3.01 (1.72)	3.29 (1.58)	3.04 (1.64)	3.28 (1.63)	3.18 (1.64)
Shame	3.09 (1.80)	3.17 (1.77)	3.10 (1.76)	3.87 (1.80)	3.14 (1.78)
Contempt	2.83[a] (1.66)	3.15[b] (1.69)	2.84 (1.54)	3.18 (1.75)	3.03 (1.68)
Guilt	2.97 (1.77)	2.97 (1.85)	2.99 (1.76)	2.99 (1.85)	2.97 (1.82)
Disgust	2.75 (1.60)	2.91 (1.74)	2.80 (1.66)	2.93 (1.68)	2.85 (1.69)
Mean	3.03 (1.31)	3.24 (1.19)	3.08 (1.24)	3.07 (1.20)	3.16 (1.24)

Note. Different superscripts denote significant differences (*a* vs. *b* = sex difference; *c* vs. *d* = ethnic difference).

Americans reported significantly greater emotion regulation than European Americans with friends ($M = 2.7$, $SD = 1.1$ vs. 2.3, $SD = 0.9$), family ($M = 2.6$, $SD = 1.1$ vs. $M = 2.1$, $SD = 1.0$), and alone ($M = 1.9$, $SD = 1.3$ vs. $M = 1.5$, $SD = 0.8$). There were no sex effects.

We also considered whether sex and ethnicity affected the valence of the emotion being regulated. We found no sex differences: 82% of men and 85% of women reported controlling negative emotions to a greater extent than positive emotions. However, we did find ethnic differences: 90% of European Americans reported controlling negative emotions more than positive emotions, whereas only 76% of Asian American participants did so. That is, only 10% of European Americans reported controlling positive emotions more than negative emotions, versus 24% of Asian Americans. In terms of the specific emotion regulation strategies that participants used, we found no sex differences, but Asian Americans did make greater use of suppression (3.3) than European Americans (2.7) for positive emotions.

For control of emotion experience, Asian Americans reported significantly greater control of five of the six positive emotions (all except pride, which still showed the same trend toward relatively greater control by Asian Americans). There were no ethnic differences for the negative emotions. As shown in Table 1.1, there was only one sex difference: Women reported less control of amusement experience than men. For control of emotion expression, ethnic effects paralleled those found in the experience domain: Asian Americans again reported greater control of five of the six positive emotions (all except pride, which, as with emotion experience, showed the same trend toward greater control by Asian Americans). There were no ethnic differences for the negative emotions. As shown in Table 1.2, sex differences were more pronounced: Women reported less control of amusement expression than men, but greater control of anger, contempt, and sadness expression. This general pattern of women exerting less control over positive emotions than men is born out by the significant difference in mean control of positive emotion, which is 2.1 for women and 2.4 for men. The tendency for women to report more control of negative emotions than men was not significant, reflected in an overall mean difference of 3.2 for women and 3.0 for men.

Approach 3: The Laboratory Experiment

Our survey approach suggested that in everyday life Asian Americans regulate positive emotions to a greater degree than European Americans. These findings jibe nicely with previous research (Tsai, Chentsova-Dutton, Freire-Bebeau, & Przymus, 2002) showing that Asian Americans express less positive emotion than do European Americans. Given that Asian Americans seem to regulate their positive emotions more frequently than European Americans (e.g., by hiding their positive emotion-expressive behavior), we might expect Asian Americans to show a practice effect when asked to suppress their emotion-expressive behavior under controlled conditions. By dint of their prior accumulated experience with suppressing positive emotions, Asian Americans should find it less difficult to inhibit positive emotions than European Americans. Given that ethnic differences seem to be evident only for positive emotions, no such differences in emotion regulation difficulty should emerge in other emotional contexts (e.g., in negative or neutral emotional contexts).

To test this hypothesis, an experimental approach is needed. To illustrate this method, we present secondary analyses of a data set examined earlier by Gross and Levenson (1997), focusing on a subset of 127 women who were either European American (58) or Asian American (69). In this study, participants had watched films drawn from a set of standardized film stimuli (Gross & Levenson, 1995) in individual experimental sessions. One film elicited a relatively neutral affective state, whereas the other films elicited either amusement (a stand-up comedy routine) or sadness (a funeral scene). Of interest here is the viewing condition, in which participants had been told to "watch the film carefully" and also told "if you have any feelings as you watch the film clip, please try your best not to let those feelings show" (the Suppression condition). After each film, participants rated how difficult it had been to suppress their behavioral responses: "On a scale from 1 to 10, where 1 is *not at all difficult* and 10 is *very difficult*, how difficult was it for you to hide your feelings during the film clip you just saw?"

Using these suppression difficulty ratings, we now tested whether, relative to European American participants, Asian Americans would find it easier to suppress their emotions during a positive-emotion-eliciting film, but not in the negative or neutral film contexts (reflecting a practice effect due to prior experience suppressing positive emotions). As predicted, we found that for the positive film, Asian Americans indeed reported less difficulty ($M = 6.0$, $SD = 3.1$) than European Americans ($M = 8.0$, $SD = 2.0$). It is important to note that this effect of ethnicity was specific to the positive emotion condition: There were no ethnic differences for either the Neutral film ($M = 2.6$, $SD = 2.4$ vs. $M = 2.8$, $SD = 2.3$), or the Sadness film ($M = 4.0$, $SD = 2.9$ vs. $M = 4.9$, $SD = 2.8$). These findings are consistent with the hypothesis that everyday practice in regulating positive emotion makes it easier for Asian Americans to regulate a positive emotion such as amusement when called on to do so in a specific situation.

FUTURE DIRECTIONS AND POLICY IMPLICATIONS

Considered together, these three studies illustrate how multiple methods (interview, survey, and experiment) are needed to achieve a more complete understanding of emotion regulation. Our findings converged in showing that in general people try to regulate negative emotions (especially anger, sadness, and anxiety) much more frequently than positive emotions, with a particular focus on regulating both experiential and behavioral, but not physiological, aspects of emotion. Although a large number of emotion regulation strategies may be discerned, two of the most common ones are cognitive reappraisal and expressive suppression. Results from these three studies also showed that emotion regulation efforts vary by context (occurring more frequently in close than distant relationship contexts) and by ethnicity (with greater regulation of positive emotions in Asian Americans than European Americans). Although these studies represent an initial step toward elucidating the ways emotions are regulated by young adults in everyday life, they nonetheless have several limitations. In the sections that follow, we consider these limitations and suggest directions for future research and implications for policy.

Implications for Health and Dysfunction

One notable limitation of the present studies is that we asked participants to recall a single recent emotion regulation episode (Approach 1), to make general ratings concerning their typical emotion regulation (Approach 2), or to regulate on command in a specific laboratory context (Approach 3). One direction for future research will be to use other methods to better characterize emotion regulation in everyday life. This will make it possible to address the important question of what health implications chronic use of particular emotion regulation strategies might have. In a series of individual-difference studies (Gross & John, 2003), we have begun to link use of reappraisal and suppression to various indicators of health and dysfunction, including emotion, social support, depression, life satisfaction, and well-being.

Our findings suggest that everyday use of reappraisal is related to greater experience of positive emotion and lesser experience of negative emotion. Reappraisers also have closer relationships with their friends and are better liked than individuals using reappraisal less frequently. In terms of maladaptive symptoms, individuals who habitually use reappraisal show fewer symptoms of depression. They are also more satisfied with their lives and more optimistic. In terms of Ryff's (1989) domains of psychological health, reappraisers have higher levels of environmental mastery, personal growth, and self-acceptance, a clearer purpose in life, a greater sense of autonomy, and better relations with others.

By contrast, everyday use of suppression is related to lesser experience of positive emotion and greater experience of negative emotion. These elevations in negative emotion appear to be due to suppressors' greater feelings of inauthenticity. Greater use of suppression is also linked to lesser social support in general, and to lesser emotional support in particular. In terms of symptoms, suppression is related to elevated levels of depressive symptoms. Suppressors have lower levels of satisfaction and well-being, as one would expect from their keen awareness of their inauthenticity, less life satisfaction, and a less optimistic attitude about the future, consistent with their avoidance and lack of close social relationships and support. In terms of Ryff's (1989) six domains of psychological health, suppressors showed lower levels of well-being across the board, with the biggest effect for positive relations with others. Overall, this pattern of findings shows that the use of reappraisal is associated with multiple indicators of healthy functioning, and that the use of suppression is associated with multiple indicators of unhealthy functioning. What is needed now, however, are prospective studies in which initial patterns in emotion regulation use predict subsequent functioning across multiple life domains.

Development: Stability and Change

A second important direction for future research is to examine stability and change in emotion regulation processes. There is growing evidence that emotion regulation varies over the course of childhood (e.g., Eisenberg & Morris, 2002) and adulthood (e.g., John & Gross, 2004), and that there are both individual and group differences (e.g., Gross & John, 2003; Tsai et al., 2002) in emotion regulation. The present studies focused on normative variation in emotion regulation in a particular age group, namely college-aged adults. However, our work on individual differences suggests that, even within the normal range of functioning, individuals vary greatly in how much they use emotion regulation strategies such as reappraisal and suppression.

Thus, although we sometimes summarize our findings by referring to "reappraisers" and "suppressors," we do not conceive of these patterns of typical emotion regulation as fixed. Indeed, in our college samples, the 3-month test–retest stability of reappraisal and suppression is about .70 (Gross & John, 2003), which suggests substantial room for change, especially over longer periods of time. If nothing else, increasing life experience and wisdom regarding the relative costs and benefits of different forms of emotion regulation suggest that changes will take place with age (Gross & John, 2002). In particular, as individuals mature and gain life experience, they might increasingly learn to make greater use of healthy emotion regulation strategies (such as reappraisal) and lesser use of less healthy emotion regulation strategies (such as suppression).

This speculation is broadly consistent with the fact that emotionally, older individuals fare surprisingly well in later years, despite a host of undesirable changes to physical health and social networks (Carstensen, Gross, & Fung, 1998). This hypothesis is also consistent with data that suggest that relative to younger adults, older adults report considerably less negative emotion (e.g., Helson & Klohnen, 1998), and with cross-sectional research showing that older individuals report greater emotional control than younger adults (Gross et al., 1997).

In a recent test of the idea that there is a normative shift toward healthier emotion regulation in later adulthood, we used retrospective and cross-sectional designs to examine individual differences in reappraisal and suppression (John & Gross, 2004). Using a retrospective design, the same older adults rated their use of reappraisal and suppression twice, once with respect to how they were now (early 60s), and once with respect to how they had been in their early 20s. We found that use of reappraisal increased from the 20s to the 60s, whereas use of suppression decreased from the 20s to the 60s. Using a cross-sectional design, we replicated these effects by comparing use of reappraisal and suppression in this older-adult sample to that of individuals now in their 20s. Here, too, we found that compared with younger participants, older participants reported greater use of reappraisal and lesser use of suppression. Together, these findings are consistent with the idea that, with age, individuals make increasing use of reappraisal as an emotion regulation strategy and decreasing use of suppression; that is, they show an increasingly healthy pattern of emotion regulation. What is needed now are longitudinal studies in which emotion regulation use is assessed at multiple time points using the same instruments.

Interventions and Policy Implications

A third important direction is applying our emerging understanding of emotion regulation to relieve existing human suffering (Gross & Munoz, 1995). For it is one thing to make the claim that many forms of psychopathology are characterized by emotion dysregulation, and quite another thing to actually work out the precise nature of the deficits (Rottenberg & Gross, 2003). The challenge is to describe how these conditions develop, clarify the underlying mechanisms, and use this knowledge to fashion better interventions to help those in need of assistance.

In particular, if natural changes in typical use of different emotion regulation strategies can be documented in adulthood, then we ought to be able to harness these same change processes in targeted interventions. One crucial early point of intervention may be influencing how parents shape their children's early emotion regulation. For example, parents differ in their meta-emotion philosophies, defined as "an organized set of feelings and thoughts about one's own emotions and one's children's emotions" (Gottman, Katz, & Hooven, 1996, p. 243). The *emotion-coaching* philosophy is held by parents who attend to and positively evaluate emotions, and discuss explicitly with their children how to best manage one's emotions. This parental philosophy, we predict, should encourage children to rely more on reappraisal to regulate their emotions. The *dismissing* philosophy, by contrast, is held by parents who view emotions as dangerous and focus on avoiding and minimizing them. Here we suggest a link to using suppression as the habitual regulation strategy. The finding that emotion coaching by parents was related to children showing less stress during emotionally challenging situations is consistent with our findings regarding the well-being and health consequences of using reappraisal rather than suppression (Gottman et al., 1996).

In the context of our studies of young adults, we have found that for many young adults, thinking explicitly about their own emotion regulation goals and the strategies they use to achieve these goals was a novel experience. This observation suggests that one simple form of preventive intervention would be to increase awareness and offer information about emotion regulation, for example, using contemporary research on emotion regulation to inform and enrich curricula in high school and college that typically do not include information on emotion and emotion regulation. Analogous to Writing 101, Mathematics 101, and Psychology 101, it may be time to offer Emotion 101—an introductory course on the nature and regulation of emotion.

Individuals who are at elevated risk for undesirable well-being and health outcomes might benefit from targeted emotion regulation intervention studies. For example, interventions could be designed that teach individuals to increase their use of reappraisal or decrease their reliance on suppression. Such interventions could be modeled after a study (Giese-Davis et al., 2002) that randomly assigned breast cancer patients to either a control group or a group that encouraged the expression of emotions and then followed patients to assess subsequent outcomes. Through such interventions—whether during early childhood in the family, during later childhood or adulthood at school, or in support groups at the clinic—it may be possible to shape individuals' emotion regulatory tendencies in ways that powerfully and beneficially affect their subsequent mental and physical health.

REFERENCES

Butler, E. A., Egloff, B., Wilhelm, F. H., Smith, N. C., Erickson, E. A., & Gross, J. J. (2003). The social consequences of expressive suppression. *Emotion, 3*, 48–67.

Carstensen, L. L., Gross, J. J., & Fung, H. (1998). The social context of emotional experience. In K. W. Schaie & M. P. Lawton (Eds.), *Annual review of gerontology and geriatrics: Vol. 17. Focus on emotion & adult development* (pp. 325–352). New York: Springer Publishing Company.

Clore, G. C. (1994). Why emotions are felt. In P. Ekman & R. J. Davidson (Eds.), *The nature of emotion: Fundamental questions* (pp. 103–111). New York: Oxford University Press.

DePaulo, B. M., Kashy, D. A., Kirkendol, S. E., Wyer, M. M., & Epstein, J. A. (1996). Lying in everyday life. *Journal of Personality and Social Psychology, 70*, 979–995.

Eisenberg, N., & Morris, A. S. (2002). Children's emotion-related regulation. *Advances in Child Development, 30*, 189–229.

Ekman, P. (1972). Universals and cultural differences in facial expressions of emotion. In J. R. Cole (Ed.), *Nebraska Symposium on Motivation, 1971: Vol. 19* (pp. 207–283). Lincoln: University of Nebraska Press.

Frijda, N. H. (1986). *The emotions.* Cambridge, England: Cambridge University Press.

Giese-Davis, J., Koopman, C., Butler, L. D., Classen, C., Cordova, M., Fobair, P., et al. (2002). Change in emotion-regulation strategy for women with metastatic breast cancer following supportive-expressive group therapy. *Journal of Consulting and Clinical Psychology, 70,* 916–925.

Gottman, J. M., Katz, L. F., & Hooven, C. (1996). Parental meta-emotion philosophy and the emotional life of families: Theoretical models and preliminary data. *Journal of Family Psychology, 10,* 243–268.

Gross, J. J. (1998). The emerging field of emotion regulation: An integrative review. *Review of General Psychology, 2,* 271–299.

Gross, J. J. (1999). Emotion regulation: Past, present, future. *Cognition & Emotion, 13,* 551–573.

Gross, J. J. (2001). Emotion regulation in adulthood: Timing is everything. *Current Directions in Psychological Science, 10,* 214–219.

Gross, J. J. (2002). Emotion regulation: Affective, cognitive, and social consequences. *Psychophysiology, 39,* 281–291.

Gross, J. J., Carstensen, L. L., Pasupathi, M., Tsai, J., Gottestam, K., & Hsu, A. Y. C. (1997). Emotion and aging: Experience, expression, and control. *Psychology and Aging, 12,* 590–599.

Gross, J. J., & John, O. P. (2002). Wise emotion regulation. In L. Feldman Barrett & P. Salovey (Eds.), *The wisdom of feelings: Psychological processes in emotional intelligence* (pp. 297–318). New York: Guilford Press.

Gross, J. J., & John, O. P. (2003). Individual differences in two emotion regulation processes: Implications for affect, relationships, and well-being. *Journal of Personality and Social Psychology, 85,* 348–362.

Gross, J. J., & Levenson, R. W. (1993). Emotional suppression: Physiology, self-report, and expressive behavior. *Journal of Personality and Social Psychology, 64,* 970–986.

Gross, J. J., & Levenson, R. W. (1995). Emotion elicitation using films. *Cognition and Emotion, 9,* 87–108.

Gross, J. J., & Levenson, R. W. (1997). Hiding feelings: The acute effects of inhibiting negative and positive emotion. *Journal of Abnormal Psychology, 106,* 95–103.

Gross, J. J., & Munoz, R. F. (1995). Emotion regulation and mental health. *Clinical Psychology: Science and Practice, 2,* 151–164.

Helson, R., & Klohnen, E. C. (1998). Affective coloring of personality from young adulthood to midlife. *Personality and Social Psychology Bulletin, 24,* 241–252.

John, O. P., & Gross, J. J. (2004). Healthy and unhealthy emotion regulation: Personality processes, individual differences, and lifespan development. *Journal of Personality, 72,* 1301–1334.

Jones, H. E. (1950). The study of patterns of emotion expression. In M. Reymert (Ed.), *Feelings and emotions* (pp. 161–168). New York: McGraw-Hill.

Lang, P., Greenwald, M., Bradley, M., & Hamm, A. (1993). Looking at pictures: Affective, facial, visceral, and behavioral reactions. *Psychophysiology, 30*, 261–273.

Lazarus, R. S., & Alfert, E. (1964). Short-circuiting of threat by experimentally altering cognitive appraisal. *Journal of Abnormal and Social Psychology, 69*, 195–205.

Lazarus, R. S., & Folkman, S. (1984). *Stress, appraisal, and coping.* New York: Springer Publishing Company.

Mischel, W., & Moore, B. (1973). Effects of attention to symbolically presented rewards on self-control. *Journal of Personality and Social Psychology, 28*, 172–179.

Parkinson, B., Totterdell, P., Briner, R. B., & Reynolds, S. (1996). *Changing moods: The psychology of mood and mood regulation.* London: Longman.

Parrott, W. G. (1993). Beyond hedonism: Motives for inhibiting good moods and for maintaining bad moods. In D. M. Wegner & J. W. Pennebaker (Eds.), *Handbook of mental control* (pp. 278–308). Englewood Cliffs, NJ: Prentice Hall.

Richards, J. M., & Gross, J. J. (2000). Emotion regulation and memory: The cognitive costs of keeping one's cool. *Journal of Personality and Social Psychology, 79*, 410–424.

Rottenberg, J., & Gross, J. J. (2003). When emotion goes wrong: Realizing the promise of affective science. *Clinical Psychology: Science and Practice, 10*, 227–232.

Ryff, C. D. (1989). Happiness is everything, or is it? Explorations on the meaning of psychological well-being. *Journal of Personality and Social Psychology, 57*, 1069–1081.

Scherer, K. R., Summerfield, A. B., & Wallbott, H. G. (1983). Cross-national research on antecedents and components of emotion: A progress report. *Social Science Information, 22*, 355–385.

Thompson, R. A. (1991). Emotional regulation and emotional development. *Educational Psychology Review, 3*, 269–307.

Tsai, J., Chentsova-Dutton, Y., Freire-Bebeau, L., & Przymus, D. E. (2002). Emotional expression and physiology in European Americans and Hmong Americans. *Emotion, 2*, 380–397.

2

EMOTIONAL INTELLIGENCE AND THE SELF-REGULATION OF AFFECT

DAISY GREWAL, MARC BRACKETT, AND PETER SALOVEY

Western psychology places enormous value on the ability to control one's emotions. Stacks of self-help books published each year offer tips and strategies on how to manage one's emotional reactions and accompanying behaviors in a variety of situations. People clearly believe that managing emotions has direct implications for the quality of their lives, especially through the impact that emotion regulation has on relationships with others. Emotions researchers ask many questions regarding the ability of individuals to regulate emotion and how it affects important life outcomes. Are there "better" and "worse" ways of handling one's emotions? And if so, can we teach people about better ways to handle their own emotions? These are the questions we attempt to answer in this chapter with the aid of empirical work within the framework of emotional intelligence.

To explore these questions, we first trace the historical trends that led to changing views about the role of emotions and the development of the

Preparation of this chapter was supported by grants to Peter Salovey from the National Cancer Institute (R01-CA68427), the National Institute of Mental Health (P01-MH/DA56826), the National Institute of Drug Abuse (P50-DA13334), and the Donaghue Women's Health Investigator Program at Yale. We wish to thank Eric Uhlmann for his helpful comments on earlier drafts of this chapter.

concept of emotional intelligence. We then discuss how the ability to regulate one's emotions effectively fits in with the profile of an emotionally intelligent person. We then report on current knowledge regarding the measurement of emotional intelligence and how findings thus far support the idea that the skills linked to emotional intelligence are directly associated with positive social interaction and well-being. We also discuss how, conversely, the absence of such skills can result in negative outcomes. Finally, we discuss the social implications of these findings and offer ideas for programs that may help increase emotional intelligence in both children and adults, and within families.

CONCEPTUAL AND THEORETICAL ISSUES

The concept of emotional intelligence represents the convergence of two historical trends in psychology: changing views about the functional "rationality" of emotions, including their role in cognitive processes, and changing definitions of what abilities constitute "intelligence." A dichotomy between emotion and reason can be traced back to ancient Greece, where Stoic philosophers espoused the idea that emotions interfere with rational thought. Such a view continued to exert an influence in psychology as evidenced by early researchers who believed that emotions have the potential to interfere with desirable thought processes (Shaffer, 1936; Young, 1940). In recent decades, particularly in the last 10 years, this view has been changing as modern cognitive psychologists and neuroscientists have begun to incorporate in their research measures that reflect the important influence of emotions on activities such as decision making (Damasio, 1994; Loewenstein, Weber, Hsee, & Welch, 2001; Mellers, Schwartz, & Ritov, 1999), stereotyping and prejudice (Bodenhausen, Kramer, & Süsser, 1994), problem solving (Isen & Daubman, 1984; Isen, Daubman, & Nowicki, 1987), and creativity (Getz & Lubart, 1998, 2000). Furthermore, views of human intelligence have greatly expanded in recent years because of the efforts of Gardner (1983), Sternberg (1985), and other investigators who have argued for broader definitions of what it means to be smart. These two converging trends set the stage for the introduction of a new kind of intelligence—one that would recognize the functional utility of emotions in everyday life and people's differing abilities in harnessing them.

What Is Emotional Intelligence?

Salovey and Mayer (1990, p. 189) proposed an initial scientific definition of *emotional intelligence* as "the ability to monitor one's own and others' feelings, to discriminate among them, and to use this information to guide one's thinking and action." Their model outlined the following components:

EXHIBIT 2.1
The Four-Branch Model of Emotional Intelligence

Branch 1: Emotional Perception and Expression (Perceiving Emotions)
- Ability to identify emotion in one's physical and psychological states.
- Ability to identify emotion in other people.
- Ability to express emotions accurately, and to express needs related to those feelings.
- Ability to discriminate between accurate/honest and inaccurate/dishonest feelings.

Branch 2: Emotional Facilitation of Thought (Using Emotions)
- Ability to redirect and prioritize one's thinking on the basis of associated feelings.
- Ability to generate emotions to facilitate judgment and memory.
- Ability to capitalize on mood changes to appreciate multiple points of view.
- Ability to use emotional states to facilitate problem solving and creativity.

Branch 3: Emotional Understanding (Understanding Emotions)
- Ability to understand relationships among various emotions.
- Ability to perceive the causes and consequences of emotions.
- Ability to understand complex feelings, emotional blends, and contradictory states.
- Ability to understand transitions among emotions.

Branch 4: Emotional Management (Managing Emotions)
- Ability to be open to feelings, both pleasant and unpleasant.
- Ability to monitor and reflect on emotions.
- Ability to engage, prolong, or detach from an emotional state.
- Ability to manage emotions in oneself.
- Ability to manage emotions in others.

Note. From *Emotional Development and Emotional Intelligence: Educational Implications* (p. 11), edited by P. Salovey and D. Sluyter, 1997, New York: Basic Books. Copyright 1997 by P. Salovey and D. J. Sluyter. Adapted with permission of Basic Books, a member of Perseus Books, LLC.

appraising emotions in the self and in others; regulating emotions in the self and in others; and using emotions to facilitate thinking, reasoning, problem solving, and creativity, as well as to motivate behavior. The model stimulated research attempting to find out more about how emotion can facilitate cognitive processes such as perceiving and reasoning (Mayer, DiPaolo, & Salovey, 1990; Mayer, Gaschke, Braverman, & Evans, 1992) and how individual differences in emotional intelligence might be captured empirically (Mayer, Caruso, & Salovey, 1998, 1999). After a few years of such exploratory research, the original model of emotional intelligence was refined so that four distinct but separate abilities are now thought to fall under the framework of emotional intelligence (Mayer & Salovey, 1997): (a) perceiving emotions, (b) using emotions to facilitate thought and language, (c) understanding emotions, and (d) managing emotions in the self and in others. These four abilities make up the four domains of emotional intelligence (see Exhibit 2.1). We now discuss each of these components with a special focus on the fourth branch, managing emotions, as it fits within the overarching model of emotional intelligence.

The first domain of emotional intelligence, perceiving emotions, involves the ability to detect and accurately perceive emotions in faces, voices, art, music, and stories. Perhaps the most basic skill involved in emotional intelligence, perceiving emotions in both the self and others, makes all other processing of emotional information possible. A severe deficit in the ability to perceive emotions in the self may be associated with alexithymia (Apfel & Sifneos, 1979) as well as increased ambivalence over emotional expression (King, 1998; King & Emmons, 1990). Furthermore, perceiving emotions accurately in others may have important implications for creating and sustaining important social relationships (Lopes, Salovey, Côté, & Beers, 2005).

The second domain of emotional intelligence, the ability to use emotions to facilitate both thought and language, is demonstrated by findings that have shown how emotions can play an adaptive role in many important cognitive processes (Palfai & Salovey, 1993; Schwarz, 1990). For example, emotions can help people focus on important information when trying to solve problems (Easterbrook, 1959; Mandler, 1975; Simon, 1982) and come up with creative ideas and solutions (Isen & Daubman, 1984; Isen et al., 1987). The emotionally intelligent person might more easily recognize how a slightly depressed mood can help deductive reasoning (Schwarz, 1990) and use this information to better accomplish certain tasks.

Understanding emotions, the third domain of emotional intelligence, is the ability to label emotions linguistically as well as understand complex relationships among emotions. For example, it entails the ability to recognize blends of different emotions as well as temporal and progressive associations among emotions, such as that between irritation and rage. The third branch is therefore linked to an individual's knowledge of emotion and use of emotion terminology.

The fourth domain of emotional intelligence, managing emotions, is the component of emotional intelligence most relevant to the themes of this chapter. It entails the adaptive ability to regulate emotions optimally both in the self and in others. However, it is important to note that an optimal outcome of emotion regulation involves more than the simple goal of decreasing negative emotions and increasing positive ones. Although this might seem counterintuitive, eliminating negative emotions may not always serve adaptive purposes (Bonnano, 2001; Parrott, 2002). For example, in some circumstances we may need to experience grief to show support for a friend's loss or use angry feelings to take necessary steps toward fighting injustice. Therefore, managing emotions also includes the ability to increase negative emotions or decrease positive emotions, depending on the context. Its definition may also be seen as very similar to the concept of response modulation developed by James Gross and his colleagues (see chap. 1, this volume). Emotion management has received particular attention in the field of psychology because of its wide-reaching implications for many subfields such as clinical, developmental, and health psychology. For example, those individuals interested in solving mental health problems increasingly have focused on how problems with managing emotions result in various psychological disorders (Gross & Munoz, 1995). Furthermore, as we shall see, this domain plays an important role in maintaining good interpersonal relationships.

Managing Emotions

Before we discuss findings supporting the importance of managing emotions in real-world contexts, we need first to try to specify what this ability entails and the best ways to measure it. We believe that managing emotions involves several skills, including the ability to monitor and label one's own feelings effectively and self-efficacy about the ability to modify these feelings, as well as the knowledge and motivation to use effective strategies to alter emotions. Managing emotions can be distinguished from coping in that the regulation attempt involves attention to one's own subjective state rather than to the specific life events that may be causing the unpleasant emotions (Larsen, 2000). Therefore, the study of emotion management seems especially important in contexts in which rearranging circumstances may not be feasible; close interpersonal relationships, especially with one's children, represent one such context. For instance, a child's poor performance in a sports game requires encouragement and emotional support rather than direct intervention by the parent.

What types of behavior constitute managing emotions? Under the framework of emotional intelligence, we consider any action an attempt at management if the specific goal when committing the action is the desire to manipulate one's own or others' emotions. People use an enormously broad range of strategies to regulate their emotions, ranging from listening to music to drinking caffeinated beverages to withdrawing from social interaction. Parkinson and Totterdell (1999) classified various emotion regulation strategies on the basis of conceptual similarities and produced the following four categories: avoidance, distraction, confrontation, and acceptance. Creating a taxonomy of strategies based on functionality, rather than similarity, seems an important first step in trying to assess the different goals people seek to gain relief from emotions. For example, two people might seek social support for two very different reasons: One person may desire emotional support, whereas the other may be seeking problem-solving information. Classification schemes based on the purpose behind the action will help us better understand the complicated processes that accompany such regulation.

Although classification of strategies remains an important first step in understanding emotion regulation, the emotional intelligence framework is more concerned with questions of effectiveness than with typologies. What emotion regulation strategies work better than others? We believe that for most emotion regulation researchers, this is the question of ultimate interest.

Given the great number of strategies that people use to regulate emotions, this question is a challenging one. However, whereas labeling specific emotion regulation strategies as better than others may be premature, some research has demonstrated that there are clearly different consequences linked to different types of strategies (Gross & John, 2002). For example, people who engage in rumination following an upsetting situation may find themselves more depressed than those who use distraction as a strategy (Nolen-Hoeksema, 1993). Thayer, Newman, and McClain (1994) found that active techniques combining relaxation, stress management, reappraisal, and exercise may reap the most benefits for people experiencing a bad mood. Pennebaker (1989, 1993, 1997) has conducted numerous studies demonstrating how emotional disclosure through writing can promote both mental and physical health. Nevertheless, at times intuition fails to capture the truth: Other researchers have shown that what sometimes seems to be a maladaptive regulation strategy can later have little to no negative effect on an individual's functioning. For example, Bonnano (2001) has demonstrated that repressing emotions after traumatic abuse or a personal loss does not necessarily lead to poor adjustment later. Therefore, though we hesitate to draw firm conclusions about which strategies seem best, we adhere to the position that we can make rough generalizations about what kinds of regulation techniques are more likely to lead to adaptive outcomes. Identifying the absolute best strategies for regulating emotions would be impossible because each situation requires attention to the specific circumstances at hand.

For the purposes of defining emotional intelligence, we make no special distinction between emotions and moods, although we adhere to the generally accepted definitions that emotions are more specific responses to particular events, whereas moods can be seen as more diffuse. The skills pertinent to emotional intelligence may be relevant to both emotions and moods; for example, strategies for changing either an unwanted emotion or an unwanted mood both fall under the fourth branch of emotional intelligence, emotional management.

We must also carefully make a distinction between intra- and interpersonal forms of managing emotions, both of which are included in the fourth domain of our model of emotional intelligence. In contrast to intrapersonal regulation, which focuses on one's own subjective state, interpersonal regulation represents a far more complex set of dynamic processes because it involves interaction with and subsequent feedback from another person. The field of emotion regulation thus far has been overwhelmingly focused on intrapersonal management, although some research, mostly conducted by developmental psychologists, has argued for the important role of the social context in managing both one's own and others' emotions (Fox & Calkins, 2003; Thompson, 1994, 1998). We believe that interpersonal regulation is more likely to depend on the harnessing rather than the suppressing of emotion in others as a means for persuasion (Salovey, Mayer, & Caruso, 2002). Individuals successful at interpersonal management may also possess skills necessary for soothing distressed others. Such skills might involve the ability to remain calm themselves, offer strategies for help, and provide comfort while remaining empathetic to their partner's situation.

For the sake of simplicity, we define *intra-* and *interpersonal* regulation as forming two separate but related components of the fourth domain of emotional intelligence. One can easily imagine an individual who is quite skilled at regulating her own emotions but fumbling and inadequate in cheering up a friend or handling conflicts between team members. In a similar way, an individual might successfully influence and regulate the emotions of others while failing miserably in managing his own depression or impulsivity (certain eminent politicians, such as Winston Churchill, may serve as examples of this latter condition).

Researchers have found individual differences in the ability to manage emotions (Cantanzaro & Greenwood, 1994; Gross & John, 2002; Salovey, Mayer, Goldman, Turvey, & Palfai, 1995); therefore, our current model of emotional intelligence predicts that individuals will vary significantly in their abilities to manage their own emotions, which in turn has an important impact on life outcomes. Although most research has focused on differences in intrapersonal regulation, we think that research focusing on interpersonal regulation will reveal such differences as well. It is also worth mentioning that the studies previously cited used self-report rather than ability-based measures. There is a difference between people's beliefs about their emotion abilities and their actual knowledge of emotions or ability to deal effectively with emotions. We also believe there is a significant difference between people's knowledge of emotion regulation strategies and their actual ability to apply those strategies to real-world situations. For example, one might recognize that exercising will more effectively change a bad mood than drinking alcohol but for a variety of reasons choose to head to a local bar, rather than the gym, after an upsetting situation. Before we discuss our evidence demonstrating that individual differences in emotional intelligence significantly impact life outcomes, we first explain the pros and cons of measuring emotional intelligence through self-report inventories and task-based performance tests.

METHODOLOGICAL AND EMPIRICAL FOUNDATIONS

Measuring emotional intelligence reliably and accurately is vital to understanding its application to important life outcomes. In this section, we discuss how emotional intelligence is measured as an ability and how scores on such measures can predict the quality of social interaction.

How Do We Measure Emotional Intelligence?

Research on emotional intelligence has proliferated mainly because of the use of self-report measures that are relatively easy to design, test, and implement as compared with ability-based measures. Examples of the more frequently used self-report tests of emotional intelligence are the Emotional Quotient Inventory (Bar-On, 1997) and the Self-Report Emotional Intelligence Test (Schutte et al., 1998). Although ease of administration poses a huge advantage over ability-based tests, self-report tests of emotional intelligence suffer from lack of construct validity, with research showing that they cannot be properly differentiated from well-established measures of personality such as the Big Five (Brackett & Mayer, 2003). Furthermore, self-report tests based on the four-part model of emotional intelligence suffer from the limitation that people may not have the capacity or willingness to provide accurate information about their own emotional skills (Brackett & Mayer, 2003; Mayer et al., 1999). For example, in a recent study, the correlation between a self-report test of emotion regulation and an ability test was quite small (Rivers, Brackett, & Salovey, 2004). Because of these limitations associated with self-report tests, we favor the use of ability-based or performance measures of emotional intelligence.

The first ability-based test of our model of emotional intelligence was called the Multifactor Emotional Intelligence Test (MEIS; Mayer et al., 1999), which eventually led to the development of the Mayer Salovey Caruso Emotional Intelligence Test (MSCEIT; Mayer, Salovey, & Caruso, 2002). The MSCEIT offers a number of advantages over its predecessor. Problematic items were eliminated, and the test itself was made shorter and easier to use by way of computer-based administration. The MSCEIT assesses the four domains of Mayer and Salovey's (1997) emotional intelligence model (perceiving, using, understanding, and managing emotions) through eight separate tasks, two for each of the domains. A researcher can, therefore, easily compare an individual's scores on each of these abilities and isolate particular sets of skills when examining associations with different outcomes.

The MSCEIT has good discriminant validity. It is distinct from common measures of personality, correlates only slightly with analytical intelligence, and shows only modest overlap with self-report tests of emotional intelligence (Brackett & Mayer, 2003; Brackett, Mayer, & Warner, 2004; Lopes, Salovey, & Straus, 2003). Scores on the MSCEIT are not associated with the Big Five traits of conscientiousness, extraversion, and neuroticism and seem to be only moderately associated with the traits of agreeableness and openness (Brackett & Mayer, 2003). Furthermore, with respect to verbal intelligence, only Branch 3, understanding emotions, produces a significant correlation, usually around $r = .30$ (Grewal, Ivcevic, Lopes, Brackett, & Salovey, 2004; Lopes et al., 2003). This association seems reasonable and expected, considering the conceptualization of Branch 3 as measuring knowledge and use of emotion terminology. A lack of overlap with self-report tests, which tend to correlate highly with personality measures (Brackett & Mayer, 2003), also distinguishes the MSCEIT from common measures of personality.

Confirmatory factor analyses of the MSCEIT have demonstrated that the four branches load onto four distinct factors. Notably, the fourth branch, managing emotions, combines intra- and interpersonal management into one factor. However, a self-report test of emotional intelligence based on the four-branch model (developed by Brackett) revealed factor analyses that distinguished the intra- and interpersonal dimensions of the fourth branch (managing emotions). We believe that although the two dimensions can be successfully combined as a single factor on ability-based tests, people's self-knowledge of emotion regulation may be more compartmentalized, leading them to make an important distinction between the two.

Although we believe that ability-based measures of emotional intelligence pose distinct advantages over self-report measures, we would like to add a cautionary note against always interpreting ability-based findings as more indicative of true emotional skill. In some particular instances, people's self-knowledge of their own emotional skills may provide better predictions for various life outcomes. This may be especially true for the Managing Emotions subscale of the MSCEIT, because this skill is presumably the most difficult, complex, and context dependent. Ability measures may not capture the intricacies of emotion regulation in terms of time, place, event, and specific emotions. In some cases, especially when provided with specific questions about particular contexts, we might expect participants to be able to provide a better idea of their tendency to regulate poorly because they, in fact, do know themselves best.

Emotional Intelligence and Social Interaction

Managing emotions, as defined under the framework of emotional intelligence, entails the optimal regulation of emotions in both intra- and interpersonal situations. The latter, in particular, suggests that the emotionally intelligent individual who excels at this particular domain of emotional intelligence ought to experience greater levels of success and satisfaction in the domain of social interaction. Research conducted thus far, which has used the fourth subscale of the MSCEIT to measure the ability to manage emotions, appears to support this assumption.

Several positive findings using the MSCEIT directly link the fourth domain of emotional intelligence, managing emotions, with positive social outcomes. The fourth subscale of the MSCEIT measures people's ability to manage emotions in both the intra- and interpersonal domains. Lopes, Salovey, and Straus (2003) found that higher scores on the Managing Emotions subscale were positively related to self-reported positive interaction with friends and negatively related to self-reported negative interaction with friends. Furthermore, individuals who scored higher on the fourth subscale reported a greater level of perceived parental support, a finding with significant implications for how such skills impact the emotional development of families.

The skills involved in managing emotions may be especially relevant to maintaining high-quality relationships with peers. MSCEIT Managing Emotions scores correlated positively with friendship quality (Lopes, Brackett, et al., 2004). Specifically, individuals who scored higher on managing emotions were rated as more supportive and caring friends in reports provided by two friends. Higher scores were also related to self-rated quality of the friendships with those two same friends. In a second study, Managing Emotions scores correlated positively with the self-perceived quality of interaction with individuals of the opposite sex.

One of the more significant social challenges for most college students is learning to live with roommates peacefully—a task that undoubtedly requires a great deal of emotion regulation, particularly when circumstances include relative strangers in tight quarters. A study conducted in a large undergraduate class looked at whether MSCEIT scores were related to interaction among roommates and close friends (Lerner & Brackett, 2004). Higher scores on the Managing Emotions subscale were related to participants' self-reported tendency to provide emotional support to their roommates. Furthermore, such scores were also negatively related to participants' self-reported tendency to leave in response to their roommates' behavior.

In the Lerner and Brackett (2004) investigation, relationships with close friends were analyzed for those students not currently living with a roommate. Higher Managing Emotions scores were positively related to self-reports of providing emotional support and promoting conflict resolution. Higher scores were negatively related to self-reported "exit" behavior (i.e., physically leaving at signs of trouble in the relationship), as well as neglecting and mistreating the friend. These results are especially interesting because they point to potential mediators of the relationship between emotional skills and the quality of relationships.

In addition, residential college students who scored higher on Managing Emotions were viewed more favorably by other students in their college (Lopes, Salovey, Côté, & Beers, 2005). For example, students with higher Managing Emotions scores received more friendship nominations from others, signifying that these individuals seemed to be more popular than their lower-scoring peers. Furthermore, these individuals received more positive than negative peer ratings overall. Both of these results remained significant after controlling for Big Five personality traits.

Another important and interesting domain for analyzing how emotion regulation impacts social interaction is the workplace. Early emotional intelligence research using the MEIS indicated that customer satisfaction related positively to the level of emotional skill possessed by individual employees (Rice, 1999). Lopes, Grewal, Kadis, Gall, and Salovey (in press) administered the MSCEIT to the employees of a Fortune 400 insurance company, who were also asked to rate their peers and supervisees on a number of social and emotional skills such as stress tolerance, conflict management, and leadership ability. Employees scoring high on the Managing Emotions subscale experienced fewer negative interactions with others, as reported by their peers. They were also rated highly by their peers for contributing to a positive work environment and for being in a cheerful mood much of the time while at work. Higher scores on the Managing Emotions subscale were positively related to supervisor ratings of interpersonal sensitivity, sociability, contributing to a positive work environment, stress tolerance, and leadership potential. Of note, the Managing Emotions subscale was also positively related to salary and rank within the company. This suggests that the ability to manage emotions well contributes to both professional and personal success at work. These results are particularly compelling because Lopes et al. (in press) used a naturalistic sample of working men and women, in contrast to the college student samples used in the other studies reviewed here.

The ability to manage emotions may also have a significant impact on romantic relationships. Brackett, Warner, and Bosco (2005) examined how scores on the MSCEIT related to the quality of young adults' romantic relationships. Couples in which both partners were low on emotional intelligence (MSCEIT total score) self-reported the least amount of emotional depth, partner support, and overall relationship quality. They also appeared to experience the greatest amount of relationship conflict and, overall, rated their relationships more negatively than couples with higher emotional intelligence.

FUTURE DIRECTIONS AND POLICY IMPLICATIONS

The field of emotional intelligence requires a great deal of additional research to develop better and more refined measures of the construct and to use such tests to determine how, when, and where these skills are important. Although the MSCEIT has demonstrated appropriate reliability and predictive validity, improvements still need to be made to capture the complicated and context-based processes involved in emotional intelligence. The development of emotion-specific measures may be helpful, as there is good reason to suspect that individuals differ not only in their general abilities with regard to emotion regulation but also in the extent to which they can regulate particular emotions (Rivers et al., 2004). An individual may successfully deal with anger but fall apart at the slightest twinge of sadness or guilt, for example.

Furthermore, the possibility remains that certain mediators may contribute to the exhibition of emotional skills, and such mediators may even interact with particular contexts. The Lerner and Brackett (2004) investigation that was discussed previously demonstrates how a search for mediators between the possession of certain emotional skills and specific outcomes might shed new light on how and when these skills operate. Future research might investigate the importance of other mediators that may contribute to relationship quality, such as the status of the relationship partners (e.g., as defined by gender or professional position) combined with the environmental setting in which the social interaction is taking place. For example, a person might be particularly good at reading the facial expressions of those superior to him or her at work while being less successful at attending to the feelings of coworkers.

Another important avenue for further research, touched on earlier in this chapter, is the important distinction between one's knowledge of how to manage emotional situations and one's ability to apply that knowledge successfully in real-world settings. Although the Managing Emotions subscale of the MSCEIT goes beyond the typical content of self-report tests of emotional intelligence, the extent to which it taps directly into ability requires further attention. Even if the material covered on the test does successfully measure people's ability to manage their emotions in situations similar to the hypothetical ones given, the test is still limited in terms of its content. Of course, it is doubtful that any measure could successfully capture all of the complex processes people engage in when confronted with unexpected emotional situations. Such situations involve a myriad of complicated stimuli including, but not limited to, facial expressions, tone of voice, familiar and unfamiliar others, and, most important, a heightened sense of personal relevance. As Shields (2002, p. 6) has summarized: "Emotion is 'taking it personally,'" and we cannot, therefore, expect to achieve in the laboratory the sense of urgency and impact that go along with most emotional events. We can only hope to approximate such processes.

However, therein lies a challenging yet exciting task for emotions researchers: to find ways both inside and outside the laboratory to capture the processes of emotion regulation as accurately as possible. If emotion is indeed "taking it personally," then many regulation attempts most likely revolve around some of the most important aspects of people's lives, including family—and particularly, children. Therefore, the development of new measures of emotional intelligence that will successfully provide us with the type of information we need to understand emotion regulation carries with it the added bonus of studying some of the more important issues that directly affect people's everyday lives.

Additional studies are also needed to examine the development of emotional intelligence over the life span, a topic of particular interest to psychologists who study children and adolescents. As with analytical intelligence, a number of factors most likely contribute to the development of emotional intelligence, and identifying such factors has important implications for those who want to increase the emotional skills of vulnerable children. Prospective studies might consider the use of longitudinal designs to assess how children of differing backgrounds and family environments develop emotional skills over time. Such studies would help illuminate the role of significant others, including teachers and parents, in a child's development of emotional competencies.

We would also like to offer some suggestions for areas in which the application of emotional intelligence research may prove especially fruitful. The first domain is in the field of clinical psychology, in which a growing number of researchers have begun to recognize the important role that emotional skills play in a number of different pathologies (Cicchetti, Ackerman, & Izard, 1995; Gross & Munoz, 1995). Berenbaum, Raghavan, Le, Vernon, and Gomez (2003) have even proposed a new taxonomy of mental disorders using problems with emotion as a central feature of diagnosis. We believe that emotional intelligence may have much to contribute in the assessment of mental health by pinpointing specific deficits in emotional skills that clients may possess. Furthermore, emotional intelligence tests such as the MSCEIT may serve as a treatment outcome measure in longitudinal studies of therapies aimed at helping people manage their emotions better. The development of new tests of emotional intelligence may help clinicians distinguish how people who suffer from certain disorders differ from controls in the way they appraise and handle emotion, which may even lead to diagnosing certain vulnerabilities in emotion regulation before they become severely problematic.

Another domain of particular interest for the application of emotional intelligence is in the schools, where children spend a great deal of their time, not only acquiring knowledge but also learning how to negotiate with and handle their emotions with those outside of their families. Although families themselves clearly have an impact on how children interact with strangers, we also believe that an integration of social and emotional programs offers the potential for great benefit to numerous children (Lopes & Salovey, 2004). This is not a new idea, and there has already been some research demonstrating that teaching social and emotional competencies can induce significant and important changes in pupils (Aber, Brown, & Henrich, 1999; Aber, Jones, Brown, Chaudry, & Samples, 1998).

Educational interventions aimed at promotion of social and emotional learning have incorporated findings from psychology to build curriculums that attempt to both reduce and prevent behavioral and emotional problems in students. One important program, the PATHS (Promoting Alternative THinking Strategies) curriculum, draws on psychoanalytic, social–cognitive, and neurocognitive theories in the formulation of its lessons. Topics for such lessons include the development of self-control, emotional and interpersonal understanding, and problem solving. There is also a focus on building positive self-esteem in children and building peer relationships within the classrooms. Randomized trials involving extensive data collection have demonstrated that the PATHS curriculum successfully improves problem-solving ability, cognitive planning abilities, self-reported conduct problems, and self-reported anxiety and depression in both normal and at-risk populations of students (Greenberg, Kusché, & Riggs, 2004).

Other programs aimed at increasing emotional intelligence in the classroom that have also demonstrated encouraging results include the Child Development Program (Schaps, Battistich, & Solomon, 2004), the Resolving Conflict Creatively Program (Brown, Roderick, Lantieri, & Aber, 2004), the Social Decision Making and Social Problem Solving program (Elias, 2004), and the Seattle Social Development Project (Hawkins, Smith, & Catalano, 2004). Each of these programs offers detailed methods for classroom-based interventions that attempt to improve the emotional abilities of school-age children. Our contribution to such efforts is to offer the four-branch emotional intelligence model, with a special focus on learning to regulate emotion, as an important guideline in designing future programs.

One such program currently undergoing testing is Emotional Literacy in the Middle School: A six-step program to promote social, emotional, and academic learning in middle school students (Maurer, Brackett, & Plain, 2004). Of particular interest to this program is the inclusion of classroom projects that prompt students to explore the regulation of both anger and sadness. Students are asked to think of a situation that caused them to feel angry or sad and write a story about the event. In the story, they are asked to explore questions related to the thoughts, feelings, and behaviors that accompanied the episode of anger or sadness and the events and persons that helped them feel better about the situation. The second half of each project asks students to explore how other people handle their anger or sadness through discussion and through actual interviews of the student's friends and families. This task stresses the skills involved in the interpersonal aspect of emotion regulation and promotes the development of empathy by having students adopt another's perspective. A recent experiment using this curriculum showed that students who received the intervention for 7 months (compared with students in the control group) were rated by their teachers to be more prosocial and less anxious and depressed. The students in the intervention group also had higher grades at the end of the school year (Brackett, Rivers, & Salovey, 2005). Much more formal evaluation is needed to determine how successful both the previously mentioned programs and others currently being implemented across the nation are at reducing conflict and improving emotional skills in the classroom.

The training of adults in emotional intelligence remains an important application as well. We believe that emotional intelligence comprises skills that can be learned rather than fixed abilities or personality traits, and that it is subject to improvement with effort and the acquisition of new knowledge. Workplace interventions focusing on the development of emotional skills in employees are already popular in the corporate world, and although we think any focus on emotional training is better than none at all, we are cautious about programs not based on sound scientific research. We advocate the development of workplace training programs emphasizing the particular skills of the four-part emotional intelligence model, which, as discussed in a previous section, seem to be directly related to several important employee outcomes. As more research is conducted on how the management of emotion impacts the welfare of individual employees and the company as a whole, we believe that this knowledge has great potential to improve the working environment through training programs that increase the emotional intelligence of a company's employees.

REFERENCES

Aber, J. L., Brown, J. L., & Henrich, C. C. (1999). *Teaching conflict resolution: An effective school-based approach to violence prevention*. New York: National Center for Children in Poverty, Joseph L. Mailman School of Public Health, Columbia University.

Aber, J. L., Jones, S. M., Brown, J. L., Chaudry, N., & Samples, F. (1998). Resolving conflict creatively: Evaluating the developmental effects of a school-based violence prevention program in a neighborhood and classroom context. *Development and Psychopathology, 10*, 187–213.

Apfel, R. J., & Sifneos, P. E. (1979). Alexithymia: Concept and measurement. *Psychotherapy and Psychosomatics, 32*, 180–190.

Bar-On, R. (1997). *Emotional Intelligence Quotient Inventory: A measure of emotional intelligence*. Toronto, Ontario, Canada: Multi-Health Systems.

Berenbaum, H., Raghavan, C., Le, H., Vernon, L. L., & Gomez, J. J. (2003). A taxonomy of emotional disturbances. *Clinical Psychology: Science and Practice, 10*, 206–226.

Bodenhausen, G. V., Kramer, G. P., & Süsser, K. (1994). Happiness and stereotypic thinking in social judgment. *Journal of Personality and Social Psychology, 66*, 621–632.

Bonnano, G. (2001). Self-regulation of emotions. In T. J. Mayne & G. Bonnano (Eds.), *Emotions: Current issues and future directions* (pp. 251–285). New York: Guilford Press.

Brackett, M. A., & Mayer, J. D. (2003). Convergent, discriminant, and incremental validity of competing measures of emotional intelligence. *Personality and Social Psychology Bulletin, 29*, 1147–1158.

Brackett, M. A., Mayer, J. D., & Warner, R. M. (2004). Emotional intelligence and the prediction of behavior. *Personality and Individual Differences, 36*, 1387–1402.

Brackett, M. A., Rivers, S., & Salovey, P. (2005). *The effects of emotional literacy training on middle school students*. Unpublished data, Yale University, New Haven, CT.

Brackett, M. A., Warner, R. M., & Bosco, J. (2005). Emotional intelligence and relationship quality among couples. *Personal Relationships, 12,* 197–212.

Brown, J. L., Roderick, T., Lantieri, L., & Aber, J. L. (2004). The Resolving Conflict Creatively Program: A school-based social and emotional learning program. In J. E. Zins, R. P. Weissberg, M. C. Wang, & H. J. Walberg (Eds.), *Building academic success on social and emotional learning* (pp. 76–93). New York: Teachers College Press.

Cantanzaro, S. J., & Greenwood, G. (1994). Expectancies for negative mood regulation, coping, and dysphoria among college students. *Journal of Consulting Psychology, 41,* 34–44.

Cicchetti, D., Ackerman, B. P., & Izard, C. E. (1995). Emotions and emotion regulation in developmental psychopathology. *Development and Psychopathology, 7,* 1–10.

Damasio, A. R. (1994). *Descartes' error: Emotion, reason, and the human brain.* New York: Putnam.

Easterbrook, J. A. (1959). The effects of emotion on cue utilization and the organization of behavior. *Psychological Review, 66,* 183–200.

Elias, M. J. (2004). Strategies to infuse social and emotional learning. In J. E. Zins, R. P. Weissberg, M. C. Wang, & H. J. Walberg (Eds.), *Building academic success on social and emotional learning* (pp. 76–93). New York: Teachers College Press.

Fox, N. A., & Calkins, S. D. (2003). The development of self-control of emotions: Intrinsic and extrinsic influences. *Motivation and Emotion, 27,* 7–26.

Gardner, H. (1983). *Frames of mind.* New York: Basic Books.

Getz, I., & Lubart, T. I. (1998). The emotional resonance model of creativity: Theoretical and practical extensions. In S. W. Russ (Ed.), *Affect, creative experience, and psychological adjustment* (pp. 41–56). Philadelphia: Brunner/Mazel.

Getz, I., & Lubart, T. I. (2000). An emotional-experiential perspective on creative symbolic-metaphorical processes. *Consciousness & Emotion, 1,* 283–312.

Greenberg, M. T., Kusché, C., & Riggs, N. (2004). The PATHS curriculum: Theory and research on neurocognitive development and school success. In J. E. Zins, R. P. Weissberg, M. C. Wang, & H. J. Walberg (Eds.), *Building academic success on social and emotional learning* (pp. 76–93). New York: Teachers College Press.

Grewal, D., Ivecic, Z., Lopes, P. N., Brackett, M. A., & Salovey, P. (2004). *Emotions and the artist: The relationship between emotional intelligence and creativity.* Unpublished manuscript, Yale University, New Haven, CT.

Gross, J. J., & John, O. P. (2002). Wise emotion regulation. In L. Feldman Barrett & P. Salovey (Eds.), *The wisdom in feeling: Psychological processes in emotional intelligence* (pp. 297–318). New York: Guilford Press.

Gross, J. J., & Munoz, R. F. (1995). Emotion regulation and mental health. *Clinical Psychology: Science and Practice, 2,* 151–164.

Hawkins, J. D., Smith, B. H., & Catalano, R. F. (2004). Social development and social and emotional learning. In J. E. Zins, R. P. Weissberg, M. C. Wang, & H. J. Walberg (Eds.), *Building academic success on social and emotional learning* (pp. 76–93). New York: Teachers College Press.

Isen, A. M., & Daubman, K. A. (1984). The influence of affect on categorization. *Journal of Personality and Social Psychology, 47*, 1206–1217.

Isen, A. M., Daubman, K. A., & Nowicki, G. P. (1987). Positive affect facilitates creative problem solving. *Journal of Personality and Social Psychology, 52*, 1122–1131.

King, L. A. (1998). Ambivalence over emotional expression and reading emotions in situations and faces. *Journal of Personality and Social Psychology, 74*, 753–762.

King, L. A., & Emmons, R. A. (1990). Conflict over emotional expression: Psychological and physiological correlates. *Journal of Personality and Social Psychology, 58*, 864–877.

Larsen, R. J. (2000). Toward a science of mood regulation. *Psychological Inquiry, 11*, 129–141.

Lerner, N., & Brackett, M. A. (2004). *Emotional intelligence, social interaction, and behavioral strategies among roommates, suitemates, and close friends.* Unpublished senior thesis, Yale University, New Haven, CT.

Loewenstein, G. F., Weber, E. U., Hsee, C. K., & Welch, N. (2001). Risk as feelings. *Psychological Bulletin, 127*, 267–286.

Lopes, P. N., Brackett, M. A., Nezlek, J., Schutz, A., Sellin, I., & Salovey, P. (2004). Emotional intelligence and social interaction. *Personality and Social Psychology Bulletin, 30*, 1018–1034.

Lopes, P. N., Grewal, D., Kadis, J., Gall, M., & Salovey, P. (in press). Evidence that emotional intelligence is related to job performance, and affect and attitudes at work. *Psicothema.*

Lopes, P. N., & Salovey, P. (2004). Toward a broader education: Social, emotional, and practical skills. In J. E. Zins, R. P. Weissberg, M. C. Wang, & H. J. Walberg (Eds.), *Building academic success on social and emotional learning* (pp. 76–93). New York: Teachers College Press.

Lopes, P. N., Salovey, P., Côté, S., & Beers, M. (2005). Emotion regulation abilities and the quality of social interaction. *Emotion, 5*, 113–118.

Lopes, P. N., Salovey, P., & Straus, R. (2003). Emotional intelligence, personality, and the perceived quality of social relationships. *Personality and Individual Differences, 35*, 641–658.

Mandler, G. (1975). *Mind and emotion.* New York: Wiley.

Maurer, M., Brackett, M. A., & Plain, F. (2004). *Emotional literacy in the middle school: A 6-step program to promote social, emotional, and academic learning.* New York: Dude Press.

Mayer, J. D., Caruso, D. R., & Salovey, P. (1998). *Multifactor Emotional Intelligence Scale (MEIS).* (Available from John D. Mayer, Department of Psychology, University of New Hampshire, Conant Hall, Durham, NH 03824)

Mayer, J. D., Caruso, D., & Salovey, P. (1999). Emotional intelligence meets traditional standards for an intelligence. *Intelligence, 27*, 267–298.

Mayer, J. D., DiPaolo, M. T., & Salovey, P. (1990). Perceiving affective content in ambiguous visual stimuli: A component of emotional intelligence. *Journal of Personality Assessment, 54*, 772–781.

Mayer, J. D., Gaschke, Y., Braverman, D. L., & Evans, T. (1992). Mood-congruent judgment is a general effect. *Journal of Personality and Social Psychology, 63*, 119–132.

Mayer, J. D., & Salovey, P. (1997). What is emotional intelligence? In P. Salovey & D. Sluyter (Eds.), *Emotional development and emotional intelligence: Educational implications* (pp. 3–31). New York: Basic Books.

Mayer, J. D., Salovey, P., & Caruso, D. (2002). *The Mayer-Salovey-Caruso Emotional Intelligence Test (MSCEIT)*. Toronto, Ontario, Canada: Multi-Health Systems.

Mellers, B., Schwartz, A., & Ritov, I. (1999). Emotion-based choice. *Journal of Experimental Psychology: General, 128*, 332–345.

Nolen-Hoeksema, S. (1993). Sex differences in control of depression. In D. M. Wegner & J. W. Pennebaker (Eds.), *Handbook of mental control* (pp. 306–324). Englewood Cliffs, NJ: Prentice-Hall.

Palfai, T. P., & Salovey, P. (1993). The influence of depressed and elated mood on deductive and inductive reasoning. *Imagination, Cognition, and Personality, 13*, 57–71.

Parkinson, B., & Totterdell, P. (1999). Classifying affect-regulation strategies. *Cognition and Emotion, 13*, 277–303.

Parrott, W. G. (2002). The functional utility of negative emotions. In L. Feldman Barrett & P. Salovey (Eds.), *The wisdom in feeling: Psychological processes in emotional intelligence* (pp. 341–359). New York: Guilford Press.

Pennebaker, J. W. (1989). Confession, inhibition, and disease. In L. Berkowitz (Ed.), *Advances in experimental social psychology* (Vol. 22, pp. 211–244). New York: Academic Press.

Pennebaker, J. W. (1993). Putting stress into words: Health, linguistic, and therapeutic implications. *Behavior Research and Therapy, 31*, 539–548.

Pennebaker, J. W. (1997). Writing about emotional experiences as a therapeutic process. *Psychological Science, 9*, 162–166.

Rice, C. L. (1999). *A quantitative study of emotional intelligence and its impact on team performance*. Unpublished master's thesis, Pepperdine University, Malibu, CA.

Rivers, S., Brackett, M. A., & Salovey, P. (2004). *Emotion regulation: Discrete emotions and individual differences*. Unpublished manuscript, Yale University, New Haven, CT.

Salovey, P., & Mayer, J. D. (1990). Emotional intelligence. *Imagination, Cognition, and Personality, 9*, 185–211.

Salovey, P., Mayer, J. D., & Caruso, D. (2002). The positive psychology of emotional intelligence. In C. R. Snyder & S. J. Lopez (Eds.), *Handbook of positive psychology* (pp. 159–171). New York: Oxford University Press.

Salovey, P., Mayer, J. D., Goldman, S. L., Turvey, C., & Palfai, T. P. (1995). Emotional attention, clarity, and repair: Exploring emotional intelligence using the Trait Meta-Mood Scale. In J. W. Pennebaker (Ed.), *Emotion, disclosure, and health* (pp. 125–154). Washington, DC: American Psychological Association.

Schaps, E., Battistich, V., & Solomon, D. (2004). Community in school as key to student growth: Findings from the child development project. In J. E. Zins, R. P. Weissberg, M. C. Wang, & H. J. Walberg (Eds.), *Building academic success on social and emotional learning* (pp. 76–93). New York: Teachers College Press.

Schutte, N. S., Malouff, J. M., Hall, L. E., Haggerty, D. J., Cooper, J. T., Golden, C. J., & Dornheim, L. (1998). Development and validation of a measure of emotional intelligence. *Personality and Individual Differences, 25,* 167–177.

Schwarz, N. (1990). Feelings as information: Informational and motivational functions of affective states. In E. T. Higgins & E. M. Sorrentino (Eds.), *Handbook of motivation and cognition* (Vol. 2, pp. 527–561). New York: Guilford Press.

Shaffer, L. F. (1936). *The psychology of adjustment: An objective approach to mental hygiene.* Boston: Houghton Mifflin.

Shields, S. A. (2002). *Speaking from the heart: Gender and the social meaning of emotion.* Cambridge, England: Cambridge University Press.

Simon, H. A. (1982). Comments. In M. S. Clark & S. T. Fiske (Eds.), *Affect and cognition* (pp. 333–342). Hillsdale, NJ: Erlbaum.

Sternberg, R. J. (1985). *Beyond IQ: A triarchic theory of human intelligence.* Cambridge, England: Cambridge University Press.

Thayer, R. E., Newman, J. R., & McClain, T. M. (1994). Self-regulation of mood: Strategies for changing a bad mood, raising energy, and reducing tension. *Journal of Personality and Social Psychology, 67,* 910–925.

Thompson, R. A. (1994). Emotion regulation: A theme in search of definition. *Monographs of the Society for Research in Child Development, 59*(2–3, Serial No. 240), 25–52.

Thompson, R. A. (1998). Early sociopersonality development. In W. Damon (Series Ed.) & N. Eisenberg (Vol. Ed.), *Handbook of child psychology: Vol. 3. Social, emotional, and personality development* (5th ed., pp. 25–104). New York: Wiley.

Young, K. (1940). *Personality and problems of adjustment.* New York: Appleton-Century-Crofts.

3

ADULT ATTACHMENT THEORY AND AFFECTIVE REACTIVITY AND REGULATION

PAULA R. PIETROMONACO, LISA FELDMAN BARRETT, AND SALLY I. POWERS

Attachment theory (Bowlby, 1969, 1973, 1979, 1980) emphasizes the emotional nature of close bonds between two people. Bowlby's original theory, which focused on understanding the close, enduring bonds between infants and their caregivers, highlighted two ways in which emotion is implicated in attachment. First, when infants experience emotional distress, they seek proximity to their caregiver. Second, caregivers who are sensitive and responsive are able to help infants regulate their feelings of distress, enabling them to experience an emotional sense of well-being or "felt security" (Sroufe & Waters, 1997). Research on attachment in adult close relationships (e.g., romantic relationships), which are the focus of this chapter, also has highlighted the connection between attachment and emotion (e.g., Hazan & Shaver, 1987; Pietromonaco & Feldman Barrett, 2000). Like children, when adults become distressed in the face of a threat, they may seek out an attachment figure in an attempt to regain an emotional sense of felt security (Simpson & Rholes, 1994).

Although researchers have examined the link between adult attachment and emotion, the precise role of emotion in attachment processes remains unclear. Most researchers have assumed that mental representations of the self in relation to others, or internal working models (Bowlby, 1973), trigger the experience and regulation of emotion. However, the object relations tradition from which Bowlby emerged reflects a conception of working models as part of a dynamic system that is organized by both the experience and regulation of emotion (Pietromonaco & Feldman Barrett, 2000; Reis & Patrick, 1996). Following this perspective, we (Pietromonaco & Feldman Barrett, 2000) have proposed that emotion and regulation strategies are formative in the development and maintenance of working models, and that emotion is an organizing force in working models rather than an outcome of them. Accordingly, we assume that two affect-based processes underlie working models of attachment and the operation of the attachment system: (a) *affective reactivity*, defined as the frequency with which individuals experience a feeling of threat, thereby activating the need for felt security, and (b) *affect regulation strategies*, defined as the patterns of relationship behavior that individuals enact in an attempt to maintain or restore felt security. We use the terms *affective reactivity* and *affect regulation* rather than *emotional reactivity* and *emotion regulation* because we are referring to the experience and regulation of global feelings of distress (i.e., global negative affect) rather than to the experience and regulation of specific emotions (e.g., fear, anger).

The goal of this chapter is to assess the affective underpinnings of adult attachment. We evaluate the current evidence, elaborate our theoretical perspective, and present new evidence from our ongoing research program. In addition, we propose several directions for future research, evaluate the potential for interdisciplinary collaboration, and discuss the implications of understanding the affective bases of attachment for clinical interventions.

CONCEPTUAL FOUNDATIONS OF ATTACHMENT THEORY AND AFFECT REGULATION

Attachment theory, at heart, concerns the experience and regulation of emotion. Several fundamental assumptions underlie the theory (for a comprehensive discussion of the theory, see Mikulincer & Shaver, 2003). First, the attachment system, as conceived by Bowlby (e.g., 1969, 1973), fulfills the evolutionarily adaptive function of keeping human infants close to their caregivers. Infants and children who remain physically close to their caregivers, or who seek proximity when a potentially dangerous situation arises, are more likely to survive and to reproduce in adulthood. Second, Bowlby proposed that the attachment-behavioral system is a hard-wired regulatory system that directs infants to seek out their caregivers in the face of threat. Thus, the attachment system is particularly likely to be activated when infants perceive either a physical or psychological threat. When a threat is perceived, infants will seek contact with their primary caregiver. If the caregiver is not available or is insufficiently responsive, then the infant is likely to experience distress (fear, anxiety). If the caregiver is available and responsive, then contact should help to reduce distress and to restore a sense of emotional safety, or felt security. Third, children learn from their interactions with attachment figures, and this knowledge develops into mental representations, or internal working models, that include information about whether attachment figures will be available and responsive (view of others) and whether the self is worthy of love (view of self). These mental representations are assumed to guide thoughts, feelings, and behavior and to shape the nature of affect regulation attempts in subsequent situations. Thus, children learn what to expect from attachment figures, and given the particular characteristics of their partnership, they learn which strategies are most likely to enable them to cope with distress (Cassidy, 1994).

Although Bowlby focused on the operation of the attachment-behavioral system during infancy and childhood, he viewed the system as enduring over the life course (Bowlby, 1979). Hazan and Shaver (1987) elaborated on Bowlby's original theory by conceptualizing adult romantic relationships as attachment bonds governed by processes similar to those that occur in infant–caregiver relationships. Thus, romantic partners may seek out each other in the face of distress, and they may help or hinder each other's efforts to regulate distress. Adults also hold working models of their romantic attachment relationships, and these models may include knowledge from earlier attachment relationships as well as additional knowledge acquired from interactions with attachment figures in adulthood (e.g., romantic partners).[1]

Individual Differences in Adult Attachment Style

Adult attachment theory (e.g., Fraley & Shaver, 2000; Hazan & Shaver, 1987; Mikulincer & Shaver, 2003), like the original developmental theory (Ainsworth, Blehar, Waters, & Wall, 1978; Bowlby, 1973), assumes that individual differences exist in the degree to which people use attachment figures as sources of security and in the degree to which they are able to achieve felt security. These individual differences are thought to arise from actual differences in recurring interaction patterns with attachment figures, and they are reflected in the content of internal working models.

In their pioneering work, Hazan and Shaver (1987) proposed that individual differences in adult attachment styles paralleled the three behavioral

---

[1]Although adult attachment theory (Hazan & Shaver, 1987) assumes that some continuity exists between working models developed during childhood and those later in life, the degree of continuity remains an open question (Pietromonaco & Feldman Barrett, 2000). Attachment processes (e.g., seeking proximity when distressed), however, appear to operate in similar ways in childhood and adulthood (Mikulincer & Shaver, 2003).

patterns (i.e., secure, anxious-ambivalent, avoidant) that Ainsworth (Ainsworth et al., 1978) observed in infant–caregiver relationships. Ainsworth's investigations using the Strange Situation and home observations revealed that securely attached infants were easily comforted when they were reunited with their caregiver after a separation, and they appeared to have caregivers who were available and responsive. Anxious-ambivalent infants became intensely distressed when separated from their caregiver, and they were not easily comforted when the caregiver returned. Their caregivers appeared to respond inconsistently, and this pattern of responding over time may have heightened the distress reactions of these infants. Avoidant infants did not show much distress when they were separated from the caregiver, and they tended to ignore the caregiver when the two were reunited. The caregivers of avoidant infants tended to be distant or unavailable. Each of these behavioral patterns is thought to reflect an affect regulation strategy that is functional in that particular kind of relationship (Cassidy, 1994; Mikulincer & Shaver, 2003). Infants with responsive caregivers (secure infants) are able to restore a sense of well-being or felt security by seeking proximity to the caregiver. Those with inconsistently available caregivers (anxious-ambivalent infants) appear to rely on hyperactivating strategies (intense distress, repeated protest, heightened vigilance), and those with distant or unavailable caregivers appear to use deactivating strategies (detachment, self-reliance). Attachment patterns in adult romantic relationships show similarities to those observed in infants (Hazan & Shaver, 1987). Secure adults evidence comfort with closeness and intimacy, anxious-ambivalent adults show an excessive concern with closeness and worry that partners will leave, and avoidant adults evidence discomfort with closeness and intimacy.

Although initial work on adult attachment focused on these three attachment styles, more recent work has conceptualized individual differences in adult attachment in terms of four prototypes (i.e., secure, preoccupied, fearful-avoidant, dismissing-avoidant; Bartholomew & Horowitz, 1991) or in terms of two dimensions underlying the categories (Brennan, Clark, & Shaver, 1998; Fraley, Waller, & Brennan, 2000). These dimensions are often characterized as anxious-ambivalence and avoidance. People high in anxious-ambivalence desire closeness and intimacy, but they are unable to achieve a stable sense of closeness and security. People high in avoidance are reluctant to rely on others and prefer to maintain emotional distance.

The interaction between the two dimensions yields four attachment prototypes identified in previous research (Bartholomew & Horowitz, 1991). Thus, people who are low on both the anxious-ambivalence and avoidance dimensions, who fall within the *secure* prototype, are comfortable with closeness and able to rely on others when the need arises. People high in anxious-ambivalence but low in avoidance, who fall within the *preoccupied* (or *anxious-ambivalent*) prototype, desire a high degree of closeness, are preoccupied with relationships, and worry about being abandoned. People high in anxious-ambivalence and high in avoidance, who fall within the *fearful-avoidant* prototype, both desire and fear closeness, whereas those high in avoidance and low in anxious-ambivalence, who fall within the *dismissing-avoidant* prototype, are reluctant to rely on others, self-reliant, and prefer to maintain emotional distance. These patterns are assumed to represent an adaptive response to the demands of a particular attachment relationship, and they are thought to reflect underlying working models.

Affect-Based Processes

In our view, two affect-based processes, affective reactivity and regulation, underlie working models. We tie affective reactivity specifically to sensitivity to threat because threat is assumed to activate the attachment system (Bowlby, 1973; Mikulincer & Shaver, 2003; Simpson & Rholes, 1994). People experience a feeling of threat when they feel unable to cope, and this experience may be triggered externally by factors in the environment, or internally from negative affect (see Pietromonaco & Feldman Barrett, 2000). The implication is that people who are more emotionally reactive will more frequently perceive a threat, thereby leading them to experience more frequent activation of the attachment system, and as a consequence, a more frequent need to regulate their feelings of distress. In addition, the regulation element in our model focuses specifically on interpersonally based affect regulation (i.e., approaching or avoiding others) rather than on a wider range of regulatory strategies.

The reactivity and regulation elements in our model should be connected to individual differences in attachment style in predictable ways. Figure 3.1 depicts the two dimensions of affective reactivity and affect regulation through reliance on others and their link to each of the adult attachment style prototypes. People who are high in anxious-ambivalence (i.e., preoccupied or fearful-avoidant) are predicted to more frequently experience a feeling of threat, and as a consequence, they will more frequently need to engage in behaviors that will help them to restore felt security. Affect regulation strategies for people high in anxious-ambivalence will differ depending on whether they are high or low in avoidance; those low in avoidance (i.e., preoccupied prototype) are likely to rely on others to restore felt security, whereas those high in avoidance (i.e., fearful-avoidant prototype) will be less willing to rely on others. People who are low in both anxious-ambivalence and low in avoidance (i.e., secure prototype) are expected to experience threat less often; when they do, however, they will be willing to rely on others to restore felt security. People high in avoidance and low in anxious-ambivalence (i.e., dismissing-avoidant prototype), who may use defensive strategies to suppress threat (Fraley, Davis, & Shaver, 1998), are expected to be less likely to experience a feeling of threat, and when they do, they will be less likely to rely on others.

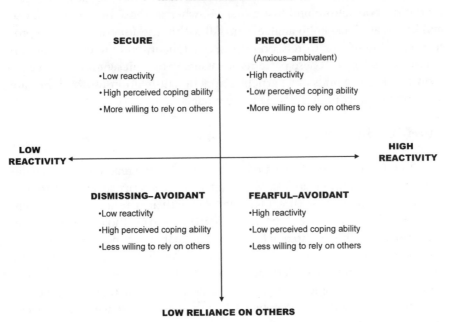

Figure 3.1. Connection between affective reactivity and regulation through reliance on others and adult attachment prototypes.

EMPIRICAL FOUNDATIONS

It follows from our model that people who more frequently perceive threats in the environment should be more likely to experience emotional distress. Most of the evidence relevant to this proposition comes from studies in which participants provide self-reports of their emotional experience. In general, this work has shown that people higher in anxious-ambivalence (preoccupation) experience greater emotional reactivity. For example, people with an anxious-ambivalent attachment style consistently report more intense emotions (e.g., Collins & Read, 1990; Pietromonaco & Feldman Barrett, 1997), greater fluctuations in their emotions (Hazan & Shaver, 1987), and greater emotional expressivity (Bartholomew & Horowitz, 1991). In contrast, people with a more avoidant style report little emotionality (Bartholomew & Horowitz, 1991; Collins & Read, 1990; Hazan & Shaver, 1987; Pietromonaco & Carnelley, 1994; Pietromonaco & Feldman Barrett, 1997).

In addition, we would expect that people high in anxious-ambivalence would show greater emotional reactivity than others across more contexts because they perceive a wider range of contexts as threat related. The few relevant studies (Mikulincer, Birnbaum, Woddis, & Nachmias, 2000; Mikulincer, Gillath, & Shaver, 2002; Simpson, Rholes, & Phillips, 1996) are consistent with this idea. Findings from these studies suggest that, regardless of whether the context was defined experimentally as threatening, people higher in anxious-ambivalence show greater emotional reactivity; they report greater distress (Simpson et al., 1996), and they respond more rapidly to the names of attachment figures (Mikulincer et al., 2002) and to proximity-related words (Mikulincer et al., 2000). Given that all of the experimental contexts in these studies concerned attachment, it may be that such contexts, in themselves, trigger a feeling of threat for those with an anxious-ambivalent style.

We also have proposed that the way in which adults regulate affect (e.g., through approaching or avoiding others) differs with attachment style. Overall, the evidence is consistent with our model. People higher in anxious-ambivalence are more likely to turn to others for help with regulating their negative feelings, whereas those who are more avoidant distance themselves from others (e.g., Collins & Feeney, 2000; Mikulincer, 1998; Mikulincer, Florian, & Weller, 1993; Mikulincer, Orbach, & Iavnieli, 1998; Ognibene & Collins, 1998; Pietromonaco & Feldman Barrett, in press; Simpson, Rholes, & Nelligan, 1992). Indeed, for people high in attachment anxiety, the experimental activation of attachment security (i.e., by subliminally priming the word *love*), which may evoke a representation of an attachment figure, appears to provide a comforting or soothing effect by reducing the accessibility of terror-related words (see chap. 4, this volume).

Many questions about the link between attachment and affective reactivity and regulation remain unanswered. One key question concerns what is defined as an attachment-relevant threat by people of different attachment styles (Pietromonaco, Greenwood, & Feldman Barrett, 2004). Are some individuals more likely to perceive threat in what may be normatively nonthreatening situations (Quigley & Feldman Barrett, 1999)? If so, how is this more frequent experience of threat connected to the ability to benefit from attempts to regulate negative affect?

A second key question concerns how efforts to regulate affect vary depending on characteristics of the partner (e.g., partner's affective reactivity and preferred regulation strategies). Some work (Carnelley, Pietromonaco, & Jaffe, 1996; Collins & Feeney, 2000; Feeney & Collins, 2001; Simpson et al., 1992; Simpson, Rholes, Oriña, & Grich, 2002) suggests that one partner's attachment style may contribute to the other partner's ability to regulate emotional distress. For example, more avoidant men have been found to be less likely to provide support when their female partner displays greater emotional distress (Simpson et al., 1992), and thus their female partners may be slower to recover from such distress. Other work (Simpson et al., 2002) suggests that more securely attached women respond more flexibly to their partner's needs; secure women provide more support when their male partner desires support, but they provide less support when the male partner does not desire it. In addition, work examining behavior during conflict interactions (for a review, see Pietromonaco et al., 2004) suggests that couples are more adept at communicating during conflict when both partners are secure; for example, their interactions show greater synchrony in the timing of behaviors and less asymmetry in dominance (Bouthillier, Julien, Dube, Belanger, & Hamelin, 2002), and they report less withdrawal and verbal aggression during conflict (Senchak & Leonard, 1992). In addition, couples including at least one secure partner evidence more constructive behavior (e.g., express greater validation, greater affection, less contempt; Creasey, 2002) when negotiating conflict than do couples including two insecure partners (see Pietromonaco, Greenwood, et al., 2004). Resolving conflict in a constructive manner may be facilitated by the ability of secure partners to behave in ways that reduce their partner's distress. Furthermore, characteristics of the partner should be especially important for individuals who more frequently regulate their feelings by relying on others.

A third key question is whether people higher in anxious-ambivalence show greater affective reactivity when reactivity is assessed through non-self-report or more implicit measures. Evidence from studies that do not rely on global self-reports suggests that avoidance also may be associated with greater reactivity. For example, two diary studies (Pietromonaco & Feldman Barrett, 1997; Tidwell, Reis, & Shaver, 1996) have found that in immediate, online reports following social interactions, avoidant individuals (but not anxious-ambivalent individuals) evidenced more negative emotion than did secure individuals. This pattern was evident across social interactions in general (Pietromonaco & Feldman Barrett, 1997; Tidwell et al., 1996) as well as during high-conflict interactions (Pietromonaco & Feldman Barrett, 1997) and interactions with different kinds of partners (e.g., same-sex, opposite-sex; Tidwell et al., 1996). Although researchers have rarely examined the link between adult attachment and any kind of physiological response, a few studies (e.g., Feeney & Kirkpatrick, 1996; Mikulincer, 1998) assessing cardiovascular measures suggest that individuals with an insecure romantic attachment style (i.e., anxious-ambivalent or avoidant) show greater physiological reactivity than do those with a secure romantic attachment style.

Findings from our recent research begin to address the last two key questions raised here. One study (Pietromonaco, Feldman Barrett, & Holmes, 2005) examined the degree to which individuals' own attachment style as well as the attachment style of the romantic partner predicted individuals' self-reported patterns of affective reactivity and regulatory strategies in response to attachment-related threats. Another study (Powers, Pietromonaco, Gunlicks, & Sayer, in press) examined the link between attachment and affective reactivity assessed through a physiological measure, and it also considered the contribution of the partner's attachment style.

Attachment and Self-Reported Affective Reactivity and Regulation

In one study (Pietromonaco et al., 2004), we directly tested the idea that differences in affective reactivity and regulation are connected to adult attachment patterns in theoretically predicted ways (see Figure 3.1), and we examined whether the partner's attachment style contributed to individuals' patterns of affective reactivity and regulation. Although previous work has investigated self-reported patterns of affective reactivity and regulation strategies, this study extended that work by examining a wide range of attachment-relevant threatening situations, and by investigating whether the partner's attachment style, alone or in combination with the individuals' attachment style, predicted responses. If attachment figures help people to regulate their feelings, then the strategies that a person uses may be shaped, to some extent, by how emotionally responsive, available, and sensitive his or her partner is. For example, people paired with a more avoidant partner, who may be less willing to discuss problems, may feel less equipped to cope with a threatening event in the relationship.

In this study, both partners in dating couples (N = 76 couples) separately read a variety of potentially threatening, attachment-relevant scenarios (e.g., "Your romantic partner didn't comfort you when you were feeling down"; "Your romantic partner was just offered a great job in another part of the country and may be making plans to move") and imagined themselves experiencing each situation. After reading each scenario, participants reported on how distressed they would feel in the situation, the degree to which they felt able to cope with the situation (appraisal of their coping ability), and the extent to which they would use different coping strategies (e.g., trying to change the situation, talking to someone for support or reassurance, suppressing one's feelings).

Consistent with the predictions advanced in our model, individuals who scored higher in anxious-ambivalence reported that they would experience more emotional distress and that they felt less able to cope with the situations. Attachment avoidance was not associated with reported distress. In addition, individuals higher in anxious attachment were more likely to deal with the problem by relying on others. In contrast, individuals higher in avoidance were less likely to report that they would rely on others (e.g., they were less likely to talk to someone for reassurance). They also were more likely to distance themselves by trying to suppress their feelings. Overall, in line with our model and with other research, people higher in anxious attachment were more likely to use others in the interest of regulating their feelings, whereas those higher in avoidance were less likely to do so.

In addition, the degree to which individuals' own attachment avoidance predicted their perceived ability to cope and their use of particular coping strategies was moderated by their partner's attachment avoidance. People who were low in avoidance felt less able to cope when their partner was more avoidant. In contrast, people who were high in avoidance generally felt well able to cope, and their perceptions were not associated with their partner's degree of avoidance. In a similar manner, people low in avoidance who were paired with a highly avoidant partner were less likely to try to distract themselves by taking their mind off the situation and more likely to try to get information from someone else to cope with the situation. In contrast, people high in avoidance who had a highly avoidant partner were more likely to distract themselves and less likely to try to get information from someone. These findings suggest that how a person copes with emotional distress and whether that method is effective or not needs to be evaluated within the context of the relationship. People low in avoidance who are paired with avoidant partners may feel less able to cope because their partners are likely to be unwilling to confront the situation, and they may believe that they must take an active stance to achieve any kind of resolution. People high in avoidance who are with avoidant partners may benefit (at least some of the time) by using distancing strategies.

Overall, these findings suggest that affect regulation strategies need to be considered not only in terms of an individuals' own attachment style but also within the interpersonal context of the specific attachment relationship. Perceptions of the ability to cope and the preference for particular strategies appear to depend, to some extent, on the attachment styles of both partners involved in the relationship.

This study focused on people's conscious, self-reported feelings and regulatory strategies. Self-report measures provide information about these more conscious aspects of affective experience, but it is also important to examine the affective underpinnings of attachment by looking at less consciously controlled response systems.

Attachment and Physiological Reactivity and Regulation

In another study, we (Powers, Pietromonaco, Gunlicks, & Sayer, in press) investigated whether individuals' own attachment style and their dating partner's attachment style predicted physiological responses to a stressful situation. This work focused on a physiological measure that taps into a major stress-response system, reactivity of the hypothalamic-pituitary-adrenal (HPA) axis (assessed through salivary cortisol). The stressful situation consisted of a standard conflict discussion in which dating couples discussed and tried to resolve an issue that represented a significant source of disagreement in their relationship. Conflict interactions generally induce stress, and they are likely to activate attachment behavior because they often raise concerns about the partner's emotional availability and responsiveness (Simpson et al., 1996).

In this study, dating partners (124 couples) provided seven saliva samples over the course of the session. These samples allowed us to assess participants' stress responses shortly before they entered the lab, through anticipation of the conflict discussion (i.e., after the experimenter provided a detailed description of the conflict task), during the discussion, and throughout a recovery period of 40 minutes after the discussion.[2]

In line with previous work examining adult attachment and cardiovascular reactivity, we found that people with a more insecure romantic attachment style showed greater cortisol reactivity. However, the type of insecure attachment (i.e., anxious-ambivalence or avoidance) associated with reactivity differed for women and men. Women high in avoidance entered the lab with higher cortisol levels, and their cortisol levels remained high throughout the conflict task. Men higher in anxious-ambivalence showed greater reactivity in anticipation of and during the conflict than did men lower in anxious-ambivalence. The nature of the conflict task may contribute to this gender difference in the link between attachment and cortisol reactivity. Women typically initiate and guide discussions about relationship problems, a task that may be particularly stressful for avoidant women. Men high in anxious-ambivalence may show greater stress reactivity because their desire to express relationship concerns runs counter to gender role norms for such interactions.

We also examined the extent to which the romantic partner's attachment style predicted individuals' patterns of cortisol reactivity and recovery. If partners help each other with affect regulation, then the partner's attachment style is likely to contribute to the extent to which people show reactivity to threat. In particular, individuals with more emotionally responsive partners (i.e., secure partners) should show less HPA reactivity in the face of conflict, whereas those with less responsive (e.g., more avoidant) partners should show greater HPA reactivity. We found the predicted pattern for men, but not for women. Men with more secure partners (i.e., partners low in anxious-ambivalence and low in avoidance) evidenced the lowest levels of cortisol throughout the session. Furthermore, men with more insecure partners (i.e., high in avoidance and low in anxiety, high in anxiety and low in avoidance, or high in both anxiety and avoidance) showed greater reactivity; their cortisol levels remained higher through the session than those for men with a more secure partner. Thus, men with partners who were likely to be more emotionally responsive (e.g., secure partners) showed less HPA reactivity in the face of conflict, suggesting that their secure partners may help them to feel less distressed in a normatively stressful situation.

Overall, these findings differ somewhat from those obtained with self-report measures of affect. Although self-report studies have generally found similar patterns for men and women, this study suggests that the link be-

---

[2]Cortisol appears in the saliva approximately 15 to 20 minutes after it is secreted from the adrenal gland. Thus, each salivary sample indexed participants' cortisol reactions about 15 to 20 minutes prior to the time of collection. For example, the sample taken when participants entered the lab indicated their stress response about 5 to 10 minutes before their arrival at the lab.

tween attachment style and less conscious measures of affective reactivity may differ for men and women. Even though men and women interacted in an objectively similar situation, they may have differed in their perceptions of the situational context, which in turn may have contributed to their patterns of physiological reactivity. This work highlights the importance of examining the link between attachment and affective reactivity and regulation using a wider range of measures that tap into different response systems.

IMPLICATIONS AND FUTURE DIRECTIONS FOR RESEARCH

Our work suggests several directions for future research on the role of affect in adult attachment. In addition, our work has implications for interdisciplinary collaboration and clinical interventions. We discuss each of these topics in the following sections.

Research on the Affective Bases of Attachment

Our work (Pietromonaco et al., 2004; Powers et al., in press) suggests that individuals' own attachment style as well as their partner's attachment style contributes to their ability to regulate negative affect. Future work should examine these processes over time to capture the reciprocal nature of affect regulation efforts in adults' attachment relationships (see Diamond, 2001). In particular, it will be important to examine how the characteristics of both partners facilitate or impair attempts to regulate emotional distress, and whether these effects vary across different interpersonal stressors.

In addition, we know little about the conditions under which turning to an attachment figure reduces negative affect or increases feelings of emotional security. For example, under what conditions do people high in anxious-ambivalence benefit from seeking help from an attachment figure, and under what conditions do such efforts exacerbate their distress? What makes it possible for a partner to serve as an effective source of comfort, and does the nature of this ability vary depending on the recipient's attachment security?

It also will be important to examine more directly whether people higher in anxious-ambivalence or avoidance are more sensitive to threat. If so, is this sensitivity specific to attachment-relevant contexts, or does it also extend to non-relational-threatening contexts? Moreover, do people who have different attachment styles differ in their base rates for perceiving threat in situations that most people view as benign? And what mechanisms (e.g., the ability to effortfully control attention or to inhibit an inappropriate response) are implicated in threat sensitivity?

Many of these questions concern whether individual differences in temperament, which has also been defined in terms of emotional reactivity and self-regulation (e.g., Eisenberg & Fabes, 1992; Rothbart, Ahadi, & Evans,

2000), underlie attachment styles. Although considerable controversy exists about the degree of overlap between temperament and attachment, temperament serves as part of the context in which attachment relationships develop (Rothbart et al., 2000). For example, infants who are prone to distress may differ from those less prone to distress in their experiences in attachment-related situations, and their greater reactivity may make it harder for caregivers to respond to them sensitively. Likewise, adults who are prone to emotional distress may construe attachment-related situations differently from those who are less distress prone, making it more difficult for distress-prone individuals to use emotion regulation strategies (Quigley & Feldman Barrett, 1999) and for their partners to help them regain emotional well-being.

Implications for Interdisciplinary Collaboration and Clinical Intervention

Our work is grounded within social and personality psychology, but the study of the affective bases of attachment cuts across multiple areas. We see a pressing need for interdisciplinary collaborations with developmental and clinical psychologists and cognitive neuroscientists. We make this claim for several reasons. First, attachment theory is rooted in developmental psychology, and any comprehensive view of attachment processes in adulthood must be tied to those in childhood. Collaborative work with developmental psychologists (particularly behavioral geneticists) will be critical for understanding the trajectory of emotional reactivity and regulation in attachment relationships from childhood to adulthood.

Second, attachment theory evolved, in part, from observations of clinical phenomena. Most of the work in social and personality psychology has examined attachment processes in young adults who fall within the normal range of psychological adjustment. However, work in this area would be informed by examining these processes in individuals in whom affective processes have broken down (e.g., in people who have anxiety or depressive disorders). Furthermore, much work has focused on young dating couples who vary in relationship length and commitment. It would be advantageous to extend this work to married couples, particularly those experiencing some type of distress. In a similar way, couples who are facing normative stressors (e.g., the birth of a child) or atypical stressors (e.g., impaired physical health) provide an excellent context for investigating affective reactivity and regulation under clinically significant conditions.

Third, knowledge in this area will be advanced by investigating the neuropsychological mechanisms that support emotional reactivity and regulatory processes in attachment relationships (see Diamond, 2001).

Several barriers must be overcome to facilitate such collaborations. For example, a lack of consensus exists between some developmental and social psychologists in the conceptualization of attachment phenomena and how those phenomena should be studied. Also, collaborations between social psychologists and neuroscientists are not as frequent as they might be, in part because researchers in these subareas must become familiar with vastly different knowledge bases. In addition, even though social–personality and clinical researchers share much in common, pragmatic issues such as access to organizations and patient populations also impede such collaborations.

If individuals with heightened sensitivity to threat perceive threat in situations that are normatively nonthreatening, intervention efforts will need to address how to alter such patterns. Changing emotional reactivity to relationship threats is likely to be difficult (Quigley & Feldman Barrett, 1999) because emotional associations are not completely unlearned through extinction or counterconditioning. Instead, change often occurs through the development of more deliberate strategies to regulate emotion and through training to recognize biases that lead to the inappropriate identification of threat cues (Quigley & Feldman Barrett, 1999). For example, cognitive interventions that encourage couple members to generate alternative interpretations of threatening events (e.g., Epstein & Baucom, 2002) may disrupt affective reactivity and instill more deliberate affect regulation strategies. Another type of intervention that may alter perceptions and responses to threat is emotionally focused therapy (Greenberg & Johnson, 1988). Emotionally focused therapy, which is grounded in attachment theory, aims to alter the affect underlying attachment representations by providing significant affective experiences within marital therapy. In particular, this therapy seeks to promote the expression of each partner's needs for closeness and security and to facilitate interactions that increase security and bolster the ability of each partner to be available and responsive to the other's needs (i.e., to serve as a secure base). As partners develop a more secure relationship, they may perceive threats less frequently. This may permit individuals to regulate their emotional distress by relying more on their partners, who have learned to be more responsive and emotionally available.

Research that tests the efficacy of these interventions should provide important information about the mechanisms underlying the regulation of emotional distress. In turn, a more precise understanding of the mechanisms that lead some individuals to experience difficulty with distress regulation in attachment relationships should facilitate the development of more refined interventions.

REFERENCES

Ainsworth, M. S., Blehar, M. C., Waters, E., & Wall, S. (1978). *Patterns of attachment: A psychological study of the strange situation.* Oxford, England: Erlbaum.

Bartholomew, K., & Horowitz, L. M. (1991). Attachment styles among young adults: A test of a four-category model. *Journal of Personality and Social Psychology, 61,* 226–244.

Bouthillier, D., Julien, D., Dube, M., Belanger, I., & Hamelin, M. (2002). Predictive validity of adult attachment measures in relation to emotion regulation behaviors in marital interactions. *Journal of Adult Development, 9,* 291–305.

Bowlby, J. (1969). *Attachment and loss: Vol. 1. Attachment.* New York: Basic Books.

Bowlby, J. (1973). *Attachment and loss: Vol. 2. Separation: Anxiety and anger.* New York: Basic Books.

Bowlby, J. (1979). *The making and breaking of affectional bonds.* London: Tavistock.

Bowlby, J. (1980). *Attachment and loss: Vol. 3. Loss: Sadness and depression.* New York: Basic Books.

Brennan, K. A., Clark, C. L., & Shaver, P. R. (1998). Self-report measurement of adult attachment: An integrative overview. In J. A. Simpson & W. S. Rholes (Eds.), *Attachment theory and close relationships* (pp. 46–76). New York: Guilford Press.

Carnelley, K. B., Pietromonaco, P. R., & Jaffe, K. (1996). Attachment, caregiving, and relationship functioning in couples: Effects of self and partner. *Personal Relationships, 3,* 257–277.

Cassidy, J. (1994). Emotion regulation: Influences of attachment relationships. *Monographs of the Society for Research in Child Development, 59*(2–3, Serial No. 240), 228–283.

Collins, N. L., & Feeney, B. C. (2000). A safe haven: An attachment theoretical perspective on support seeking and caregiving in intimate relationships. *Journal of Personality and Social Psychology, 78,* 1053–1073.

Collins, N. L., & Read, S. J. (1990). Adult attachment, working models, and relationship quality in dating couples. *Journal of Personality and Social Psychology, 58,* 644–663.

Creasey, G. (2002). Associations between working models of attachment and conflict management behavior in romantic couples. *Journal of Counseling Psychology, 49,* 365–375.

Diamond, L. M. (2001). Contributions of psychophysiology to research on adult attachment: Review and recommendations. *Personality and Social Psychology Review, 5,* 276–295.

Eisenberg, N., & Fabes, R. A. (1992). Emotion, regulation, and the development of social competence. In M. S. Clark et al. (Eds.), *Review of personality and social psychology: Vol. 14. Emotion and social behavior* (pp. 119–150). Newbury Park, CA: Sage.

Epstein, N. B., & Baucom, D. H. (2002). *Enhanced cognitive–behavioral therapy for couples: A contextual approach.* Washington, DC: American Psychological Association.

Feeney, B. C., & Collins, N. L. (2001). Predictors of caregiving in adult intimate relationships: An attachment theoretical perspective. *Journal of Personality and Social Psychology, 80,* 972–994.

Feeney, B. C., & Kirkpatrick, L. A. (1996). Effects of adult attachment and presence of romantic partners on physiological responses to stress. *Journal of Personality and Social Psychology, 70,* 255–270.

Fraley, R. C., Davis, K. E., & Shaver, P. R. (1998). Dismissing-avoidance and the defensive organization of emotion, cognition, and behavior. In J. A. Simpson & W. S. Rholes (Eds.), *Attachment theory and close relationships* (pp. 249–279). New York: Guilford Press.

Fraley, R. C., & Shaver, P. R. (2000). Adult romantic attachment: Theoretical developments, emerging controversies, and unanswered questions. *Review of General Psychology, 4,* 132–154.

Fraley, R. C., Waller, N. G., & Brennan, K. (2000). An item response theory analysis of self-report measures of adult attachment. *Journal of Personality and Social Psychology, 78,* 350–365.

Greenberg, L. S., & Johnson, S. M. (1988). *Emotionally focused therapy for couples.* New York: Guilford Press.

Hazan, C., & Shaver, P. R. (1987). Romantic love conceptualized as an attachment process. *Journal of Personality and Social Psychology, 52,* 511–524.

Mikulincer, M. (1998). Adult attachment style and individual differences in functional versus dysfunctional experiences of anger. *Journal of Personality and Social Psychology, 74,* 513–524.

Mikulincer, M., Birnbaum, G., Woddis, D., & Nachmias, O. (2000). Stress and accessibility of proximity-related thoughts: Exploring the normative and intraindividual components of attachment theory. *Journal of Personality and Social Psychology, 78,* 509–523.

Mikulincer, M., Florian, V., & Weller, A. (1993). Attachment styles, coping strategies, and posttraumatic psychological distress: The impact of the Gulf War in Israel. *Journal of Personality and Social Psychology, 64,* 817–826.

Mikulincer, M., Gillath, O., & Shaver, P. R. (2002). Activation of the attachment system in adulthood: Threat-related primes increase the accessibility of mental representations of attachment figures. *Journal of Personality and Social Psychology, 83,* 881–895.

Mikulincer, M., Orbach, I., & Iavnieli, D. (1998). Adult attachment style and affect regulation: Strategic variations in subjective self–other similarity. *Journal of Personality and Social Psychology, 75,* 436–448.

Mikulincer, M., & Shaver, P. R. (2003). The attachment behavioral system in adulthood: Activation, psychodynamics, and interpersonal processes. In M. Zanna (Ed.), *Advances in experimental social psychology* (Vol. 35, pp. 53–152). New York: Academic Press.

Ognibene, T. C., & Collins, N. L. (1998). Adult attachment styles, perceived social support, and coping strategies. *Journal of Social and Personal Relationships, 15,* 323–345.

Pietromonaco, P. R., & Carnelley, K. B. (1994). Gender and working models of attachment: Consequences for perceptions of self and romantic relationships. *Personal Relationships, 1,* 63–82.

Pietromonaco, P. R., & Feldman Barrett, L. (1997). Working models of attachment and daily social interactions. *Journal of Personality and Social Psychology, 73,* 1409–1423.

Pietromonaco, P. R., & Feldman Barrett, L. (2000). Internal working models: What do we really know about the self in relation to others? *Review of General Psychology, 4,* 155–175.

Pietromonaco, P. R., & Feldman Barrett, L. (in press). What can you do for me? Attachment style and motives for valuing partners. *Journal of Research in Personality.*

Pietromonaco, P. R., Feldman Barrett, L., & Holmes, B. (2005). *Romantic partners' attachment styles and patterns of emotional reactivity and regulation.* Manuscript in preparation. University of Massachusetts, Amherst.

Pietromonaco, P. R., Greenwood, D., & Feldman Barrett, L. (2004). Conflict in adult close relationships: An attachment perspective. In W. S. Rholes & J. A. Simpson (Eds.), *Adult attachment: New directions and emerging issues* (pp. 267–299). New York: Guilford Press.

Powers, S., Pietromonaco, P. R., Gunlicks, M., & Sayer, A. (in press). Romantic attachment styles and cortisol reactivity during conflict. *Journal of Personality and Social Psychology.*

Quigley, K. S., & Feldman Barrett, L. (1999). Emotional learning and mechanisms of intentional psychological change. In J. Brandtstadter & R. M. Lerner (Eds.), *Action and development: Origins and functions of intentional self-development* (pp. 435–464). Thousand Oaks, CA: Sage.

Reis, H. T., & Patrick, B. C. (1996). Attachment and intimacy: Component processes. In E. T. Higgins & A. W. Kruglanski (Eds.), *Social psychology: Handbook of basic principles* (pp. 523–563). New York: Guilford Press.

Rothbart, M. K., Ahadi, S. A., & Evans, D. E. (2000). Temperament and personality: Origins and outcomes. *Journal of Personality and Social Psychology, 78,* 122–135.

Senchak, M., & Leonard, K. E. (1992). Attachment styles and marital adjustment among newlywed couples. *Journal of Social and Personal Relationships, 9,* 51–64.

Simpson, J. A., & Rholes, W. S. (1994). Stress and secure base relationships in adulthood. In K. Bartholomew & D. Perlman (Eds.), *Advances in personal relationships* (Vol. 5, pp. 181–204). London, England: Jessica Kingsley.

Simpson, J. A., Rholes, W. S., & Nelligan, J. S. (1992). Support seeking and support giving within couples in an anxiety-provoking situation: The role of attachment styles. *Journal of Personality and Social Psychology, 62,* 434–446.

Simpson, J. A., Rholes, W. S., Oriña, M. M., & Grich, J. (2002). Working models of attachment, support giving, and support seeking in a stressful situation. *Personality and Social Psychology Bulletin, 28,* 598–608.

Simpson, J. A., Rholes, W. S., & Phillips, D. (1996). Conflict in close relationships: An attachment perspective. *Journal of Personality and Social Psychology, 71,* 899–914.

Sroufe, L. A., & Waters, E. (1997). Attachment as an organizational construct. *Child Development, 48*, 1184–1199.

Tidwell, M. O., Reis, H. T., & Shaver, P. R. (1996). Attachment, attractiveness, and social interaction: A diary study. *Journal of Personality and Social Psychology, 71*, 729–745.

II

LINKING EMOTION REGULATION TO DYSFUNCTION AND WELL-BEING ACROSS THE LIFE SPAN

4

ATTACHMENT BASES OF EMOTION REGULATION AND POSTTRAUMATIC ADJUSTMENT

MARIO MIKULINCER, PHILLIP R. SHAVER, AND NETA HORESH

Attachment theory (Bowlby, 1969/1982, 1973, 1980) is one of the most useful contemporary conceptual frameworks for understanding emotion regulation. Bowlby (1973) highlighted the anxiety-buffering function of close relationships and emphasized the importance of interpersonal experiences as a source of individual differences in psychological resilience, emotion regulation, and adjustment (see also chap. 3, this volume). In this chapter, we explore the relevance of attachment theory for understanding emotion regulation specifically during traumatic events and posttraumatic adjustment. We also review recent findings concerning the involvement of attachment-related processes in posttraumatic disorders.

THEORETICAL AND CONCEPTUAL FOUNDATIONS

According to Bowlby (1969/1982, 1973) human beings are born with an innate psychobiological system (the *attachment behavioral system*) that motivates them to seek proximity to significant others (*attachment figures*) in times of need as a way of protecting themselves from threats and alleviating distress. Bowlby (1973) also described important individual differences in attachment-system functioning that result from social experiences with attachment figures beginning in childhood. Interactions with attachment figures who are available and responsive in times of need promote a sense of attachment security, a feeling or sense—"felt security" (Sroufe & Waters, 1977)—based on expectations that attachment figures will be helpful when needed. These expectations are parts of relatively stable *working models*: mental representations of self and others in the context of close relationships. When attachment figures are not reliably available and supportive, however, a sense of security is not attained, negative working models of self and/or others are formed, and strategies of affect regulation other than appropriate proximity seeking are encouraged. These *secondary attachment strategies* can be conceptualized in terms of two major dimensions, *avoidance* and *anxiety*. The first dimension, *avoidance*, reflects the extent to which a person distrusts relationship partners' goodwill and strives to maintain behavioral independence and emotional distance from partners. The second dimension, attachment-related *anxiety*, reflects the degree to which a person worries that a partner will not be available in times of need. People who score low on these two dimensions are said to be secure or securely attached.

Attachment styles begin to be formed in interactions with primary caregivers during early childhood, as a large body of research has shown (Cassidy & Shaver, 1999), but Bowlby (1988) claimed that memorable interactions with others throughout life can alter a person's working models and move the person from one region of the two-dimensional space to another. Moreover, although attachment style is often conceptualized as a single global orientation toward close relationships, and can definitely be measured as such, a person's attachment orientation is actually rooted in a complex cognitive and affective network that includes many different episodic, context-related, and relationship-specific attachment representations, as well as fairly general ones (Mikulincer & Shaver, 2003). In fact, research shows that attachment style can change, subtly or dramatically, depending on context and recent experiences (e.g., Baldwin, Keelan, Fehr, Enns, & Koh Rangarajoo, 1996; Mikulincer & Shaver, 2001).

Attachment-System Functioning in Adulthood

On the basis of an extensive review of adult attachment studies, Mikulincer and Shaver (2003) proposed a three-phase model of attachment-system dynamics in adulthood (see Figure 4.1). In this model, the monitoring of experiences results in activation of the attachment system when a potential or actual threat is registered. Once the attachment system is activated, an affirmative answer to the implicit or explicit question "Is an attachment figure available and likely to be responsive to my needs?" height-

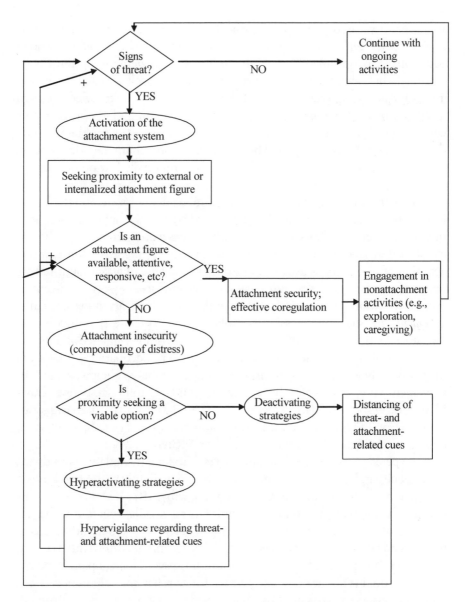

Figure 4.1. An integrative model of the activation and dynamics of the attachment system.

ens the accessibility of the sense of attachment security and facilitates the application of security-based strategies of affect regulation (Mikulincer & Shaver, 2003). These strategies are aimed at alleviating distress, maintaining supportive intimate relationships, and bolstering a person's sense of love-worthiness and self-efficacy. They also foster optimal functioning of other behavioral systems (such as exploration, sexuality, and caregiving) and are an important part of personality development and social adaptation.

Security-based strategies consist of declarative and procedural knowledge about the self, other people, and affect regulation. The declarative knowledge consists of optimistic beliefs about distress management, optimistic and trusting beliefs about others' goodwill, and a sense of self-efficacy about dealing with threats (Shaver & Hazan, 1993). The procedural knowledge is organized around three coping strategies: acknowledgment and display of distress without personal disorganization, support seeking, and problem solving (Mikulincer & Shaver, 2003). These tendencies are characteristic of secure, or securely attached, people—those who score relatively low on measures of attachment anxiety and avoidance.

Perceived unavailability of an attachment figure results in attachment insecurity, which compounds the distress aroused by the appraisal of a situation as threatening. This state of insecurity forces a decision about the viability of further (more active) proximity seeking as a protective strategy. The appraisal of proximity as feasible or essential—because of attachment history, temperamental factors, or contextual cues—results in energetic, insistent attempts to attain proximity, support, and love. These attempts are called *hyperactivating strategies* (Cassidy & Kobak, 1988) because they involve up-regulation of the attachment system, including constant vigilance and intense concern until an attachment figure is perceived to be adequately available and supportive. Hyperactivating strategies include attempts to elicit a partner's involvement, care, and support through clinging and controlling responses (Davis, Shaver, & Vernon, 2003); overdependence on relationship partners as a source of protection (Shaver & Hazan, 1993); and perception of oneself as relatively helpless at emotion regulation (Mikulincer & Shaver, 2003).

Hyperactivating strategies cause a person to remain vigilant about threat-related cues and cues of attachment figures' unavailability, the two kinds of cues that activate the attachment system (Bowlby, 1973). Hence, once they become the focus of a person's attention, they more or less guarantee that the attachment system will remain continuously active. Hyperactivation also intensifies negative emotional responses to threats and heightens mental rumination on threat-related concerns. As a result, psychological pain is exacerbated and doubts about one's ability to achieve relief are heightened. These aspects of attachment-system hyperactivation account for many of the empirically documented correlates of attachment anxiety (Mikulincer & Shaver, 2003).

Appraising proximity seeking as unlikely to alleviate distress results in deliberate deactivation of the attachment system, inhibition of the quest for support, and commitment to handling distress alone, especially distress arising from the failure of attachment figures to be available and responsive. These strategies of affect regulation are called *deactivating* (Cassidy & Kobak, 1988) because their goal is to keep the attachment system down-regulated so as to avoid the frustration and pain of attachment-figure unavailability. Deactivating strategies include avoidance of intimacy and dependence in close relationships and maximization of emotional distance from others. They also involve dismissal of threat- and attachment-related cues, and suppression of threat- and attachment-related thoughts, because such cues and thoughts automatically reactivate the attachment system. These tendencies are further reinforced by assuming a self-reliant stance that decreases dependence on others and discourages acknowledgment of personal weaknesses and faults. These strategies account for the empirically documented correlates of attachment avoidance (Mikulincer & Shaver, 2003).

Attachment, Mental Health, and Adjustment

Individual differences in attachment-system functioning are highly relevant to mental health and adjustment. The sense of being loved and supported by significant others results naturally in positive mental representations of others, a stable sense of self-esteem and self-efficacy, and adoption of constructive coping strategies (see Shaver & Hazan, 1993; Mikulincer & Shaver, 2003, for reviews). These assets, in turn, act as resilience resources during periods of stress. Moreover, people with positive mental representations of attachment experiences tend to feel generally safe and protected, allowing them to benefit from what we, following Fredrickson (2001), call a "broaden and build" cycle of attachment security, which, beyond bolstering psychological resilience, broadens a person's skills and interests (by virtue of what Bowlby, 1969/1982, called the exploration behavioral system) as well as his or her prosocial tendencies (through the caregiving system). In this way, securely attached people are able to devote mental resources that would otherwise be used in defensive maneuvers to activities that facilitate the development of a "fully functioning personality" (Rogers, 1961, pp. 187–192).

Bowlby's (1973, 1980) theory also implies that insecure attachment is a risk factor that reduces resilience in times of stress, fosters negative affectivity, and contributes to emotional problems, maladjustment, and psychopathology. The early attachment experiences of insecure people (whether anxious, avoidant, or both) are characterized by unstable and inadequate distress regulation (Bowlby, 1973; Shaver & Hazan, 1993), which can interfere with the development of inner resources necessary for coping successfully with life's problems and maintaining mental health. With regard to anxious individuals, such experiences encourage hyperactivating strategies that exaggerate threats and intensify the sense of helplessness and vulnerability. With regard to avoidant individuals, they foster deactivating strategies that block access to emotions and discourage acknowledgment of needs, even though needs are present.

Chronic reliance on hyperactivating strategies places anxious individuals at risk for a variety of emotional and adjustment problems, because hyperactivation impairs the regulation of negative emotions and encourages intense distress, even after actual threats subside. As a result, attachment-anxious people are subject to prolonged and uncontrollable negative thoughts and moods, which can lead to cognitive disorganization and, in some cases, psychopathology, especially strong depressive reactions to losses. Moreover, problems in emotional control may be manifested in angry outbursts and personality disorders. These negative psychological outcomes of hyperactivating strategies have been documented in dozens of cross-sectional and longitudinal studies (see Mikulincer & Shaver, 2003; Shaver & Hazan, 1993, for reviews).

Avoidant individuals' deactivating strategies can also be a source of emotional and adjustment problems (Mikulincer & Shaver, 2003). Although these strategies encourage a defensive façade of security and strength, they block access to emotions, leave suppressed distress unresolved, and impair one's ability to confront many of life's adversities. This impairment is particularly likely to be noticeable during prolonged, highly demanding stressful experiences that require active confrontation of a problem and mobilization of external sources of support. In such cases, deactivating strategies can collapse, revealing a sense of inadequacy in coping and a marked decline in functioning. In addition, although deactivating strategies involve suppressing the conscious experience and display of distress, distress can still be indirectly manifested in somatic symptoms and health problems. Several studies have documented emotional and adjustment problems associated with attachment avoidance (see Mikulincer & Shaver, 2003; Shaver & Hazan, 1993, for reviews).

Beyond documenting the association between insecure attachment and emotional problems, a number of studies have examined psychological variables—including both declarative and procedural knowledge associated with hyperactivating and deactivating strategies—that mediate this association. For example, with respect to declarative knowledge, Roberts, Gotlib, and Kassel (1996) and Reinecke and Rogers (2001) reported that negative working models of the self, others, and the future mediated both cross-sectional and prospective associations between attachment insecurity and depression, and Whisman and McGarvey (1995) found that negative beliefs about performance evaluation and others' approval mediated the association between attachment anxiety and depression. With regard to procedural knowledge, the association between attachment anxiety and negative affectivity is mediated by heightened reliance on emotion-focused coping and rumination on threat-related thoughts, whereas the association between avoidance and negative affectivity is mediated by heightened reliance on distancing coping, high levels of emotional control, and reluctance to engage in support seeking (e.g., Berant, Mikulincer, & Florian, 2001; Cozzarelli, Sumer, & Major, 1998).

Attachment, Trauma, and Posttraumatic Processes

The mental health implications of attachment-system functioning are highly pertinent to understanding a person's psychological reactions to traumatic events. Clinical and empirical evidence consistently indicates that traumatic experiences, such as rape, assault, car accidents, floods, war, and a host of other natural and manmade disasters, require the mobilization of internal and external resources for coping with trauma and place people at risk for short-term and long-term emotional and adjustment problems (see Horowitz, 1982, for a review). In some cases emotional balance is restored when or shortly after a traumatic event ends, but in other cases there may be profound and prolonged mental health sequelae including posttraumatic stress disorder (PTSD). According to the *Diagnostic and Statistical Manual of Mental Disorders* (4th ed., *DSM–IV*; American Psychiatric Association, 1994), PTSD is characterized by repeated reexperiencing of the traumatic event (unwanted intrusion of trauma-related material into conscious thoughts, mental images, and dreams), numbing of responsiveness to or reduced involvement with the external world (trauma-related avoidance responses), and a variety of autonomic, affective, and cognitive signs of hyperarousal.

On the basis of previous research on individual differences in attachment, we advance three theoretical propositions concerning the involvement of the attachment system in the formation and course of PTSD. Our first proposition is that the attachment behavioral system is automatically activated when a person is exposed to natural or human-caused traumatic events. According to Horowitz (1982), a person's state of mind when undergoing trauma is characterized by overwhelming shock and intense feelings of panic, vulnerability, helplessness, and exhaustion. According to our three-phase model of attachment-system dynamics (see Figure 4.1 and Mikulincer & Shaver, 2003), these are conditions that automatically activate the attachment system at a high level, impelling a person to search for external or internalized attachment figures that can protect one from trauma. This attachment-system activation is likely to be experienced as an intense cry for help.

Our second proposition is that individual variations in attachment-system functioning play a crucial role in determining the extent to which PTSD ensues from exposure to trauma. Optimal functioning of the attachment system can allow even a highly threatened person to feel relatively safe and secure, thereby decreasing the likelihood of long-term PTSD. A normally secure person's mental cry for help during distress should result in mobilization of internal representations of security-providing attachment figures or actual external sources of support. As a result, the secure person is likely to activate optimistic and hopeful representations of self and others, rely on constructive strategies of affect regulation, deal effectively with the trauma, and restore emotional balance. In other words, the sense of attachment security should act, at least to some extent, as a protective shield against PTSD. Moreover, contextual activation of mental representations of attachment security, due to symbolic or actual encounters with security-providing attachment figures, during or after a traumatic event, should help a traumatized person more readily restore emotional equanimity.

By the same token, disruptions in optimal functioning of the attachment system can prevent restoration of emotional equanimity and thereby contribute to PTSD formation. In such cases, a traumatized person may fail to find inner representations of security or external sources of support and comfort, which may then interfere with the regulation of distress. This regulatory failure may initiate a cascade of mental events—including strong feelings of loneliness and rejection as well as negative working models of self and others, intensification of distress, and reliance on less effective (hyperactivating or deactivating) strategies of affect regulation—that prevents resolution of the trauma and enhances the likelihood of prolonged PTSD. In other words, an insecure attachment style (anxious, avoidant, or a combination of the two, called *fearful avoidance*), reflecting chronic disruption of attachment-system functioning, can predispose a traumatized person to PTSD. Furthermore, contextual activation of mental representations of attachment insecurity, due to symbolic or actual encounters with rejecting and unsupportive figures, during or after trauma exposure can increase the likelihood of PTSD.

Our third proposition is that variations in attachment-system functioning shape the posttraumatic process and the specific form that PTSD takes. According to Horowitz (1982), the posttraumatic process is defined by two kinds of intrapsychic manifestations of PTSD: intrusion and avoidance. *Intrusion* refers to unwanted and uncontrollable thoughts, images, emotions, and nightmares related to the traumatic event. *Avoidance* refers to psychic numbing, denial of the significance and consequences of the traumatic event, and behavioral inhibition. The relative salience of intrusion versus avoidance is not constant (Horowitz, 1982). Intrusion is generally experienced immediately after the trauma, but the two states can alternate during the posttraumatic period until successful "working through" of the trauma is achieved.

Attachment-related strategies are important in regulating the intensity and frequency of posttraumatic intrusion and avoidance tendencies. On one hand, security-based strategies can help people work through trauma, reducing the frequency and intensity of both intrusions and avoidance responses. On the other hand, insecure attachment may render a person insufficiently equipped for working through the trauma. Hyperactivating strategies facilitate reactivation of the traumatic experience and the frustrated cry for help, which encourage what Horowitz (1982) called *intrusive responses*. Deactivating strategies incline a traumatized person to deny the trauma and avoid direct or symbolic confrontation with trauma reminders, thereby encouraging posttraumatic avoidance responses.

This analysis of the attachment system's role in traumatic and posttraumatic processes can be summarized in five hypotheses. First, traumatic events trigger attachment-system activation. Second, mobilizing external or internal security-providing attachment figures during a traumatic period or episode helps a person to resolve the trauma and prevents the development of PTSD. Third, failure to resolve a trauma results not only in feelings of helplessness and vulnerability but also in feelings of loneliness and rejection, because the trauma can shatter both a person's sense of personal safety and his or her confidence in attachment figures' protection and support. Fourth, insecure individuals are more likely than their relatively secure counterparts to develop PTSD, and anxiously attached people are more likely to suffer from posttraumatic intrusion symptoms whereas avoidant people are more likely to suffer from posttraumatic avoidance symptoms. Fifth, the actual or symbolic mobilization of security-providing attachment figures during a posttraumatic period can help a person heal traumatic wounds and restore emotional balance.

In the following section, we review existing empirical findings concerning the association between attachment style and PTSD. We also present new findings of our own that reveal the contribution of global attachment style and contextually activated mental representations of attachment security to explicit and implicit manifestations of PTSD.

EMPIRICAL FOUNDATIONS

Researchers who study adult attachment and psychopathology have only begun to examine posttraumatic stress. The first systematic attempt to document attachment-style differences in the severity of PTSD symptoms concerned the reactions of young adults to Iraqi Scud missile attacks on Israel during the 1991 Gulf War (Mikulincer, Florian, & Weller, 1993). One hundred and forty Israeli undergraduates were approached 2 weeks after the end of the Gulf War and asked to complete a series of self-report measures of attachment style, coping with the missile attacks, and PTSD symptoms. The study revealed emotional and adjustment problems associated with attachment anxiety and avoidance. Specifically, as compared with participants who self-reported a secure attachment style, participants with an anxious attachment style exhibited heightened reliance on maladaptive emotion-focused coping, experienced higher levels of depression and anxiety after the war, and had more severe PTSD symptoms of intrusion and avoidance. Participants with an avoidant attachment style relied more on distancing coping with the missile attacks, denied or suppressed anxiety and depression, and expressed distress indirectly through higher somatization and hostility after the war and more severe posttraumatic avoidance responses.

The association between insecure attachment and PTSD-symptom severity has also been observed among adults who were abused as children (Alexander et al., 1998; Muller, Sicoli, & Lemieux, 2000) and among former prisoners of war (POWs) in both the United States and Israel (Dieperink, Leskela, Thuras, & Engdahl, 2001; Solomon, Ginzburg, Mikulincer, Neria,

& Ohry, 1998). For example, Solomon et al. (1998) interviewed 164 Israeli ex-POWs of the Yom Kippur War 18 years after hostilities ended. Participants in the study completed self-report measures of attachment style and PTSD symptomatology and provided retrospective accounts of their experience of captivity. Anxious and avoidant ex-POWs reported more severe PTSD symptoms than ex-POWs who were relatively secure. It is important to note that attachment-style differences were also found in a content analysis of accounts of the traumatic experience of captivity. On one hand, securely attached ex-POWs reported having dealt with captivity by recruiting positive memories of, or imagining positive encounters with, significant others. That is, they coped with the trauma by seeking symbolic proximity to, and comfort from, internalized attachment figures. In contrast, anxious persons mainly remembered suffering and pain, and their accounts were full of feelings of helplessness, abandonment, and loss of control, which seemed to reflect their hyperactivation of distress and threat-related thoughts. The narratives of avoidant ex-POWs reflected deactivating strategies, containing little information about experiences during captivity but being laced with hostile feelings about the army in which they had served.

In a recent study, Kanninen, Punamaki, and Qouta (2003) examined the association between attachment style and PTSD among 176 Palestinian former political prisoners living in the Gaza Strip. The statistical association was observed mainly among political prisoners who had been exposed to high levels of physical torture and ill treatment. In this group, participants classified as anxious or avoidant by an interview method (on the basis of the Adult Attachment Interview; Hesse, 1999) reported more severe PTSD symptoms than participants classified as secure. This difference was not significant among prisoners who had been exposed to high levels of psychological torture involving interpersonal cruelty. It seems that whereas secure attachment acts as a protective safeguard against the development of PTSD following physical torture, it is less effective when the torture is interpersonal and involves the shattering of positive working models. Perhaps this kind of torture creates or activates negative representations of self and others that successfully undermine the protective action of a previously secure attachment style.

Although these correlational findings are compatible with the propositions we derived from attachment theory, they do not necessarily reveal a causal connection between attachment-related processes and the formation and course of PTSD. This is because the studies did not include assessment or manipulation of cognitive accessibility of attachment-related representations during or following trauma, and attachment style was not measured until after the traumatic experience. Hence, psychological processes other than those related to attachment may explain the observed associations between attachment style and PTSD. In the following sections we review findings from two new studies that examined the causal role of attachment-related processes in the development and course of PTSD.

Daily Fluctuations in the Sense of Attachment Security and the Course of Posttraumatic Stress Disorder

In a recent study, Mikulincer, Horesh, Berant, and Gillath (2004) examined Israelis' psychological reactions during the 2003 U.S.–Iraq war. The authors were particularly interested in Israelis' feelings about Iraq's threat to launch nonconventional missiles against Israel in response to an American offensive. Although no such missiles were actually launched, the Israeli government and media were convinced that such an attack was imminent and that the country was once again as vulnerable as it had been during the 1991 Gulf War. During the first week of the 2003 war, Israelis therefore took many precautions to try to cope with impending missile strikes.

Mikulincer et al. (2004) examined the effects of global, dispositional attachment anxiety and avoidance measured before the beginning of the war on the intensity of trauma-related symptoms (intrusion, avoidance, and hyperarousal) during the war. These potential symptoms were assessed daily for 21 days. In addition, each participant's feelings of being comforted and supported by, and connected to, others (i.e., daily, context-specific feelings of attachment security) were also assessed daily throughout the same period. This allowed examination of two additional issues: (a) the contribution of attachment security on a given day to the intensity of trauma-related symptoms on that day and the next day, and (b) the extent to which the actual or symbolic mobilization of security-providing figures during the traumatic period (the daily sense of attachment security) moderated the detrimental effects of global attachment anxiety and avoidance on trauma-related symptoms.

The sample included 51 Israeli undergraduates (37 women and 14 men) who volunteered to participate in a study comprising two stages. In the first stage, 2 months before the war, participants completed the Experiences in Close Relationships Scale (Brennan, Clark, & Shaver, 1998), which assesses global attachment anxiety and avoidance in close relationships. In the second stage, 5 to 7 days before the beginning of the war, participants who had agreed to participate in the study were asked to complete daily diary measures for 3 weeks. They completed a questionnaire each evening for 21 days. Each day, they received 32 items dealing with war-related thoughts and feelings and posttraumatic symptoms, and they were asked to rate the extent to which they experienced each of these thoughts, feelings, and symptoms that day. Six items tapped the unwanted intrusion of war-related feelings, thoughts, and memories (e.g., "I thought about the war when I didn't mean to," "Images of the war popped into my mind," "I had a nightmare about the war"). Six items tapped defensive avoidance of war-related thoughts and feelings (e.g., "I tried to remove the war from my memory," "I stayed away from reminders of the war," "I tried not to talk about the war"). Four items tapped posttraumatic hyperarousal symptoms (e.g., sleep difficulties, hyperalertness, concentration problems). Finally, four items tapped the daily sense of attachment security—feelings of being supported and connected to others ("I felt that I had someone who would be there for me," "I felt strongly connected to other people").

Preliminary analyses revealed significant inverse correlations between the global attachment dimensions and the average sense of attachment security across the 21 days (–.41 for attachment anxiety and –.32 for avoidance). In support of a traitlike conceptualization of attachment style, the daily report of attachment security was associated with global reports of attachment anxiety or avoidance at the beginning of the study. The correlations were only moderate in strength, however, and large portions of the variance in the daily reports of attachment security were not explained by global attachment style, suggesting that the daily sense of attachment security fluctuated across the 21 days, presumably as a result of contextual factors. This conclusion fits with a representational network model of attachment orientations (Baldwin et al., 1996; Mikulincer & Shaver, 2003), in which incongruent attachment orientations can coexist at chronic–global and transient–episodic levels of the network.

The effects of global attachment style and daily attachment security on trauma-related responses were analyzed using hierarchical linear modeling (HLM). The data were conceptualized in terms of two levels, the lower level included variables that could change daily and the upper level focused on traitlike individual differences in attachment anxiety and avoidance. At the lower level, the main question was whether the sense of attachment security on a particular day was associated with less intense war-related distress responses—intrusion, avoidance, and hyperarousal—on that day. At the upper level there were two questions: (a) whether global attachment anxiety and avoidance contributed to the intensity of intrusion, avoidance, and hyperarousal responses across the 21 days, and (b) whether these war-related responses were shaped by interactions between global attachment style and contextual activation of the sense of attachment security on a particular day.

With regard to daily variations in war-related intrusion, the HLM analysis revealed that the sense of attachment security on a given day made a significant unique contribution to the intensity of unwanted intrusions of war-related feelings and thoughts on that day: The higher the sense of being supported and connected to others, the weaker the war-related intrusions. In addition, global attachment anxiety contributed significantly and uniquely to war-related intrusions: The higher the attachment anxiety, the stronger the unwanted intrusions of war-related thoughts and feelings across the 21 days. However, these two significant main effects were qualified by a significant interaction between global attachment anxiety and the daily sense of attachment security. Activation of attachment security on a given day was significantly associated with weaker war-related intrusions on that day mainly among participants who scored high on attachment anxiety. More securely attached participants were not so strongly affected by fluctuations in the sense of attachment security across the 21 days. Looking at the same results in a different way, the detrimental effect of attachment anxiety on war-related intrusions was weakened on days when participants felt comforted and connected to others. No significant main effect or interaction was found for the attachment avoidance dimension.

With regard to war-related avoidance, viewed as a particular kind of coping response, the HLM analysis revealed that the sense of attachment security on a given day made a significant unique contribution to the intensity of war-related avoidance on that day: The higher the sense of being supported and connected to others, the weaker the avoidance of war-related thoughts and feelings. In addition, global attachment avoidance made a significant unique contribution to war-related avoidance: The higher the attachment avoidance, the stronger the avoidance of war-related feelings and thoughts across the 21 days. It is interesting to note that the interaction between attachment avoidance and the daily sense of attachment security was not significant. That is, the detrimental effect of attachment avoidance on war-related defensive avoidance remained significant even on days when participants felt more comforted and connected to others. No significant main effect or interaction was found for the attachment anxiety dimension.

With regard to hyperarousal symptoms, the HLM analyses revealed that the higher the sense of being supported by and connected to others on a given day, the weaker the hyperarousal symptoms that day. In addition, both attachment anxiety and avoidance had a significant effect on the intensity of hyperarousal symptoms: The higher the attachment anxiety or avoidance, the more intense were these symptoms across the 21 days. Although the interaction between attachment avoidance and the daily sense of attachment security was not significant, the HLM analysis yielded a significant interaction between attachment anxiety and this daily sense of security. The form of the interaction was similar to that found for war-related intrusions. The detrimental effect of attachment anxiety on posttraumatic hyperarousal symptoms was weakened on days when participants felt comforted and connected to others. In contrast, the detrimental effect of attachment avoidance remained significant even on days when participants felt a strong sense of attachment security.

In these analyses, the associations between daily fluctuations in attachment security and war-related responses were based on participants' same-day reports. The findings can therefore be interpreted just as well by saying that the experience of intense trauma-related symptoms on a given day interfered with the sense of being comforted and connected to others on that day. To evaluate this possibility, additional HLM analyses were conducted to examine the contribution of the sense of attachment security on a given day to war-related responses the next day. War-related responses on the previous day were introduced as a covariate so that the unique contribution of the sense of attachment security to war-related responses the next day could be determined while controlling for war-related responses the previous day. In other words, these HLM analyses examined the contribution of the sense of attachment security on a given day to changes in war-related responses from that day to the next. The results were identical to the findings previously reported: The sense of attachment security on a given day led to more positive changes in war-related responses from that day to the next. Moreover, the prospective effects of daily attachment security on intrusion and hyperarousal were stronger for people who scored high on global attachment anxiety than for people who scored low.

In the analyses reviewed so far, the data included participants' reports across 3 weeks (1 week before the war and 2 weeks after the war's onset). However, Mikulincer et al. (2004) also considered the possibility that 1 week after the war's onset, Israelis began to believe that no missiles would be launched against Israel. Therefore the intensity of PTSD responses in the first week of the war was compared with the intensity of these responses during the following week, and the contribution of attachment-related variables was examined separately for each of these two periods.

The findings revealed stronger war-related intrusions, avoidance, and hyperarousal responses during the first week of war than during the second week. In addition, HLM analyses conducted on the data for the first week revealed similar main effects and interactions to those found in the analysis of the 21-day data. However, HLM analyses conducted on data from the second week revealed that the main effects of attachment anxiety and the interactions between attachment anxiety and the daily sense of attachment security on war-related intrusion and hyperarousal responses were no longer significant. However, the detrimental main effects of attachment avoidance on war-related avoidance and hyperarousal symptoms were still significant during the second week of war. Moreover, the healing effects of daily attachment security on war-related defensive avoidance and hyperarousal symptoms were significant during the second week of war. Again, no significant interaction was found between attachment avoidance and the sense of attachment security during the second week of war.

The findings support our theoretical propositions and have important implications for understanding the involvement of the attachment system in traumatic and posttraumatic processes. Both chronic (personality) and transient (contextual) processes shape trauma-related responses. That is, both global attachment orientations and daily fluctuations in the sense of attachment security have significant and unique effects on trauma-related responses. From a personality perspective, chronically insecure people are more likely to suffer trauma-related reactions than chronically secure people, with anxiously attached individuals exhibiting more intrusion symptoms and avoidant individuals exhibiting more avoidance symptoms. It is interesting to note that, at least in this study, the detrimental effects of attachment avoidance on trauma-related responses lasted longer than the detrimental effects of attachment anxiety and were observed even after the greatest danger of missile attacks subsided. From a contextual perspective, daily activation of the sense of attachment security helped people heal traumatic wounds and weakened the intensity of trauma-related symptoms. Moreover, this contextual activation seemed to weaken the effects of anxious individuals' hyperactivating strategies and inhibit these strategies in a particular context (e.g., causing an anxious person to react to the trauma of war with fewer intrusions and hyperarousal responses than usual).

The findings also indicate that the beneficial effects of the daily sense of attachment security on PTSD symptoms were not moderated by dispositional avoidance and that the detrimental effects of attachment avoidance on trauma-related avoidance and hyperarousal responses did not depend on daily fluctuations in attachment security. That is, although the daily sense of security had beneficial effects among both high and low scorers on the avoidance dimension, more avoidant people did not exhibit greater benefits than less avoidant people from feeling supported and comforted. This result has both a bright and a dark side. On the bright side, contextual heightening of attachment security seemed to weaken PTSD symptoms even for avoidant individuals. On the dark side, attachment avoidance was associated with more severe PTSD symptoms even on days when people felt relatively well supported and comforted. This makes it seem that avoidant people's deactivating strategies sometimes continue to operate even when actual or symbolic attachment figures are available and supportive. This pattern of findings both supports our hypothesis about the healing effects of attachment security and encourages us to search for more effective security-based interventions to reduce the detrimental effects of dispositional avoidance.

Experimental Activation of Attachment Security and Implicit Responses to Trauma

The attachment system's involvement in posttraumatic processes was also documented in a recent study by Miterany (2004), which focused on Palestinian terrorist attacks on Israeli cities, a source of trauma to which most Israelis have been directly or indirectly exposed for several years. The study was designed to determine whether global and contextual attachment-related representations affect explicit and implicit responses to trauma.

Explicit trauma-related responses were assessed with a self-report scale tapping the kinds of posttraumatic symptoms previously discussed: intrusion, avoidance, and hyperarousal. Implicit trauma-related responses were assessed by measuring the cognitive accessibility of trauma-related mental representations in a Stroop color-naming task. Specifically, accessibility was operationalized by the time needed to name the color in which a trauma-related word was printed: The higher the latencies for naming the colors of these words, the higher the accessibility of trauma-related thoughts was inferred to be, because such thoughts apparently interfered with color naming. Previous researchers have considered longer reactions times for naming the colors of trauma-related words to reflect implicit manifestations of PTSD and have found that individuals experiencing posttraumatic symptoms take longer to name the colors of trauma-related words (see Emilien et al., 2000; McNally, 1998, for extensive reviews). Using this implicit measure, Miterany (2004) examined the unique and interactive effects of global attachment style (self-reports of attachment anxiety and avoidance) and contextual activation of attachment-security representations (subliminal priming with a security-related word immediately before presentation of a trauma-related word) in a Stroop task.

The study included three sessions. In the first session, which occurred at the beginning of a semester, 120 Israeli undergraduates completed the Experiences in Close Relationships Scale (Brennan et al., 1998), tapping global attachment anxiety and avoidance in close relationships. In the second session, conducted 1 month later, all 120 participants completed the PTSD Inventory (Solomon, Neria, Ohry, Waysman, & Ginzburg, 1994), a 21-item self-report scale based on *DSM–IV* symptom criteria, with regard to Palestinian terrorist attacks. Participants rated the frequency with which they had experienced posttraumatic intrusion, avoidance, and hyperarousal responses related to these attacks during the previous month. On the basis of their PTSD scores, two distinct groups of people were selected to participate in the third session. One group—the PTSD group (*n* = 30)—comprised participants who scored above the 75th percentile. The other group—the non-PTSD group (*n* = 30)—contained participants who scored below the 25th percentile.

After an interval of 2 to 3 weeks, the 60 participants were invited to an experimental session in which they performed a computerized Stroop task. In this task, they were asked to name the color in which a target word was presented on a computer monitor. The target words included 10 Hebrew words connoting terror (e.g., *Hamas, car bomb*), 10 negatively valenced Hebrew words not related to terror (e.g., *theft, illness*), and 10 emotionally neutral Hebrew words (e.g., *table, picture*). Each of these words was printed, on different trials, in four different colors (green, blue, yellow, red) and presented randomly across 12 trials (for a total of 360 trials). Participants performed each trial while being subliminally primed with a Hebrew attachment-security word (*love*), a positively valenced but non-attachment-related Hebrew word (*success*), or a neutral Hebrew word (*hat*). The prime word *love* was presented for 20 ms before the target word on 120 trials, the prime word *success* was presented on another 120 trials, and the prime word *hat* was presented on the remaining 120 trials. These primes were presented in randomly ordered blocks of trials across participants.

Findings related to self-reports of posttraumatic symptoms replicated the previously observed association of these reports with global attachment anxiety and avoidance. Attachment anxiety was significantly associated with more frequent terrorism-related intrusions and hyperarousal symptoms. Attachment avoidance was significantly associated with more frequent defensive avoidance of terrorism-related thoughts. In line with our theoretical propositions, these findings indicate that chronically insecure people were more likely than their more secure counterparts to suffer from PTSD symptoms, with anxiously attached people experiencing more intrusion symptoms and avoidant people experiencing more avoidance symptoms.

With regard to the Stroop task, statistical analyses performed on latencies for neutral and negative words revealed no significant effects of PTSD status (non-PTSD, PTSD) and prime type (attachment security, positive, neutral). However, the analysis of color-naming latencies for terror-related words (after controlling for latencies associated with neutral and negative words) revealed a significant main effect of PTSD status. This effect replicated previous findings in the literature concerning the accessibility of trauma-related thoughts among people experiencing PTSD symptoms (see Emilien et al., 2000; McNally, 1998, for extensive reviews). Specifically, participants in the PTSD group produced longer color-naming latencies for terror words (higher accessibility) than participants in the non-PTSD group. However, this main effect was qualified by a significant interaction with prime type. The effect of PTSD status was significant only when participants were primed with a neutral or positive word. The effect was not significant following priming with an attachment-security word (*love*). Therefore, priming with an attachment–security word reduced the accessibility of terror-related thoughts and eliminated the difference between PTSD and non-PTSD groups in color-naming latencies for terror-related words. This result suggests that activation of attachment-security representations countered a cognitive manifestation of PTSD.

Interesting associations were also obtained between attachment anxiety and avoidance, on one hand, and color-naming latencies for terror-related words in each PTSD group and prime category, on the other. In the non-PTSD group, attachment scores were not significantly associated with color-naming latencies. In the PTSD group, attachment scores were significantly correlated with the accessibility of trauma-related representations. Specifically, attachment anxiety was significantly associated with longer color-naming latencies for terror words (higher accessibility) following neutral or positive priming but not following subliminal presentation of the security-related word *love*. Attachment avoidance was significantly associated with longer color-naming latencies for terror words in all three priming conditions.

The findings concerning color-naming latencies for terror words imply that the attachment behavioral system is involved in the shaping of implicit trauma-related responses. First, chronic attachment insecurity assessed in terms of the anxiety and avoidance dimensions was associated with greater accessibility of trauma-related thoughts among people with PTSD symptoms. Second, symbolic mobilization of attachment-security representations during the Stroop task (attachment-security priming) seemed to have a soothing or healing effect, lowering the accessibility of trauma-related thoughts even among people who usually suffered from PTSD symptoms, and countering the detrimental effects of attachment anxiety on the accessibility of these thoughts. However, security priming failed to reduce the detrimental effects of attachment avoidance. The link between attachment avoidance and distress reactions was significant even following security priming, suggesting that avoidant people's defensive strategies for dealing with trauma remain active even when comforting representations are potentially available.

IMPLICATIONS AND FUTURE DIRECTIONS

The reviewed empirical evidence supports our theoretical propositions. Most important, the two recent studies support the hypothesis that mobilizing external or internal forms of felt security during traumatic and posttraumatic periods reduces the likelihood and intensity of PTSD symptoms, which helps to explain why dispositionally secure people are less likely than their insecurely attached counterparts to develop PTSD. The research both documents and helps to explain the fact that anxiously attached people suffer from more severe posttraumatic intrusion symptoms and avoidant people suffer from more severe posttraumatic avoidance symptoms. These different kinds of symptoms are compatible with anxious and avoidant individuals' respective strategies of hyperactivating or deactivating their attachment systems.

The studies also show that traumatized individuals respond favorably to actual support offered by familiar others in their immediate environments and to the attempted contextual manipulation of their immediate sense of attachment security. It is significant that this healing effect was observed regardless of variations in dispositional attachment avoidance and anxiety, although it was more pronounced among anxiously attached people. Anxiously attached individuals appear to be very responsive to contextually augmented mental representations of love, support, and security. This finding fits with those from previous studies of marital relationships, interactions in groups, and postpartum depression (Mikulincer, Florian, & Hirschberger, 2002; Rom & Mikulincer, 2003; Simpson, Rholes, Campbell, Tran, & Wilson, 2003) and highlights the importance of love, kindness, and support for buffering the detrimental effects of attachment anxiety. At the same time, it is important to note that although highly avoidant persons also seemed to benefit from contextual activation of the sense of attachment security, they still showed more severe PTSD symptoms than less avoidant people during and following security augmentation.

The discovery that more chronically avoidant individuals appear to be less influenced than chronically anxious individuals by either the amount of support they receive on a given day or by subliminal exposure to attachment-security words deserves further attention and elaboration. Together, these findings imply that highly avoidant individuals are less amenable to security-based changes in coping strategies than are highly anxious individuals. It seems possible, on the basis of child-developmental studies (beginning with Ainsworth, Blehar, Waters, & Wall, 1978), that caregivers of avoidant infants consistently rebuffed or deflected the infants' attachment behaviors, and that, because of this early rejection, highly avoidant people need stronger "doses" of support and attachment-figure availability to prevent the development of PTSD following traumatic experiences. Alternatively or in addition, avoidant individuals' relative impermeability to security-enhancing stimuli may directly reflect their deactivating strategies. According to our model (see Figure 4.1), these strategies interfere with the monitoring of cues concerning the availability or unavailability of attachment figures, increasing the likelihood that genuine and clear-cut signals of attachment-figure availability and support will be missed or deemphasized. This impermeability has not been evident in all of our previous studies of experimental security enhancement (e.g., Mikulincer & Shaver, 2001), so it may be due to particular circumstances in which avoidant people are coping with distress. Future research should be directed at understanding the nature and contextual variability of avoidant barriers to security-enhancing experiences as well as at creating and evaluating security-enhancing interventions tailored especially for avoidant people who have been traumatized.

Although the studies we have reviewed here constitute important initial steps in understanding the role played by the attachment system in traumatic and posttraumatic mental processes, more research is needed on our hypothesized equation of traumatic helplessness with feelings of loneliness and rejection. It is important to determine whether such feelings actually arise during and after trauma, whether they intensify PTSD symptoms, and whether interventions aimed at enhancing a person's sense of connectedness, belonging, and community can reduce or prevent PTSD symptomatology. Beyond preventing PTSD, attachment security may contribute to the reconstruction and strengthening of comforting, health-sustaining beliefs shattered by trauma—that is, to posttraumatic growth (Tedeschi & Calhoun, 2004). In fact, attachment security has already been associated with cognitive openness and creative exploration of personal memories and experiences (Mikulincer & Shaver, 2003). Tedeschi and Calhoun (2004) view these qualities and activities as important ingredients of posttraumatic growth. Finally, future research should examine the healing effects of actual or symbolic encounters with security-providing figures (e.g., family members, therapists, God) during the posttraumatic process and explore how best to use such encounters to improve outcomes for PTSD victims.

The study of attachment-related processes related to the etiology, course, and treatment of PTSD is an ideal arena for interdisciplinary collaboration. Because attachment theory was originally conceptualized as a theory of social and emotional development, and because attachment-related processes are manifested most directly in family contexts, attachment-oriented research on trauma and posttraumatic adjustment can create useful bridges between personality and social psychology, developmental psychology, clinical psychology, and family psychology. More interdisciplinary research guided by attachment theory should be conducted on the ways in which adaptive and maladaptive strategies of emotion regulation are developed within families.

In the same way that "attachment injuries" have proven useful as a focus for marital therapy (Johnson, 2004, p. 378), it would be worthwhile to examine the role of attachment wounds in the development of attachment insecurity and vulnerability to trauma and PTSD. Attachment theory leads us to expect that major failures of support during previous traumatic events (e.g., being abandoned by a parent, exploited by a trusted teacher, or cuckolded by a spouse) will cause a person to feel especially vulnerable to a lack of support during subsequent traumas. As Bowlby (1969/1982) so forcefully argued when criticizing his psychoanalytic colleagues' emphasis on fantasy rather than reality, working models of attachment are tolerably accurate reflections of a person's actual experiences. Overcoming working models based on actual attachment injuries and providing countervailing experiences and images of love and support should be major goals of parenting, mentoring, counseling, and marriage.

Research has demonstrated that attachment theory applies beyond the realm of close relationships to social life more generally. In the preceding chapter of this volume, Pietromonaco and colleagues emphasized the interpersonal aspects of attachment and the attachment system's role in regulating interpersonal conflict in close relationships. In this chapter, we have focused on intrapsychic aspects of attachment-system functioning and the healing effects of attachment security during and following exposure to traumatic events, while showing indirectly how community-level and even international events can affect and interact with attachment-related processes. These chapters should be integrated with our previous writings (e.g., Mikulincer & Shaver, 2003), which showed that people who are either secure in a dispositional sense or induced to feel more secure in a particular context are less threatened than their insecure counterparts by novel information and are better able to tolerate intergroup diversity, more likely to maintain broadly humane values, more able to creatively and flexibly explore their own beliefs and feelings, and more likely to regard others compassionately and behave prosocially. In light of this research it seems likely that if human beings were helped by their families, communities, schools, religious institutions, and cultural media to become more secure, they would be better able to avoid manmade disasters, cope effectively with natural ones, and perhaps even grow from unavoidable trauma and adversity.

REFERENCES

Ainsworth, M. S., Blehar, M. C., Waters, E., & Wall, S. (1978). *Patterns of attachment: A psychological study of the strange situation*. Oxford, England: Erlbaum.

Alexander, P. C., Anderson, C. L., Brand, B., Schaeffer, C. M., Grelling, B. Z., & Kretz, L. (1998). Adult attachment and long-term effects in survivors of incest. *Child Abuse and Neglect, 22*, 45–61.

American Psychiatric Association. (1994). *Diagnostic and statistical manual of mental disorders* (4th ed.). Washington, DC: Author.

Baldwin, M. W., Keelan, J. P. R., Fehr, B., Enns, V., & Koh Rangarajoo, E. (1996). Social–cognitive conceptualization of attachment working models: Availability and accessibility effects. *Journal of Personality and Social Psychology, 71*, 94–109.

Berant, E., Mikulincer, M., & Florian, V. (2001). The association of mothers' attachment style and their psychological reactions to the diagnosis of infant's congenital heart disease. *Journal of Social and Clinical Psychology, 20*, 208–232.

Bowlby, J. (1973). *Attachment and loss: Vol. 2. Separation: Anxiety and anger*. New York: Basic Books.

Bowlby, J. (1980). *Attachment and loss: Vol. 3. Sadness and depression*. New York: Basic Books.

Bowlby, J. (1982). *Attachment and loss: Vol. 1. Attachment* (2nd ed.). New York: Basic Books. (Original work published 1969)

Bowlby, J. (1988). *A secure base: Clinical applications of attachment theory*. London: Routledge.

Brennan, K. A., Clark, C. L., & Shaver, P. R. (1998). Self-report measurement of adult attachment: An integrative overview. In J. A. Simpson & W. S. Rholes (Eds.), *Attachment theory and close relationships* (pp. 46–76). New York: Guilford Press.

Cassidy, J., & Kobak, R. R. (1988). Avoidance and its relationship with other defensive processes. In J. Belsky & T. Nezworski (Eds.), *Clinical implications of attachment* (pp. 300–323). Hillsdale, NJ: Erlbaum.

Cassidy, J., & Shaver, P. R. (Eds.). (1999). *Handbook of attachment: Theory, research, and clinical applications*. New York: Guilford Press.

Cozzarelli, C., Sumer, N., & Major, B. (1998). Mental models of attachment and coping with abortion. *Journal of Personality and Social Psychology, 74*, 453–467.

Davis, D., Shaver, P. R., & Vernon, M. L. (2003). Physical, emotional, and behavioral reactions to breaking up: The roles of gender, age, emotional involvement, and attachment style. *Personality and Social Psychology Bulletin, 29*, 871–884.

Dieperink, M., Leskela, J., Thuras, P., & Engdahl, B. (2001). Attachment style classification and posttraumatic stress disorder in former prisoners of war. *American Journal of Orthopsychiatry, 71*, 374–378.

Emilien, G., Penasse, C., Charles, G., Martin, D., Lasseaux, L., & Waltregny, A. (2000). Post-traumatic stress disorder: Hypotheses from clinical neuropsychology and psychopharmacology research. *International Journal of Psychiatry in Clinical Practice, 4*, 3–18.

Fredrickson, B. L. (2001). The role of positive emotions in positive psychology: The broaden-and-build theory of positive emotions. *American Psychologist, 56*, 218–226.

Hesse, E. (1999). The Adult Attachment Interview: Historical and current perspectives. In J. Cassidy & P. R. Shaver (Eds.), *Handbook of attachment: Theory, research, and clinical applications* (pp. 395–433). New York: Guilford Press.

Horowitz, M. J. (1982). Psychological processes induced by illness, injury, and loss. In T. Millon, C. Green, & R. Meagher (Eds.), *Handbook of clinical health psychology* (pp. 53–68). New York: Plenum Press.

Johnson, S. M. (2004). Attachment theory: A guide for healing couple relationships. In W. S. Rholes & J. A. Simpson (Eds.), *Adult attachment: Theory, research, and clinical implications* (pp. 367–387). New York: Guilford Press.

Kanninen, K., Punamaki, R. L., & Qouta, S. (2003). Personality and trauma: Adult attachment and posttraumatic distress among former political prisoners. *Peace and Conflict: Journal of Peace Psychology, 9*, 97–126.

McNally, R. J. (1998). Experimental approaches to cognitive abnormality in posttraumatic stress disorder. *Clinical Psychology Review, 18*, 971–982.

Mikulincer, M., Florian, V., & Hirschberger, G. (2002, January). *The dynamic interplay of global, relationship-specific, and contextual representations of attachment security*. Paper presented at the annual meeting of the Society for Personality and Social Psychology, Savannah, GA.

Mikulincer, M., Florian, V., & Weller, A. (1993). Attachment styles, coping strategies, and posttraumatic psychological distress: The impact of the Gulf War in Israel. *Journal of Personality and Social Psychology, 64*, 817–826.

Mikulincer, M., Horesh, N., Berant, E., & Gillath, O. (2004). *An attachment perspective on posttraumatic stress disorder: The contribution of global attachment style and contextual representations of attachment security*. Manuscript in preparation.

Mikulincer, M., & Shaver, P. R. (2001). Attachment theory and intergroup bias: Evidence that priming the secure base schema attenuates negative reactions to out-groups. *Journal of Personality and Social Psychology, 81*, 97–115.

Mikulincer, M., & Shaver, P. R. (2003). The attachment behavioral system in adulthood: Activation, psychodynamics, and interpersonal processes. In M. P. Zanna (Ed.), *Advances in experimental social psychology* (Vol. 35, pp. 53–152). San Diego, CA: Academic Press.

Miterany, D. (2004). *The healing effects of the contextual activation of the sense of attachment security: The case of posttraumatic stress disorder*. Unpublished master's thesis, Bar-Ilan University, Ramat-Gan, Israel.

Muller, R. T., Sicoli, L. A., & Lemieux, K. E. (2000). Relationship between attachment style and posttraumatic stress symptomatology among adults who report the experience of childhood abuse. *Journal of Traumatic Stress, 13,* 321–332.

Reinecke, M. A., & Rogers, G. M. (2001). Dysfunctional attitudes and attachment style among clinically depressed adults. *Behavioral and Cognitive Psychotherapy, 29,* 129–141.

Roberts, J. E., Gotlib, I. H., & Kassel, J. D. (1996). Adult attachment security and symptoms of depression: The mediating roles of dysfunctional attitudes and low self-esteem. *Journal of Personality and Social Psychology, 70,* 310–320.

Rogers, C. R. (1961). *On becoming a person.* Boston: Houghton Mifflin.

Rom, E., & Mikulincer, M. (2003). Attachment theory and group processes: The association between attachment style and group-related representations, goals, memory, and functioning. *Journal of Personality and Social Psychology, 84,* 1220–1235.

Shaver, P. R., & Hazan, C. (1993). Adult romantic attachment: Theory and evidence. In D. Perlman & W. Jones (Eds.), *Advances in personal relationships* (Vol. 4, pp. 29–70). London: Jessica Kingsley.

Simpson, J. A., Rholes, W. S., Campbell, L., Tran, S., & Wilson, C. L. (2003). Adult attachment, the transition to parenthood, and depressive symptoms. *Journal of Personality and Social Psychology, 84,* 1172–1187.

Solomon, Z., Ginzburg, K., Mikulincer, M., Neria, Y., & Ohry, A. (1998). Coping with war captivity: The role of attachment style. *European Journal of Personality, 12,* 271–285.

Solomon, Z., Neria, Y., Ohry, A., Waysman, M., & Ginzburg, K. (1994). PTSD among Israeli former prisoners of war and soldiers with combat stress reaction: A longitudinal study. *American Journal of Psychiatry, 151,* 554–559.

Sroufe, L. A., & Waters, E. (1977). Attachment as an organizational construct. *Child Development, 48,* 1184–1199.

Tedeschi, R. G., & Calhoun, L. G. (2004). Posttraumatic growth: Conceptual foundations and empirical evidence. *Psychological Inquiry, 15,* 1–18.

Whisman, M. A., & McGarvey, A. L. (1995). Attachment, depressotypic cognitions, and dysphoria. *Cognitive Therapy and Research, 19,* 633–650.

5

HAPPY VICTIMIZATION: EMOTION DYSREGULATION IN THE CONTEXT OF INSTRUMENTAL, PROACTIVE AGGRESSION

WILLIAM F. ARSENIO

In their review of the extensive literature on emotion regulation, Cole, Martin, and Dennis (2004) recently attempted to clarify how and why emotions, which are supposedly regulatory and biologically adaptive to begin with, often need to be regulated. Numerous commentaries following their review then proceeded to debate the nature, origins, and consequences of children's emotion regulation in ways that reveal how much remains to be learned about these emerging abilities. Yet, despite the numerous unresolved questions raised in this debate, a working consensus seems to have emerged regarding two major issues: (a) individual differences in children's abilities to regulate their emotions are related to variations in their social competence as well as their risk for psychopathology; and (b) parents, other caregivers, and the larger sociocultural context have a substantial influence on children's emerging abilities to regulate emotions.

This chapter focuses on children's emotion experiences and their abilities to regulate these emotions in the context of aggressive interactions. The fact that "many studies of emotion regulation center on the control of aggressive or hostile behavior" (Campos, Frankel, & Camras, 2004, p. 385) is not surprising given the major social and individual costs of aggression and other disruptive behaviors (see Dodge & Pettit, 2003, for a review). To date, however, nearly all of the developmental research has addressed the role of children's frustration, anger, and other dysregulated negative emotions. Although this classical view of reactive or "hot-headed" aggression has long historical roots, there is also a growing interest in a more instrumental, proactive form of aggression (Coie & Dodge, 1998) that may have very different connections with children's emotions and emotion regulatory abilities.

Much of the research my students and I have conducted suggests that children's and adolescents' positive emotions also play an important role in their aggressive tendencies. As described in the following sections, we have found that preschoolers typically expect to feel happy following successful acts of victimization (i.e., harming others for physical or psychological gains), and our observational research suggests that preschoolers who actually display more frequent positive emotions during aggressive interactions are both more aggressive and disliked by their peers. Moreover, recent work reveals that behaviorally disruptive adolescents expect to feel more positive than their peers following acts of aggressive victimization.

I argue that, collectively, this research raises several themes that are especially relevant for research on emotion regulation in families:

1. Most emotion regulation research addresses children's need to control or modulate already experienced negative emotions. How does "happy victimization" fit into this framework? Are the display and expectation of positive emotions in aggressive contexts related to difficulties in regulating ongoing emotions or to children's problematic emotion-related appraisals?
2. What are the parental and cultural forces implicated in the developmental emergence of happy victimization? Are these different from the contributors already implicated in children's angry aggressive trajectories? Does the disruption of early attachment relationships and empathic ties play a unique role in happy victimization?

CONCEPTUAL AND EMPIRICAL FOUNDATION

Happy Victimization—Theory and Early Research

[Many of our behavioral decisions are influenced by] an anticipation of the way we will feel in some future situation. A child's readiness to go to school, to brave the dentist, to seek out a new friend, or to run away from punishment is based on an appraisal of how he or she will feel when facing those situations. (Harris, 1985, p. 162)

Almost 20 years ago, some moral development researchers began to focus on children's understanding of moral emotions and what that knowledge might reveal about the connections among moral reasoning, emotions, and behavior. Much of this work was implicitly guided by the reasoning reflected in the preceding quote by Harris. In brief, children often remember the emotional antecedents and consequences of events, and this information can be very useful for anticipating the emotional outcomes of different behaviors. Moral development researchers were aware that the events they studied, ranging from aggression and victimization to transgressions of social conventions, were especially likely to elicit strong emotions that would be easily remembered and stored in memory as part of children's affect-event representations (see Arsenio, Gold, & Adams, 2006).

In one early study on this topic, Nunner-Winkler and Sodian (1988) proposed that moral events were likely to produce intense but conflicting emotions, including some happiness and satisfaction resulting from the gains resulting from victimization, as well as sadness, guilt, and other negative emotions from observing the consequences for others. Instead, however, results of this three-part study revealed that young children uniformly expected victimizers to feel happy, although by age 8 nearly all children expected victimizers to feel a mix of negative emotions. Moreover, another study (Barden, Zelko, Duncan, & Masters, 1980) revealed that most young children expected to feel happy when they themselves were placed in the hypothetical role of the victimizer (e.g., successfully stealing someone's candy).

Although my colleagues and I obtained similar findings in some of our initial research, we shared Nunner-Winkler and Sodian's (1988) expectation that even young children's representations of moral victimizers must include both positive and negative emotion expectancies. Perhaps young children's happy victimizer conceptions were just the result of some combination of methodological limitations and children's underlying cognitive difficulties with the task. To address these issues we (Arsenio & Kramer, 1992) asked 4-, 6-, and 8-year-olds to judge the likely emotional consequences of acts of victimization and to provide rationales for those judgments for both victims and victimizers. And to increase the moral salience of these events, story characters were described as good friends, making it less likely that the victimizer would simply be seen as a bully. Finally, after eliciting these initial emotion attributions, children were probed regarding other possible emotional reactions of the victimizer, using a series of increasingly direct questions (beginning with "Could [the victimizer] be feeling anything else? What?").

Results revealed that all but 2 (out of 32) 4- and 6-year-olds still expected victimizers to feel happy, as did about one half of the 8-year-olds, even though almost all children expected victims to feel exclusively negative emotions. The probe-related findings, however, indicated that nearly all of the 8-year-olds who initially expected victimizers to feel happy and three quarters of all 6-year-olds responded to the least direct probe ("anything else?") by providing an additional negative-valence emotion ("She was happy she got the candy but sad that her friend might not talk to her"). By contrast, two thirds of the 4-year-olds insisted that victimizers could only feel happy, even after being explicitly directed to the loss and suffering experienced by the victim on the final probe. (A separate assessment indicated that probing did not change children's views of victims' feelings, suggesting that probing, per se, did not lead to a change in victimizers' emotions.)

On the basis of these and other related findings, I concluded that 4-year-olds appear to view victims and victimizers as having two noninteracting sets of emotional responses to this single victimizing act (perhaps because of cognitive constraints involving the coordination of mixed, i.e., positive and negative, emotion-event representations [Harter & Buddin, 1987]). By contrast, the findings that 6- and 8-year-olds so easily changed from positive to negative emotion attributions for victimizers suggested an age-related moral attributional shift. That is, the emotions attributed to victimizers appear to be influenced by the expected emotional reactions of victims. Furthermore, this age-related shift could reflect a changing developmental understanding of a basic moral conflict—to victimize is to gain desirable outcomes and to feel happy, but to be victimized is to lose what is yours and to feel sadness, anger, and other clearly negative emotions.

If correct, these claims support a view of moral development as involving an underlying ability and spontaneous tendency (Hoffman, 1981, 2000) to integrate the two halves of this moral conflict, that is, both understanding and feeling that the victims' pain and loss will moderate one's own happiness regarding the gains produced by victimization. At a cognitive level, these empathic tendencies depend on children's ability to recognize and understand others' emotional states, as well as children's understanding that they are responsible for producing the other person's current distress. At an affective level, these empathic tendencies depend on an *emotional response* to the distress that has been inflicted on the victim: "I feel your pain and it affects me." As a consequence, disruptions in either the cognitive or affective aspects of this integration are likely to have significant effects on children's victimizing behavior (see the following section for more information).

Observational Studies Involving "Happy Victimization"

Although there are more than 20 studies on various aspects of children's "happy victimization" to date (see Arsenio et al., 2006, for a review), questions have been raised about the psychological meaning and significance of these findings (e.g., Keller, Lourenco, Malti, & Saalbach, 2003). One obvious initial question is whether young children, in fact, do display frequent positive emotions when initiating aggressive and victimizing acts. To address this issue, my colleagues and I have conducted a series of observational studies on the emotions that young children display in the context of peer conflicts and aggression.

The most extensive of these studies (Arsenio, Cooperman, & Lover, 2000) was designed to address the connections between 51 preschoolers' emotional dispositions and knowledge, and aspects of their aggression and social competence. Over the course of a year observational assessments were made of the emotions preschoolers displayed both during and outside of their aggressive interactions with peers, as well as of children's involvement in aggressive encounters. Additional assessments addressed children's emotion knowledge (e.g., recognition and labeling) and ratings of how much they liked their peers, as well as teacher ratings of children's social competence.

Substantial differences were found in the connections between children's emotional dispositions (i.e., their tendency to display happiness or anger) and their aggressive behaviors, depending on the context in which those emotions were observed. Specifically, children with higher levels of happiness outside of aggression (as a percentage of emotions displayed) initiated fewer aggressive acts, but, as expected, children who displayed more aggression-related happiness initiated more aggression. Furthermore, although children often displayed either anger or happiness when initiating aggression, only their tendency to display more happiness was associated with greater aggressiveness and peer disliking. Mediation analyses also revealed that only aggression-related happiness had somewhat of a direct connection with peer liking, with the rest of the connections between emotion-related variables and peer liking being mediated by children's aggressiveness. Finally, victims of aggression were more distressed (showed more displays of sadness or anger) when aggressors were happy than when aggressors displayed other emotions.

Similar findings by Miller and Olson (2000) support the role of observed happy victimization in predicting children's social competence. In that study, young children who engaged in more "gleeful taunting" during a structured peer interaction task at the beginning of the year were rated 9 months later as less socially competent by peers and teachers. Moreover, in a composite measure of children's problematic behavior, gleeful taunting accounted for more than six times the variance of any other emotion variable. Collectively, the results of these studies suggest that young children's frequent normative tendency to be happy when initiating aggression is consistent with children's conceptions that victimizers are often happy. In addition, however, this observational research indicates that individual differences in children's actual tendencies to be happy victimizers are strongly connected with their peer-related aggression and overall social competence.

Reactive and Proactive Aggression

The work previously described raises a number of questions, beginning with how this focus on happy victimization can be reconciled with the long-standing traditional emphasis on the close ties between anger and aggression (e.g., see Bradley, 2000). One resolution begins with Dodge's social informa- tion processing (SIP) model of children's social adjustment and competence (e.g., see Dodge, Lochman, Harnish, Bates, & Pettit, 1997). In this model children's reasoning and behavior involving aggressive events are described in terms of six more or less sequential information-processing steps (i.e., encoding, interpretation, clarification of goals, response access and selec- tion, and behavioral enactment). Research based on this model (see Coie & Dodge, 1998, for a review) has been particularly successful in explaining how children's aggression is related to various biases and deficits during their "on-line" social reasoning about potentially provocative social events. Perhaps the best-known finding involves the "hostile attributional bias," that is, some children's tendency to (mis)attribute hostile intentions to others in ambiguous provocation situations is a major predictor of their hostile aggres- sive behavior.

Subsequent SIP research, however, suggests that this hostile attributional bias characterizes only one important subtype of aggression, reactive aggres- sion, which is linked with classical frustration-aggression-anger theories. On the basis of both observational assessments and teacher ratings, a second more "proactive" form of aggression has also been identified—a type of ag- gression that is thought to be motivated more by expectations of reward than by anger or deficits in intention–cue detection. Although assessments of proac- tive and reactive aggression typically show high levels of overlap, proactive aggression appears to be associated with a unique set of social-information- processing biases and deficits. Specifically, compared with their peers, proac- tive aggressive children exhibit a preference for instrumental rather than social goals, a bias toward viewing aggression as an effective means for ob- taining goals, and a belief in their own efficacy for enacting aggressive be- havior (Arsenio & Lemerise, 2001).

Although reactive aggression is sometimes described as "hot-headed" and proactive aggression as "cold-blooded," research on the emotional as- pects of these forms of aggression is really just beginning. For proactive ag- gression, a single emotional correlate has been studied, although it is one with direct relevance for understanding children's conceptions of happy vic- timization. Children are sometimes asked to rate how they would feel (from "very bad" to "very good") after responding aggressively to a peer's hypo- thetical provocation. Results from one study (Dodge et al., 1997) indicate that proactive aggressive children expect to feel more positive following their proactive aggression than either reactive or nonaggressive children.

Adolescents' Emotion Attributions

In a recent study, my colleagues and I (Arsenio, Gold, & Adams, 2004) sought to extend the Dodge et al. (1997) research by examining adolescents' conceptions of the emotional outcomes of different types of aggression and non-aggression-related events. Our goals were both to obtain a normative picture of participants' expected emotional consequences and to examine whether adolescents with behavior problems would view the consequences of such events differently from their peers. (Adolescents were chosen because of the lack of research on their conceptions of moral emotions.) Another focus was on examining whether adolescents' emotion expectancies had different connections with reactive and proactive aggressive tendencies.

A total of 100 adolescents (about two thirds boys, all African American or Latino) from a low-income urban environment participated. One half of the adolescents had previously been diagnosed by school psychologists as meeting DSM–IV (*Diagnostic and Statistical Manual of Mental Disorders*, 4th ed.; American Psychiatric Association, 1994) criteria for either conduct disorder or oppositional defiant disorder. The comparison group came from the same public school system attended by the behaviorally disruptive (BD) adolescents, and the two groups did not differ in terms of age, gender, ethnic composition, or socioeconomic status.

Adolescents were individually administered a multipart interview that included an assessment of their verbal abilities, as well as assessments of their emotion expectancies regarding both proactive aggression and non-aggression-related events. Participants judged how they expected to feel as a consequence of these different story scenarios by dividing 10 plastic chips as desired between 5 emotion categories—happy, sad, mad, scared, and neutral affect (e.g., 7 chips on happy and 3 on neutral affect). For proactive aggression stories, adolescents were asked to imagine themselves in the role of the person who initiated the aggression, and for nonaggression stories adolescents assumed the role of the central character in events expected (on the basis of previous research) to elicit emotion attributions involving either happiness, sadness, anger, fear, or a mixture of fear and sadness. Finally, the adolescents' teachers completed assessments of the participants' reactive and proactive aggressive tendencies as well as their overall externalizing patterns (Achenbach, 1991).

Analyses indicated that BD and comparison adolescents expected to feel quite differently in response to these various types of events. For nonaggression stories, BD adolescents were somewhat more likely than their peers to expect to feel angry in response to events that normatively did not elicit anger attributions. Furthermore, across all emotion-eliciting categories, BD adolescents expected to feel fewer normative emotions than comparison adolescents. Finally, as hypothesized, BD adolescents expected to feel significantly happier than their peers following acts of proactive aggression that produced clear material and psychological gains. Although BD adolescents did not rate themselves as feeling especially happy following their victimization, it was still their modal emotion choice (BD 3.31 chips vs. comparison 1.67).

Subsequent regression analyses revealed that this "proactive aggression happiness" was a unique predictor of adolescents' externalizing tendencies. Even after accounting for the influence of verbal ability and other forms of significant non-aggression-related emotion knowledge, adolescents' expectation of happiness following proactive aggression was a significant predictor of their externalizing tendencies. Moreover, these findings were not moderated by adolescents' behavioral status. In other words, despite mean group differences for some of these variables, the associations between variables (e.g., proactive happiness and externalizing) did not differ between the groups. In terms of adolescents' reactive and proactive aggression tendencies, proactive aggression happiness was uniquely associated with teacher ratings of adolescents' proactive aggression but not their reactive aggression.

These findings involving adolescents' conceptions and the observational findings for young children collectively support the idea that "happy victimization" plays an important, if little understood, role in the development of some children's aggressive and socially incompetent behavior. There is also some initial evidence that this victimization is a form of proactive aggression, or at least that it is more closely associated with proactive than reactive aggression. Yet, despite these contributions, almost nothing is known about how and why this happy victimization first emerges.

The remainder of this chapter provides some first steps toward addressing these issues. To anticipate the discussion, the "how" and "why" questions are seen as closely related, and both are explained in terms of a form of emotion dysregulation that has its roots in pervasive attachment disruptions that affect children's sense of emotional reciprocity and subsequent empathic tendencies. For the sake of simplicity, however, the "how" question is addressed first ("How does happy victimization emerge and what does this have to do emotion regulation?"), followed by an exploration of "why" in terms of possible family influences.

LINKING EMOTION DYSREGULATION AND HAPPY VICTIMIZATION

It is easy to see how the classic "frustration-anger-aggression" model involves emotion dysregulation, with children misinterpreting or overreacting to situations in which they believe someone is deliberately trying to block a desirable, maybe even legitimate, goal. Intense, excessive anger follows, and perhaps without their fully realizing it, that anger leads some children to become aggressive. By contrast, happy victimization seems more controlled, more intentional, and the resulting emotion is often a product of the successful instrumental use of aggression to take what belongs to others. Yet, as Cole, Michel, and Teti (1994) noted, emotion dysregulation involves more than controlling negative emotions. "Positive emotions can be dysregulatory

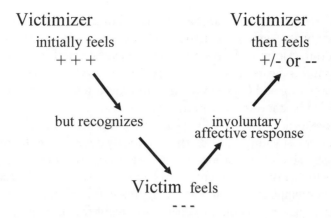

Figure 5.1. Simplified view of victimizers' empathic responses to the pain and loss experienced by their victim.

and dysregulating . . . [for example] laughing at another person's distress [when] positive affect is not modulated so as to take account of the other's distress" (p. 84; see also chap. 6, this volume, on antecedent regulation, i.e., regulating emotions before they are elicited). Regardless of whether the resulting emotions are positive or negative, a child's failure to recognize or to be suitably responsive to the emotional states of others can be a basic cause of emotion dysregulation. In this sense, happy victimization presents a clear, if somewhat complex, problem with children's emotion regulatory abilities.

My colleague Elizabeth Lemerise and I have begun to address some of these issues as part of a larger discussion (Arsenio & Lemerise, 2001, 2004) on the potential affective underpinnings of aggression. In brief, we have argued that the social cognitive biases and deficits associated with aggression and victimization are—at their core—a product of pervasive failures or disruptions in underlying empathic tendencies. Happy victimization, in particular, is viewed as stemming from a basic lack of emotional responsiveness to others that runs counter to certain biologically rooted empathic tendencies (Hoffman, 1981). Finally, these empathic difficulties are seen as resulting from shared adult–child interactional histories (e.g., attachment patterns) characterized by ongoing problems with emotion regulation and responsiveness.

Figure 5.1 shows a simplified picture of how empathy typically influences nonaggressive children's victimization (e.g., see Hoffman, 2000). Young children may initially start out feeling happy about the potential or realized gains produced by victimization—the desired toy or the turn on the swing without waiting. Then, however, as part of a gradual developmental transformation, they both directly observe or are directed to observe their victims' emotional responses (by victims themselves as well as by other socializing agents). Once the victimizer becomes aware of the victim's negative emotions, underlying empathic mechanisms take effect and cause the victimizer to respond and, to some extent, share the strong negative emotions expressed by the victim. Along with this affective recognition and response, the victimizing child is aware that (a) he or she is the source of the other child's pain and suffering and (b) the victimization was intentional and could have been avoided by choosing an alternative behavior.

With repeated exposures to acts of victimization both as victimizers and victims, most young children then gradually develop mental representations of aggressive victimization that include strong mixed emotions and often guilt. Finally, these representations begin to play an anticipatory role, so that even contemplating victimization may elicit either hot or cold (i.e., emotionally arousing or nonarousing) cognitions about the negative emotions associated with these acts (Hoffman, 2000). At times, however, this normative developmental integration of cognitive and affective contributors to empathy can fail or become disrupted. At the heart of these empathic difficulties, in the present model, is the early role of attachment relationships and their effects on parent–child and child–child emotional reciprocity.

Attachment, Temperament, Empathy, and Behavior Problems

A number of studies have addressed the connections between children's attachment patterns and their emerging behavior problems and externalizing tendencies. Although initial studies of this topic provided somewhat mixed findings, there is a growing agreement that when insecure early attachments combine with low socioeconomic status (SES) and other sociocultural stressors, affected children are at a greatly elevated risk for behavior problems (see Greenberg, 1999, for a review). For example, in one longitudinal study Lyons-Ruth and colleagues followed a high-risk sample that included many depressed mothers. Results revealed that the majority (55%) of children who had been classified as disorganized in infancy and who had a mother with psychosocial problems subsequently exhibited hostile behaviors in kindergarten (compared with only 5% of those children without either risk factor). Other studies also suggest that disorganized attachments may play a unique role in the emergence of children's behavior problems. This is not surprising given that disorganized attachments are often associated with parental abuse and neglect and an inability to develop any effective strategy for attaining the central biological goal of the attachment system—that is, maintaining proximity to caregivers (Lyons-Ruth & Jacobvitz, 1999).

Despite the growing support for connections among children's attachment, high-risk status, and externalizing tendencies, there is much less consensus about the mechanisms underlying these connections (Dodge & Pettit, 2003). Furthermore, there is almost no research on the related question that is the focus of this chapter: Why is it that some children do not alter their initially positive emotional views of victimization? In what follows, a brief outline of an explanatory model is offered, a model that borrows freely from various ideas elaborated in much greater detail by Hoffman (2000), Fonagy (2004), Cassidy (1994), Kochanska (1995), and others.

The central ideas of this model can be summarized as follows: (a) children's attachment status is, in large part, the product of a shared pattern of parent–child emotional reciprocity in which adults typically play a greater role; (b) in some cases, however, children's temperamental and dispositional tendencies may have a significant influence on parent–child emotional reciprocity; (c) resulting patterns of emotional reciprocity affect children's empathic tendencies; and (d) in turn, differences in emotional reciprocity and attachment are connected with children's mental representations of victimization and aggression. In this view, patterns of parent–child emotional reciprocity provide the foundation for children's understanding of moral reciprocity (i.e., fair and equitable treatment) and influence their subsequent aggressive tendencies.

Secure attachment is typically described as the product of (relatively) consistent caregiver responsiveness to young children's biological and emotional needs. And as many have noted, emotional factors including children's "felt security" and caregivers' sensitivity to infants' emotional signals play a key role in this responsive interplay (Sroufe & Waters, 1977). As securely attached infants grow into toddlers and preschool-age children, these early patterns of emotional reciprocity then allow children to freely share both their positive and negative emotionally charged experiences with caregivers (Cassidy, 1994). Overall, securely attached children can expect to share negative feelings, including those directed at their caregivers, within the boundaries of a relationship characterized by trust and mutual emotion regulation.

Children's temperament and dispositional tendencies, however, can have an important influence on both attachment and parent–child emotional reciprocity. For example, Vaughn and Bost (1999) noted that although attachment and temperament are generally orthogonal, infant irritability in combination with low parental social or economic resources increases the likelihood of insecure attachment. In a related vein, Kochanska (1995) has examined an influential model of how children's temperament, attachment status, and parent–child emotional reciprocity are linked with the development of children's guilt and moral internalization. One key finding is that for children who are temperamentally relatively fearless, moral internalization and compliance with adults depend on a history of mutually positive parent–child interactions and secure child attachment.

Yet, even though attachment and temperament sometimes interact (see the following section), insecurely attached children, in general, encounter a very different pattern of parent–child emotional reciprocity than their securely attached peers. For some insecurely attached children, the core implicit message from adults is that children must learn to filter or distort their emotional experiences before adults will respond. Although many of these children will develop a more or less successful strategy for maintaining emotional and physical proximity, some insecurely attached children will be faced with adults who are fundamentally emotionally unresponsive. A combination of mental disorders (e.g., depression), extreme sociocultural stressors including poverty, previous abuse and neglect, and related factors makes it impossible for some parents to provide their children with even minimal psychologically adequate levels of contingent emotional responsiveness. In turn, these children are likely to develop severely disrupted attachment patterns and to develop internal working models of these relationships that implicitly reflect messages such as "in this life you're on your own" and "others are out to get me."

Although there is only limited support for this model, the broad outlines are consistent with several studies (e.g., see Troy & Sroufe, 1987, on connections among attachment, empathy, and aggression). In a more general sense, the present approach is somewhat related to a model outlined by Fonagy (e.g., 2004) in which he argued that insecure attachments undermine children's understanding of both their own and others' mental states in ways that increase the likelihood of peer aggression and victimization. In his view, the lack of contingent responsiveness between caregivers and infants, in particular, acts to weaken insecurely attached children's understanding of others' mental states. Because less responsive adults inadvertently make their needs, beliefs, and desires somewhat more opaque to their children, these children develop less elaborated theories of mind involving these mental states than securely attached children. As a consequence, insecurely attached children are less likely to consider or understand the needs and feelings of others, and they are subsequently more likely to victimize their peers.

Returning to Figure 5.1, Fonagy's model is especially helpful for explaining the behavior of those children who are aggressive because of a relative inability to recognize or understand victims' emotions, which then results in a failure to activate underlying empathic tendencies. There are, however, some aggressive children who do not appear to be experiencing failures in either their mentalizing or other social cognitive abilities (e.g., see Sutton, Smith, & Swettenham, 1999). As noted earlier, this other group may be characterized by a more "cold-blooded" proactive form of aggression in which some children may be quite aware of the consequences of their actions for the victim but be emotionally unmoved and unaffected by those reactions. For these children, the problem is more one of emotional responsiveness than of social understanding, per se (see also Arsenio & Lemerise, 2001, 2004).

Empathy and Aggression: Further Distinctions

This distinction between being relatively unaware versus unconcerned regarding the emotional costs of victimization for victims is important for addressing the next set of questions: What are the specific empathic mechanisms associated with proactive aggression and happy victimization? What role do parents' and children's temperaments play in these connections? To date, there is neither empirical nor theoretical work on these specific questions. As a consequence, what follows is necessarily more suggestive than definitive.

Fonagy's account of the empathically unaware seems consistent with descriptions of more reactively aggressive children. Because these children have deficits in understanding the needs, beliefs, and desires of others, they are also likely to have difficulty understanding others' intentions and, consequently, to exhibit the hostile attributional biases typically associated with reactive aggression. In other words, these children often assume others are being deliberately provocative and aggressive when, in fact, they are not. At an affective level, the empathically unaware are likely to respond with what they believe is legitimate (i.e., provoked) anger, frustration, and retaliatory aggression. By contrast, children who are more proactively aggressive are less likely to have difficulties in recognizing or understanding the emotional reactions of others. So, although they are less likely to engage in "misfired" aggression, their lack of emotional responsiveness to victims makes it easier for them to use aggression instrumentally and to feel emotionally positive about the resulting physical and psychological gains.

What about the attachment and parenting antecedents of these patterns? The model presented to this point does not really explain these different paths to aggression (i.e., "empathically unaware" is associated with reactive aggression, whereas "empathically unconcerned" is linked to proactive aggression). Part of what may be missing is an understanding of how child temperament or dispositional characteristics combine with particular aspects of parenting. For example, one promising approach (Frick, O'Brien, Wootton, & McBurnett, 1994) begins by distinguishing two groups of children with behavior problems, "[those] prone to poor impulse control (e.g., becomes angry when corrected) [versus those] characterized by a lack of guilt, lack of empathy, and superficial charm" (p. 704). In subsequent studies, these researchers (Wootton, Frick, Shelton, & Silverthorn, 1997) examined how ineffective parenting, including inconsistent discipline and lack of parental involvement, was related to these two types of problems—impulsivity versus callous–unemotional [CU] traits—in a group of mostly clinically referred 6- to 13-year-olds. As expected, ineffective parenting was associated with higher levels of conduct problems, but, unexpectedly, this held only for those children without CU traits: Children high in CU traits had high levels of conduct problems regardless of parental effectiveness.

Kochanska's research with normally functioning children provides a potential explanation for this last finding involving children high in CU traits. As mentioned earlier, Kochanska (1995) found that temperamentally more fearless toddlers develop higher levels of moral internalization (and presumably less victimization) when they are securely attached and when parents have developed reciprocal affectively positive relationships with their children. In a subsequent longitudinal study Kochanska (2004) confirmed the importance of what she calls the two-process model of conscience development. Children's secure attachment at 14 months increased the cumulative positive influence of effective parenting (e.g., nonpunitive responsiveness) when children were between 14 and 45 months of age and resulted in higher levels of both moral conduct and reasoning when children were 56 months of age. Extrapolating from these findings, it may be that for children prone to CU traits, secure attachments in infancy (which were not assessed by Wootton et al., 1997) act as a necessary precondition for responsiveness to parents' subsequent attempts at moral socialization.

In summary, pervasive early failures in parent–child emotional reciprocity (with attachment reflecting that reciprocity) may promote children's victimizing behaviors by undermining nascent empathic tendencies in one of two ways: (a) some children may become so self-focused they do not easily recognize their victims' pain and losses and (b) other children may learn to view their victims' emotional reactions as simply irrelevant when they conflict with the victimizer's own desires and goals. The second set of empathic failures (i.e., a lack of empathic concern or responsiveness) is expected to be especially predictive of higher levels of "happy victimization" and proactive–instrumental aggression. In terms of the origins of this pattern, these children may be temperamentally less responsive to parenting that utilizes power assertion and other fear-inducing techniques, especially when that parenting is built on an earlier base of insecure child attachment. Over time these parents may attempt to escalate their ineffective punitive socialization efforts, leading to even more disrupted parent–child emotional reciprocity, and a severing or truncation of childrens' emotional responsiveness to others (including potential victims).

Potential Parental Contributors to the Model

Up to this point, a somewhat complex model has been proposed in which children's conceptions and behaviors involving happy victimization are seen as the product of parent–child emotional patterns and child temperament affecting children's attachment, internal working models, and empathic tendencies. Although some aspects of this model have been assessed by Kochanska (e.g., 1995, 2004), Frick (e.g., Frick et al., 1994), and others, almost nothing is known about other essential components of the model, such as the unique developmental origins of children's proactive and reactive aggressive tendencies (Coie & Dodge, 1998), and especially parental and other sociocultural contributors to children's happy victimization.

To date, my research on this last issue has focused on a much more modest, reduced version of the model described previously. In my initial research, I (Arsenio, Ramos-Marcuse, & Hoffman, 2006; Ramos-Marcuse & Arsenio, 2001) have attempted to examine the connections of preschoolers' conceptions of happy victimization and other moral emotions with parental disciplinary strategies. Participants included a group of developmentally at-risk, lower-SES African American and Latino 4- and 5-year-olds and their mostly single parents. About one half of the 63 children had been referred to a university-based clinic because of early behavioral problems, and the other children came from preschools in the same area served by the clinic. The groups did not differ in terms of gender, race and ethnicity, SES, or expressive language abilities.

Previous research has shown so little variability in preschoolers' conceptions of happy victimization (in contrast to adolescents) that it has been difficult to examine connections between those conceptions and young children's emerging aggression and behavioral problems. As a consequence, my colleagues and I adapted techniques from the widely used MacArthur Story Stem Battery (MSSB), in which children are presented with the beginning of some story or event and then asked to enact what they expect to follow using engaging, age-appropriate materials. An extensive literature has shown this technique provides an especially sensitive and effective way of getting at young children's underlying mental representation of emotionally charged relationships (Emde, Wolf, & Oppenheim, 2003). This study modified a moral version of this assessment (Kochanska, Padavich, & Koenig, 1996) so that children were presented with situations in which they had victimized another child (e.g., taking his or her bike), and participants were then asked how they would feel and what would happen next.

In addition to this child assessment, parents and other adults (teachers or therapists) completed appropriate versions of the Child Behavior Checklist (e.g., see Achenbach, 1991). Parents also completed the Parenting Dimensions Inventory (PDI), which assesses several self-reported dimensions of parenting style including parental support, control, and specific disciplinary techniques. Multiple studies have shown that the PDI predicts important variations in low-SES adults' parenting style as well as various aspects of children's behavior (see Power, 1992).

Children's judgments about how they would feel as victimizers in these stories were consistent with previous literature, although contrary to initial expectations. In nearly 80% of their judgments, both clinic and nonclinic children said they expected to feel happy (clinic M = 3.15 vs. nonclinic M = 3.21 out of 4 stories), which both groups typically justified by referring to the desirable gains produced by victimization. Coding of children's subsequent responses ("What happens then?"), however, revealed important group differences for one broad category. Nonclinic children were nearly twice as likely as clinic children (23% vs. 12% of all responses) to say they would make reparations to their victims, a category that included offering apologies, returning stolen or seized property, or admitting blame (e.g., "I would say sorry and give him his bike back"). It appears that although neither group was able to resist the initial salience of the (hypothetical) gain and happiness resulting from victimization, nonclinic children quickly saw a need to address the victims' losses.

The parenting strategies of the two groups also differed in some revealing ways. A factor analysis of the parenting scale resulted in several broad categories that are generally consistent with previous PDI research, including parental warmth, amount of control, focus on child input, and use of reasoning. Only a single group difference emerged, however, in relation to these factors: Nonclinic parents described themselves as being warmer to their children than clinic parents. Subsequently, guided by research on parenting styles, my colleagues and I combined warmth and a form of control into a single measure of an authoritative ("loving but firm") parenting style. Nonclinic parents also scored higher than clinic parents on this overall measure. In addition, however, subsequent analyses revealed that (a) higher levels of authoritative parenting were associated with children's tendencies to offer more reparations for their aggression in the MSSB interview and (b) this connection was not moderated by clinic versus nonclinic status. In other words, despite mean group differences in children's use of reparations and parents' authoritative parenting style, in both groups parents who were more authoritative had children who were more likely to try to make amends to the victims of their hypothetical victimization.

Other parts of the study (Ramos-Marcuse & Arsenio, 2001) also revealed that children's attachment representations (combining parent and other adults) and their moral reasoning both contributed to adult ratings of children's behavior problems. Contrary to expectations, however, there was no evidence that children's emotionally charged moral reasoning mediated the connection between children's attachment representations and their behavior problems.

FUTURE RESEARCH AND POLICY IMPLICATIONS

After almost 20 years of research, there is a growing awareness that children's and adolescents' conceptions and behaviors involving happy victimization are more than a curious exception to frustration-anger models of childhood aggression. In this chapter, I have attempted to show that much of the behavior noted in this literature can best be understood as a form of proactive aggression with regard to the reactive–proactive distinction (e.g., Dodge et al., 1997). Furthermore, I have examined this "happy proactive aggression" in relation to the two major themes of this book: (a) the importance of children's emotion regulatory abilities for explaining broad differences in their psychological functioning and (b) the role of parents and other contributors to individual differences in these abilities.

Much of the discussion on these last two points has been admittedly speculative. On one hand, there is evidence linking attachment difficulties and behavior problems in otherwise at-risk children and some support for the role of empathy in these connections. The specific interplay between happy victimization, disruptions in parent–child emotion reciprocity, child temperament, and active disregard for victims' emotions, however, is mostly theoretical at this point. But before offering a few specific directions for future research on these connections, it might be worth addressing some more basic questions: Why bother? What does the work on happy victimization really add to the voluminous literature on aggression that warrants further exploration?

The simplest explanation requires a brief reexamination of Dodge and colleagues' distinction between reactive and proactive aggression. As I have argued elsewhere (Arsenio & Lemerise, 2001, 2004), children who are more reactively aggressive appear to share a central moral concern with their nonaggressive peers: "It's not OK for someone to hurt or victimize me on purpose." The problem for reactively aggressive children is not with their "moral values," per se, but with the social reasoning they used to judge the intentionality of others' behaviors. In provocative but ambiguous situations, these are the children who (mis)perceive hostile intentions in their peers. As a consequence, some of the treatment and social policy implications for these children are relatively clear: Design anger management and other social cognitive interventions that attempt to alter underlying deficits in their social reasoning. And, of course, these programs do exist and are at least somewhat effective at addressing these problems (e.g., see Lochman & Lenhart, 1993).

By contrast, for proactive aggression the problem "may lie in the values of the bully rather than the accuracy of the cognitions" (Sutton et al., 1999, p. 122). Although not all proactively aggressive children are necessarily bullies, the available research indicates that, as a group, bullies believe that aggression is an effective means of getting needs met, that they themselves are "good" at aggression, and that they will feel happy afterward, or "it's easy, it works, and it makes me feel good." Moreover, these children seem to understand the importance of others' intentions while still initiating intentional aggression of their own. Given that more than two thirds of all aggressive children are mostly (about 10%–15% of children) or at least partly (about 50%) proactively aggressive (e.g., see Dodge et al., 1997), the need for a better understanding of this form of aggression becomes clearer.

With these issues in mind, several directions for future research can be offered. One suggestion involves the need for more explicit research on the connections between happy victimization and proactive aggression. At a theoretical level, there is no question that the unprovoked acts of instrumental aggression used to assess happy victimization are a form of proactive aggression. To date, however, only a couple of studies have shown an empirical connection between children's conceptions of happy victimization and ratings of their proactive aggression. More work is needed to examine specific connections between happy victimization, which has emerged from the moral development literature, and proactive aggression, which has emerged from a more "value neutral" SIP model (see Arsenio & Lemerise, 2004, on such an integration).

It would also be helpful if research on the connections between children's attachment patterns and their behavior problems focused more explicitly on underlying mechanisms. Does this connection really depend on the sort of empathic mechanisms outlined previously? Specifically, are proactive happy aggressors more "numb" than "blind" to their victims' reactions, and is this pattern perhaps more likely to emerge in children with certain types of early temperaments? It may be especially useful to combine some of the work by Kochanska and Frick and their colleagues to address these issues. For example, are temperamentally more fearless young children who develop insecure attachments (and who also experience pervasive sociocultural risks) subsequently more likely to be high in CU traits? And given the nature of those callous-unemotional traits (e.g., "absence of guilt . . . failure to show empathy, use of others for one's own gain"; Frick et al., 2003, p. 247), are these children more likely to exhibit higher levels of instrumental–proactive aggression and happy victimization than their peers?

It may be easier to excuse the aggression of a child who loses his or her temper and hits a peer than the aggression of a child who looks happy after pushing a peer down to get a quicker turn on the swing. The first child is seen as failing to control his or her emotions, whereas the second child is not typically seen as having problems with emotional control. Much of the present chapter, however, has been an attempt to explain happy victimization in terms of disruptions in parent–child emotional reciprocity that have a lasting effect on children's empathic tendencies. In this view, the emotional reciprocity that children experience within their larger environment underlies both their emotion regulatory abilities (including antecedent emotion appraisals) and their emerging sense of moral reciprocity. Moreover, interventions that attempt to address happy victimization as just another social cognitive bias are unlikely to address the deeper affective and moral roots of this potentially important form of aggression.

REFERENCES

Achenbach, T. (1991). *Manual for the Child Behavior Checklist: 4–18 and 1991 profile.* Burlington: University of Vermont, Department of Psychiatry.

American Psychiatric Association. (1994). *Diagnostic and statistical manual of mental disorders* (4th ed.). Washington, DC: Author.

Arsenio, W., Cooperman, S., & Lover, A. (2000). Affective predictors of preschoolers' aggression and peer acceptance: Direct and indirect effects. *Developmental Psychology, 36,* 438–448.

Arsenio, W., Gold, J., & Adams, E. (2004). Adolescents' emotion expectancies regarding aggressive and nonaggressive events: Connections with behavior problems. *Journal of Experimental Child Psychology, 89,* 338–355.

Arsenio, W., Gold, J., & Adams, E. (2006). Children's conceptions and displays of moral emotions. In M. Killen & J. Smetana (Eds.), *Handbook of moral development* (pp. 581–610). Hillsdale, NJ: Erlbaum.

Arsenio, W., & Kramer, R. (1992). Victimizers and their victims: Children's conceptions of the mixed emotional consequences of victimization. *Child Development, 63,* 915–927.

Arsenio, W., & Lemerise, E. (2001). Varieties of childhood bullying: Values, emotion processes, and social competence. *Social Development, 10,* 59–73.

Arsenio, W., & Lemerise, E. (2004). Aggression and moral development: Integrating the social information processing and moral domain models. *Child Development, 75,* 986–1002.

Arsenio, W., Ramos-Marcuse, F., & Hoffman, R. (2006). *Young at-risk children's emotionally charged moral narratives: Relations with behavior problems, parental social support, and family disciplinary techniques.* Manuscript in preparation.

Barden, C., Zelko, F., Duncan, S., & Masters, J. (1980). Children's consensual knowledge about the experiential determinants of emotion. *Journal of Personality and Social Psychology, 39,* 968–976.

Bradley, S. (2000). *Affect regulation and the development of psychopathology.* New York: Guilford Press.

Campos, J. J., Frankel, C. B., & Camras, L. (2004). On the nature of emotion regulation. *Child Development, 75,* 377–394.

Cassidy, J. (1994). Emotion regulation: Influences of attachment relationships. *Monographs of the Society for Research in Child Development, 59*(2–3, Serial No. 240), 228–283.

Coie, J. D., & Dodge, K. A. (1998). Aggression and antisocial behavior. In W. Damon (Series Ed.) & N. Eisenberg (Vol. Ed.), *Handbook of child psychology: Vol. 3. Social, emotional, and personality development* (pp. 779–862). New York: Wiley.

Cole, P. M., Martin, S. E., & Dennis, T. A. (2004). Emotion regulation as a scientific construct: Methodological challenges and directions for child development research. *Child Development, 75,* 317–333.

Cole, P. M., Michel, M. K., & Teti, L. O. (1994). The development of emotion regulation and dysregulation: A clinical perspective. *Monographs of the Society for Research in Child Development, 59*(2–3, Serial No. 240), 73–100, 250–283.

Dodge, K. A., Lochman, J. E., Harnish, J. D., Bates, J. E., & Pettit, S. (1997). Reactive and proactive aggression in school children and psychiatrically impaired chronically assaultive youth. *Journal of Abnormal Psychology, 106,* 37–51.

Dodge, K. A., & Pettit, G. S. (2003). A biopsychosocial model of the development of chronic conduct disorders in adolescence. *Developmental Psychology, 39,* 349–371.

Emde, R., Wolf, D., & Oppenheim, D. (2003). *Revealing the inner worlds of young children: The MacArthur Story Stem Battery and parent–child narratives.* New York: Oxford University Press.

Fonagy, P. (2004). The developmental roots of violence in the failure of mentalization. In F. Pfafflin & G. Adshead (Eds.), *A matter of security: The application of attachment theory to forensic psychiatry and psychotherapy* (pp. 13–56). New York: Jessica Kingsley.

Frick, P., Crowell, A., Loney, B., Bodin, S., Dane, H., & Barry, C. (2003). Callous-unemotional traits and development pathways to severe conduct problems. *Developmental Psychology, 39,* 246–260.

Frick, P., O'Brien, B., Wootton, J., & McBurnett, K. (1994). Psychopathy and conduct problems in children. *Journal of Abnormal Psychology, 103,* 700–707.

Greenberg, M. (1999). Attachment and psychopathology in childhood. In J. Cassidy & P. Shaver (Eds.), *Handbook of attachment: Theory, research, and clinical applications* (pp. 469–496). New York: Guilford Press.

Harris, P. L. (1985). What children know about the situations that provoke emotions. In M. Lewis & C. Saarni (Eds.), *The socialization of emotion* (pp. 161–186). New York: Plenum Press.

Harter, S., & Buddin, N. (1987). Children's understanding of the simultaneity of two emotions: A five-stage developmental acquisition sequence. *Developmental Psychology, 23,* 388–399.

Hoffman, M. (1981). Is altruism part of human nature? *Journal of Personality and Social Psychology, 40,* 121–137.

Hoffman, M. (2000). *Empathy and moral development: Implications for caring and justice.* New York: Cambridge University Press.

Keller, M., Lourenco, O., Malti, T., & Saalbach, H. (2003). The multifaceted phenomenon of "happy victimizers": A cross-cultural comparison of moral emotions. *British Journal of Developmental Psychology, 21,* 1–18.

Kochanska, G., (1995). Children's temperament, mothers' discipline, and security of attachment: Multiple pathways to emerging internalization. *Child Development, 66,* 597–615.

Kochanska, G., (2004). Maternal parenting and children's conscience: Early security as a moderator. *Child Development, 75,* 1229–1242.

Kochanska, G., Padavich, D., & Koenig, A. (1996). Children's narratives about hypothetical moral dilemmas and objective measures of their conscience: Mutual relations and socialization antecedents. *Child Development, 67,* 1420–1436.

Lochman, J., & Lenhart, L. (1993). Anger coping intervention for aggressive children: Conceptual models and outcome effects. *Clinical Psychology Review, 13,* 785–805.

Lyons-Ruth, K., & Jacobvitz, D. (1999). Attachment disorganization: Unresolved loss, relational violence, and lapses in behavioral and attentional strategies. In J. Cassidy & P. Shaver (Eds.), *Handbook of attachment: Theory, research, and clinical applications* (pp. 520–534). New York: Guilford Press.

Miller, A. L., & Olson, S. L. (2000). Emotional expressiveness during peer conflicts: A predictor of social maladjustment among high-risk preschoolers. *Journal of Abnormal Child Psychology, 28,* 339–352.

Nunner-Winkler, G., & Sodian, B. (1988). Children's understanding of moral emotions. *Child Development, 59,* 1323–1338.

Power, T. G. (1992). *Parenting Dimensions Inventory (PDI): A research manual.* Unpublished manuscript, University of Houston, TX.

Ramos-Marcuse, F., & Arsenio, W. (2001). Young children's emotionally charged moral narratives: Relations with attachment and behavior problems and competencies. *Early Education & Development, 12,* 165–184.

Sroufe, A., & Waters, E. (1977). Attachment as an organizational construct. *Child Development, 48,* 1184–1199.

Sutton, J., Smith, P. K., & Swettenham, J. (1999). Bullying and "theory of mind": A critique of the "social skills deficit" model of anti-social behavior. *Social Development, 8,* 117–127.

Troy, M., & Sroufe, A. (1987). Victimization among preschoolers: Role of attachment relationship history. *Journal of the American Academy of Child and Adolescent Psychiatry, 26,* 156–172.

Vaughn, B., & Bost, K. (1999). Attachment and temperament: Redundant, independent, or interacting influences on interpersonal adaptation and personality development. In J. Cassidy & P. Shaver (Eds.), *Handbook of attachment: Theory, research, and clinical applications* (pp. 198–225). New York: Guilford Press.

Wootton, J., Frick, P., Shelton, K., & Silverthorn, P. (1997). Ineffective parenting and childhood conduct problems: The moderating role of callous-unemotional traits. *Journal of Consulting and Clinical Psychology, 65,* 301–308.

6

PARENTING AND CHILDREN'S ADJUSTMENT: THE ROLE OF CHILDREN'S EMOTION REGULATION

CARLOS VALIENTE AND NANCY EISENBERG

In the last decade the topics of emotion and emotion regulation have been a focal issue in the study of children's social development. Once viewed as a nuisance variable, emotion regulation is now viewed as a key construct in some developmental models and many research programs. A large body of literature links emotion regulation to measures of social functioning; a smaller literature highlights the role socializers play in fostering emotion regulation; and an even smaller, but growing, literature considers how parenting and children's emotion regulation simultaneously contribute to children's quality of social functioning.

Our goal in this chapter is to provide an overview of our work on parenting, children's emotion regulation, and children's social and emotional development. A focus of our work, like that of many other developmentalists, has been to explain individual differences in indices of children's problem behaviors, social competence, and empathy-related responses. Initially our

Work on this chapter was supported by grants from the National Institute of Mental Health (NIMH 1 R01 MH 60838 and 2 R01 MH60838), as well as a Research Scientist Award to Nancy Eisenberg.

work, and the work of others, focused on the direct, linear relations of either parenting or children's emotion regulation to typical measures of children's adjustment. This early work laid the foundation for more recent inquiries that are focused on explaining why relations among these variables exist. In addition to examining direct effects, we now often test hypotheses involving mediational chains or moderated models. Moreover, as developmentalists, we are particularly interested in how the relations among our key constructs may change as children age and develop.

In this chapter we begin with a discussion of definitions and conceptual issues, including a brief review of the contribution of emotion regulation to adjustment, and then turn our attention to a review of empirical findings on the relation between parenting and children's emotion regulation and adjustment. Next, we discuss ideas for future research, and finally, we conclude with thoughts on the clinical, social, and public policy implications of this line of research.

CONCEPTUAL, THEORETICAL, AND METHODOLOGICAL ISSUES

On the basis of a large body of literature linking regulation with developmental outcomes, a 2000 National Academy of Sciences committee report, *From Neurons to Neighborhoods*, concluded that "the growth of self-regulation is a cornerstone of early childhood development that cuts across all domains of behavior" (Shonkoff & Phillips, 2000, p. 3). Huffman, Mehlinger, and Kerivan's (2000) NIH-funded report concerning risk factors for academic and behavioral problems at the beginning of school similarly concluded that "children's competency also seems to depend on social skills and emotion regulation capacities" (p. 4). Despite the importance of self-regulation to one's social functioning, research devoted to understanding how individual differences in self-regulation emerge is somewhat limited, although this is changing rapidly.

Given the variance in views on emotions and on how they are regulated, one would expect to find a number of different definitions of emotion regulation. Despite differences, there are a number of similarities in how emotion regulation is defined. For example, Thompson (1994) defined *emotion regulation* as the "extrinsic and intrinsic processes responsible for monitoring, evaluating, and modifying emotional reactions, especially their intensive and temporal features, to achieve one's goals" (pp. 27–28). Included in Thompson's discussion of emotion regulation were neurophysiological responses, attention processes, construals of emotionally arousing events, encoding of internal emotion cues, access to coping resources, regulating the demands of familiar settings, and selecting adaptive response alternatives. Emotion regulation has also been defined as "the intra- and extraorganismic factors by which emotional arousal is redirected, controlled, modulated, and modified to enable an individual to function adaptively in emotionally arousing situations" (Cicchetti, Ganiban, & Barnett, 1991). Cicchetti et al. emphasized the role of emotion regulation in maintaining internal arousal "within a manageable, performance-optimizing range" (p. 15).

Building on the work of Thompson (1994), P. M. Cole and colleagues (Cole, Michel, & Teti, 1994), Campos, Mumme, Kermoian, and Campos (1994), and others, we define emotion-related regulation (henceforth called *emotion regulation* for brevity) as "the process of initiating, avoiding, inhibiting, maintaining, or modulating the occurrence, form, intensity, or duration of internal feeling states, emotion-related physiological, attentional processes, motivational states, and/or the behavioral concomitants of emotion in the service of accomplishing affect-related biological or social adaptation or achieving individual goals" (Eisenberg & Spinrad, 2004, p. 338). This definition is broad because we believe emotion regulation can occur in regard to numerous aspects of functioning and at various times before, during, and after the occurrence of emotion. In thinking about emotion regulation, we have found it useful to distinguish between *antecedent* and *concurrent* emotion regulation, *control* versus *regulation*, and *voluntary control–regulation* and *less voluntary, reactive control.*

Antecedent and Concurrent Emotion Regulation

In our view, individuals can regulate emotion before its elicitation, while it is being elicited, or after the elicitation of emotion (Eisenberg & Spinrad, 2004). This difference is consistent with the distinction between antecedent-focused emotion regulation (e.g., the management of emotion before the emotion response tendencies are fully activated) and response-focused emotion regulation (e.g., activities one uses after emotion is elicited; Gross, 1999; chap. 1, this volume). Drawing on the coping literature, one can view proactive coping, defined as "efforts undertaken in advance of a potentially stressful event to prevent it or to modify its form before it occurs," as a form of antecedent emotion regulation (Aspinwall & Taylor, 1997, p. 417). Antecedent emotion regulation involves managing emotional reactions before they occur by using not only proactive coping but also attentional and cognitive processes to choose the situations that are focused on and how they are interpreted (Gross, 1999).

Control Versus Regulation

For both theoretical (Eisenberg & Spinrad, 2004) and empirical reasons (Valiente et al., 2003), we also find it useful to distinguish between control and regulation. *Control* can be defined as inhibition or restraint (regardless of the cause of the inhibition) and is presumed to increase in a linear manner from low to high restraint. Control (i.e., constraint or inhibition) is part of regulation when it is voluntary, but regulation involves more than voluntary inhibition (e.g., it includes the abilities to activate behavior and shift attention, as well as planning). Adaptive regulation includes optimal amounts of control as well as the ability to initiate action as needed. Like others (Block & Block, 1980), we believe well-regulated individuals are not overly controlled or undercontrolled and that they are quite flexible in how they manage emotions. From our perspective, regulation is adaptive, whereas control may be adaptive or maladaptive, depending on its flexibility and whether it can be voluntarily managed.

Voluntary Control–Regulation and Less Voluntary, Reactive Control

When considering relations between emotion regulation and measures of socialization (as well as other constructs), we find it useful to consider the degree to which the control or regulation is voluntary. Children who are well-regulated are believed to be able to voluntarily control their attention and behavior as needed. Voluntary control overlaps considerably with Rothbart's construct of *effortful control*, defined as "the ability to inhibit a dominant response to perform a subdominant response" (Rothbart & Bates, 1998, p. 137) or, more recently, as the "efficiency of executive attention, including the ability to inhibit a dominant response and/or to activate a sub-dominant response, to plan, and to detect errors" (Rothbart & Bates, in press). Voluntary control involves the "effort" or "will" to control or modulate temperamental reactivity, including emotionality. Although the use of effortful control does not always involve highly conscious cognitions (indeed, its use may be somewhat automatic in many situations), the individual can willfully modulate its use. Measures of effortful control typically include the abilities to voluntarily shift and focus attention and inhibit or activate behavior as needed to adapt or behave appropriately (processes believed to be controlled by the anterior cingulated gyrus and prefrontal cortical systems), even if the individual is not motivated to do so. For example, in tasks that tap effortful control, participants are often required to engage in behavior (e.g., persisting on a difficult task when one could easily cheat or stop working) when another behavior would be more appealing. Past early infancy, well-regulated people usually should be high in effortful control because it can be used at will and is flexible (although excessive voluntary suppression of emotion may be problematic; Gross, 1999). In our view, emotion regulation involves effortful control and perhaps other skills that include, but are broader than, effortful control (e.g., proactive coping).

Whereas effortful control is viewed as voluntary, reactive control is more difficult to voluntarily modulate. Included in this domain are types of impulsivity and approach behavior (e.g., based on interest or potential rewards) or rigid overcontrol, such as that evidenced by children who are timid and constrained and lack flexibility in novel or stressful situations (Derryberry & Rothbart, 1997). The systems related to reactive control are believed to be primarily subcorticol (Pickering & Gray, 1999).

Effortful control and reactive control are considered aspects of temperament; they therefore have a biological basis, although they also are influenced by the environment (Rothbart & Bates, 1998). We believe the distinction between effortful control and reactive control is useful in many situations but think it is especially important when considering possible socialization correlates because we expect parenting to be more strongly related to children's effortful control than reactive control. We would expect a weaker relation between reactive control and parenting, perhaps because the effect of parenting on reactive control is indirect, through effortful control. More specifically, we would predict that as effortful control increases one would be able to mask the overt expressions of reactive tendencies, especially as one ages. In contrast to the more complex relations of parenting and reactive control, we expect direct, and stronger, relations between parenting and children's effortful control. Therefore, failing to distinguish between effortful and reactive control is likely to result in inconsistent and weak findings.

EMPIRICAL FOUNDATIONS: THE KNOWN AND UNKNOWN

Direct relations between measures of parenting and children's social functioning have been noted in thousands of published studies. Frequently, significant relations are reported between parents' warmth or negativity, control or permissiveness, and style of parenting (e.g., authoritative vs. authoritarian) and measures of children's social and emotional adjustment (Parke & Buriel, 1998). However, generally these relations are modest in magnitude, and the reader is often left wanting more of an explanation for why the relations were significant (or not significant).

In an effort to organize and summarize a large portion of the socialization literature, especially literature on the topic of children's experience, expression, and regulation of emotion, Eisenberg, Spinrad, and Cumberland (1998) developed the heuristic model presented in Figure 6.1. In their model, Eisenberg et al. reviewed the concept of parents' emotion-related socializing behaviors (ERSBs) and identified four ways parents socialize their children's emotions: (a) parents' reactions to children's emotions, (b) parents' discussion of emotion, (c) parents' expression of emotion, and (d) parents' selection or modification of situations. Parents' ERSBs are hypothesized to have both indirect effects (e.g., through their effect on children's emotional arousal) and direct effects on children's experience, expression, understanding, and regulation of emotion. Eisenberg et al. argued that if parental ERSBs promote optimal levels of emotional arousal, they are likely to foster learning

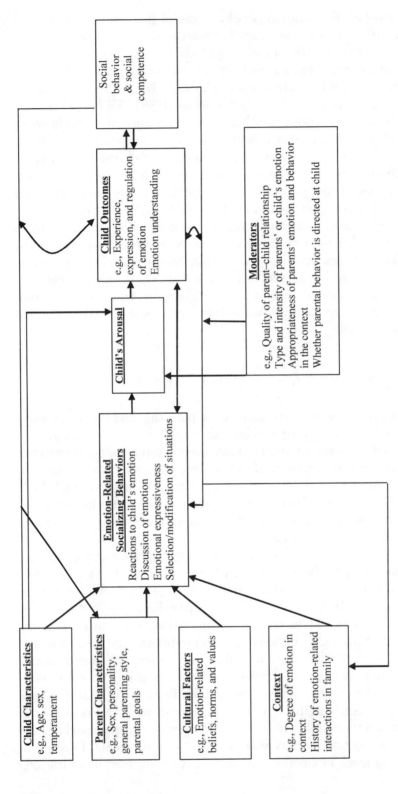

Figure 6.1. A heuristic model of the socialization of emotion. There also may be linear relations and interactions among the four predictors on the left. From "The Socialization of Emotion: Reply to Commentaries," by N. Eisenberg, T. L. Spinrad, and A. Cumberland, 1998, *Psychological Inquiry, 9,* p. 320. Copyright 1998 by Erlbaum. Adapted with permission.

and constructive behavior; if they overarouse the children, they will tend to undermine opportunities for learning about emotions and their regulatory capacities. In addition, it is predicted that children's regulatory abilities have direct effects on their adjustment and can also mediate or moderate the relations between emotion-related parenting practices and children's social behavior and social competence. We now turn our attention to reviewing findings on this topic.

Children's Effortful Control and Developmental Outcomes

If children's effortful control mediates the relations of parenting and children's adjustment, it is likely to be a significant predictor of their adjustment (although this need not always be true; see MacKinnon, Lockwood, Hoffman, West, & Sheets, 2002). Empirical findings are consistent with the premise that regulation or control is related to children's quality of social and psychological adjustment. Because a thorough review of these relations is beyond the scope of this chapter, and is available elsewhere (Eisenberg, Fabes, Guthrie, & Reiser, 2000; Rothbart & Bates, 1998), we only briefly highlight some robust relations. For example, children who are viewed as well regulated typically are low in externalizing problems and internalizing problems, and high in social competence, prosocial behavior, compliance, and sympathetic responses (Eisenberg et al., 2000; Eisenberg, Gershoff, et al., 2001; Eisenberg & Valiente, 2002; Kochanska, Murray, & Harlan, 2000; Valiente et al., 2004). These relations often can be found at early ages, later in adolescence, across time (i.e., longitudinally), and when different reporters or methods are used to assess the relevant constructs (Eisenberg, Valiente, et al., 2003; Murray & Kochanska, 2002). Because of the strong evidence that individuals' abilities to manage emotion are important to their social and emotional development, we believe it is useful to hypothesize that children's effortful control (or other aspects of emotion regulation) may mediate or moderate the relations between parenting and children's adjustment.

Parents' Emotion-Related Socializing Behaviors and Children's Effortful Control

There are numerous reasons that interactions with socializers might promote children's effortful control, social competence, and adjustment. Children who have higher-quality relationships with socializers are likely to be emotionally attached to them and to believe that the socializers are concerned with their welfare; consequently, they are likely to be motivated by feelings of trust and reciprocity (Dix, 1991) and to comply with socializers' standards of self-regulation (Grusec & Goodnow, 1994). Moreover, sensitive, responsive socializers model positive ways of responding, whereas socializers who express high levels of negative emotion model hostility and dysregulation (P. M. Cole et al., 1994). Investigators have also suggested that negative, nonsupportive behavior by socializers is associated with children's emotional reactivity and dysregulation (Buck, 1984; Eisenberg, Cumberland, & Spinrad, 1998; Eisenberg, Spinrad, et al., 1998; Gottman, Katz, & Hooven, 1997), which can undermine the learning of socially appropriate behavior and cognitive or language skills. Parents can also influence how their children cope with stress by protecting them from stressors (e.g., inappropriate stressors for their age) and by influencing how they appraise a stressful event (Power, 2005).

Recently we have used data from two different samples to test some of the predictions depicted in Eisenberg et al.'s heuristic model. In our at-risk sample (selected to oversample children with problem behaviors), at Time 1 (T1), we collected data from 214 children (M age = 6 years), their parents, and their teachers. Of the 214 children, 74 had t-scores below 60 on the Achenbach Child Behavior Checklist for both internalizing and externalizing, 36 had t-scores above 60 for internalizing (but not externalizing), 30 had scores over 60 for externalizing (but not internalizing), and 74 had scores over 60 for both externalizing and internalizing. Scores of 60 to 63 are viewed as indicating moderate risk for clinical problems. The other sample is an unselected group of 199 schoolchildren (M age = 7 years at T1; assessments are 2 years apart). In each study we have taken a multimethod approach to assess the key constructs. To measure socialization, we generally collect both parent-reported and observational data. Children's effortful control has been assessed with parent- and teacher-report data (inhibitory control, attention shifting and focusing), as well as an observational measure of persistence. Overcontrol and children's externalizing or internalizing problem behaviors generally are assessed with parents' and teachers' reports. These same reporters also report on children's social competence and sometimes on sympathy.

Stemming from early work highlighting the role of parenting in the development of children's adjustment, and later work demonstrating the important role effortful control likely plays in fostering adaptive adjustment, we, like others, have been interested in studying how parenting and effortful control jointly contribute to children's outcomes. Sometimes we have reported significant relations between parents' effortful control and their offspring's effortful control (Cumberland-Li, Eisenberg, Champion, Gershoff, & Fabes, 2003), but more often we have examined the relation between measures of parents' ERSBs (mostly parents' warmth or negativity or their expression of emotion [both positive and negative]) and children's effortful control. We now turn our attention to the role of effortful control as a mediator and moderator of the relation between ERSBs and children's adjustment.

The Mediating Role of Children's Effortful Control

In general, we and others have found that positive, supportive parenting is related to children's social competence, prosocial and empathic behavior, and adjustment, and that this relation tends to be mediated by children's effortful control. For example, with the at-risk sample we used structural equation modeling (SEM) to test if 5- to 8-year-old children's effortful control mediated the relation between mothers' expression of emotion and children's adjustment at the initial assessment (Time 1 or T1; Eisenberg, Gershoff, et al., 2001). Consistent with expectations, we found that high levels of mothers' expression of positive emotion and low expression of negative dominant (e.g., displays of anger or hostility) emotion predicted higher levels of children's effortful control, which in turn predicted high levels of children's social competence and low levels of externalizing problems (findings for internalizing problems were not quite significant). Consistent with Eisenberg et al.'s (1998) heuristic model, follow-up tests indicated that effortful control mediated the relations between parents' expressivity and children's externalizing problems and social competence.

Two years later (T2), we reassessed the constructs with the same measures and in a concurrent SEM found that children's effortful control mediated the relation between mothers' positive expressivity and children's externalizing problems and social competence (Eisenberg, Valiente, et al., 2003). In regression analyses (although not in SEM, likely because of low power) we found that children's effortful control continued to mediate the relation between mothers' positive expressivity and children's adjustment even when controlling initial levels of the variables. Finding mediation at T2 when controlling for the T1 variables is important because it suggests that the findings at T2 were not simply due to consistency in the pattern of relations as children aged. In other words, the data are consistent with the notion that parental positive expressivity continues to have an effect on children's effortful control as children age. Similar to a previous finding that parental negative expressivity was positively related to teachers' reports of children's compliance at school (M. T. Greenberg, personal communication, July 2, 2001), we found that mothers' reported negative expressivity was positively related to teachers' reports of children's effortful control. This unexpected finding may have emerged because teachers view compliant children as well regulated; it also highlights the possible moderating effect of child age (or developmental level) on the relation between ERSBs and child characteristics.

Although these findings are consistent with theory, the sample contained many children who had borderline or clinical levels of problem behaviors. Thus, in a more normative sample (the unselected sample), we examined the relations among ERSBs, children's expressivity, and externalizing problem behaviors (Eisenberg, Losoya, et al., 2001). The pattern of relations, consistent with those found in the at-risk sample, suggested that warm parents and parents who talked about emotions and linked others' emotions to the child's own experience had children who typically regulated the expression of emotion and, in turn, were relatively low in externalizing problems.

Using the same sample, we used longitudinal data to examine the mediational sequence: Maternal warmth and positive expressivity to slides → child's reactive overcontrol → children's tendency to express high (and often inappropriate) levels of emotion (Eisenberg, Zhou, et al., 2003). In concurrent models at T1 and T2 (assessments were at 2-year intervals), parental warmth or positive expression of emotion predicted high levels of children's reactive overcontrol, which in turn was negatively related to children's tendency to express high levels of emotion. When T1 and T2 data were combined into a longitudinal panel model, there were strong paths from the T1 to T2 variables (indicating high levels of consistency); nevertheless, the relation between children's T2 reactive overcontrol and expressivity remained significant and negative (indicating that associations at T2 were not simply due to the stability of relations as children age). In summary, cross-sectional and longitudinal data, from both the at-risk and more normative samples, suggest that relations between parents' expressivity and measures of children's social functioning are mediated by children's ability to manage emotion.

Other investigators have also found that parents' emotional expressivity and emotion-related beliefs are related to children's emotion regulation. For example, Garner (1995) found that mothers' reported positive expressivity in the family was related to higher levels of toddlers' self-soothing behavior, whereas mother-reported sadness was inversely related to self-soothing. In older children, maternal acceptance and support have been linked to successful coping (Hardy, Power, & Jaedicke, 1993; Kliewer, Fearnow, & Miller, 1996), and college students and adults from negatively expressive families report less control than their peers over feelings of anger, even when controlling for its intensity (Burrowes & Halberstadt, 1987; Power, 2005). Moreover, consistent with Eisenberg et al.'s (1998) model, and with findings reviewed earlier (Eisenberg, Gershoff, et al., 2001), Brody and Ge (2001) found that parents' nurturance versus negativity predicted high levels of children's self-regulation, which subsequently predicted low levels of children's adjustment problems (e.g., depression, hostility, low self-esteem). Furthermore, in a study of parents' emotion-related beliefs and teachings, Gottman et al. (1997) found that parents' supportiveness of the expression of emotion and coaching of emotions predicted high levels of children's emotion regulation.

Issues of Directionality

Trying to uncover the direction of effects between ERSBs, children's regulatory abilities, and adjustment is, for a variety of reasons, very difficult (it is often impractical or unethical to change ERSBs). In our program of research we have adopted two ways to overcome some of these obstacles. Initially, we tested both parent-driven and child-driven models. By comparing the fit (primarily the Akaike information criteria; Kline, 1998) as well as paths, one is in a better position to discuss issues of causality. For example, in addition to using SEM to test the premise that ERSBs → children's regulatory abilities → adjustment, we have tested child-driven models in which child characteristics predict ERSBs. On several occasions we have found that child-driven models generally do not fit the data as well as the hypothesized parent-driven models (Eisenberg, Gershoff, et al., 2001; Eisenberg, Losoya, et al., 2001), although this is not always the case (Eisenberg, Zhou, et al., 2003).

One is in a better position to discuss issues of directionality when supported by longitudinal data. Thus, more recently we have begun using three waves of longitudinal data to test if effortful control mediates the relation between ERSBs and children's adjustment. This way, we can test, for example, if ERSBs at the initial assessment predict children's effortful control at the second assessment (controlling for effortful control at Assessment 1), which in turn would predict adjustment at Assessment 3 (see Figure 6.2 and D. A. Cole & Maxwell, 2003, for a thorough discussion of this analytic strategy). The methods described by Cole and Maxwell should allow researchers to move beyond predictions for which there is evidence (see the dotted circle in Figure 6.2) to hypotheses that have either received less attention or for which there is little empirical support. In addition, Figure 6.2 displays dashed paths to note areas that require further exploration. When following the procedures outlined by Cole and Maxwell (2003), we are finding further evidence that children's effortful control mediates the relations between ERSBs and children's adjustment.

A related issue is whether there are bidirectional relations between the variables of interest. Although the most widely accepted view is that there are bidirectional relations between parenting and children's characteristics or behavior, there are very few data on this topic. However, in a study involving a longitudinal sample not previously discussed, we obtained a pattern of findings consistent with the conclusion that children's emotion regulation at age 6 to 8 years predicted mothers' punitive reactions to children's negative emotion 2 years later, and mothers' punitive reactions at ages 8 to 10 predicted children's regulation when they were age 10 to 12 years (Eisenberg et al., 1999). Thus, there is some, albeit limited, evidence that children's emotion regulation influences socializers' behaviors.

Cultural Issues

The data reviewed thus far pertain to the role of effortful control in samples of children from the United States. Given evidence that norms for emotional expressivity and the regulation of emotion differ across cultures, especially in collectivistic, Eastern cultures versus Western cultures, it is interesting to examine if a similar mediation process operates in non-Western samples. To address this question, Eisenberg, Liew, and Pidada (2001) ob-

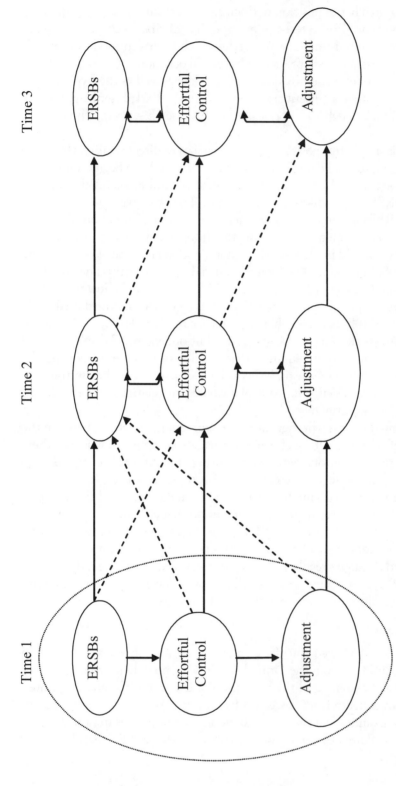

Figure 6.2. The role of effortful control as a mediator between ERSBs and children's adjustment. The constructs within the dotted circle indicate relations that have empirical support. The dotted lines represent hypothesized paths that have yet to receive consistent support. There may also be paths from Time 2 effortful control and adjustment to Time 3 ERSBs. These were not drawn to simplify the presentation. ERSB = emotion-related socializing behavior.

tained self-reports of Indonesian parents' (mostly mothers') emotional expressivity, parents' and teachers' reports of children's attentional control and inhibitory control, and adults' or peers' reports of quality of social functioning (e.g., externalizing problems, popularity, and sympathy). In contrast to findings in U.S. samples, parents' positive expressivity was unrelated to children's effortful control. This finding may stem from positive emotion being less valued in Asian cultures (Tsai, 2004). Moreover, the relations between parents' negative submissive (e.g., sulking, expressing sorrow, crying) expressivity and children's quality of social functioning were mediated by children's effortful control (in U.S. samples, negative submissive expressivity is inconsistently related to children's effortful control; Eisenberg & Fabes, 1998; Eisenberg, Gershoff, et al., 2001). However, consistent with findings in U.S. samples, children's effortful control at least partially mediated the relations between parents' negative dominant expressivity and the quality of children's social functioning. When the correlations among the measures in the Indonesian sample and the U.S. at-risk sample were examined, parents' positive expressivity was more consistently positively related to children's effortful control in the U.S. sample than in the sample from Indonesia, whereas negative submissive expressivity was a more consistent negative predictor of effortful control and social functioning for the Indonesian sample. It is possible that expressions of submissive negative emotion are viewed as more undesirable in Indonesia than in the United States and therefore that such expressions promote dysregulation in Indonesia (perhaps because they reflect unregulated parental behavior). Correlations of parents' negative dominant expressivity with effortful control and adjustment were quite similar across the samples.

In a study conducted in the People's Republic of China with first and second graders, we tested effortful control as a mediator of the relations of authoritative (i.e., supportive, involving the use of reasoning and constructive methods of control) and authoritarian (nonsupportive, controlling) parenting to quality of children's social functioning (Zhou, Eisenberg, Wang, & Reiser, 2004). Consistent with findings involving parents' expressivity, authoritative (positive) and authoritarian (negative) styles of parenting predicted children's effortful control, which in turn predicted children's social functioning. In follow-up tests, over 50% of the effects for authoritative and authoritarian parenting on children's social functioning were mediated by children's effortful control.

A number of investigators have found that children's ability to regulate emotion is related to high levels of parents' expression of positive emotion (at least in the United States) or support and low levels of their expression of negative emotion. These relations have been found in both normative and clinical samples. In addition, the pattern of relations has been partially replicated in China and Indonesia (although some differences have also been found).

Interactions Between Children's Emotion Regulation and Emotion-Related Socializing Behaviors

A growing body of research supports the premise that ERSBs and children's effortful control jointly (e.g., interactively) contribute to aspects of children's social functioning. For example, we have found links between children's sympathy and parenting in our at-risk sample that illustrate (a) socializers' positivity and negativity both are modestly related to children's empathy-related reactions, although such relations are not necessarily linear, and (b) children's effortful control might moderate such relations (Valiente et al., 2004). In our 2004 article, we, and our colleagues, used the at-risk sample to examine whether parents' positive and negative expressions of emotion and children's effortful control interact statistically when predicting children's sympathy or personal distress (a self-focused, aversive emotional response to others' need or distress). Children viewed empathy-inducing films to assess situational sympathy or personal distress (and reported their situational reactions); dispositional (personality) sympathy was assessed with children's self-reports. Prediction of children's sympathy from parents' negative expressivity was significant and negative at low levels of children's effortful control and nonsignificant at medium and high levels of children's effortful control. Prediction of children's situational personal distress from parents' negative expressivity was strongest (and positive) at high levels of children's effortful control (because personal distress tended to be higher for all unregulated children, regardless of parenting). In essence, we believe that children high in effortful control are able to avoid becoming overaroused when exposed to intense negative (or positive) emotion, and thus they are able to learn from these experiences. Consequently they may be better equipped to manage negative emotion and to understand and respond to another's needs in other circumstances than those low in effortful control. A key finding of the study was that prediction of children's empathy-related responses from parents' expressivity differed depending on whether effortful control was taken into consideration.

FUTURE DIRECTIONS IN RESEARCH AND DIRECTIVES FOR INTERDISCIPLINARY COLLABORATION

In summary, existing data are consistent with the premise that parents' behaviors contribute to the development of their children's emotion regulation. Some data also suggest that prediction of developmental outcomes can be improved by considering both measures of parenting and children's emotion regulation. Although emotion regulation has a genetic, temperamental basis that may place some limits on how well children regulate their emotions, it also seems likely that parents can promote (or inhibit) the development of high levels of children's emotion regulation.

Future research endeavors need to develop and test more explicit models explaining why there are relations between ERSBs and aspects of children's emotion regulation and adjustment. The availability of these data, especially when embedded in a prospective study that spans relevant developmental stages, offers the best hope of generating theoretical advances. It will be particularly important to design longitudinal studies capable of describing the reciprocal nature of relations among parenting, children's emotion regulation, and their adjustment and social functioning. It seems quite possible that parenting practices play a prominent role early in childhood, but that parents' influence diminishes as their child ages and becomes exposed to the influence of other socializers (e.g., peers).

In addition, genetically informed data sets, and those including variables such as parental personality (which likely reflect, in part, parental genetics), would provide insights into the biological bases of the relations of parenting to children's emotion regulation, social competence, and adjustment. Longitudinal data are also useful in making distinctions between the types of regulation or control discussed earlier. For example, as children age and develop, one would expect effortful control to be more strongly related to outcomes than reactive control, a hypothesis with some support (Valiente et al., 2003). Only with longitudinal data that span from early childhood to early (or late) adolescence can one thoroughly test this hypothesis.

Methodological improvements will continue to be an important component driving advances in this area of research. Whereas paper-and-pencil measures of children's effortful control are fairly well developed and allow multiple informants (e.g., parents, teachers, and children) to report on effortful control, more refined observational measures are necessary to make distinctions between effortful control and reactive control. Kochanska et al. (2000) have developed a battery of measures of regulation or control for younger children, but additional measures are needed for older children and adolescents. Moreover, investigators need to consider whether they are assessing effortful or reactive control, or both.

The use of electronic daily diaries can provide a rich set of data that can be used to examine more moment-to-moment processes that are key to understanding how parents can promote or inhibit children's emotion regulation and adjustment. Recent work by Cummings and colleagues highlights the usefulness of this type of approach (Cummings, Goeke-Morey, & Papp, 2002). Moreover, as new measures are developed, their usefulness with high-risk populations, as well as middle-class study participants, requires systematic examination.

Perhaps of most importance, intervention and prevention programs need to be designed to test the premises suggested in correlational studies. In interventions, investigators can experimentally change parents' and other socializers' behavior with children and assess the effects of these changes. Research concerning the role of children's regulation in the success of interventions is sparse, although such an approach is consistent with Huffman et al.'s (2000) recommendations for future research examining risk in the early school years.

It seems that interdisciplinary efforts could be especially important when developing and conducting interventions that target children's ability to manage emotion (and quality of social functioning that is linked to these abilities). Given the focus on promoting school success and links among children's regulation, social competence, and academic success, interdisciplinary interventions in schools involving scholars in educational and developmental psychology (as well as statisticians with expertise on clustering data within classrooms) could be particularly fruitful. In a similar way, interventions in the home with parents naturally combine the talents and knowledge of individuals in the developmental and family sciences. Funding resources are available to support this type of research, but large amounts of money are needed to conduct well-designed intervention studies. When seeking large project grants involving investigators with different training and experiences, it may be challenging to overcome the use of different languages and jargon when outlining conceptual issues, making predictions, and selecting methods. Investigators must also overcome some inherent difficulties in deciding how many (and which) auxiliary measures of relevant and related constructs can be included without having to implement an intervention that is too large.

CLINICAL, SOCIAL, AND PUBLIC POLICY IMPLICATIONS

The relatively consistent finding that children's abilities to regulate their emotions are related to their social and emotional development and that parenting likely can promote (or inhibit) regulatory abilities has social and public policy implications. Clinicians working with children exhibiting behavioral problems may wish to integrate methods for improving children's regulatory abilities into therapy while also considering targeting the parent–child relationship as a way to produce change. At a broader level, data from intervention studies are necessary to elucidate the ERSBs that are most successful in promoting children's regulation. Although data from existing interventions indicate that one can successfully intervene in children's lives and even promote emotion regulation (Greenberg, Kusche, Cook, & Quamma, 1995), investigators do not know enough about how interventions designed to promote children's regulation actually work. Indeed, although researchers may feel comfortable advising policymakers that teaching socializers to be positive and supportive and to express negative emotion appropriately can promote children's adjustment, it would be difficult to precisely explain why these relations exist, and at what ages one can most successfully intervene (Power, 2005). The continued support of policymakers would allow the work currently underway the opportunity to provide answers to a number of the remaining questions.

REFERENCES

Aspinwall, L. G., & Taylor, S. E. (1997). A stitch in time: Self-regulation and proactive coping. *Psychological Bulletin, 121,* 417–436.

Block, J. H., & Block, J. (1980). The role of ego-control and ego-resiliency in the organization of behavior. In W. A. Collins (Ed.), *Development of cognition, affect, and social relations: The Minnesota Symposia on Child Psychology* (Vol. 13, pp. 39–101). Hillsdale, NJ: Erlbaum.

Brody, G. H., & Ge, X. (2001). Linking parenting processes and self-regulation to psychological functioning and alcohol use during early adolescence. *Journal of Family Psychology, 15,* 82–94.

Buck, R. (1984). *The communication of emotion.* New York: Guilford Press.

Burrowes, B. D., & Halberstadt, A. G. (1987). Self- and family-expressiveness styles in the experience and expression of anger. *Journal of Nonverbal Behavior, 11,* 254–268.

Campos, J. J., Mumme, D. L., Kermoian, R., & Campos, R. G. (1994). A functionalist perspective on the nature of emotion. *Monographs of the Society for Research in Child Development, 59*(2–3, Serial No. 240), 284–303.

Cicchetti, D., Ganiban, J., & Barnett, D. (1991). Contributions from the study of high-risk populations to understanding the development of emotion regulation. In J. Garber & K. A. Dodge (Eds.), *The development of emotion regulation and dysregulation* (pp. 15–48). New York: Cambridge University Press.

Cole, D. A., & Maxwell, S. E. (2003). Testing mediational models with longitudinal data: Questions and tips in the use of structural equation modeling. *Journal of Abnormal Psychology, 112,* 558–577.

Cole, P. M., Michel, M. K., & Teti, L. O. (1994). The development of emotion regulation and dysregulation: A clinical perspective. *Monographs of the Society for Research in Child Development, 59*(2–3, Serial No. 240), 73–100.

Cumberland-Li, A., Eisenberg, N., Champion, C., Gershoff, E., & Fabes, R. A. (2003). The relation of parental emotionality and related dispositional traits to parental expression of emotion and children's social functioning. *Motivation and Emotion, 27,* 27–56.

Cummings, E. M., Goeke-Morey, M., & Papp, L. M. (2002). A family-wide model for the role of emotion in family functioning. *Marriage and Family Review, 34,* 13–34.

Derryberry, D., & Rothbart, M. K. (1997). Reactive and effortful processes in the organization of temperament. *Development and Psychopathology, 9,* 633–652.

Dix, T. (1991). The affective organization of parenting: Adaptive and maladaptive processes. *Psychological Bulletin, 110,* 3–25.

Eisenberg, N., Cumberland, A., & Spinrad, T. L. (1998). Parental socialization of emotion. *Psychological Inquiry, 9,* 241–273.

Eisenberg, N., & Fabes, R. A. (1998). Prosocial development. In N. Eisenberg (Ed.), *Handbook of child psychology: Vol. 3. Social, emotional, and personality development* (5th ed., pp. 701–778). New York: Wiley.

Eisenberg, N., Fabes, R. A., Guthrie, I. K., & Reiser, M. (2000). Dispositional emotionality and regulation: Their role in predicting quality of social functioning. *Journal of Personality and Social Psychology, 78,* 136–157.

Eisenberg, N., Fabes, R. A., Shepard, S. A., Guthrie, I. K., Murphy, B. C., & Reiser, M. (1999). Parental reactions to children's negative emotions: Longitudinal relations to quality of children's social functioning. *Child Development, 70,* 513–534.

Eisenberg, N., Gershoff, E. T., Fabes, R. A., Shepard, S. A., Cumberland, A. J., Losoya, S. H., et al. (2001). Mother's emotional expressivity and children's behavior problems and social competence: Mediation through children's regulation. *Developmental Psychology, 37,* 475–490.

Eisenberg, N., Liew, J., & Pidada, S. U. (2001). The relations of parental emotional expressivity with quality of Indonesian children's social functioning. *Emotion, 1,* 116–136.

Eisenberg, N., Losoya, S., Fabes, R. A., Guthrie, I. K., Reiser, M., Murphy, B., et al. (2001). Parental socialization of children's dysregulated expression of emotion and externalizing problems. *Journal of Family Psychology, 15,* 183–205.

Eisenberg, N., & Spinrad, T. L. (2004). Emotion-related regulation: Sharpening the definition. *Child Development, 75,* 334–339.

Eisenberg, N., Spinrad, T. L., & Cumberland, A. J. (1998). The socialization of emotion: Reply to commentaries. *Psychological Inquiry, 9,* 317–333.

Eisenberg, N., & Valiente, C. (2002). Parenting and children's prosocial and moral development. In M. H. Bornstein (Ed.), *Handbook of parenting: Vol. 5. Practical issues in parenting* (2nd ed., pp. 111–142). Mahwah, NJ: Erlbaum.

Eisenberg, N., Valiente, C., Morris, A. S., Fabes, R. A., Cumberland, A., Reiser, M., et al. (2003). Longitudinal relations among parental emotional expressivity, children's regulation, and quality of socioemotional functioning. *Developmental Psychology, 39,* 3–19.

Eisenberg, N., Zhou, Q., Losoya, S. H., Fabes, R. A., Shepard, S. A., Murphy, B. C., et al. (2003). The relations of parenting, effortful control, and ego control to children's emotional expressivity. *Child Development, 74,* 875–895.

Garner, P. W. (1995). Toddlers' emotion regulation behaviors: The roles of social context and family expressiveness. *The Journal of Genetic Psychology, 156,* 417–430.

Gottman, J. M., Katz, L. F., & Hooven, C. (1997). *Meta-emotion: How families communicate emotionally.* Mahwah, NJ: Erlbaum.

Greenberg, M. T., Kusche, C. A., Cook, E. T., & Quamma, J. P. (1995). Promoting emotional competence in school-aged children: The effects of the PATHS curriculum. *Development and Psychopathology, 7*, 117–136.

Gross, J. J. (1999). Emotion and emotion regulation. In L. A. Pervin (Ed.), *Handbook of personality: Theory and research* (2nd ed., pp. 525–552). New York: Guilford Press.

Grusec, J. E., & Goodnow, J. J. (1994). Impact of discipline methods on the child's internalization of values: A reconceptualization of current points of view. *Developmental Psychology, 30*, 4–19.

Hardy, D. F., Power, T. G., & Jaedicke, S. (1993). Examining the relation of parenting to children's coping with everyday stress. *Child Development, 64*, 1829–1841.

Huffman, L. C., Mehlinger, S. L., & Kerivan, A. S. (2000). *Risk factors for academic and behavioral problems at the beginning of school.* Bethesda, MD: National Institute of Mental Health.

Kliewer, W. K., Fearnow, M. D., & Miller, P. A. (1996). Coping socialization in middle childhood: Tests of maternal and paternal influences. *Child Development, 67*, 2339–2357.

Kline, R. B. (1998). *Principles and practice of structural equation modeling.* New York: Guilford Press.

Kochanska, G., Murray, K. T., & Harlan, E. T. (2000). Effortful control in early childhood: Continuity and change, antecedents, and implications for social development. *Developmental Psychology, 36*, 220–232.

MacKinnon, D. P., Lockwood, C. M., Hoffman, J. M., West, S. G., & Sheets, V. (2002). A comparison of methods to test mediation and other intervening variable effects. *Psychological Methods, 7*, 83–104.

Murray, K. T., & Kochanska, G. (2002). Effortful control: Factor structure and relation to externalizing and internalizing behaviors. *Journal of Abnormal Child Psychology, 30*, 503–514.

Parke, R. D., & Buriel, R. (1998). Socialization in the family: Ethnic and ecological perspectives. In N. Eisenberg (Ed.), *Handbook of child psychology: Vol. 3. Social, emotional, and personality development* (5th ed., pp. 463–552). New York: Wiley.

Pickering, A. D., & Gray, J. A. (1999). The neuroscience of personality. In O. P. John & L. A. Pervin (Eds.), *Handbook of personality: Theory and research* (2nd ed., pp. 277–299). New York: Guilford Press.

Power, T. G. (2005). Stress and coping in childhood: The parents' role. *Parenting: Science and Practice, 4*, 271–317.

Rothbart, M. K., & Bates, J. E. (in press). Temperament. In W. Damon & R. M. Lerner (Series Eds.) & N. Eisenberg (Vol. Ed.), *Handbook of child psychology: Social, emotional, personality development* (Vol. 3, 6th ed.). New York: Wiley.

Rothbart, M. K., & Bates, J. E. (1998). Temperament. In N. Eisenberg (Ed.), *Handbook of child psychology: Vol. 3. Social, emotional, personality development* (pp. 105–176). New York: Wiley.

Shonkoff, J. P., & Phillips, D. A. (2000). *From neurons to neighborhoods: The science of early childhood development.* Washington, DC: National Academy Press.

Thompson, R. A. (1994). Emotion regulation: A theme in search of definition. *Monographs of the Society for Research in Child Development, 59*(2–3, Serial No. 240), 25–52.

Tsai, J. L. (2004, May). *Affect valuation: Theory, measurement, and cultural variation.* Paper presented at the annual meeting of the American Psychological Society, Chicago.

Valiente, C., Eisenberg, N., Fabes, R. A., Shepard, S. A., Cumberland, A., & Losoya, S. H. (2004). Prediction of children's empathy-related responding from their effortful control and parents' expressivity. *Developmental Psychology, 40,* 911–926.

Valiente, C., Eisenberg, N., Smith, C. L., Reiser, M., Fabes, R. A., Losoya, S., et al. (2003). The relations of effortful control and reactive control to children's externalizing problems: A longitudinal assessment. *Journal of Personality, 71,* 1171–1196.

Zhou, Q., Eisenberg, N., Wang, Y., & Reiser, M. (2004). Chinese children's effortful control and dispositional anger/frustration: Relations to parenting styles and children's social functioning. *Developmental Psychology, 40,* 352–366.

7

FAMILY AND PEER RELATIONSHIPS: THE ROLE OF EMOTION REGULATORY PROCESSES

ROSS D. PARKE, DAVID J. McDOWELL,
MINA CLADIS, AND MELINDA S. LEIDY

The acquisition of social skills in childhood appears to be a key developmental task that is linked to successful adjustment over the life span. Research has established links between poor peer relationships in childhood and a range of negative consequences for adaptation and competence in later life, including delinquency, poor academic achievement, and dropping out of high school, as well as criminality and other forms of social and emotional disorders in adulthood (Parker & Asher, 1987). Recently, scholars have begun to identify the developmental pathways through which children acquire social skills and behavioral styles that promote interpersonal competence with peers during the early school years (Parke et al., 2002; Parke & Ladd, 1992). A growing body of literature identifies a number of modes by which children's early socialization experiences are linked to peer competence in early and middle childhood.

In this chapter we briefly review literature concerning ways in which families are hypothesized to influence social adaptation in childhood and adolescence. In doing so, we emphasize recent work from a longitudinal study of familial influences on children's social development currently being conducted in our laboratory. Specifically, we examine the role that parents play as interaction partners and review research on the processes that account for relations between experiences with familial social partners and social competencies in childhood, with an emphasis on emotion regulatory processes and attention regulatory processes. We illustrate each mediational process with data from our work and related work by others. Our own studies are based on the University of California, Riverside (UCR) Social Development Project, a longitudinal study aimed at understanding links between children's experiences in their families from early childhood to early adolescence and their developing competence with peers. Measures of family interaction as well as indices of a variety of social and emotional abilities were assessed yearly from kindergarten through sixth grade. A final follow-up was completed when the children were in eighth grade. Sociometric assessments and teacher ratings provided independent indices of peer social competence. The sample consisted of approximately 120 children and their mothers and fathers. The socioeconomic status of the families ranged from lower to upper-middle class; 50% of the sample was Euro-American, 40% Latino, and 10% African American, Asian American, or other. Attrition rates were relatively modest (15%–20%), and no evidence of attrition-related bias was found. For each study, the age of the child is noted. For a detailed description of the project and related findings, see Parke and O'Neil (1999).

CONCEPTUAL, THEORETICAL, AND METHODOLOGICAL ISSUES

To set the stage for our chapter, we outline several conceptual and methodological assumptions that guide our work in this area. As noted, our research program has focused on the links between family and peer systems with a view to describing both the nature of these relations and the processes that may account for them. Various phases of this work can be distinguished. In the first phase the link between parental relationship qualities and peer competence was the focus. Two research traditions illustrate this approach. First, in the child attachment tradition, the focus has been on the impact of infant–mother attachment on social adaptation to the peer group (Sroufe & Fleeson, 1986). The second tradition is illustrated by studies of the effect of particular child-rearing styles (Baumrind, 1973) or parent–child interaction patterns on children's social competence with peers (MacDonald & Parke, 1984). Together, studies of parent–child relationships and children's peer competence in early childhood suggest that parents who are responsive, warm, and synchronous have children who are better accepted by peers (Harrist, Pettit, Dodge, & Bates, 1994). In contrast, parents of children who are low in peer acceptance can be characterized as more directive and demanding, expressing more negative affect, eliciting more negative affect in their children, exhibiting less ability to engage in and sustain play interaction with their children, and displaying less ability to modulate their level of playful stimulation with their children (Harrist et al., 1994; Parke et al., 2002). Family interaction patterns not only relate to concurrent peer relationships but also predict children's competence with peers over time (Barth & Parke, 1993). Another aspect of this first phase was the focus not only on family interaction patterns in general but specifically on the affective quality of the parent–child relationship as indexed by the display of positive or negative affect during interactions between parents and children (see Parke & O'Neil, 1999, for a review).

In a second phase, the focus shifted from a descriptive phase to an examination of the mediating processes that could account for the links between parent–child interaction patterns and peer competence. Specifically, it was assumed that in the course of parent–child interaction, children acquire a variety of emotional competencies or skills that, in turn, are influential in their subsequent interactions with peers. Several sets of emotional processes are assumed to be important for successful social interaction, including encoding and decoding, understanding the causes and consequences of emotions, understanding and utilizing display rules, and regulating emotional expression and level of emotional arousal. Our view is that these emotional skills represent an interrelated family or cluster of abilities that work together in achieving successful enactment of social behavior with a variety of social agents, including both families and peers. Although conceptualized as distinct aspects of emotional competence, which can be measured and evaluated independently, these emotional skills operate in a coordinated fashion in real-life situations. In a similar way, social cognitive skills such as choices of goals and strategies and response solutions and enactment function together in accounting for social behavior (Crick & Dodge, 1994). Our guiding assumption that emotional components form a family or cluster of skills is compatible with Salovey's multicomponential concept of emotional intelligence (see chap. 2, this volume). We briefly review three of these components (encoding and decoding, emotional understanding, and emotional expressiveness) to illustrate the multiply determined nature of the links between emotional competence and social competence. Consistent with the theme of this volume, we focus in more detail on two components of emotional competence: emotion regulatory and attention regulatory processes. Figure 7.1 provides a conceptual model that guides our work.

A further assumption that guides our work in this area is that emotional and attentional competencies are acquired over the course of children's development. The rudiments of these processes are acquired in infancy and childhood, whereas more sophisticated understanding of complex emotions and social rules for emotional expression develops over middle childhood and adolescence. For example, according to Parker and Gottman (1989), the

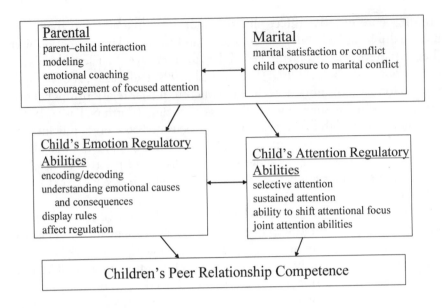

Figure 7.1. Emotional and attentional mediators of the family–peer interface.

emotional tasks of early and middle childhood differ from the tasks of adolescence. In early childhood, the major affective goal is "management of arousal interaction." In middle childhood, the affective task is to acquire "display and feeling rules," and in adolescence the affective task is the management and regulation of self-disclosure and intimacy.

Third, we recognize the importance of not only demonstrating links among parenting, various aspects of emotional competence, and children's social competence but also exploring the causal pathways among these components. Specifically our goal is to begin to better understand the mediating role of emotional competence in accounting for these linkages between parenting and social competence.

Fourth, our work is guided by the assumption that both fathers and mothers play complementary as well as distinctive roles in both the acquisition of emotional competencies and in the development of social competence with peers. Because the prior literature has focused largely on mothers as socialization agents, we view our focus on fathers as well as mothers as an important corrective to this earlier maternal bias. Our assumption is that mothers and fathers have distinctive interactive styles which, in turn, result in distinctive contributions to children's emotional and social competence (Parke, 2002). To demonstrate the unique roles of mothers and fathers, it is important to control for the effects of one parent to determine if there is unique variance associated with the behavior of the other parent. As we note in the following section, we have followed this guideline in our work and found that mothers and fathers do indeed make independent contributions to both emotional and social competence in children.

Fifth, our work is guided by a family systems theoretical framework that highlights the role not only of multiple parental agents but also of multiple subsystems, including parent–parent or marital subsystems, as well as the parent–child subsystem. As we illustrate, and consistent with research by Cummings and colleagues (Cummings & Davies, 1994; chap. 8, this volume), variations in children's emotional and social competence are, in part, determined by the quality of the marital interaction patterns to which they are exposed.

Methodologically, several assumptions guide our work in this area. It is important to assess parenting, marital, and child outcomes at multiple time points so that shifts in parenting or the quality of marital relationships can be linked to changes in child competence. Many of the studies that we present are longitudinal to address this limitation in earlier studies. In addition, it is critical to use multimethod, multireporter designs to avoid the confounds that are found when parents report both on their own parenting and on child competencies. In our studies, we use independent assessments of parenting—either self-report or observations of parent–child interactions, child or parent reports of emotional competencies, or experimental assessments of these skills. Finally, to assess social competence, we rely on teacher or peer reports of children's social acceptance and behavioral characteristics. Our use of longitudinal designs involving multiple measures and reporters should increase confidence in our results and move the field to a firmer methodological footing.

EMPIRICAL EVIDENCE IN SUPPORT OF EMOTIONAL PROCESSES

In this section, we summarize the empirical support for the role of the emotional processes outlined in Figure 7.1. We briefly examine emotional encoding and decoding, emotional understanding, and emotional expressiveness but focus the bulk of our review on recent empirical findings concerning emotion regulatory abilities and attention regulatory skills.

Emotion Encoding and Decoding

One set of skills relevant to successful peer interaction is the ability to encode emotional signals and to decode the emotional signals of others. These skills are part of the "perceiving emotions" branch in the model of emotional intelligence discussed by Grewal, Brackett, and Salovey in chapter 2 of this volume. Arousing physical play is thought to be a particularly important context for the development of encoding and decoding skills. Through physically playful interaction with their parents, especially fathers, children may learn how to use emotional signals (encoding) to regulate the social behavior of others. For example, during the course of physical play children may signal through a facial display of displeasure (i.e., scowl or fear) when a father is playing too roughly. They may also learn how to decode the social and emotional signals of other social partners. For example, a child will monitor the emotional expressions of a play partner to modify his or her own play style during a play interaction. Earlier work has found that variations in parent–child interaction are related to emotional encoding and decoding skills (Parke Cassidy, Burks, Carson, & Boyum, 1992), and that these skills, in turn, are related to children's sociometric status (Cassidy, Parke, Butkovsky, & Braungart, 1992; Parke et al., 1992). Together, these two sets of evidence suggest that emotion production and recognition skills may serve as mediating mechanisms between early experiences with parents and the quality of interaction with peers. Other recent work (Parke et al., 1992) suggests that the families of peer-rejected children may use idiosyncratic or "familycentric" affect cues that are recognized within the context of the family but are not as well recognized outside the family.

Emotional Understanding

Evidence also suggests that successful peer functioning requires an understanding of the causes, consequences, and meaning of emotional experiences. (See the concept of understanding emotions in the four-branch model, chap. 2, this volume.) Cassidy et al. (1992) found that higher levels of social competence among 5- and 6-year-olds were associated with the ability to identify emotions, the ability to describe appropriate causes of emotions, the acknowledgment of experiencing emotion, and the expectation that they would respond appropriately to the display of emotions. Denham, McKinley, Couchoud, and Holt (1990) similarly found that children's understanding of the type of emotion that would be elicited by different situations was positively related to peer likeability. These findings confirm the findings of other research that suggests connections between other components of social understanding and peer relations (Hubbard & Dearing, 2004). However, the early familial antecedents of emotional understanding are unclear and need closer scrutiny (Denham, 1998).

Emotional Expressiveness

A growing body of research indicates that parental patterns of emotional expressiveness are associated with children's own expressiveness styles, social behavior, and acceptance by peers (Boyum & Parke, 1995; Cassidy et al., 1992). However, studies typically have assessed emotional expressiveness with self-report measures and have tended to focus exclusively on maternal expressiveness (see Halberstadt, Denham, & Dunsmore, 2001, for a review of this literature). Research in our lab using observational assessments of mothers' and fathers' affect expression provides evidence in support of the role of emotional expression in regulating social interaction (Carson & Parke, 1996). Carson and Parke found that patterns of reciprocated negative affect between children and their fathers, but not their mothers, were linked to child verbal and physical aggression with peers. Other research (Isley, O'Neil, & Parke, 1996) has extended this work to older children (7- to 9-year-olds) and found that negative paternal affect expressed in the context of parent–child interaction was correlated with lower peer social acceptance and social competence. These data underscore the importance of examining fathers as well as mothers.

EMOTION REGULATORY ABILITIES

In this section, we examine two issues, namely the links between emotion regulatory abilities and children's social competence with peers and the familial correlates of emotional regulation. Following Thompson (1994), emotional regulation is defined as "the extrinsic and intrinsic processes responsible for monitoring, evaluating and modifying emotional reactions, especially their intensive and temporal features, to accomplish one's goals" (pp. 27–28). Moreover, it is important to distinguish between intrapersonal and interpersonal emotional regulation. In the case of intrapersonal emotional regulation, the goal is to modulate one's emotional reaction, for example, increasing or decreasing one's level of excitement or upset to enhance positive and reduce negative emotional feelings. In the case of interpersonal emotional regulation, the goal of the modulation is to control the evaluative reaction of a social audience who may be witness to the eliciting event and to the actor's emotional response. In our work we have examined several aspects of this issue. In one series of studies we focused on children's ability to control their level of emotional arousal and the strategies that they use to cope with their emotional upset; these studies could be viewed as explorations of intrapersonal emotional regulation. In a second series of studies we examined children's understanding of and utilization of emotional display rules; these investigations could be viewed as examples of interpersonal emotional regulation. Again it is recognized that these two approaches are tapping different aspects of emotional regulation and reflect the multifaceted nature of this construct (Cole, Martin, & Dennis, 2004).

Links Between Emotional Regulation (Arousal Modulation) and Peer Social Competence

Children's skill in regulating emotions is important to successful development of peer relationships. To evaluate emotional regulation, children's strategies for coping with emotionally charged events were assessed using children's responses to a series of vignettes (Kim, McDowell, & Parke, 2004; McDowell, Kim, O'Neil, & Parke, 2002; McDowell & Parke, 2005). Five vignettes that were designed to generate anger, frustration, or excitement were presented to the children. Interviewers asked children to respond to a series of closed-ended items that assessed intensity of emotion ("How upset or excited would this make you feel?"), latency ("How long would it take you to calm down?"), and ease of calming ("How easy or hard would it be for you to calm down?") following an event using a 10-point, barometer-type response scale (lower scores are indicative of a lower level of excitement or agitation and a higher ease of calming down). In the Gross model (chap. 1, this volume), these measures are examples of response-focused emotional regulation; specifically, these actions illustrate the concept of response modulation.

In a study with fourth and fifth graders, using these same vignettes, our data indicate that the ability to control the level of emotional arousal and the strategies selected for coping with high levels of emotional arousal are related to a number of indicators of children's social competence with peers (Kim, McDowell, et al., 2004; McDowell et al., 2002; McDowell & Parke, 2005). Fourth- and fifth-grade children who rated themselves as higher in emotion regulation were rated by teachers and peers as more socially competent (McDowell et al., 2002; McDowell & Parke, 2005). In a similar way, children who responded to the arousing vignettes with a negative emotion regulatory strategy (anger, sadness, or nervousness and fidgeting) were rated by peers and teachers as less socially accepted (McDowell & Parke, 2005) and less socially competent (Kim, McDowell, et al., 2004).

It is important to distinguish between positive and negative emotion regulatory strategies (Gross, 2002). Children who endorsed positive regulatory strategies (reasoning, thinking of alternative responses) were rated by both teachers and peers as more accepted by their classmates (McDowell & Parke, 2005). Parental reports of children's coping with emotionally arousing situations yielded a similar picture. Mothers and fathers who reported that their children used negative coping strategies (avoidance, engaging in problem behavior) were rated as less socially competent by teachers and peers (Kim, McDowell, et al., 2004). In short, similar results were evident across both child and parent reports of emotional regulation.

Nor are the relations evident only at one time point, but rather the links between emotional regulation and child competencies are evident across time as well. Moreover, children who report using reasoning or trying to understand the problem in response to distressing situations were better adjusted in the classroom (as rated by teachers) 1 year later—in fifth grade (Kim, McDowell, et al., 2004). More evidence that emotional regulation has cross-time effects comes from recent longitudinal analyses (Leidy & Parke, 2004). Sixth graders who reported poor emotion regulatory abilities (as assessed by the barometer-type measure previously described) were rated by themselves and by their parents as higher on the Child Behavior Checklist Internalizing scale 2 years later when they were in eighth grade. In sum, emotional regulation conceptualized as arousal regulatory ability is linked both cross-sectionally and longitudinally with indices of peer social competence and adjustment.

Family Correlates of Emotional Regulation

Recent investigations indicate that the extent to which parents tolerate the expression of negative emotions and assist their children with the resolution of emotional upset is associated with children's emotion regulatory abilities as well as their social competence (Eisenberg & Fabes, 1992). Furthermore, in a rare examination of the role that fathers play in the socialization of children's emotion regulatory abilities, Gottman, Katz, and Hooven (1996) found that father acceptance and assistance with children's sadness and anger when children were 5 years old was related to children's social competence with peers at 8 years of age. Although it is assumed that the direction of effect flows from parent to child, it is feasible that children's behavior elicited the parental responses as well.

Findings from the UCR Social Development Project also suggest that the strategies parents use to manage children's negative emotion are associated with children's emotional reactivity, coping, and social competence (O'Neil, Parke, Isley, & Sosa, 1997). When mothers reported that they encouraged the expression of negative affect when their fourth-grade child was upset, children indicated that they would be less likely to use social withdrawal as a strategy to deal with emotional upset. In a similar way, mothers who reported that they would help the child find solutions to deal with emotional distress had children who reported that they would be more likely to use reasoning to cope with emotional upset. Mothers who expressed more awareness and sensitivity to their child's emotional state in a family problem-solving task had children who expressed less positive affect and more negative affect in the problem-solving task. When mothers modeled problem-solving approaches to handling disagreement and upset, children were less likely to report becoming angry when faced with an upsetting event. Moreover, children of problem-solving mothers were less likely to express negative affect during the parent–child discussion task, clearer in their emotional expressions, and more likely to adopt problem-solving strategies in the discussion task. Fathers' regulation of children's emotions was only modestly related to social competence. Fathers who reported being more distressed by their child's expressions of negative affect had children who were more likely to report using anger and other negative emotions to cope with distressing events. When fathers reported using strategies to minimize distressing circumstances, children were more likely to report using reasoning to cope with a distressing situation. Fathers who reported emotion- and problem-focused reactions to the expression of negative emotions had children who were described by teachers as less aggressive and disruptive.

Moreover, both parental control and affect were related to children's emotional regulation and coping. Using data from the UCR Social Development Project, McDowell and Parke (2005) examined this issue. Children's strategies for managing emotionally charged events were assessed using a barometer-like scale described earlier. When fathers were more controlling, their fourth-grade children exhibited less emotion regulation. However, more paternal positive affect and less paternal negative affect were associated with more positive coping strategies on the part of their children. In a similar manner, when mothers exhibited more positive affect, children were rated as higher in emotional regulation and endorsed fewer negative coping strategies.

Links Between Display Rule Knowledge and Use and Peer Social Competence

During early and middle childhood, children acquire and use rules for the socially appropriate expression of emotion. Emotional display rule use can be viewed as another form of emotional regulation as children learn to hide or suppress their feelings about an event and express a socially acceptable overt emotional expression. For example, children learn to hide their disappointment when receiving an unwanted or undesirable gift, or on receiving a poor grade or losing a competitive event. In the Gross model (chap. 1, this volume), display rule use is a further example of response-focused emotional regulation; specifically, response modulation occurs as children attempt to decrease or hide their expressive reactions to the event. Most work in this area has focused either on the developmental course of display rule acquisition (Saarni, 1984) or on individual differences in display rule knowledge within the preschool and elementary school years (Garner, 1996). A few studies have examined links between display rule knowledge and social competence. McDowell and Parke (2000) examined the links between display rule knowledge and children's social competence. Third-grade children's display rule knowledge was assessed from responses to several hypothetical situations in which it would be appropriate for children to use display rules. Children indicated both how the child in the story would feel and how the child's face would look and why the child would look that way. Data concerning children's display rule knowledge and their reasons for their responses were generated from these interviews. Social competence was assessed by peer sociometric ratings and by teacher ratings of children's likeability and behavioral attributes. These investigators found that children who had a better knowledge of the display rules for both positive and negative emotions were rated as more competent by both teachers and peers.

Other work on our project examined the relations between children's use of socially appropriate rules for displaying negative emotions and social competence with peers (McDowell, O'Neil, & Parke, 2000). We used Saarni's (1984) "disappointing gift paradigm," which enables the assessment of children's ability to mask negative emotions in the face of disappointment. In this paradigm, children were presented with an age-inappropriate gift, and their resulting emotional displays were monitored to determine if they masked their feelings of disappointment by displaying neutral or positive emotional expressions. Although Saarni's work suggests that this ability improves with age and may be a critical component of successful emotional regulation, to date, researchers have not examined the links between individual differences in the ability to mask or control negative emotions and children's competence with peers. Our data indicate that among fourth graders, children who displayed negative affect or behavior following the presentation of a disappointing gift (thus, not using display rules) were rated by teachers as more socially withdrawn. Girls who were able to maintain levels of positive affect after receiving a disappointing gift were viewed as more socially competent by teachers and peers. Children who expressed more tension and anxiety in response to a disappointing gift were described by peers as more socially avoidant and rated as more aggressive or disruptive by teachers. Moreover, emotional display rule utilization is linked with social competence not only concurrently but across time as well, controlling for baseline competence and display rule utilization (McDowell & Parke, 2005). These longitudinal results provide support for our implicit assumption that skill in the utilization of emotional display rules leads to social competence.

Parental Correlates of Display Rule Knowledge and Utilization

What role do parents play in accounting for the individual differences in display rule knowledge and utilization? To assess this issue, McDowell and Parke (2000) examined the role of parental control of their children's emotions in the development of children's display rule knowledge. The PACES questionnaire developed by Saarni (1989) that taps the degree to which parents are controlling or accepting of children's hypothetical emotional displays was used to measure parental control. Our findings indicated that children whose mothers and fathers were more controlling were less likely to endorse the use of display rules. Parental control was more consistently linked with knowledge of display rules for negative emotions than for knowledge of display roles for positive emotions. Parents' controlling emotional displays rather than accepting and exploring emotions (described by Gottman et al., 1996, as emotional coaching) was consistently linked with poorer emotion regulatory outcomes. Furthermore, fathers' control significantly predicted knowledge of display rules above and beyond mother's control. Finally, and consistent with previous work (Eisenberg, Fabes, & Murphy, 1996), we found that children whose parents were more controlling of emotional expression were rated as less socially competent. This suggests that parents who are more controlling are providing children with fewer opportunities to "try out" different emotional responses that are shaped by natural consequences in peer social encounters.

Not only are there links between parenting and children's knowledge of display rules, recent evidence suggests relations between parental behavior and children's display rule use as well. Recently, McDowell and Parke (2005) examined this issue using fourth- and fifth-grade children from the UCR Social Development Project. To assess display rule use, the disappointing gift paradigm was used (Saarni, 1984; refer to previous description). A triadic discussion task involving mother, father, and child was used to assess the following parental behaviors: affect (positive and negative affect, clarity of expression, intensity of expression, and awareness of child's feelings) and control (regulation of child's emotions, controlling interaction style). Parental affect played a clear role in predicting children's display rule use. Both mothers' and fathers' observed affect was related to higher display rule use (more positive and fewer negative behaviors) during the disappointing gift session. Moreover, parental control predicted children's positive and tense behavior in the display rule context. Fathers' affect and control predicted children's positive and negative responses to disappointment over and above mothers' affect and control assessments.

The Marital Relationship and Children's Emotional Regulation

Consistent with a family systems view, it is clear that a variety of subsystems beyond the parent–child subsystems, such as the marital subsystem, are linked to children's peer relationships. As Cummings (chap. 8, this volume) and others (Fincham, 1998) have recognized, there are clear links between marital conflict and children's adjustment. In this section, we briefly demonstrate that the relation between marital conflict and peer competence is, in part, mediated by children's emotion regulatory abilities.

To assess this issue we measured children's perceptions of marital conflict, children's emotion regulatory abilities, and peer competence. Prior evidence suggests a reliable relation between both self-report and observed indices of parental marital conflict and children's perception of marital conflict (see Parke et al., 2002, for a review). As a first step, we examined the links between indices of marital conflict and children's emotional regulation. According to Kim, Parke, and Leidy (2004), fifth-grade boys' perceptions of marital conflict properties (frequency, intensity, content, resolution of conflict, and feeling of threat from conflict) were associated with poor emotion regulatory skills (engaging in problem behaviors). In a similar way, girls' self-blame for marital conflict was positively associated with engaging in problem behavior in response to emotionally arousing challenges and negatively related to cognitive problem solving as an emotion regulatory strategy. Similar findings are evident for sixth graders as well. Both parental reports of marital conflict and children's perceptions of marital conflict were negatively related to emotional regulation (Leidy & Parke, 2004).

As a next step we examined the relation between marital conflict, children's emotional regulation, and their social competence with peers. Kim, Parke, and Leidy (2004) found that children's reports of marital conflict were related to a variety of outcomes. For boys, self-reported depression and both peer- and teacher-rated social competence were linked with marital conflict. For example, boys' reports of marital conflict and their tendency to blame themselves were positively related to peer and teacher ratings of aggression and gossip. In turn, marital conflict was negatively related to maternal reports of emotional regulation. For girls, marital conflict was positively correlated with teacher ratings of social competence and negatively related to their friendship qualities. In turn, attributions of self-blame for marital conflict were related to poor emotional regulation. Finally, there was evidence of the mediating role of children's emotion regulatory strategy between marital conflict and children's social competence. Boys' emotion regulatory skill mediated the link between perceptions of marital conflict and teacher ratings of aggressive behavior and peer-rated gossip.

In sum, marital conflict as well as parent–child interaction patterns are correlates of children's peer competence. Moreover, just as in the case of parent–child relationships, emotion regulatory abilities mediate, in part, the links between marital conflict and peer competence.

ATTENTION REGULATION AS A POTENTIAL MEDIATING MECHANISM

In concert with emotional regulation and other emotional processes, attention regulatory processes have come to be viewed as an additional mechanism through which familial socialization experiences might influence the development of children's social competence. These processes include the ability to attend to relevant cues, to sustain attention, to refocus attention through such processes as cognitive distraction and cognitive restructuring, and other efforts to purposefully reduce the level of emotional arousal in a situation that is appraised as stressful (chap. 1, this volume). Attentional processes are thought to organize experience and to play a central role in cognitive and social development beginning early in infancy (Rothbart & Bates, 1998). Thus, Wilson and Gottman (1994) aptly considered attention regulatory processes as a "shuttle" linking emotional regulation and sociocognitive processes because attentional processes organize both cognitions and emotional responses, and thus influence the socialization of relationship competence.

Although studies are only beginning to emerge, evidence suggests that attention regulation may have direct effects on children's social functioning (Wilson & Gottman, 1994). In support of direct influences, Eisenberg and colleagues (1993) found that children who were low in attention regulation were also low in social competence. Other work (Eisenberg et al., 1995) suggests that attentional control and emotional negativity may interact when predicting social competence. Attention regulatory skills appear to be more critical among children who experience higher levels of emotional negativity. Eisenberg et al. argued that when children are not prone to experience intense negative emotions, attention regulatory processes may be less essential to positive social functioning. In contrast, the social functioning of children who experience anger and other negative emotions may only be undermined when these children do not have the ability to use attention regulatory processes such as cognitive restructuring and other forms of emotion-focused coping.

Work emanating from the UCR Social Development Project also suggests that attentional processes may work in tandem with emotion regulatory abilities to enhance social functioning (O'Neil & Parke, 2000). Parenting style may be an important antecedent of children's abilities to refocus attention away from emotionally distressing events. Data from fifth graders in our study indicated that when mothers adopted a negative, controlling parenting style in a problem-solving discussion, children were less likely to use cognitive decision making as a coping strategy. In addition, these children were more likely to report greater difficulty in controlling negative affect when distressed. Lower levels of cognitive decision making and higher levels of negative affect, in turn, were associated with more problem behaviors and higher levels of negative interactions with classmates (as reported by teachers). Similarly, when fathers adopted a negative, controlling style, children were more likely to use avoidance as a mechanism for managing negative affect. In addition, fathers who reported expressing more negative dominant emotions such as anger and criticism in everyday interactions had children who reported greater difficulty controlling negative emotions. Avoidant coping and negative emotionality, in turn, were related to higher levels of parent-reported problem behaviors.

Recent findings from the NICHD study of child care and youth development also bear on this issue (NICHD Child Care Research Network, 2003). The role of attention in a laboratory task as a mediator between parenting and peer outcomes was examined. A sample of nearly 1,000 children and parents from 10 states across the United States was used. Parenting was measured by the HOME Scale, by maternal sensitivity, and by cognitive stimulation. Attention regulation was indexed by sustained attention and impulsivity. Both were measured using the Continuous Performance Task (CPT), in which children viewed a matrix of familiar objects and were required to note when an object appeared and to refrain when a nontarget stimulus was pre-

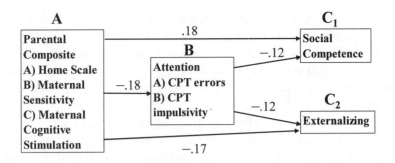

Figure 7.2. Relations among maternal parenting, attention regulation, and social competence (NICHD Child Care Research Network, 2003). Attention (B) mediates the relation between the parental composite (A) and both social competence (C_1) and externalizing behaviors (C_2). CPT = Continuous Performance Task.

sented. Errors of omission occurred when children failed to respond to a target stimulus; errors of commission occurred when children responded to a nontarget stimulus. Children who had fewer errors of omission had greater ability to sustain attention; children with more errors of commission were more impulsive. Social competence and externalizing behaviors were rated by child care providers at 54 months. There were significant links between higher-quality family environments, better social competence, and lower externalizing symptoms. Second, sustained attention and less impulsivity were associated with higher social competence scores and lower externalizing scores. Third, impulsivity served as a mediator between family and social outcome measures (see Figure 7.2).

In a recent follow-up (NICHD Child Care Research Network, 2005) we found that attention regulation mediated between mothers' and fathers' parental sensitivity measures and teacher ratings of children's peer competence and self-reports of loneliness in Grade 1. In this study attention was measured by both the CPT and by maternal reports of attention regulatory abilities. Using third-grade outcomes of aggression, exclusion by peers and friendship, earlier measures (first grade) of mother and father sensitivity predicted these outcomes. Moreover, attention regulation competence served as a mediator between parenting (at Grade 1) and later peer outcomes (at Grade 3). Together these studies provide supportive evidence for the role of attention as a mediator of the links between family and peer systems.

FUTURE DIRECTIONS

Several issues remain to be addressed in future research. First, it is important to specify how emotion and attention regulatory processes are modified by development. Most of the work with children in this area has focused on early and middle childhood. More work on the links between these processes and social competence in infants and young children as well as in adolescence would be worthwhile.

Second, the issue of intracultural and cross-cultural variation needs more attention. It is not clear that these processes operate similarly either across different ethnic groups in the United States or in different cultures. Culturally linked differences in temperament are well documented (Rothbart & Bates, 1998). For example, Asian infants are more proficient self-regulators than Caucasian infants, but we know less about culturally linked self-regulatory differences across cultures in older children and adolescents. Also the parental and marital correlates of differences in emotion regulatory abilities in different cultures remain relatively unexplored. Finally the links between these processes and social competence in different cultures needs more attention.

Third, more work is needed to specify the familial pathways through which children learn emotion and attention regulatory skills. Our focus has been on parental control strategies, but parental modeling is another avenue that needs more attention. Studies that provide measures of both parental and child regulatory skills and strategies would be a worthwhile way of addressing this issue. Nor should we ignore the contribution of siblings to the socialization of these regulatory capacities. Needed are genetically sensitive within-family designs in which two or more siblings in the same family are measured on the same regulatory processes and parental differences in management of these issues with different children are noted. This type of design would begin to address the important issue of genetic contributions as well as socialization influences on the development of emotional regulation skills.

Fourth, the biological correlates of emotional regulation and attentional processes are beginning to be examined (chap. 6, this volume), especially the psychophysiological correlates of these issues. Less is known about the neurological correlates of these processes, especially the role of developmental shifts in frontal lobe functioning (Nelson & Bloom, 1997). Recent advances in neuro-imaging will make examination of these issues more feasible and permit us to understand the neurological underpinnings of individual and developmental differences in emotional and attentional functioning (see chap. 1, this volume). Moreover, the neurological changes that accompany behavioral shifts in these processes will provide an "online" view of these cross-level linkages.

Finally, a variety of conceptual issues need further examination. The concept of emotional regulation needs further refinement, especially the multifaceted nature of the construct. As others have noted (Cole et al., 2004; Denham, 1998), it is useful to distinguish among emotional, cognitive and perceptual, and behavioral components of emotional regulation. As our work suggests, attentional processes need to be considered as well. The interplay among these components and the differential integration of these aspects of emotional regulation across development merit more systematic examination. As our own work suggests, attentional processes merit more examination not only as correlates of social competence but as a component of emotional regulation as well. The extent to which attention regulation is a more general process or one that plays a unique role in emotional regulation remains unclear. Application of Gross's (2002) construct of attentional deployment, an antecedent-focused aspect of emotional regulation, to future development studies would be worthwhile.

Our goal in this chapter was to demonstrate the central role played by emotional processes, especially emotion and attention regulation, in accounting for variations in peer social competence. As our work has shown through social experience in the family either in the course of parent–child interaction or as a consequence of witnessing marital conflict, children acquire a variety of emotional competencies that, in turn, are used in their interactions with peers. One of the contributions of our work has been to highlight the role of fathers as well as mothers in this cross-systems process. The challenge for future research is to trace more closely how these emotional competencies shift across development and to better uncover the predictive value of emotional competence in childhood for later social and emotional functioning in adulthood. In view of the central importance of emotional competence for successful social adaptation in a wide variety of settings, this is clearly a worthwhile goal.

REFERENCES

Barth, J. M., & Parke, R. D. (1993). Parent–child relationship influences on children's transition to school. *Merrill-Palmer Quarterly, 39*, 173–195.

Baumrind, D. (1973). The development of instrumental competence through socialization. In A. D. Pick (Ed.), *Minnesota symposium on child psychology* (Vol. 17, pp. 3–46). Minneapolis: University of Minnesota Press.

Boyum, L. A., & Parke, R. D. (1995). The role of family emotional expressiveness in the development of children's social competence. *Journal of Marriage and the Family, 57*, 593–608.

Carson, J. L., & Parke, R. D. (1996). Reciprocal negative affect in parent–child interactions and children's peer competency. *Child Development, 67*, 2217–2226.

Cassidy, J., Parke, R. D., Butkovsky, L., & Braungart, J. M. (1992). Family peer connections: The roles of emotional expressiveness within the family and children's understanding of emotions. *Child Development, 63*, 603–618.

Cole, P. M., Martin, S. E., & Dennis, T. A. (2004). Emotional regulation as a scientific construct: Methodological challenges and directions for child development. *Child Development, 75*, 317–333.

Crick, N. R., & Dodge, K. A. (1994). A review and reformulation of social information-processing mechanisms in children's social adjustment. *Psychological Bulletin, 115*, 74–101.

Cummings, E. M., & Davies, P. (1994). *Children and marital conflict: The impact of family dispute and resolution.* New York: Guilford Press.

Denham, S. A. (1998). *Emotional development in young children.* New York: Guilford Press.

Denham, S. A., McKinley, M., Couchoud, E. A., & Holt, R. (1990). Emotional and behavioral predictors of preschool peer ratings. *Child Development, 61,* 1145–1152.

Eisenberg, N., & Fabes, R. A. (1992). Young children's coping with interpersonal anger. *Child Development, 63,* 116–128.

Eisenberg, N., Fabes, R., Bernzweig, J., Karbon, M., Poulin, R., & Hannish, L. (1993). The relations of emotionality and regulation to preschoolers' social skills and sociometric status. *Child Development, 64,* 1418–1438.

Eisenberg, N., Fabes, R. A., & Murphy, B. C. (1996). Parents' reactions to children's negative emotions: Relations to children's social competence and comforting behavior. *Child Development, 67,* 2227–2247.

Eisenberg, N., Fabes, R., Murphy, B., Maszk, P., Smith, M., & Karbon, M. (1995). The role of emotionality and regulation in children's social functioning: A longitudinal study. *Child Development, 66,* 1360–1384.

Fincham, F. D. (1998). Child development and marital relations. *Child Development, 69,* 543–574.

Garner, P. W. (1996). The relations of emotional role taking, affective/moral attributions, and emotional display rule knowledge to low-income school-age children's social competence. *Journal of Applied Developmental Psychology, 17,* 19–36.

Gottman, J. M., Katz, L. F., & Hooven, C. (1996). *Meta-emotion: How families communicate emotionally, links to child peer relations, and other developmental outcomes.* Mahwah, NJ: Erlbaum.

Gross, J. J. (2002). Emotional regulation: Affective, cognitive, and social consequences. *Psychophysiology, 39,* 281–291.

Halbertstadt, A., Denham, S. A., & Dunsmore, J. C. (2001). Affective social competence. *Social Development, 10,* 79–119.

Harrist, A. W., Pettit, G. S., Dodge, K. A., & Bates, J. E. (1994). Dyadic synchrony in mother–child interaction: Relations with children's subsequent kindergarten adjustment. *Family Relations, 43,* 417–424.

Hubbard, J. A., & Dearing, K. F. (2004). Children's understanding and regulation of emotion in the context of their peer relations. In J. B. Kupersmidt & K. A. Dodge (Eds.), *Children's peer relations* (pp. 81–99). Washington, DC: American Psychological Association.

Isley, S., O'Neil, R., & Parke, R. D. (1996). The relation of parental affect and control behaviors to children's classroom acceptance: A concurrent and predictive analysis. *Early Education and Development, 7,* 7–23.

Kim, M., McDowell, D. J., & Parke, R. D. (2004). *A longitudinal examination of emotion regulation across middle childhood: Links with social adjustment.* Unpublished manuscript, University of California, Riverside.

Kim, M., Parke, R. D., & Leidy, M. S. (2004). *Children's perceptions of marital conflict: Gender differences on children's social and emotional outcomes*. Unpublished manuscript, University of California, Riverside.

Leidy, M. S., & Parke, R. D. (2004). *Marital relationships, emotional regulation and peer competence: A longitudinal examination*. Unpublished manuscript, University of California, Riverside.

MacDonald, K., & Parke, R. D. (1984). Bridging the gap: Parent–child play interaction and peer interactive competence. *Child Development, 55,* 1265–1277.

McDowell, D. J., Kim, M., O'Neil, R., & Parke, R. D. (2002). Parental influences on children's emotional and social competence. *Marriage and Family Review, 34,* 345–364.

McDowell, D. J., O'Neil, R., & Parke, R. D. (2000). Display rule application in a disappointing situation and children's emotional reactivity: Relations with social competence. *Merrill-Palmer Quarterly, 46,* 306–324.

McDowell, D. J., & Parke, R. D. (2000). Differential knowledge of display rules for positive and negative emotions: Influence from parents, influences on peers. *Social Development, 9,* 415–432.

McDowell, D. J., & Parke, R. D. (2005). Parental control and affect as predictors of children's display rule use and social competence with peers. *Social Development, 14,* 440–457.

Nelson, C. A., & Bloom, F. E. (1997). Child development and neuroscience. *Child Development, 68,* 970–987.

NICHD Child Care Research Network. (2003). Do children's attention processes mediate the link between family predictors and school readiness? *Developmental Psychology, 39,* 581–593.

NICHD Child Care Research Network. (2005). *Family–peer linkages: Attributional and attentional processes as mediators*. Unpublished manuscript, National Institute of Child Health and Human Development, Washington, DC.

O'Neil, R., & Parke, R. D. (2000). Family–peer relationships: The role of emotional regulation, cognitive understanding, and attentional processes as mediating processes. In K. A. Kerns, J. M. Contreras, & A. M. Neal-Barnett (Eds.), *Family and peer: Linking two social worlds* (pp. 195–226). Westport, CT: Praeger Publishers.

O'Neil, R., Parke, R. D., Isley, S., & Sosa, R. (1997, April). *Parental influences on children's emotion regulation in middle childhood*. Paper presented at the biennial meeting of the Society for Research in Child Development, Washington, DC.

Parke, R. D. (2002). Fathers and families. In M. Bornstein (Series & Vol. Ed.), *Handbook of parenting: Vol. 3. Being and becoming a parent* (2nd ed., pp. 27–73). Mahwah, NJ: Erlbaum.

Parke, R. D., Cassidy, J., Burks, C. M., Carson, J. L., & Boyum, L. (1992). Familial contribution to peer competence among young children: The role of interactive and affective processes. In R. D. Parke & G. W. Ladd (Eds.), *Family–peer relationships: Modes of linkage* (pp. 107–134). Hillsdale, NJ: Erlbaum.

Parke, R. D., & Ladd, G. W. (Eds.). (1992). *Family–peer relationships: Modes of linkage*. Hillsdale, NJ: Erlbaum.

Parke, R. D., & O'Neil, R. (1999). Social relationships across contexts: Family–peer linkages. In W. A. Collins & B. Laursen (Eds.), *Minnesota symposium on child psychology* (Vol. 30, pp. 211–241). Mahwah, NJ: Erlbaum.

Parke, R. D., Simpkins, S. D., McDowell, D. J., Kim, M., Killian, C., Dennis, J., et al. (2002). Relative contributions of families and peers to children's social development. In P. K. Smith & C. H. Hart (Eds.), *Handbook of childhood social development* (pp. 156–177). Oxford, England: Blackwell.

Parker, J. G., & Asher, S. R. (1987). Peer relations and later personality adjustment: Are lower-accepted children at risk? *Psychological Bulletin, 102,* 357–389.

Parker, J. G., & Gottman, J. M. (1989). Social and emotional development in a relational context: Friendship interactions from early childhood to adolescence. In T. J. Berndt & G. W. Ladd (Eds.), *Peer relationships in child development* (pp. 95–131). New York: Wiley.

Rothbart, M., & Bates, J. (1998). Temperament. In W. Damon (Ed.), *Handbook of child psychology* (pp. 105–176). New York: Wiley.

Saarni, C. (1984). An observational study of children's attempt to monitor their expressive behavior. *Child Development, 55,* 1504–1513.

Saarni, C. (1989). Children's understanding of strategic control of emotional expression in social transactions. In C. Saarni & P. L. Harris (Eds.), *Children's understanding of emotion* (pp. 181–208). New York: Cambridge University Press.

Sroufe, L. A., & Fleeson, J. (1986). Attachment and the construction of relationships. In W. W. Hartup & Z. Rubin (Eds.), *Relationships and development* (pp. 51–72). Hillsdale, NJ: Erlbaum.

Thompson, R. A. (1994). Emotional regulation: In search of definition. *Monographs of the Society or Research in Child Development, 59*(2–3, Serial No. 240), 25–52.

Wilson, B. J., & Gottman, J. M. (1994). Attention—The shuttle between emotion and cognition: Risk, resiliency and physiological bases. In E. M. Hetherington & E. Blechman (Eds.), *Stress, coping, and resiliency in children and families* (pp. 189–228). Hillsdale, NJ: Erlbaum.

8

MARITAL DISCORD AND CHILDREN'S EMOTIONAL SELF-REGULATION

E. MARK CUMMINGS AND PEGGY S. KELLER

Although a normal part of every marriage, interparental conflict can result in serious harm to children's functioning. Children exposed to high levels of intense, unresolved conflict are at increased risk for social, emotional, and behavioral problems (Grych & Fincham, 1990). Given the prevalence of discordant marriages, this represents a significant challenge for our society. However, simply providing evidence of the link between marital discord and child adjustment has reached a point of diminishing returns. Theoretical, process-oriented models accounting for these relationships must now be tested.

The emotional security hypothesis (ESH; Davies & Cummings, 1994) posits that children's emotion regulation plays a key role in the deleterious effects of interparental conflict on children. According to this theory, when children interpret marital discord as threatening to family stability and personal well-being, children's emotional security is reflected by patterns of emotional, cognitive, and behavioral self-regulation in response. However, consistent with a functionalist perspective on emotions, emotion regulation is expected to play an especially important role in organizing and directing children's reactions to conflict and in reflecting the meaning of conflict from the children's perspective (Cummings & Davies, 1996). This chapter examines how an understanding of these patterns of responding helps account for how and why marital discord affects children's functioning and development.

CONCEPTUAL, THEORETICAL, AND METHODOLOGICAL ISSUES

Conflict is inevitable in every relationship, but there is a great variability in the ways that couples handle and resolve their disagreements. Some couples use effective problem-solving skills, demonstrate affection, and show concern for each other, successfully resolving issues as they come up. Other couples engage in conflicts of escalating intensity, using threats, insults, and aggression without resolving problems. Most couples fall somewhere in between, handling some of their differences poorly and others well, sometimes using effective and other times maladaptive conflict strategies.

From children's perspectives, these different conflict strategies have different meanings, and different implications for their long-term adjustment. Children have adverse reactions to certain conflict tactics such as physical aggression, verbal hostility, and threats to leave the relationship, whereas they may potentially benefit from exposure to conflict tactics such as problem solving, support, and affection (Goeke-Morey, Cummings, Harold, & Shelton, 2003). According to ESH, children's interpretation of the meaning of marital conflict as constructive or destructive conflict can be determined from their emotional, behavioral, and cognitive responding, but emotional reactions are held to be especially informative. Destructive conflict is linked with long-term negative child outcomes, including children's social, emotional, and behavioral problems (Grych & Fincham, 1990). According to the theory, destructive marital conflict is harmful because children perceive negative implications for the family and for personal well-being. Children who are exposed to high levels of destructive conflict develop reduced emotional security. Insecure children have negative perceptions and beliefs about family stability. They are also hypervigilant to conflict, have a lower threshold for the perception of threat, and are preoccupied with the maintenance of family stability.

Consistent with the view of emotional security as an organizational construct (Cummings, Davies, & Campbell, 2000), children's emotional security is operationally defined in terms of several component processes (Cummings & Davies, 1996; Davies & Cummings, 1994). The first component of emotional security is children's emotional reaction to interparental disagreements. When disagreements are perceived as threatening, children may react with fear, anger, or sadness. Characteristics of the disagreement and children's history of exposure to conflict both influence the form, intensity, and duration of these emotions. Children's representations of family relationships are a second component of emotional security. These representations include expectations of parental behavior in both parent–child and interparental contexts and the consequences of that behavior for the family. Consistent with attachment theory notions about children's representations of family (chaps. 3 and 4, this volume), they are based on previous experience (Cummings et al., 2000). For example, children develop expectations of how the interparental relationship relates to broader family functioning. Emotionally insecure children may perceive even positive interactions between their parents as threatening, believe that conflict between their parents is unlikely to be resolved and may lead to divorce, expect parents who are angry at each other to take it out on the children, or view themselves as partially or entirely responsible for the discord. The third component of emotional security is children's effort to regulate exposure to marital conflict. Insecure children may attempt to end the disagreement through their own involvement, either directly as a mediator or indirectly as a distracter. In an alternative way, children may remove themselves from the immediate environment to avoid exposure to destructive conflict. Finally, children's higher-order patterns of emotional security may reflect meaningful organizations of these several components, adding to the prediction of individual differences in children's functioning and adjustment (Davies & Forman, 2002).

These component processes fit with theoretical definitions of emotion regulation. For example, Thompson (1994) stated that "emotion regulation consists of the extrinsic and intrinsic processes responsible for monitoring, evaluating and modifying emotional reactions, especially their intensive and temporal features, to accomplish one's goals" (pp. 27–28). Regulation occurs through neurophysiological constituents, attention, cognitive interpretations of external and internal events, access to coping resources, regulation of environmental demands, and choice of emotional expressions. More recently, Cole, Martin, and Dennis (2004) stated that "emotion regulation refers to changes associated with activated emotions. These include changes in the emotion itself . . . or in other psychological processes" and further contended that "the term emotion regulation can denote two types of regulatory phenomena: emotion as regulating and emotion as regulated" (p. 320). In addition, Gross, Richards, and John (chap. 1, this volume), have defined emotion regulation as the use of cognition and behavior to determine the quality, timing, and expression of emotion. In terms of these definitions of emotion regulation, children with low emotional security devote greater attention to marital relations and are more likely to interpret marital disagreements as cause for concern. Negative emotional reactions organize and motivate efforts to cope with marital conflict, including attempts to alter conflict to protect their own welfare (e.g., mediation). In this way, children's goal-directed behavior prompts them to create an environment with fewer threats to emotional security. Their experience of fear, anger, and sadness prompts efforts toward regulation of the environment that, in turn, are aimed at regulating the experience of emotion.

A lower threshold of emotional arousal may in the short term be beneficial by increasing vigilance for potentially harmful situations. Negative representations about family relationships may also be beneficial by providing a framework within which children can select and use behavioral strategies that reduce threat. However, a key contention of ESH is that these short-term benefits are outweighed by the long-term costs in terms of heightened risk of adjustment problems. From the perspective of emotional intelligence (see chap. 2, this volume), emotionally insecure children fail to develop the abilities necessary for adaptive functioning, because insecurity creates potentially maladaptive patterns of responding in multiple contexts and also diverts resources away from addressing other developmental goals (Cummings & Davies, 1996). For example, the pattern of insecure responding to interparental conflict may generalize to peer conflict, leading to inappropriate social withdrawal or aggressive behavior as responding aimed at reducing the threat other children are perceived as posing. Social adaptation difficulties may translate into romantic difficulties as children emerge into adolescence and adulthood. Increased emotional arousal may contribute to chronic anxiety or depression. The attention required to monitor family interactions may reduce resources available for academics. Thus, children's emotional insecurity may undermine adaptive functioning in multiple domains, increasing the risk for less optimal child outcomes over time.

EMPIRICAL FOUNDATIONS

Recent analyses have begun to distinguish between constructive and destructive conflict tactics on the basis of children's reactions. As previously described, research has traditionally focused on a limited number of strategies, such as physical aggression and hostility. However, everyday disagreements include a wide range of behaviors, both positive and negative, such as humor, support, problem-solving, threat, withdrawal, and pursuit. According to ESH, tactics that threaten family stability will be associated with more adverse child reactions than tactics that help couples resolve disagreements. Thus, children's reactions to conflict strategies serve as the basis for determining whether they are constructive or destructive.

Goeke-Morey et al. (2003) examined a wide range of conflict tactics in two different cultural contexts using analog procedures. The study included 175 American children ages 8 to 16 and 327 Welsh children ages 11 and 12 living with married or cohabiting parents. The U.S. sample was drawn from a larger study of 300 mothers, fathers, and children, recruited to achieve a representative community sample (see also Cummings, Goek-Morey, & Papp, 2003, 2004; Cummings, Goeke-Morey, Papp, & Dukewich, 2002; Du Rocher

Schudlich & Cummings, 2003; Papp, Cummings, & Goeke-Morey, 2002), fostering the generalizability of the results to such samples. The sample reflected the demographic characteristics of the county from which it was drawn, including 83% White, 11% Black, and 3% Hispanic. Annual family income ranged from less than $10,000 to more than $80,000, with the median income in the $40,000 to $65,000 range. Demographic statistics suggested that the Welsh sample was similarly representative of the communities from which it was drawn with regard to family constitution, ethnic representation, economic diversity, and parent education (see also Davies, Harold, Goeke-Morey, & Cummings, 2002).

Children were asked to watch a videotaped series of vignettes in which an adult enacted a specific behavior toward a second adult of opposite gender and asked to pretend that the actors were their parents. In half the vignettes a female portrayed the tactic; in the other half a male portrayed the tactic. Actors were selected to match the children culturally and ethnically. Each scene demonstrated only one of the following tactics: humor, support, affection, problem solving, calm discussion, physical aggression toward an object, physical aggression toward a person, verbal hostility, nonverbal hostility, threat, or pursuit. After each scene, children were interviewed regarding their emotional, cognitive, and behavioral reactions.

Results indicate that American children had more negative than positive emotional reactions to aggression toward a person, aggression toward an object, threat, verbal hostility, nonverbal hostility, and pursuit, indicating that these strategies are destructive or threatening to family stability. American children had more positive than negative emotional reactions to problem solving, support, and affection, suggesting that these tactics are experienced as constructive. The only tactic that could not be classified on the basis of reactions by American children was calm discussion. A similar pattern of results was found for Welsh children, with the exception that calm discussion emerged as a constructive conflict tactic. Consistent with ESH, children's emotional, behavioral, and cognitive responses yielded similar ordering of conflict tactics from relatively most negative (i.e., most destructive) to relatively most positive (i.e., most constructive). Both American and Welsh children engaged in more behavioral regulation (attempting to avoid exposure to the conflict) in response to aggression toward a person, aggression toward an object, threat, verbal hostility, and pursuit than in response to problem solving, support, and affection. Both samples also reported more negative cognitive representations (greater concern) for aggression toward a person, aggression toward an object, threat, verbal hostility, nonverbal hostility, and pursuit than for problem solving, support, and affection.

Cummings et al. (2003) attempted to replicate these findings using a different method: home diary reports of children's reactions to everyday conflict. The diary method allows for a more ecologically valid assessment of constructive and destructive conflict. This study focused on children's emotional reactions. As we noted previously, emotions are seen by ESH as primary indicators of children's perceptions about the meaning of conflict, and also as motivating, organizing, and directing children's responses to marital conflict. Furthermore, analyses included children's specific emotions (anger, fear, and sadness) as well as overall negativity. The study included 116 families with children between the ages of 8 and 16. Parents were trained to complete diary reports of any major or minor difference of opinion that occurred between them for a period of 15 days. The diaries consisted of a checklist of various tactics (threat, insult, verbal and nonverbal hostility, defensiveness, withdrawal, physical distress, calm discussion, support, and affection) and children's reactions to the disagreement if they were present. Training involved verbal, written, and video descriptions of conflict tactics along with practice using videos of disagreements.

Mothers completed 580 and fathers completed 377 records for disagreements in which children were present. A wide variety of conflict tactics were reported. The results thus supported the view that everyday conflicts include a rich array of both positive and negative strategies (Cummings & Davies, 2002). Children responded with greater negativity and less happiness to threat, insult, verbal hostility, and defensiveness (both mothers' and fathers' reports), as well as nonverbal hostility, withdrawal, and physical distress (mothers' report only). Children responded with less negativity and greater happiness to fathers' and mothers' reports of calm discussion, support, and affection. Relations with children's specific emotional reactions of fear, anger, and sadness were generally consistent with this pattern, so little support was found for a specific emotions theory (Crockenberg & Langrock, 2001).

Interesting questions arise about family members' perspectives and classification of constructive and destructive conflicts. A spouse's perspective on conflict may influence whether he or she appraises it as constructive or destructive. Thus, the marital literature, particularly with regard to pursuit–withdrawal patterns and power differentials in couples (Loving, Heffner, Kiecolt-Glaser, Glaser, & Malarkey, 2004), suggests that conflict-management tactics that are functionally or emotionally advantageous to one partner may be disadvantageous to the other (Ball, Cowan, & Cowan, 1995). However, children are less likely to have a strong interest in one parent's perspective in relation to the other. That is, children are more interested in family stability and both parents staying together. Accordingly, we hypothesize that children are more likely to react in an "expert way" to the meaning of conflict for the parental (and family) relationship.

Therefore, in terms of appraising family conflicts for their emotional security implications, especially in terms of their emotional responses, children may be more reliable reporters on the relative constructiveness versus destructiveness of conflict tactics than their parents. As Cummings and Davies have shown (2002), using theoretically based, operational criteria derived from ESH, children's responses to most conflict tactics have supported unambiguous classifications as constructive or destructive across cultures (e.g., see the typically moderate to high effect sizes reported in Goeke-Morey et al., 2003, Table 2) that are also generally consistent across children's ages and gender. In a similar way, parental emotional expressions during conflicts in the home have been consistently classified as destructive (e.g., anger, sadness) or constructive (e.g., positive affect), respectively, on the basis of children's emotional (Cummings et al., 2002) or aggressive (Cummings et al., 2004) responses. It is important to note that responses to nonverbal anger and marital withdrawal in the home indicate that children consistently respond to these behaviors as destructive, although parents themselves may sometimes assume that conflict avoidance is "functionally constructive" in that the immediate threat is minimized.

It is also important to note the long-term impact of destructive marital conflict on children's emotion regulation. A key tenet of ESH is that children's emotional security is affected by their previous exposure to marital conflict. Children who are exposed to high levels of destructive conflict are proposed to develop a pattern of emotional insecurity in which reactions to conflict are intensely negative. Children develop a pattern of emotional insecurity because their previous exposure has taught them about the important threat that their parents' conflict poses to family stability. In this sense, children become "experts" on their parents' conflict styles and are well equipped to assess both the constructiveness and destructiveness of a given conflict.

The notion that children become more reactive to conflict over time is known as the sensitization hypothesis, and it is supported by research (Cummings, 1994). A series of experiments has demonstrated that children who have seen intense and unresolved disagreements later have more negative reactions to conflict than children who have seen constructive and resolved disagreements (El Sheikh & Cummings, 1995; El Sheikh, Cummings, & Reiter, 1996). For example, Davies, Myers, Cummings, and Heindel (1999) randomly assigned children in three age groups (early childhood, preadolescence, and late adolescence) to see either four intense and unresolved conflicts between a couple on videotape, or four mild and resolved conflicts. Children in both groups then watched a standard conflict of moderate intensity between the familiar couple. Children in all age groups who had been exposed to destructive conflict had more negative emotional reactions and showed increased attempts at avoidance of the standard conflict. Late adolescents in the destructive conflict group also demonstrated more negative representations about relationship stability in response to the standard conflict than children in the constructive conflict group. These findings suggest that children who have witnessed their parents' destructive conflict will, over the long term, develop an insecure pattern of responding to conflict. Correlational research also supports this suggestion: Research indicates that children's reactions to conflict in the laboratory setting are related to previous exposure to marital discord and distress in the home (Davies & Cummings, 1998).

Additional evidence of the sensitization hypothesis can be found in children's cognitive representations of marital relationships. Children who have been exposed to high levels of marital discord may view conflict as likely to go unresolved, spill over into parent–child interactions, and eventually bring about family dissolution. These appraisals help account for children's angry, fearful, and sad reactions, which then must be regulated or are used to regulate interparental behavior. One innovative way of assessing children's cognitive representations of marital conflict was used by Shamir, Du Rocher Schudlich, and Cummings (2001). Children's experiences within their families and sense of emotional security are hypothesized to contribute to beliefs and expectations about family events, which are organized into mental representations. In this study, 47 children between the ages of 5 and 8 completed a narrative story stem task in which experimenters used dolls to enact different family events (mother–father conflict, mother–child conflict, father–child conflict, and mother–father conflict with children present), and children were then given the dolls and asked to finish the stories. An assumption underlying story stem tasks is that children draw on their existing mental representations when completing the narrative task. The stories the children told in response to story stems were videotaped and coded for positive (sharing, caregiving, affection, helpfulness, forgiving, instructiveness, collaboration, and conflict resolution) and negative (avoidance, intervention, verbal aggression, physical aggression, stalemating, ignoring, inconsistence, nagging, rejection, neglect, harsh discipline, hostility, helplessness, and blaming) representations.

Results indicate similarities and differences across the types of stories (mother–father, mother–child, etc). Frequent negative representations included verbal aggression (all story types), physical aggression (parent–child stories), harsh discipline (parent–child and mother–father–child stories), blame (mother–father and mother–father–child stories), intervention and ignoring (mother–father stories), and avoidance (mother–father–child stories). The use of negative strategies by one person in a story was associated with greater use of negative strategies by other family members. The same pattern was found for positive representations. The most frequent positive representations were of resolution for all conflict story stems. Consistent with ESH, both mothers' and fathers' reports of stalemating, avoidance, physical aggression, and verbal aggression during their marital conflict predicted more negative child representations across all story types. In addition, negative representations between story types were positively correlated. The same pattern was found for positive representations.

The results of these studies suggest robust classifications of multiple, everyday marital conflict strategies as constructive or destructive on the basis of children's responding across cultures, parental gender, methodologies (laboratory, naturalistic), and types of responses examined (e.g., emotional, cognitive). They suggest that disruptions in the marital relationship affect children's emotion regulation, behavioral regulation, and representations in response to marital, parent–child, and triadic interactions in both the short and long term. As hypothesized by ESH, children differentiate between conflict through their emotional, behavioral, and cognitive reactions. In addition, conflict that is most likely to jeopardize family stability, conflict characterized by greater intensity and less resolution, is associated with decreased emotional security. When children are exposed to destructive conflict styles, they have more intense negative emotional reactions and develop the negative cognitive representation that interparental disagreements are a cause for concern, and attempts by children to mediate or avoid the conflict are evident. However, there may also be individual differences in how the component processes of emotional security are interrelated. Similar to the case of attachment within the parent–child relationship, specific patterns of emotional security related to the marital relationship may have important additional implications for children's adjustment.

Davies and Forman (2002) reported on three clusters of children on the basis of their emotional security in the interparental relationship, examined across two data sets of children of different ages and assessed across a wide range of measures of child and family functioning. These clusters correspond highly to clusters of attachment orientation (Mikulincer, Shaver, & Pereg, 2003). About half of the children were in the secure cluster, which was characterized by mild and healthy concern in the face of destructive conflict and mental representations of family relationships as stable (i.e., they believed the conflict would not spill over into the parent–child relationship and that conflict would eventually be resolved). About a quarter of children fell into the second cluster, preoccupied children, who experienced intense negative emotional reactions, viewed relationships as less stable, and attempted to intervene or avoid the disagreements. Preoccupied children likely have a low threshold for the perception of threat and have difficulties preserving their sense of security. The third cluster, dismissive children, was also characterized by intense overt negative reactions, avoidance, and involvement, but when asked about their feelings, representations, and impulses to intervene or avoid they more closely resembled secure children. This suggests that these children are highly threatened by conflict but seek to restore their sense of security by dissociating and blunting their distress.

The three patterns of emotional security differed in a variety of important respects, including family characteristics and child outcomes. Secure children had historically lower exposure to destructive marital conflict than dismissive and preoccupied children and also came from more cohesive families. They also evidenced fewer internalizing and externalizing symptoms, fewer personality problems, and fewer coping difficulties than children in the dismissive and preoccupied groups. These children were frequently exposed to conflict handled well and resolved, presumably bolstering their sense of the family as well equipped to deal with any difficulties that arise and supporting the child in achieving developmental goals such as interpersonal skills and coping resources. In contrast, preoccupied children were exposed to high levels of destructive conflict, and also to high levels of parental control. Although their families were relatively cohesive, these children were at heightened risk for developing internalizing problems. From an emotional security perspective, these children may be drawn into family conflict, with their feelings of responsibility and guilt hindering their ability to preserve emotional security, resulting in internalizing problems. Finally, dismissing children experienced high levels of unresolved marital conflict and the lowest levels of family cohesion and marital relationship satisfaction. Dismissing children were at greatest risk for externalizing problems and substance use. Children who exhibit this pattern of emotional security may view the family as a source of stress rather than a resource for coping and therefore attempt to distance themselves from family relationships, especially family conflict. To preserve their sense of security, their dismissing pattern may reflect efforts to minimize the threat that interparental discord poses.

Three different types of broad family configurations may coincide with the three emotional security groups (Davies & Forman, 2002). First, close healthy families handle disagreements well, foster warm and caring family relationships, and engage in appropriate parenting strategies, fostering the development of secure children. Second, enmeshed and discordant families have frequent, intense, and unresolved conflicts that draw in multiple family members and spill over into other dimensions of family functioning, increasing the likelihood of preoccupied patterns of emotional insecurity about family relationships. Third, cold and discordant families also have intense and unresolved conflict. However, they are characterized by a rigid family structure in which members disengage from one another and little warmth is present in family interaction. Children from these distant and highly conflictual homes are at increased risk for developing dismissive patterns of emotional insecurity.

Recently, Davies, Cummings, and Winter (2004) extended this work toward broader family-wide models of emotional security, distinguishing among family configurations pertinent to emotional security. Participants were 235 families with a child in kindergarten (see also Cummings, Keller, & Davies, 2005). As in the study by Goeke-Morey et al. (2003), described earlier, research staff made efforts to recruit a representative sample of families by targeting areas with low socioeconomic status and ethnically and racially diverse populations. Consistent with the demographics of the surrounding counties, 76% were White, 16.7% were Black, 3.8% were Hispanic, and 2.1% were of mixed race. Total family income ranged from less than $6,000 a year to more than $75,000 a year, with the median income between $40,000 and $54,999 a year.

On the basis of a multi-informant and multimethod procedure, cluster analyses yielded four distinct groups of families. Close to half of the sample was characterized as cohesive families because of low levels of conflict, high levels of relationship satisfaction and effective parenting, and warm relationships. About one third of the sample fell into the disengaged cluster; they experienced somewhat elevated levels of conflict and were extremely low on warmth and affection. The third cluster (17% of the sample) was similar to the cohesive families, but high levels of psychological control were present. This cluster was therefore labeled the controlling configuration. A small number (8%) of the families were enmeshed; they were characterized as high in intense conflict, inconsistent discipline, and parental psychological control but reported moderate levels of acceptance and affection.

These family configurations differed with respect to children's emotional security and psychological symptoms. Children in enmeshed families were more emotionally reactive, had more negative mental representations, and exhibited greater behavioral regulation in response to conflict than children from the cohesive group. These children also demonstrated more internalizing and externalizing symptoms relative to children in cohesive families. Children in disengaged families experienced more self-reported distress and impulses to become involved in the conflict and perceived conflict to be more threatening than children in the cohesive group. Children in disengaged families also suffered higher levels of internalizing symptoms than children in cohesive families. Children in controlling families were similar to children in the cohesive group. Additional analyses implicate emotional security as a mediator between family enmeshment and children's internalizing and externalizing symptoms 1 year later. Thus, evidence has been found that children develop unique patterns of emotional security that are associated with their family experiences, especially marital conflict. In addition, these studies support the role of dimensions of emotion regulation in the adverse effects of children's exposure to marital conflict.

The role of children's emotion regulation as a dimension of emotional security in the relationship between marital conflict and child adjustment has recently been examined relative to other possible theories about mediators. One alternative theory of why marital discord is harmful to children is the social learning theory (Bandura, 1973), which posits that children will respond with anger and behaviorally imitate the same-sex parent's angry behaviors, especially when the parent is physically aggressive. As another example of a prediction for children's responding, social learning theory holds that children will react more aggressively to more aggression between adults and that the themes of disagreements will otherwise have little impact on the effects of marital conflict on children. In contrast, ESH contends that children will react behaviorally to reduce the threat posed rather than imitate the emotions and behaviors of parents. Conflict topics that pose a greater threat to security, such as those with child-related themes, will be associated with more intense negative reactions.

Contrary to social learning theory and consistent with ESH, Davies et al. (2002) found that children have more negative responses to child-related than adult-related themes and that conflicts involving an explicit threat to end the marital relationship are just as disturbing as physically aggressive conflicts. In fact, boys responded more negatively to disagreements involving a threat to family intactness than to disagreements involving physical aggression. Also inconsistent with social learning theory, children responded with greater fear but not greater anger to physical aggression than to verbal hostility. Thus, greater support was found for ESH than for social learning theory processes. Children did not react differently to the anger expressions of the same- versus the opposite-gender parent, as predicted by social learning theory. The maladjustment exhibited by children exposed to high levels of marital discord was not simply a function of behavioral imitation. Children were far more likely to intervene in conflict or avoid conflict than to imitate parental conflict tactics. Thus, the evidence supports the contention that children view conflict as a threat to the family and their own well-being and as a result are more likely to attempt to regulate their parents' behavior in such a way as to preserve emotional security than simply to imitate the emotions and behaviors of parents.

Another alternative to ESH is the cognitive contextual framework (Grych & Fincham, 1990). According to the cognitive contextual framework, high levels of marital discord are associated with perceived threat and self-blame on the part of children. These cognitions are posited to account for the deleterious effects on children's adjustment. Although the cognitive contextual framework and ESH have some important similarities, the former places greater emphasis on cognition, whereas the latter focuses more on emotion regulation. In a comparison of the two theories, Davies et al. (2002) tested a model that included children's appraisals of threat, self-blame, and emotional security as mediators between interparental conflict and children's internalizing and externalizing symptoms. Cognitive appraisals of threat and self-blame appeared to play a role in the adverse effects of marital discord on children. However, emotional security, with its additional focus on emotion regulation, emerged as the most consistent mediator.

FUTURE DIRECTIONS

Research on the relationship between marital conflict and children's emotion regulation has recently made significant theoretical and empirical progress. However, there are many unanswered questions. For example, apart from the characteristics of marital conflict and conflict histories, are there characteristics of children that might influence the meaning they give to interparental discord? The majority of studies reviewed have found little or no evidence that child gender acts as moderator of the relationship between marital conflict and child adjustment. However, sample sizes may not have been large enough to adequately test this question. Previous studies have found differences in emotion regulation on the basis of child gender. For example, Cole, Zahn-Waxler, and Smith (1994) conducted a study in which preschoolers at low or high risk for adjustment problems were given a disappointing gift. Children's reactions to the gift were observed while the experimenter was present and absent. High- and low-risk boys differed in the experimenter-present condition: High-risk boys showed more negative emotion. Girls differed in the experimenter-absent condition: High-risk girls showed less negative emotion than low-risk girls. Thus, child gender may play a role in children's regulation of emotion in the face of marital discord.

An additional child characteristic that might influence children's appraisals of and reactions to marital conflict is age. Children's emotion regulation abilities and strategies develop over time; initially infants have a limited repertoire of emotion regulation skills that are eventually replaced with more flexible, volitional strategies (Cole et al., 2004). There is limited and inconsistent evidence regarding how exposure to marital conflict at different stages might impact this development or how the emotion regulation strategies of different developmental levels compare in effectiveness (Cummings & Davies, 2002).

In addition to child characteristics, other family characteristics such as parental mental illness may influence children's perceptions of marital conflict. Individuals experiencing psychological disorders often experience high levels of marital conflict (Cummings et al., 2000), and exposure to destructive marital discord helps explain why parental symptoms of psychopathology are associated with decreased child functioning (Cummings et al., 2005; Du Rocher Schudlich et al., 2003; El Sheikh & Flanagan, 2001). Additional research is needed to explore how the combination of exposure to both marital conflict and parental psychopathology impacts children's emotion regulation. Specifically, what additional meaning might an interparental disagreement have to a child when one of those parents is experiencing depression, alcohol dependence, or other conditions? How might children's emotional reactions differ in terms of their content, intensity, duration, and expression? How would children respond behaviorally in this context? From the emotional security perspective, children in this context may see family stability as under constant threat from parental mental illness. The additional threat of marital discord may therefore result in extremely intense negative reactions because children will need to be extremely sensitive to family events. Children exposed to high levels of marital conflict in combination with parental mental illness may be even more prone to intervention or avoidance than those exposed to high levels of destructive conflict alone.

Another important future direction involves child agency. Previous studies have made it clear that children react behaviorally to interparental disagreements, sometimes avoiding them by leaving the room or psychologically distancing themselves, other times intervening in conflict by interrupting or by attempting to resolve the problem themselves. ESH offers a clear theoretical explanation for these phenomena: Children are doing their best to reduce the threat they believe marital conflict poses. This reduction in threat may be perceptual (psychological distancing) or actual (interrupting parents might stop them from fighting). The implication is that the relationship between marital conflict and children's emotion regulation need not be in one direction. Children's emotion regulation behavior may reduce (or inadvertently increase) levels of marital conflict. Little research has addressed this possibility. Impulses to intervene in conflict have been reported in previous studies, and high levels of discord are related to children's decreased feelings of efficacy in dealing with conflict (Cummings & Schermerhorn, 2003). It is still unclear how child intervention into conflict or mere presence during conflict might affect parent behavior. One recent study found that when children are present, interparental conflict tends to be more destructive (Papp et al., 2002). However, although based on a substantial sampling of naturalistic observations in the home, this study was correlational in nature, and causality cannot be inferred.

Directives for Interdisciplinary Collaboration

Most research in this area, particularly on the role of emotion regulation, has been conducted by developmental and clinical psychologists. Their expertise has helped bring about a greater awareness of the importance of marital relations to child development and has resulted in many of the findings described here. Nevertheless, future research will be greatly improved by collaborative research between developmental psychologists, clinical psychologists, sociologists, cultural anthropologists, physiological psychologists, and biologists.

There is increasing evidence for the importance of physiology in emotional self-regulation. Researchers now know that the experience of emotion is associated with a wide range of physiological events, including changes in skin conductance, heart rate, vagal tone, and hormone levels. Furthermore, studies show that family interactions are associated with these physiological experiences of emotion. Collaboration with physiological psychologists and biologists is therefore a valuable direction for future research. In particular, the emergence of unique profiles of emotion regulation such as secure, preoccupied, and dismissing may be associated with patterns of physiological responding. The work of Gross (chap. 1, this volume; Gross, 1998) indicates that differing strategies of regulating emotion have important consequences for physiology and long-term adjustment. Specifically, cognitive reappraisals of events as nonthreatening may decrease physiological arousal, whereas the suppression of emotional expression might actually increase it. From an emotional security perspective, dismissing children might engage in higher levels of reappraisal, thereby minimizing the potential threat of marital conflict. Thus, dismissing children might be expected to have physiological responding similar to secure children. Preoccupied children, however, make no attempt to reduce their emotional expression and likely are more physiologically reactive. Collaborative research is needed to formally test these hypotheses.

Vagal tone and cortisol levels represent two important avenues for such collaborative research. *Vagal tone* refers to the activity of the vagus nerve, an important nerve in the parasympathetic nervous system that connects the brain with the heart and helps control heart rate. Research indicates that toddlers with high baseline vagal tone approach strangers more quickly than other children (Fox & Field, 1989). In addition, the suppression of vagal tone (which is typically associated with focused attention, such as during a stressful situation or emotional interaction) may play an important role in children's emotion regulation (Gottman & Katz, 2002). *Cortisol* is a stress hormone that can be detected in saliva. As with vagal tone, individual differences in baseline levels of cortisol as well as increases and recovery of cortisol levels are important. Research indicates that children's cortisol production can be influenced by the quality of child care (Dettling, Parker, Lane, Sebanc, & Gunnar, 2000) and parental maltreatment (Hart, Gunnar, & Cicchetti, 1995). In addition, cortisol levels are associated with insecure attachment (Lyons-Ruth, 1996).

Another important direction for interdisciplinary collaboration is the study of how children's abilities to regulate emotion in the face of marital discord vary from culture to culture. Cultural anthropologists and sociologists may provide the essential expertise for this endeavor. To date, studies have examined marital conflict and children's emotional security in Wales (Goeke-Morey et al., 2003), and Chile (Cummings, Wilson, & Shamir, 2003). Several similarities in children's reactions have been noted; children across cultures are adversely affected by marital conflict, especially unresolved conflict. However, important differences have also emerged. For example, Chilean children appear to be more sensitive to marital conflict than American children. Chilean children react with greater sadness to unresolved disagreements and have more negative expectations for future conflict than children in the United States. A comparison of American and Israeli children revealed a similar pattern: Both groups experienced more negative reactions to intense and unresolved conflict than to constructive conflict (Shamir, Cummings, Davies, & Goeke-Morey, 2005). However, Israeli children reacted less negatively to unresolved conflicts and less positively to resolved conflicts than American children, indicating resolution as less meaningful in the appraisal of conflict.

These studies suggest cultural context as an important factor in the relationship between marital discord and children's emotion regulation. Future research is needed to broaden the number of differing cultures examined. For example, little research has been conducted on the effects of marital discord on children in China, India, Russia, or Africa. Collaborative work with cultural anthropologists and sociologists can help ensure that such research is conducted in a culturally sensitive and relevant format. Furthermore, such collaboration is imperative for the interpretation of results. The detection of any existing cultural differences represents an important step forward, but it is equally important to develop insight into why these similarities and differences exist. For example, cultural differences in children's responding to marital conflict may reflect distinctions between collectivistic and individualistic traditions. Children in more collectivistic cultures may view disruptions to family functioning as particularly threatening or may have been socialized to attend closely to family interactions. However, cultures in which commitment is highly valued and divorce is discouraged may view conflict as unlikely to impact family stability. Children's responses to interparental conflict may also be influenced by cultural beliefs about children's role in the family. For example, in societies in which children's submission and obedience are valued, children may be less likely to intervene in marital conflict. Furthermore, ongoing struggles with political or ethnic violence in communities may contribute to children's emotional insecurity. The understanding of societal or national characteristics and patterns of changes in those characteristics that sociologists and cultural anthropologists observe will be essential for the explanation of cultural differences.

Clinical, Social, and Public Policy Implications

Given both the inevitability of disagreements and the current high rates of destructive marital discord, children's exposure to marital conflict represents an important clinical, social, and public policy concern. An additional concern is that public opinion regarding marital disagreements, as well as some of the professional advice given to the public, is often inaccurate and frequently ignores children's perspectives.

Findings indicating that children's emotional self-regulation is an important mediator of the relationship between marital discord and children's adjustment have important implications for addressing these concerns. Recent studies identifying the conflict tactics potentially harmful to children's abilities to regulate emotion can inform parent-education programs designed to instruct parents how to better handle their disagreements. Parents may not be aware of how sensitive children can be to disagreements between their parents, or of how specific conflict strategies that they use may place their children at increased risk for the development of adjustment problems.

Merely educating parents about these findings may make a difference in families. However, prevention programs and therapeutic interventions can also teach parents to use more constructive conflict tactics as an important way of addressing this social problem.

Because children's emotional security is based largely on their family experiences and is hypothesized to serve an adaptive, goal-oriented function (at least in the short term), it may be both impossible and undesirable to use child-focused clinical interventions to change insecure children to secure children. Children's perceptions of marital conflict as threatening may well be accurate, and the associated emotional, behavioral, and cognitive reactions are designed to reduce the threat children experience. Thus, children in high-conflict homes might be especially well served by programs targeting parent behavior to create families that foster emotional security, rather than directly targeting children's own emotion regulation. Nevertheless, an additional component to help children better cope with interparental discord may be a valuable feature of intervention programs. For example, children might be taught to avoid involvement in their parents' disagreements (involvement may place children at risk for parental retaliation, particularly in violent homes) and to minimize or reduce contexts for exposure to conflict. In addition, it is important for children to understand that their parents' disagreements are not their fault.

It is important that clinicians address these issues in their practice with couples and families and that public policy incorporate them into programs for at-risk children. However, development of such interventions is in an early stage, and the payoff for intervention to improve marital relations and children's emotional security in families is still unknown.

REFERENCES

Ball, F. L. J., Cowan, P., & Cowan, C. P. (1995). Who's got the power? Gender differences in partners' perceptions of influence during marital problem-solving discussions. *Family Process, 34,* 303–321.

Bandura, A. (1973). *Aggression: A social learning analysis.* Oxford, England: Prentice-Hall.

Cole, P. M., Martin, S. E., & Dennis, T. A. (2004). Emotion regulation as a scientific construct: Methodological challenges and directions for child development research. *Child Development, 75,* 317–333.

Cole, P. M., Zahn-Waxler, C., & Smith, D. K. (1994). Expressive control during a disappointment: Variations related to preschoolers' behavior problems. *Developmental Psychology, 30,* 835–846.

Crockenberg, S., & Langrock, A. (2001). The role of specific emotions in children's responses to interparental conflict: A test of the model. *Journal of Family Psychology, 15,* 163–182.

Cummings, E. M. (1994). Marital conflict and children's functioning. *Social Development, 3*, 16–36.

Cummings, E. M., & Davies, P. T. (1996). Emotional security as a regulatory process in normal development and the development of psychopathology. *Development and Psychopathology, 8*, 123–139.

Cummings, E. M., & Davies, P. T. (2002). Effects of marital conflict on children: Recent advances and emerging themes in process-oriented research. *Journal of Child Psychology and Psychiatry and Allied Disciplines, 43*, 31–63.

Cummings, E. M., Davies, P. T., & Campbell, S. B. (2000). *Developmental psychopathology and family process: Theory, research, and clinical implications*. New York: Guilford Press.

Cummings, E. M., Goeke-Morey, M. C., & Papp, L. M. (2003). Children's responses to everyday marital conflict tactics in the home. *Child Development, 74*, 1918–1929.

Cummings, E. M., Goeke-Morey, M. C., & Papp, L. M. (2004). Everyday marital conflict and child aggression in the home. *Journal of Abnormal Child Psychology, 32*, 191–202.

Cummings, E. M., Goeke-Morey, M. C., Papp, L. M., & Dukewich, T. L. (2002). Children's responses to mothers' and fathers' emotionality and conflict tactics during marital conflict in the home. *Journal of Family Psychology, 16*, 478–492.

Cummings, E. M., Keller, P. S., & Davies, P. T. (2005). Toward a family process model of maternal and paternal depressive symptoms: Exploring multiple relations with child and family functioning. *Journal of Child Psychology and Psychiatry, 46*, 479–489.

Cummings, E. M., & Schermerhorn, A. C. (2003). A developmental perspective on children as agents in the family. In L. Kuczynski (Ed.), *Handbook of dynamics in parent–child relations* (pp. 91–108). Thousand Oaks, CA: Sage.

Cummings, E. M., Wilson, J., & Shamir, H. (2003). Reactions of Chilean and U.S. children to marital discord. *International Journal of Behavioral Development, 27*, 437–444.

Davies, P. T., & Cummings, E. M. (1994). Marital conflict and child adjustment: An emotional security hypothesis. *Psychological Bulletin, 116*, 387–411.

Davies, P. T., & Cummings, E. M. (1998). Exploring children's emotional security as a mediator of the link between marital relations and child adjustment. *Child Development, 69*, 124–139.

Davies, P. T., Cummings, E. M., & Winter, M. A. (2004). Pathways between profiles of family functioning, child security in the interparental subsystem, and child psychological problems. *Development and Psychopathology, 16*, 525–550.

Davies, P. T., & Forman, E. M. (2002). Children's patterns of preserving emotional security in the interparental subsystem. *Child Development, 73*, 1880–1903.

Davies, P. T., Harold, G. T., Goeke-Morey, M. C., & Cummings, E. M. (2002). Child emotional security and interparental conflict. *Monographs of the Society for Research in Child Development, 67*(3, Serial No. 270).

Davies, P. T., Myers, R. L., Cummings, E. M., & Heindel, S. (1999). Adult conflict history and children's subsequent responses to conflict: An experimental test. *Journal of Family Psychology, 13,* 610–628.

Dettling, A. C., Parker, S. W., Lane, S., Sebanc, A., & Gunnar, M. R. (2000). Quality of care and temperament determine changes in cortisol concentration over the day for young children in childcare. *Psychoneuroendocrinology, 25,* 819–836.

Du Rocher Schudlich, T., & Cummings, E. M. (2003). Parental dysphoria and children's internalizing symptoms: Marital conflict styles as mediators of risk. *Child Development, 74,* 1–19.

El Sheikh, M., & Cummings, E. M. (1995). Children's responses to angry adult behavior as a function of experimentally manipulated exposure to resolved and unresolved conflict. *Social Development, 4,* 75–91.

El Sheikh, M., Cummings, E. M., & Reiter, S. (1996). Preschoolers' responses to ongoing interadult conflict: The role of prior exposure to resolved versus unresolved arguments. *Journal of Abnormal Child Psychology, 24,* 665–679.

El Sheikh, M., & Flanagan, E. (2001). Parental problem drinking and children's adjustment: Family conflict and parental depression as mediators and moderators of risk. *Journal of Abnormal Child Psychology, 29,* 417–432.

Fox, N. A., & Field, T. M. (1989). Individual differences in preschool entry behavior. *Journal of Applied Developmental Psychology, 10,* 527–540.

Goeke-Morey, M. C., Cummings, E. M., Harold, G. T., & Shelton, K. H. (2003). Categories and continua of destructive and constructive conflict tactics from the perspective of U.S. and Welsh children. *Journal of Family Psychology, 17,* 327–338.

Gottman, J. M., & Katz, L. F. (2002). Children's emotional reactions to stressful parent–child interactions: The link between emotion regulation and vagal tone. *Marriage and Family Review, 34,* 265–283.

Gross, J. J. (1998). Antecedent- and response-focused emotion regulation: Divergent consequences for experience, expression, and physiology. *Journal of Personality and Social Psychology, 74,* 224–237.

Grych, J. H., & Fincham, F. D. (1990). Marital conflict and children's adjustment: A cognitive contextual framework. *Psychological Bulletin, 108,* 267–290.

Hart, J., Gunnar, M., & Cicchetti, D. (1995). Salivary cortisol in maltreated children: Evidence of relations between neuroendocrine activity and social competence. *Development and Psychopathology, 7,* 11–26.

Loving, T. J., Heffner, K. L., Kiecolt-Glaser, J., Glaser, R., & Malarkey, W. B. (2004). Stress hormone changes and marital conflict: Spouses' relative power makes a difference. *Journal of Marriage and Family, 66,* 595–612.

Lyons-Ruth, K. (1996). Attachment relationships among children with aggressive behavior problems: The role of disorganized early attachment patterns. *Journal of Consulting and Clinical Psychology, 64,* 64–73.

Mikulincer, M., Shaver, P. R., & Pereg, D. (2003). Attachment theory and affect regulation: The dynamics, development, and cognitive consequences of attachment-related strategies. *Motivation and Emotion, 27,* 77–102.

Papp, L. M., Cummings, E. M., & Goeke-Morey, M. C. (2002). Marital conflicts in the home when children are present versus absent. *Developmental Psychology, 38*, 774–783.

Shamir, H., Cummings, E. M., Davies, P. T., & Goeke-Morey, M. C. (2005). Children's reactions to marital conflict in Israel and in the U.S. *Parenting: Science and Practice, 5*, 371–386.

Shamir, H., Du Rocher Schudlich, T., & Cummings, E. M. (2001). Marital conflict, parenting styles, and children's representations of family relationships. *Parenting: Science and Practice, 1*, 123–151.

Thompson, R. A. (1994). Emotion regulation: A theme in search of a definition. *Monographs of the Society for Research in Child Development, 59*(2–3, Serial Nol. 240), 25–52.

9

INDIVIDUAL DIFFERENCES IN EMOTION REGULATION AND THEIR RELATION TO RISK TAKING DURING ADOLESCENCE

M. LYNNE COOPER, MINDY E. FLANAGAN,
AMELIA E. TALLEY, AND LADA MICHEAS

Risk taking is a prototypic feature of adolescence. Recent studies show that the majority of adolescents engage in risky behaviors, many on a regular basis (see Arnett, 1999, for a review). For example, in a national survey conducted in 1998 (Kann et al., 1998), half of all high school students had drunk alcohol in the past 30 days, and nearly one third had had five or more drinks on a single occasion during that same period. Fully half of all high school students had ever had sex, and of these, 30% and 40% of female and male students, respectively, had had four or more lifetime sex partners. Even though experts agree that risky behaviors can serve adaptive developmental needs during adolescence (e.g., Baumrind, 1987), the potentially negative consequences associated with such behaviors are, nevertheless, real. Indeed, accidents are the leading cause of death among adolescents. Homicide and AIDS also rank among the top five causes of death in this age group (see Sells & Blum, 1996, for a review).

Although heightened involvement in risky behaviors during adolescence is well established, the causes of this increase and its consequences for later development are less well understood. In the present chapter, we argue that risk-taking behavior can be usefully understood as an effort to regulate the quality of both positive and negative emotional experience. We review past research (both our own and that of others) and present previously unpublished data that bear on the validity of this proposition. We conclude with a discussion of the implications of this perspective for research and intervention.

CONCEPTUAL AND THEORETICAL ISSUES

Risk behaviors are volitional behaviors that involve trade-offs between short-term (usually affective) gains and potential long-term costs (Baumeister & Scher, 1988). For example, drinking or using drugs may appeal to an individual because of immediate benefits, such as relief from stress or sharing an enjoyable evening with friends, despite longer-term risks of an intoxication-related accident or injury. Thus, prototypic risk situations involve two or more competing goals in which the risk of a more remote, undesirable outcome is accepted (either implicitly or explicitly) as a cost of achieving a more immediate, desired outcome.

Risk Taking and the Central Role of Emotion

Traditional models of decision making under risk viewed these trade-offs in largely cognitive terms. That is, people were assumed to choose between alternative courses of action by assessing the desirability of each action's possible outcomes and weighting those outcomes by their probability of occurrence (see Edwards, 1954). Thus, cognitive evaluations were thought to drive the decision process in a more or less rational fashion. Research over the past 25 years has clearly demonstrated, however, the inadequacies of this model for predicting actual behavioral choice in risk situations (see Harless & Camerer, 1994, for a review).

Two broad categories of explanation for this failure have emerged. First, it is now widely accepted that people's risk calculus diverges from the normative expectations of the rational decision model because of cognitive errors in estimating the likelihood of future consequences and reliance on simplifying cognitive heuristics (e.g., Tversky & Kahneman, 1974). More important for the present purposes, however, failures in the predictive validity of this model also reflect the model's inattention to the role of emotions. Indeed, emotions are now thought to play at least two crucial roles in the risk decision process.

First, anticipated emotions—those the individual expects to experience under different choice scenarios—are thought to drive the weighting of consequences associated with each behavior option. Thus, anticipated emotions can be viewed as a component of the expected consequences of the decision even within the rational decision-making framework (Mellers, Schwartz, Ho, & Ritov, 1997). An individual will accordingly select a risky behavioral option when he or she believes that the option will lead to desired emotional outcomes (e.g., enhancing a neutral or positive mood, or relieving a dysphoric one). Although the mood-altering properties of certain risk behaviors are obvious—for example, recreational drugs whose pharmacological properties act directly on mood states—virtually all risk behaviors possess this potential. Taking a joy ride in a stolen car or having sex with an attractive partner can induce euphoric states or serve as diversions from more troubling mood states. Thus, to the extent that individuals recognize the mood-altering properties of risk behaviors, expectancies of positive (or negative) emotional outcomes associated with behavioral choices under risk should strongly influence the weighting of these alternatives. These considerations suggest that individuals may learn to engage in risky behaviors as one way to manage both positive and negative affective states.

Second, behavioral responses in risky situations can also be driven by feelings in the moment, such as fear or excitement. According to Loewenstein and colleagues (Loewenstein, Weber, Hsee, & Welch, 2001), immediate emotions can influence the decision process directly by providing information about the relative desirability of the impending decision alternatives, or indirectly (a) by altering the individual's expectations of the probability or desirability of future consequences or (b) by changing the way that these consequences are processed.

For example, consider how emotions experienced in the moment might shape risk decisions for adolescents at a party. The typically ebullient emotions experienced in such situations might lead them to accept a drink offered by peers to the extent that they attribute their positive mood to the prospect of drinking (cf. Schwartz & Clore's mood-as-information hypothesis, 1983). The experience of positive emotions might also lead adolescents to underestimate the likelihood that a negative outcome would result from accepting the drink, or provide them with false confidence that they could handle whatever consequences followed from having the drink. Finally, if adolescents believed that refusing the drink might lead to a potentially unpleasant interaction with peers, the desire to maintain their positive mood might also increase the likelihood of accepting the proffered drink (Isen, 1993).

Conversely, negative emotions experienced in the moment might also influence risk decisions. For example, socially awkward adolescents might approach the same party with feelings of anxiety and apprehension. Such feelings, in turn, might increase the attractiveness of a drink offered by their peers, at least to the extent that positive mood-altering properties are attributed to alcohol (cf. Leith & Baumeister, 1996). A negative mood state might also undermine adolescents' confidence in their ability to resist peer pressure, or make even more aversive the possibility of rejection or ridicule by peers if the drink were refused. Thus, momentary affect—whether positive or negative—can exert strong influences on the decision process, even when that affect is incidental (i.e., unrelated) to the decision at hand.

In sum, contemporary perspectives on risk-taking behaviors view emotions—as experienced in the moment and anticipated in the future—as central, driving forces behind the risk-decision process. Moreover, both negative and positive emotions are thought to play a role, influencing risk decisions through distinct motivation–emotion pathways. Finally, although not all pathways are thought to involve emotion regulation processes (e.g., some effects may be mediated by changes in information processing), direct efforts to manage emotions are thought to play an important role in motivating risk-taking behaviors.

Dual Pathways to Risk Taking

The idea that distinct positive and negative motivation–emotion pathways underlie risk-taking behaviors has received little formal attention even though this view is broadly consistent with major motivational theories of behavior. According to Gray (1970), two neurologically distinct motivation systems underlie behavior. The behavioral inhibition system (BIS) regulates behaviors that involve avoidance or escape from negative or painful experiences (aversive or avoidant behaviors), whereas the behavior activation system (BAS) regulates behaviors that involve the pursuit of positive or pleasurable ones (appetitive or approach behaviors). Further, individuals are thought to differ in a stable traitlike manner in the relative sensitivity of the two systems. People who are high in BIS are especially responsive to threat and punishment cues, and are therefore predisposed to experience negative affect and to avoidant and fearful responding. In contrast, individuals who are high in BAS are especially responsive to reward cues, and are thus predisposed to experience positive affect and engage in reward-seeking behaviors. Indeed, high levels of the personality traits neuroticism and extraversion are thought to derive from overactive BIS and BAS systems, respectively (Gray, 1970).

Consistent with the notion of two distinct pathways, past research indicates that people attribute both positive-mood-enhancing and negative-mood-altering properties to a wide range of risky behaviors (Fromme, Katz, & D'Amico, 1997). Perhaps more important, our research shows that people attribute their own risk behaviors to conscious efforts to pursue positive emotional experiences, as well as to escape or cope with negative ones (Cooper, 1994; Cooper, Shapiro, & Powers, 1998; Jackson, Cooper, Mintz, & Albino, 2003). Research from independent labs has not only replicated our findings for alcohol use (Stewart, Zeitlin, & Samoluk, 1996) and risky sexual behavior (Schachner & Shaver, 2004) but also extended them to other behavioral domains, including reasons for using tobacco (Cohen, McCarthy, Brown, & Myers, 2002) and illicit drugs (Boys, Marsden, & Strang, 2001), aggressing against others (Bushman, Baumeister, & Phillips, 2001), skipping school (Caffray & Schneider, 2000), and gambling (Cotte, 1997).

In the following sections, we identify and discuss a number of individual differences that should, if emotions and efforts to regulate them are central to risk taking, help us better understand differential vulnerabilities to diverse risk behaviors during adolescence and young adulthood. We first consider individual differences that are theoretically relevant to understanding risk taking driven by aversive motivation processes and then follow with a discussion of individual differences theoretically important to understanding risk taking driven by appetitive motivation processes. Finally, we discuss an important individual difference in the ability to self-regulate emotions and emotionally driven behaviors—impulsivity versus restraint—that we believe serves as a generalized vulnerability toward risk taking, exacerbating tendencies toward both aversive and appetitively motivated risk behaviors.

Individual Differences in the Experience of Negative Emotions and Efforts to Regulate Them

The Disposition to Experience Negative Emotions

To the extent that aversive motivation processes drive risk behaviors, individuals who are chronically predisposed to dysphoric mood states should engage in higher overall levels of risky behaviors. In addition, chronically dysphoric individuals—because of their greater BIS sensitivity—should be more sensitive to the experience (or even the threat of experience) of negative emotions, and thus less able to tolerate or cope with these emotions in constructive ways.

Extensive evidence—including results from a number of large-scale, prospective studies—supports the potential importance of a negative emotion pathway to risk taking. We have shown, for example, that negative emotions, stressful events that elicit negative emotions, and neuroticism predict alcohol use (Cooper, Agocha, & Sheldon, 2000; Cooper, Frone, Russell, & Mudar, 1995; Cooper, Russell, Skinner, Frone, & Mudar, 1992) and risky sexual behavior (Cooper et al., 2000). Further supporting an emotion-regulation interpretation of these data, we have also shown that the effects of negative emotions and neuroticism on alcohol use and risky sex are at least partly mediated by the use of alcohol and sex, respectively, to cope (Cooper et al., 2000). Finally, we have also shown that drinking to cope moderates the impact of stressors on alcohol-related outcomes such that stressors are more strongly linked to alcohol outcomes among individuals who drink to cope (Peirce, Frone, Russell, & Cooper, 1996).

The mediation and moderation findings for coping motives in alcohol involvement have since been replicated using both longitudinal (Wills, Sandy,

Shinar, & Yaeger, 1999) and diary (Hussong, 2003) methods. Similar results have also been reported linking stressors, negative emotions, and the disposition to experience negative emotions to tobacco (Cohen et al., 2002; Wills et al., 1999) and illicit drug use (Wills et al., 1999), violent behaviors (Caspi et al., 1997), conduct disorder (Krueger, Caspi, & Moffitt, 2000), and risky sexual behavior (Hoyle, Fejfar, & Miller, 2000). Together these data (in particular, the mediation and moderation results) suggest that risk taking may be the product of a person's efforts to down-regulate distress rather than the experience of emotional distress per se. In the next section, we consider whether some individuals are more likely than others to engage in risk behaviors in an effort to regulate negative affect, and if so, what individual differences distinguish them.

Individual Styles of Regulating Negative Emotions

Although no single agreed-upon typology of emotion regulation strategies exists, a crucial distinction shared by most typologies concerns strategies to regulate one's negative emotions through active approach or engagement (e.g., analyzing the problem) versus strategies that involve avoidance or withdrawal from the stressful situation, or denial, minimization, or escape from the emotions themselves (Thayer, Newman, & McClain, 1994). This distinction, though not without its limitations, has proven to be an important one for discriminating the adaptiveness of emotion regulation efforts.

Indeed, past research shows that avoidant strategies are not only widely seen as less effective ways to regulate negative emotions (Thayer et al., 1994) but are also consistently associated with adverse consequences, including diverse risk-taking behaviors. For example, avoidant styles of coping with negative emotions have been positively associated with alcohol use and drinking problems (Cooper et al., 1995), relapse among recovering alcoholics (Chung, Langenbucher, Labouvie, Pandina, & Moos, 2001), risky sexual behavior (Folkman, Chesney, Pollack, & Phillips, 1992), pathological gambling (Nower, Derevensky, & Gupta, 2004), and broadband indices of multiple risk or externalizing behaviors (Loesel & Bliesener, 1994). Whereas the evidence linking avoidance and risk behaviors is robust and relatively consistent across studies, data on the adaptiveness of approach strategies are inconsistent. Although the belief is widely held that approach strategies are effective ways to regulate negative emotions and reduce tension (e.g., Thayer et al., 1994), studies attempting to provide support for this notion frequently find no effects (see Carver & Scheier, 1994, for review).

Individual Differences in the Propensity to Seek Arousal and Positive Emotional Experiences

Thus far, we have focused on the role of negative emotions and efforts to regulate them. However, traditional theories of risk taking have focused almost exclusively on the regulation of arousal and positive emotions (e.g., Zuckerman, 1983). This perspective views risk taking as an appetitive or approach behavior in which individuals choose risky options as a way to achieve optimum arousal, enhance positive emotional experience, or both. Such a view highlights the role of individual differences in preferences for seeking arousal and positive emotional experiences but depicts an uncertain role for stable individual differences in the experience of positive emotions (i.e., positive emotionality), as well as for the experience of positive emotions as proximal precipitants of risk-taking behaviors.

The possibility that positive (relative to negative) emotional experience is less consequential for risk-taking behaviors is consistent with well-documented asymmetries in the motivational consequences of positive versus negative emotional states (Carver & Scheier, 1990). Negative emotions have been shown to have strong motivational consequences, prompting cognitive and behavioral efforts aimed at managing, minimizing, or eliminating the source of the problem or the emotions themselves. In contrast, people experiencing a positive mood tend to refrain from effortful activity in order to enjoy their mood (Forgas, 2003). Moreover, although people do report attempts to regulate their positive mood states, only a small percentage of naturally occurring mood regulation efforts involve positive affect, and these efforts more often involve down-regulation (chap. 1, this volume)—a goal that seems unlikely to be served by risk seeking. For these reasons, the following sections focus on individual differences in reward or arousal seeking and their relationship to risky behaviors.

Reward (or *arousal*) *seeking* (assessed by a variety of measures including thrill seeking, excitement seeking, sensation seeking, venturesomeness) refers to stable individual differences in preferences for varied, novel, complex, and intense sensations and experiences (Zuckerman, 1994). It is viewed as a component of extraversion in the big five model (Costa & McCrae, 1980), and differences in reward (arousal) seeking are thought to be rooted in the BAS, as previously discussed. Individuals who are high in reward (arousal) seeking show not only heightened sensitivity to reward cues but also diminished sensitivity to punishment cues (Gray, 1990). Together these differential sensitivities are thought to promote risk taking by increasing the attractiveness (or the weighting) of the short-term benefits promised by a risky behavioral choice, as well as by decreasing the aversiveness (or the weighting) of its potential long-term costs. Consistent with this analysis, individuals who are high in this trait tend to perceive more benefits for a variety of risk behaviors (including illicit drug use, heavy drinking, and risky sexual behavior) than do those who are low in the trait (Katz, Fromme, & D'Amico, 2000). They also perceive fewer risks, even for activities they have never tried, and anticipate experiencing less anxiety if they were to try the activity (Zuckerman & Kuhlman, 2000). Overall then, as Zuckerman and Kuhlman concluded, the approach gradient appears higher and the avoidance gradient (anticipated anxiety) lower among high reward (arousal) seekers over a range of risk-taking activities.

It is not surprising that substantial empirical evidence supports a link between various measures of reward or arousal seeking and multiple risk behaviors (see Horvath & Zuckerman, 1993, for a review). Several lines of evidence also indicate that appetitive motives mediate this link. We have shown, for example, that the effect of thrill seeking on alcohol use is mediated by enhancement (but not coping) motives for alcohol use (Cooper et al., 1995)—a finding that was recently replicated using a diary method (Hussong, 2003). People who strongly endorse drinking to enhance have also been shown to attend more closely to reward cues in a laboratory task (Colder & O'Connor, 2002), further underscoring reward sensitivity as a crucial factor in behaviors driven by appetitive motivation processes.

Individual Differences in Undercontrol or Impulsivity

Impulsivity is thought to include both the tendency to give in to urges, impulses, or desires and to respond to stimuli impetuously without reflection or planning (Revelle, 1997). The relative inability to control one's behavior is thought to stem from deficits in the self-regulation of affect, motivation, and arousal, as well as in working memory and higher-order cognitive functions that ordinarily give rise to hindsight, forethought, anticipatory behavior, and goal-directed action (Barkley, 1997). Impulsive individuals have difficulty inhibiting the prepotent response—that is, the response for which immediate reinforcement (whether positive or negative) is available. Substantial empirical support exists for a link between impulsivity and a range of risk-taking behaviors. For example, in separate meta-analyses of only partially overlapping literatures, both Miller and Lynam (2001) and Cale (in press) found an average effect in the .35 to .40 range between impulsivity or disinhibition and delinquent or antisocial behavior, and this was by far the strongest effect observed for any dimension of personality examined in either review. In a meta-analysis on personality and sexual risk taking, Hoyle and colleagues (2000) also found reliable, though more modest (from .10 to .23), effects on multiple indices of sexual risk taking for both constraint (a reverse scored index of impulsivity) and impulsivity.

Although most of the studies included in the above meta-analyses were cross-sectional, longitudinal studies also provide strong support for the role of impulsivity as a factor in adolescent risk-taking behavior. For example, undercontrol (variously conceptualized and measured) has been shown to prospectively predict drug abuse vulnerability (Tarter et al., 2003), the onset of gambling problems (Vitaro, Arseneault, & Tremblay, 1997), and the number of sexual partners (Breakwell, 1996) among adolescents. Data from a study of a complete birth cohort in Dunedin, New Zealand, showed that individual differences in constraint at age 18 predicted lower rates of substance dependence, alcohol abuse, conduct disorder, violent crime, unsafe sexual behavior, and dangerous driving habits 3 years later (Caspi et al., 1997; Krueger et al., 2000). Perhaps even more impressive, indicators of poor self-control based on behavioral observations in early childhood were found to prospectively predict antisocial behavior (e.g., destructiveness, bullying, lying), as independently evaluated by parents and teachers during middle childhood and adolescence (Caspi, Henry, McGee, Moffitt, & Silva, 1995). Thus, the data are clear in showing that deficits in impulse control play an important role in predisposing individuals to risky behavioral decisions.

As previously indicated, we believe that impulsivity (or low constraint) serves as a general risk factor, promoting risky behaviors undertaken in service of both negative affect reduction and positive emotion enhancement and arousal seeking. Consistent with this view, results of factor analytic studies of basic personality dimensions reveal that impulsivity or constraint forms a discrete factor, separable from both positive emotionality and incentive sensitivity, and negative emotionality and threat sensitivity (Clark & Watson, 1999). This view is also compatible with models that postulate the existence of an effortful cognitive control mechanism distinct from approach and avoidance systems (Rothbart, Ellis, & Posner, 2004). According to these models, impulsive behavior might arise from an overactive approach system, an insensitive inhibition system, deficient cognitive control, or a combination of these.

Although only a few studies have examined the possibility that impulsivity interacts with factors reflecting either the approach or avoidance system, results tend to support this view. Using data from the Dunedin study, Caspi and colleagues (1997) showed that the highest levels of involvement in multiple risk behaviors at age 21 occurred among those who were high on negative emotionality and low on constraint at age 18 (though the interaction of the two factors was not directly tested). In prospective studies of adjustment among children, Eisenberg and colleagues have similarly shown that high levels of negative emotionality combine with high levels of behavioral undercontrol to predict particularly poor outcomes, including aggressive and antisocial behavior (Eisenberg, Fabes, & Murphy, 1995). In one of the most direct tests of this idea, we found that impulsivity interacted with surgency (a facet of extraversion that reflects a strong approach orientation) to predict having sex for enhancement reasons and risky sexual practices, such that individuals who were high on both impulsivity and surgency were the most likely to report high levels of both behaviors (Cooper et al., 2000).

METHODOLOGICAL ISSUES

Though strongly supporting the role of emotions and efforts to regulate them as contributing factors to risk-taking behaviors, the present review also points to several gaps in the literature. First, because the majority of past studies have focused on one or at most a few predictors at a time, it is not always clear whether observed effects are independent or overlapping. In a similar manner, the majority of empirical studies have focused on only one of the two hypothesized emotion regulation pathways, thus leaving largely unanswered questions about the independence and relative importance of contributions of the two pathways to risk taking. Likewise, although impulsivity is thought to operate independently of both negative and positive emotion regulation pathways, and should therefore exert unique effects on risk-taking behaviors, only a few studies have simultaneously considered the contributions of all three sets of factors. Thus, whether impulsivity also exerts unique effects on risk-taking behaviors remains unclear.

Perhaps more important, focusing on single predictors in isolation emphasizes simplistic cause–effect relationships, rather than networks of causal variables that work together to shape risk-taking behaviors. This unfortunate emphasis has led to a neglect of both mediation and moderation, despite the central role such mechanisms are thought to play in emotion regulation processes. Indeed, the core assumption that the behavioral consequences of emotion experience are more strongly shaped by people's efforts to regulate their emotions than by the emotions themselves implies both mediation and moderation of the effects of emotion experience on risk taking by regulatory efforts, styles, or capacities. Specifically, to the extent that this view is valid, the effects of emotional experience on risky behaviors should be at least partly mediated by individual differences in regulatory styles and abilities. In other words, the experience of certain emotions should elicit efforts to regulate these emotions, which in turn could promote riskier decisions. Second, to the extent that this view is valid, one would also expect to see stronger relationships between emotional experience (or other indicators of reward or threat sensitivity) and risk-taking behaviors among those who rely on maladaptive styles of regulating their emotions, such as avoidance coping, or who have specific deficits in their emotion regulation capacities (e.g., are impulsive). Presumably those who effectively manage their emotional experience would find other more adaptive (less risky) ways to regulate their mood states.

Finally, most studies have focused on a single risk behavior, or occasionally several risk behaviors within a closely related domain (e.g., alcohol and tobacco use), rather than examining broad indices of involvement in multiple risk behaviors. Although focusing on individual risk behaviors is useful when the goal is to understand what drives involvement in that specific behavior, examining one or only a few closely related risk behaviors in isolation precludes us from determining whether deficits in emotion regulation lie at the heart of a general predisposition to risk taking, or contribute more narrowly to specific risk behaviors. Whereas the extant literature certainly suggests a broad role for emotion regulation processes, including multiple risk behaviors in a single study would allow for a more direct test of this possibility.

SOME EMPIRICAL EVIDENCE ADDRESSING THESE ISSUES

In the following sections, we summarize the results of two studies—one recently published and one unpublished—that bear directly on each of these issues. The data for both studies were taken from an ongoing, longitudinal study of a random sample of community-residing Black and White adolescents ($N = 2,051$), age 13- to 19-years-old at Time 1. Before presenting these data, we briefly describe the methodology of this larger study.

Overview of Study Methodology

Participants in this study were interviewed up to five times over 15 years, using a combination of interviewer- and self-administered (for more sensitive questions) formats for the first three waves and telephone interviews for the last two waves. The recently published study (Cooper, Wood, Orcutt, & Albino, 2003) used data from 1,978 Time 1 participants (mean age = 16.7 years) who had complete data on the subset of relevant measures, as well as from a subset of these respondents who were reinterviewed at Time 2 (mean age = 21.4 years). The unpublished study (hereinafter referred to as the *follow-up study*) used data from the first four waves of interviews. For reasons unrelated to the present study, only those participants who were 27 or younger at Time 3 were eligible to participate at Time 4. Thus, the sample for the follow-up study included 996, 886, 699, and 518 participants, respectively, at Times 1 through 4, with mean ages at successive waves of 15.1, 19.7, 25.4, and 26.9 years. Male and female youths and majority and minority (predominantly Black) youths were equally represented in the Time 1 sample. However, fewer male than female participants were retained in the sample over time.

Both studies included measures of involvement in multiple risk behaviors, though they were operationalized differently. The published study used a higher-order factor to model covariance among a set of first-order factors indexing substance use, risky sexual behavior, delinquent behaviors, and educational underachievement. In the follow-up study, we created a composite variable reflecting involvement (at each wave) in each of seven different risky behaviors, including the number of sexual partners, risky sexual practices, frequency of heavy drinking, drug use, truant behaviors, property crimes, and violent behaviors. The multiple-risk variable was created for each wave by counting the number of behaviors (of 7) for which the individual's score was at or above the 75th percentile of the distribution. Four individual difference measures were examined as predictors of risk-taking behaviors across the two studies: the dispositional tendency to experience negative emotions, avoidance coping, thrill and adventure seeking (TAS), and impulsivity.

The Initial Study

Using structural equation modeling, we examined the independent contributions of negative emotions, avoidance coping, TAS, and impulsivity to the previously described higher-order risk factor. Results showed that impulsivity and avoidance coping, but not negative emotions, significantly predicted the higher-order factor. Given that the negative emotion composite was highly correlated with avoidance coping ($r = .65$), it is possible that the experience of negative emotions indirectly contributed to involvement in the higher-order factor by eliciting avoidant coping responses. However, this possibility was not tested in the data. TAS was unrelated to the higher-order risk factor ($\beta = .04$) in the full sample. Subsequent cross-race models revealed, however, that TAS was a significant positive predictor of the higher-order factor among White but not Black adolescents. We also tested all possible two-way interactions among the four predictors. Results showed that impulsivity interacted with avoidance coping to predict involvement in the higher-order risk factor. Consistent with expectation, plotting the interaction showed that maladaptive coping was more strongly related to risky behaviors among individuals who were high rather than low in impulsivity. Finally, avoidance coping, but none of the remaining factors, prospectively predicted the onset of risky behaviors (at Time 2) among the subset of individuals who reported little or no risk involvement at Time 1 ($n = 344$).

The Follow-Up Study

In the follow-up study, we sought to both replicate these findings in a subsample of the original study and to extend them longitudinally to determine if differences in the experience and regulation of both negative and positive emotions during adolescence forecast risk-taking behaviors into young adulthood. In addition, we wanted to test whether avoidance coping and impulsivity mediated the effects of negative emotionality on patterns of risk taking. Finally, we also examined interactions among these factors to determine if the previously obtained interaction between avoidance coping and impulsivity was replicated in this subsample and, if so, whether the unique vulnerabilities created by the intersection of these factors persisted across time.

Using data from four waves of interviews, a series of random regression coefficient models (Bryk & Raudenbush, 1992) was estimated to address these issues. In all models, change in risky behaviors was modeled by three parameters: an initial level or intercept (estimated at age 14), linear change, and quadratic change. These components in turn were predicted from baseline (i.e., Time 1) differences in the four predictor variables. Gender and race were controlled in all analyses.

Do Initial Differences Forecast Patterns of Risky Behavior Into Young Adulthood?

Results of our first analysis revealed that youths who experienced high levels of negative emotions, relied on avoidant forms of coping with these emotions, and were highly impulsive reported significantly higher levels of risk behaviors at age 14. In addition, youths who were high in TAS reported marginally higher levels of risk behavior at age 14. None of the four predictors accounted for differences in rates of either linear or quadratic growth, suggesting that differences that were in place at baseline were maintained throughout adolescence and into young adulthood.

Do Coping Styles and Regulatory Capacity Mediate the Effects of Emotion Experience?

Following procedures outlined by Baron and Kenny (1986), we found evidence of substantial, though not complete, mediation of the effects of negative emotions on risk behaviors. Specifically, the total effect of negative emotions on risky behaviors was reduced from $b = .40$ to $b = .17$, by controlling for impulsivity and avoidance coping. Consistent with the distinction between aversive and appetitive processes, TAS did not mediate the relationship between negative emotions and risky behaviors.

Do These Factors Interact to Create High-Risk Subgroups?

In the final analysis, all possible two-way interactions among the four predictors were added to a model that already included the main effects and covariates. Results indicated that impulsivity interacted with avoidance coping to predict average levels of risk behavior at age 14, thus replicating our earlier finding. In addition, avoidance coping interacted with both TAS and negative emotions to predict the quadratic component of change. Plotting the interactions revealed important commonalities in the form of the three interactions. (As an example, the interaction between avoidance coping and impulsivity is shown in Figure 9.1.) For all three interactions, the subgroup that was low on both variables reported the lowest levels of risk behaviors on average across time; the subgroup that was high on both variables reported the highest levels; and the two low–high subgroups reported intermediate levels. Moreover, in all cases, the maximum difference between the low–low and the high–high groups occurred at age 21 or older, suggesting that differences between the groups extended beyond Time 1, when predictors and outcomes were concurrently assessed. Finally, for all three interactions, the absolute size of the maximum difference between the low–low and high–high groups was large, with effect sizes (d) ranging from .98 (comparing the

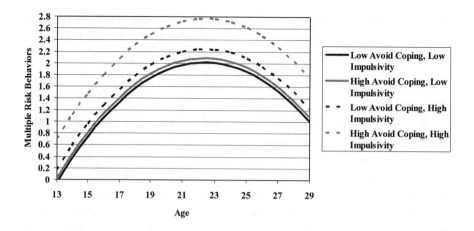

Figure 9.1. Interaction of avoidance coping and impulsivity with regard to risk behaviors.

low avoidance coping, low TAS group with the high–high group) to 1.22 (comparing the low avoidance coping–low impulsivity group with the high–high group). Despite strong similarities, one noteworthy difference was observed between the avoidance–impulsivity interaction. Consistent with the presence of significant quadratic components for the avoidance–TAS and avoidance–negative emotions interactions, the differences between the implied subgroups dissipated by their late 20s, whereas the high impulsive–high avoidance coping group continued to exhibit greatly elevated levels of risk behaviors throughout their 20s.

SUMMARY AND IMPLICATIONS FOR FUTURE RESEARCH

Broadly speaking, the results of these studies together with the reviewed literature highlight the importance of two distinct motivational pathways to risk taking—an aversive pathway driven primarily by the experience of negative emotions and efforts to down regulate them, and an approach pathway aimed at up regulating positive emotional experiences. In contrast to earlier theoretical models that emphasized the role of appetitive behaviors, results of the present studies suggest that risk behaviors may be more strongly linked to avoidance than approach phenomena. Indeed, avoidance coping exhibited the strongest relationship to both the higher-order risk factor (in the initial published study) and to the risk composite (in the follow-up study), and it was the only factor to predict the onset of risk behaviors in a true prospective analysis. In addition, avoidance coping interacted with impulsivity to define a uniquely vulnerable subgroup that remained at elevated risk throughout their 20s. Thus, avoidance coping appears to play a uniquely important role in directly fostering risky decision processes and in exacerbating risky tendencies among undercontrolled individuals.

In contrast, the experience of negative emotions was not strongly related to risk taking in either study but instead appeared to indirectly influence risk taking through its effects on regulatory efforts and capacities. Thus, consistent with the view that it is what people do to regulate their emotions that matters, negative emotions appear to indirectly foster risk taking by eliciting avoidant forms of coping and by undermining effective self-control.

Our results, along with findings from the larger literature, also indicate an important role for impulsivity. Theoretically, impulsivity is seen as a releaser of prepotent responses, whether those responses are driven by avoidant or appetitive impulses. As such, it is thought to be distinct from, but to contribute to, both appetitive and aversive motivational processes. Consistent with this view, impulsivity made a significant independent contribution to risk taking in both sets of analyses. However, it interacted only with avoidance coping. Thus, contrary to expectation, our data suggests that impulsivity may amplify prepotent aversive, but not appetitive, responses.

Finally, the weakest results were obtained for efforts to regulate positive emotions (in the form of thrill seeking). Of course, we cannot rule out the possibility that these findings are specific to the measure we used or to our sample. At least somewhat countering this possibility, we showed in our earlier study that TAS exerted specific effects (over and above its indirect effect through the higher-order risk factor) on both alcohol use and violent behavior. These data thus raise the possibility that appetitive motivation processes contribute more narrowly to specific risk behaviors rather than to a broad, general disposition to risk taking.

The foregoing highlights several important directions for future research. First, more research including a broader range of measures central to both pathways is clearly warranted. This is particularly true for the positive emotion–approach motivation pathway, which was represented in our data by only a single measure (thrill and adventure seeking). Although this measure is thought to reflect a core component of sensation seeking (Zuckerman, 1994), a broader measure would provide a more definitive test of the contributions of reward (arousal) seeking processes. Inclusion of a measure of positive emotions would also permit an explicit test of the potential contributions of positive emotional experience to risk-taking behaviors. Second, it is possible that our use of composite measures of distinct emotions (e.g., depression, hostility) and distinct coping styles (e.g., avoidance coping, anger suppression) masked effects specific to individual components. This is of particular concern for hostility, which some prior research suggests may be an especially potent predictor of risk-taking behavior (e.g., Caspi et al., 1997). Future studies should therefore attempt to determine whether the specific components contribute equally and similarly to risk-taking behaviors (an assumption underpinning our use of composite measures), or whether specific emotions or coping strategies make distinctive contributions. Third, given the crucial role that avoidance coping appears to play, future research should attempt to delineate both the immediate and developmental processes whereby avoidance coping leads to risky behaviors. Finally, the fact that some of our findings were discrepant with prior research highlights the importance of simultaneously evaluating the contributions of approach and avoidance processes along with those of undercontrol. Indeed, zero-order correlations between each of these predictors and broadband risk measures were roughly similar in magnitude, thus suggesting that failure to examine these factors in concert may lead to an overestimation of the importance of specific processes or pathways. Obviously this conclusion must be regarded as tentative pending replication in different samples using a broader representation of core constructs within both pathways.

IMPLICATIONS FOR INTERVENTION

Results of the present study suggest that universal intervention efforts aimed at promoting more adaptive ways of coping with negative emotions and of regulating one's impulses could have far-reaching consequences. Consistent with this contention, several highly efficacious intervention programs focus on just these goals. For example, anger management therapy (reviewed in Hinshaw, 1996) has been highly successful in reducing delinquent behaviors (e.g., fighting, shoplifting) common among children with attention-deficit/hyperactivity disorder. In this approach, children are first taught to recognize their own unique signs of impending anger. Once these cues have been identified, each child selects and then practices a particular cognitive or behavior strategy that can be used whenever this cue occurs. The overarching goal is to teach the child alternative responses that not only lack the negative social consequences common to delinquent behaviors but also alleviate the negative affect thought to trigger the undesirable behavior. Anger management therapy has also been effective in reducing alcohol use among heavy-drinking college students (Deffenbacher & Oetting, 2002), cocaine use among dependent adults (Reilly & Shopshire, 2000), and both substance use and sexual risk taking among incarcerated juvenile offenders (St. Lawrence, Crosby, Belcher, Yazdani, & Brasfield, 1999).

Dialectic behavior therapy (DBT; Linehan, 1993), an approach that focuses on treating deficits in emotional control and distress tolerance, appears equally promising for reducing involvement in a wide range of risk behaviors during adolescence. DBT approaches, which teach new means of managing emotional distress and of inhibiting destructive initial response tendencies, have been proven efficacious in the treatment of borderline personality disorder (a disorder characterized by involvement in a variety of risky behaviors), substance use, and eating disorders (Robins & Chapman, 2004).

Thus, interventions aimed at teaching more effective means of regulating one's emotions and behaviors appear promising as generalized or universal intervention strategies. Of course, on the basis of our data alone, we cannot say whether such approaches would ultimately prove more useful for children and adolescents who engage in multiple risk behaviors or for those whose difficulties are manifest primarily in one behavioral arena. The fact that the efficacy of such approaches has been demonstrated across diverse risk behaviors bodes well, however, for the utility of this approach both as a general and specific intervention strategy.

REFERENCES

Arnett, J. J. (1999). Adolescent storm and stress, reconsidered. *American Psychologist, 54*, 317–326.

Barkley, R. A. (1997). Behavioral inhibition, sustained attention, and executive functions: Constructing a unifying theory of ADHD. *Psychological Bulletin, 121*, 65–94.

Baron, R. M., & Kenny, D. A. (1986). The moderator–mediator variable distinction in social psychological research: Conceptual, strategic, and statistical considerations. *Journal of Personality and Social Psychology, 51*, 1173–1182.

Baumeister, R. F., & Scher, S. J. (1988). Self-defeating behavior patterns among normal individuals: Review and analysis of common self-destructive tendencies. *Psychological Bulletin, 104*, 3–22.

Baumrind, D. (1987, Fall). A developmental perspective on adolescent risk taking in contemporary America. *New Directions for Child Development, 37*, 93–125.

Boys, A., Marsden, J., & Strang, J. (2001). Understanding reasons for drug use amongst young people: A functional perspective. *Health Education Research, 16*, 457–469.

Breakwell, G. M. (1996). Risk estimation and sexual behavior: A longitudinal study of 16- to 21-year-olds. *Journal of Health Psychology, 1*, 79–91.

Bryk, A. S., & Raudenbush, S. W. (1992). *Hierarchical linear models for social and behavioral research: Applications and data analysis methods.* Newbury Park, CA: Sage.

Bushman, B. J., Baumeister, R. F., & Phillips, C. M. (2001). Do people aggress to improve their mood? Catharsis beliefs, affect regulation opportunity, and aggressive responding. *Journal of Personality and Social Psychology, 81*, 17–32.

Caffray, C. M., & Schneider, S. L. (2000). Why do they do it? Affective motivators in adolescents' decisions to participate in risky behaviours. *Cognition & Emotion, 14*, 543–576.

Cale, E. M. (in press). A quantitative review of the relations between the "Big 3" higher order personality dimensions and antisocial behavior. *Journal of Research in Personality.*

Carver, C. S., & Scheier, M. F. (1990). Principles of self-regulation: Action and emotion. In E. T. Higgins & R. M. Sorrentino (Eds.), *Handbook of motivation and cognition: Vol. 2. Foundations of social behavior* (pp. 3–52). New York: Guilford Press.

Carver, C. S., & Scheier, M. F. (1994). Situational coping and coping dispositions in a stressful transaction. *Journal of Personality and Social Psychology, 66*, 184–195.

Caspi, A., Begg, D., Dickson, N., Harrington, H., Langley, J., Moffitt, T. E., et al. (1997). Personality differences predict health-risk behaviors in young adulthood: Evidence from a longitudinal study. *Journal of Personality and Social Psychology, 73*, 1052–1063.

Caspi, A., Henry, B., McGee, R. O., Moffitt, T. E., & Silva, P. A. (1995). Temperamental origins of child and adolescent behavior problems: From age three to fifteen. *Child Development, 66*, 55–68.

Chung, T., Langenbucher, J., Labouvie, E., Pandina, R. J., & Moos, R. H. (2001). Changes in alcoholic patients' coping responses predict 12-month treatment outcomes. *Journal of Consulting and Clinical Psychology, 69*, 92–100.

Clark, L. A., & Watson, D. (1999). Temperament: A new paradigm for trait psychology. In L. A. Pervin & O. P. John (Eds.), *Handbook of personality: Theory and research* (2nd ed., pp. 399–423). New York: Guilford Press.

Cohen, L. M., McCarthy, D. M., Brown, S. A., & Myers, M. G. (2002). Negative affect combines with smoking outcome expectancies to predict smoking behavior over time. *Psychology of Addictive Behaviors, 16*, 91–97.

Colder, C. R., & O'Connor, R. (2002). Attention bias and disinhibited behavior as predictors of alcohol use and enhancement reasons for drinking. *Psychology of Addictive Behaviors, 16*, 325–332.

Cooper, M. L. (1994). Motivations for alcohol use among adolescents: Development and validation of a four-factor model. *Psychological Assessment, 6*, 117–128.

Cooper, M. L., Agocha, V. B., & Sheldon, M. S. (2000). A motivational perspective on risky behaviors: The role of personality and affect regulatory processes. *Journal of Personality, 68*, 1059–1088.

Cooper, M. L., Frone, M. R., Russell, M., & Mudar, P. (1995). Drinking to regulate positive and negative emotions: A motivational model of alcohol use. *Journal of Personality and Social Psychology, 69*, 990–1005.

Cooper, M. L., Russell, M., Skinner, J. B., Frone, M. R., & Mudar, P. (1992). Stress and alcohol use: Moderating effects of gender, coping, and alcohol expectancies. *Journal of Abnormal Psychology, 101*, 139–152.

Cooper, M. L., Shapiro, C. M., & Powers, A. M. (1998). Motivations for sex and sexual behavior among adolescents and young adults: A functional perspective. *Journal of Personality and Social Psychology, 75*, 1528–1558.

Cooper, M. L., Wood, P. K., Orcutt, H. K., & Albino, A. (2003). Personality and the predisposition to engage in risky or problem behaviors during adolescence. *Journal of Personality and Social Psychology, 84*, 390–410.

Costa, P. T., Jr., & McCrae, R. R. (1980). Influence of extraversion and neuroticism on subjective well-being: Happy and unhappy people. *Journal of Personality and Social Psychology, 38*, 668–678.

Cotte, J. (1997). Chances, trances, and lots of slots: Gambling motives and consumption experiences. *Journal of Leisure Research, 29,* 380–406.

Deffenbacher, J., & Oetting, E. R. (2002, June 26). *Cognitive–behavioral therapy for substance-using angry youth.* Retrieved July 8, 2002, from http://www.colostate.edu/Depts/TEC/behaviortherapy.htm

Edwards, W. (1954). The theory of decision making. *Psychological Bulletin, 51,* 380–417.

Eisenberg, N., Fabes, R. A., & Murphy, B. C. (1995). Relations of shyness and low sociability to regulation and emotionality. *Journal of Personality and Social Psychology, 68,* 505–517.

Folkman, S., Chesney, M. A., Pollack, L., & Phillips, C. (1992). Stress, coping, and high-risk sexual behavior. *Health Psychology, 11,* 218–222.

Forgas, J. P. (2003). Affective influences on attitudes and judgments. In R. J. Davidson, K. R. Scherer, & H. H. Goldsmith (Eds.), *Handbook of affective sciences* (pp. 596–218). New York: Oxford University Press.

Fromme, K., Katz, E., & D'Amico, E. (1997). Effects of alcohol intoxication on the perceived consequences of risk taking. *Experimental and Clinical Psychopharmacology, 5,* 14–23.

Gray, J. A. (1970). The psychophysiological basis of introversion–extraversion. *Behaviour Research and Therapy, 8,* 249–266.

Gray, J. A. (1990). Brain systems that mediate both emotion and cognition. *Cognition & Emotion, 4,* 269–288.

Harless, D. W., & Camerer, C. F. (1994). The predictive utility of generalized expected utility theories. *Econometrica, 62,* 1251–1289.

Hinshaw, S. P. (1996). Enhancing social competence: Integrating self-management strategies with behavioral procedures for children with ADHD. In E. D. Hibbs & P. S. Jensen (Eds.), *Psychosocial treatments for child and adolescent disorders: Empirically based strategies for clinical practice* (pp. 285–309). Washington, DC: American Psychological Association.

Horvath, P., & Zuckerman, M. (1993). Sensation seeking, risk appraisal, and risky behavior. *Personality and Individual Differences, 14,* 41–52.

Hoyle, R. H., Fejfar, M. C., & Miller, J. D. (2000). Personality and sexual risk taking: A quantitative review. *Journal of Personality, 68,* 1203–1231.

Hussong, A. M. (2003). Social influences in motivated drinking among college students. *Psychology of Addictive Behaviors, 17,* 142–150.

Isen, A. M. (1993). Positive affect and decision making. In M. Lewis & J. M. Haviland (Eds.), *Handbook of emotions* (pp. 261–277). New York: Guilford Press.

Jackson, B., Cooper, M. L., Mintz, L., & Albino, A. (2003). Motivations to eat: Scale development and validation. *Journal of Research in Personality, 37,* 297–318.

Kann, L., Kinchen, S., Williams, B., Ross, J., Lowry, R., Hill, C., et al. (1998). Youth risk behavior surveillance—United States, 1997. *Morbidity and Mortality Weekly Report, 47,* 1–89.

Katz, E. C., Fromme, K., & D'Amico, E. J. (2000). Effects of outcome expectancies and personality on young adults' illicit drug use, heavy drinking, and risky sexual behavior. *Cognitive Therapy and Research, 24,* 1–22.

Krueger, R. F., Caspi, A., & Moffitt, T. E. (2000). Epidemiological personology: The unifying role of personality in population-based research on problem behaviors. *Journal of Personality, 68,* 967–998.

Leith, K. P., & Baumeister, R. F. (1996). Why do bad moods increase self-defeating behavior? Emotion, risk tasking, and self-regulation. *Journal of Personality and Social Psychology, 71,* 1250–1267.

Linehan, M. M. (1993). *Cognitive–behavioral treatment of borderline personality disorder.* New York: Guilford Press.

Loesel, F., & Bliesener, T. (1994). Some high-risk adolescents do not develop conduct problems: A study of protective factors. *International Journal of Behavioral Development, 17,* 753–777.

Loewenstein, G. F., Weber, E. U., Hsee, C. K., & Welch, N. (2001). Risk as feelings. *Psychological Bulletin, 127,* 267–286.

Mellers, B. A., Schwartz, A., Ho, K., & Ritov, I. (1997). Decision affect theory: Emotional reactions to the outcomes of risky options. *Psychological Science, 8,* 423–429.

Miller, J. D., & Lynam, D. (2001). Structural models of personality and their relation to antisocial behavior: A meta-analytic review. *Criminology, 39,* 765–798.

Nower, L., Derevensky, J. L., & Gupta, R. (2004). The relationship of impulsivity, sensation seeking, coping, and substance use in youth gamblers. *Psychology of Addictive Behaviors, 18,* 49–55.

Peirce, R. S., Frone, M. R., Russell, M., & Cooper, M. L. (1996). Financial stress, social support, and alcohol involvement: A longitudinal test of the buffering hypothesis in a general population survey. *Health Psychology, 15,* 38–47.

Reilly, P. M., & Shopshire, M. S. (2000). Anger management group treatment for cocaine dependence: Preliminary outcomes. *American Journal of Drug and Alcohol Abuse, 26,* 161–177.

Revelle, W. (1997). Extraversion and impulsivity: The lost dimension? In H. Nyborg (Ed.), *The scientific study of human nature: Tribute to Han J. Eysenck at eighty* (pp. 189–212). Oxford, England: Pergamon Press.

Robins, C. J., & Chapman, A. L. (2004). Dialectical behavior therapy: Current status, recent developments, and future directions. *Journal of Personality Disorders, 18,* 73–89.

Rothbart, M. K., Ellis, L. K., & Posner, M. I. (2004). Temperament and self-regulation. In R. F. Baumeister & K. D. Vohs (Eds.), *Handbook of self-regulation: Research, theory, and applications* (pp. 357–370). New York: Guilford Press.

Schachner, D. A., & Shaver, P. R. (2004). Attachment dimensions and sexual motives. *Personal Relationships, 11,* 179–195.

Schwarz, N., & Clore, G. L. (1983). Mood, misattribution, and judgments of well-being: Informative and directive functions of affective states. *Journal of Personality and Social Psychology, 45,* 513–523.

Sells, C. W., & Blum, R. W. (1996). Current trends in adolescent health. In R. J. DiClemente, W. B. Hansen, & L. E. Ponton (Eds.), *Handbook of adolescent health risk behavior: Issues in clinical child psychology* (pp. 5–34). New York: Plenum Press.

Stewart, S. H., Zeitlin, S. B., & Samoluk, S. B. (1996). Examination of a three-dimensional drinking motives questionnaire in a young adult university student sample. *Behaviour Research and Therapy, 34*, 61–71.

St. Lawrence, J. S., Crosby, R. A., Belcher, L., Yazdani, N., & Brasfield, T. L. (1999). Sexual risk reduction and anger management interventions for incarcerated male adolescents: A randomized controlled trial of two interventions. *Journal of Sex Education and Therapy, 24*, 9–17.

Tarter, R. E., Kirisci, L., Mezzich, A., Cornelius, J. R., Pajer, K., Vanyukov, M., et al. (2003). Neurobehavioral disinhibition in childhood predicts early age at onset of substance use disorder. *American Journal of Psychiatry, 160*, 1078–1085.

Thayer, R. E., Newman, J. R., & McClain, T. M. (1994). Self-regulation of mood: Strategies for changing a bad mood, raising energy, and reducing tension. *Journal of Personality and Social Psychology, 67*, 910–925.

Tversky, A., & Kahneman, D. (1974, September 27). Judgment under uncertainty: Heuristics and biases. *Science, 185*, 1124–1131.

Vitaro, F., Arseneault, L., & Tremblay, R. E. (1997). Dispositional predictors of problem gambling in male adolescents. *American Journal of Psychiatry, 154*, 1769–1770.

Wills, T. A., Sandy, J. M., Shinar, O., & Yaeger, A. (1999). Contributions of positive and negative affect to adolescent substance use: Test of a bidimensional model in a longitudinal study. *Psychology of Addictive Behaviors, 13*, 327–338.

Zuckerman, M. (Ed.). (1983). *Biological bases of sensation seeking, impulsivity, and anxiety.* Hillsdale, NJ: Erlbaum.

Zuckerman, M. (1994). Impulsive unsocialized sensation seeking: The biological foundations of a basic dimension in personality. In J. E. Bates & T. D. Wachs (Eds.), *Temperament: Individual differences at the interface of biology and behavior* (pp. 219–255). Washington, DC: American Psychological Association.

Zuckerman, M., & Kuhlman, D. M. (2000). Personality and risk-taking: Common biosocial factors. *Journal of Personality, 68*, 999–1029.

III

CLINICAL INTERVENTIONS IN EMOTION REGULATION PROCESSES

10

EMOTION REGULATION PROCESSES IN DISEASE-RELATED PAIN: A COUPLES-BASED PERSPECTIVE

FRANCIS J. KEEFE, LAURA S. PORTER, AND JEFFREY LABBAN

When a person is diagnosed with a disease such as arthritis or cancer, one of the biggest concerns they and their families voice is "How much pain will be involved?" Population-based studies have shown that pain is very common in arthritis and cancer (Bonica, Bentafridda, & Twycross, 1990; Jakobsson & Hallberg, 2002). Pain in these diseases is unfortunately often not managed adequately, or its management is associated with major side effects such as constipation or fatigue. The impact of a chronic disease on patients and their families can be profound, particularly when that disease is painful. Research, for example, shows that partners of cancer patients who are experiencing pain report significantly higher levels of emotional distress than partners of cancer patients who are pain free (Miaskowski, Kragness, Dibble, & Wallhagen, 1997).

Preparation of this chapter was supported in part by the following grants from the National Institutes of Health: NIAMS AR 46305, AR047218, P01 AR50245, and NIMH MH63429; R21-CA88049–01 and CA91947–01 from the National Cancer Institute; and NS46422 from the National Institute of Neurological Diseases and Stroke; and by support from the Arthritis Foundation and the Fetzer Institute.

The traditional approach to understanding disease-related pain is based on a biomedical model (Keefe, Abernathy, & Campbell, 2005). This model views pain as a sensory event that signals tissue damage. Although the biomedical model can be helpful in guiding diagnostic and treatment efforts, it often ignores or minimizes the role that psychological factors (e.g., emotion) or social factors (e.g., support from a concerned partner) can play in how persons adjust to persistent pain. Dissatisfaction with the biomedical model has stimulated the emergence of newer models (e.g., the biopsychosocial model) that highlight the fact that pain is a multidimensional experience that is influenced not only by biological factors such as tissue damage but also by psychological and social factors.

Over the past 15 years, psychosocial pain researchers have become increasingly interested in the role that partners play in how patients adjust to pain, and in involving partners in psychosocial pain management efforts (Keefe et al., 1990; Radojevic, Nicassio, & Weisman, 1992). The purpose of this chapter is to provide an overview of this recent research and to discuss its implications for understanding emotion regulation processes in couples. The chapter is divided into four sections. In section 1, we describe the biopsychosocial model of pain and highlight the reasons that persistent pain conditions provide a particularly appropriate context in which to consider emotion regulation processes in couples. In section 2, we describe and evaluate several recent studies that have tested the efficacy of partner-assisted pain coping approaches to two common diseases: arthritis and cancer. We analyze intervention techniques used in these studies from an emotion regulation perspective. In section 3, we highlight future directions for research on emotion regulation processes in couples who are dealing with persistent pain. In the final section, we discuss the clinical, social, and public policy implications of research on couples-based emotion regulation processes in disease-related pain.

CONCEPTUAL BACKGROUND

The biopsychosocial model emerged in the 1970s and was applied to persistent pain conditions in the early 1980s by a number of psychosocial pain researchers (Keefe, 1982; Turk, Meichenbaum, & Genest, 1983; Turner & Chapman, 1982). The basic tenet of this model is that pain is a complex experience that is not only related to biological factors (e.g., underlying tissue damage or injury) but also is strongly influenced by psychological factors (e.g., cognitive and emotional responses) and social factors (e.g., social support). Empirical support for the biopsychosocial model has grown substantially over the past 20 years (Keefe, Rumble, Scipio, Giordano, & Perri, 2004), and studies have now identified specific psychological and social factors that are associated with pain. Emotional factors are known to play a key role in the experience of pain and in how persons adjust to persistent pain. Among the emotional factors most consistently found to be important in persons having pain are fear of pain (Vlaeyen & Linton, 2000), negative emotional states such as depression and negative mood (Zautra & Smith, 2001), and deficits in emotion regulation abilities (e.g., alexithymia, emotional inhibition, or avoidance; Dalton & Feuerstein, 1989). Numerous studies have shown that cognitive variables are critical not only in explaining pain but also in explaining emotional responses to pain. Especially important cognitive variables are overly negative cognitions (e.g., pain catastrophizing; Keefe et al., 2000), maladaptive pain beliefs (Jensen, Romano, Turner, Good, & Wald, 1999), and the tendency to appraise pain as uncontrollable (Lefebvre et al., 1999). Social factors known to affect pain include marital distress (Waltz, Kriegel, & van't Pad Bosch, 1996), partner responses to pain (e.g., solicitous, critical, or facilitative response; Keefe, Ahles, et al., 2005), and social support (Evers, Kraaimaat, Geenen, Jacobs, & Bijlsma, 2003).

A hallmark of the biopsychosocial model is its insistence that there are reciprocal relationships among the biological, psychological, and social factors that influence pain. Thus, persistent pain can precipitate an emotional response (e.g., a major depressive episode) that in turn leads to overly negative cognitions (e.g., the belief that pain can never be controlled) and changes in behavior (e.g., reductions in activity level), as well as biological responses (e.g., physical deconditioning), all of which can heighten the severity and impact of pain. The biopsychosocial model is based on a systems model of behavior change (Keefe, Abernathy, et al., 2005). Thus, positive changes in one part of this system can affect other parts of the system. For example, patients who learn to use cognitive reappraisal to alter their beliefs can develop a more positive and realistic outlook in the face of pain flares (a cognitive change) and are more likely to be able to maintain a positive mood (an emotional change) and elicit appropriate emotional support from their partners (a social change).

Treatment protocols based on the biopsychosocial model of pain typically are directed at the individual having pain and incorporate three basic elements (Keefe, Abernathy, et al., 2005). First, patients are provided with a rationale emphasizing the fact that pain is a complex experience and highlighting the role that thoughts, feelings, and behaviors can play in how persons adjust to pain. Second, systematic training in coping skills is carried out over a series of sessions. Skills commonly taught include relaxation training, imagery, activity pacing, goal setting, cognitive restructuring, and problem solving. Practice is viewed as essential in mastering these skills, and training thus emphasizes systematic instruction, guided in-session practice, therapist feedback, and home practice assignments. Coping skills training is typically conducted either on an individual basis or in small groups of patients. Finally, to enhance maintenance, patients are taught strategies for maintaining regular practice of learned skills and for dealing with setbacks and relapses in coping efforts. Evidence supporting the efficacy of biopsychosocial pain management protocols has accumulated over the past 20 years (Keefe et al., 2004).

Over the past decade there has been growing recognition among biopsychosocial pain researchers of the need to involve partners in treatment efforts, and heightened interest in addressing relationship factors such as marital adjustment and social support. Partner-assisted biopsychosocial pain management interventions have been developed and tested in several studies. To date, the rationale for these protocols primarily has centered on the role that the partner can play in assisting the patient in learning pain control skills (Keefe et al., 1996). Along these lines, involving the partner has been considered to be useful for enhancing patients' coping efforts and sense of self-efficacy. Helping partners understand the role that coping skills can play in managing pain also has been viewed as helpful in preventing problems such as the partner's enforcing rest, criticizing the use of coping skills, or insisting that pain medication is the only way to manage pain.

Although the rationale for partner-assisted coping skills training has mainly centered on the assisting role that partners can play in the patient's developing and maintaining pain coping skills, this intervention also can provide a particularly appropriate setting for identifying and modifying patients' and partners' emotion regulation processes. This notion is supported by several observations. First, persistent pain is not only emotionally demanding for patients but also quite emotionally challenging for their partners. Being the caregiver of a person having pain means not only having to help a loved one manage his or her emotions (e.g., frustration or fear) but also managing one's own emotional reactions (e.g., anxiety, guilt, anger, or depression). Partners who are overwhelmed by their own frustration, fears, and feelings of aloneness may not be able to offer the emotional or instrumental support needed by the person having pain. Second, partners must also learn to recognize and respond to signals of pain in their loved one. This task is complicated by the fact that signals of pain often occur in combination with cues of pain-related emotional distress that signal the need for additional or alternative types of assistance or support. More effective emotion regulation by patients and partners may increase their abilities to discriminate between pain and emotional distress, leading to more effective communication and support. Third, although pain is a personal experience, it can affect important dyadic processes like the way a couple approaches tasks such as requesting help, providing emotional and tangible support, dealing with conflict, and expressing affection and intimacy. Faced with a pain condition that persists, couples often need to develop a new set of skills and strategies for managing their emotions and negotiating their interactions. Skills that may have been effective in earlier years of the relationship may not be that effective in coping with the emotional demands of persistent, often disabling pain.

Partner-assisted pain coping skills protocols typically include training in a variety of strategies that can help patients and their partners regulate emotional processes. Although these protocols do not have their roots in theories of emotion regulation, the model developed by Gross, Richards, and John (Gross, 2001) provides a useful framework for understanding how the coping skills taught in these protocols can be helpful in emotion regulation. Figure 10.1, based on Gross (2001), illustrates the process model of emotion regulation and depicts how this model potentially can be used to categorize skills often included in partner-assisted coping skills training protocols. As shown in Figure 10.1, the coping skills used in these protocols can be grouped into two broad categories on the basis of whether they are antecedent-focused or response-focused emotion regulation strategies. *Antecedent-focused skills* are those that patients and partners can use to modify potential future emotional responses. These skills can be thought of as more proactive in that they attempt to minimize the incidence or severity of emotional distress. *Response-focused skills*, in contrast, refer to strategies that can be used to cope with emotional responses once they occur. Response-focused skills can be thought of as more reactive and useful in managing emotional distress once it occurs.

As shown in Figure 10.1, the coping skills used in partner-assisted interventions can be further delineated into five families of specific strategies on the basis of when they are used in the timeline of emotional processes (chap. 1, this volume). *Situation selection* refers to learning to approach or avoid certain situations or events (e.g., S1 rather than S2) so as to regulate emotion. For example, by learning better skills for pacing their daily activities, patients can avoid pain flares that can be frustrating and anxiety provoking for both patients and partners. *Situation modification skills* teach patients and partners to regulate emotion by modifying the situation itself (S1) to create different situations (S1x, S1y, or S1z). By learning to schedule pleasant activities into the day or set weekly activity goals, patients and partners can make simple daily activities much more rewarding and thereby increase positive affect and avoid the depression and discouragement that come when the patient adopts an overly sedentary and restricted lifestyle.

Attentional deployment skills regulate emotion by teaching individuals to focus on certain aspects (a1, a2, etc.) of a situation (e.g., the pleasant sensations and experiences that occur in a novel situation) rather than other aspects (e.g., increased pain). Training in imagery and distraction methods as well as learning to use a focal point can also be quite helpful in teaching patients and their partners how to redirect attention from pain to other salient neutral or more pleasurable aspects of a situation.

Cognitive change skills are designed to alter pain-related emotions by restructuring the meaning (e.g., m1, m2, or m3) attached to situations. Negative pain beliefs and cognitions (e.g., catastrophizing) are among the most consistent predictors of poor emotional adjustment to pain (Sullivan et al.,

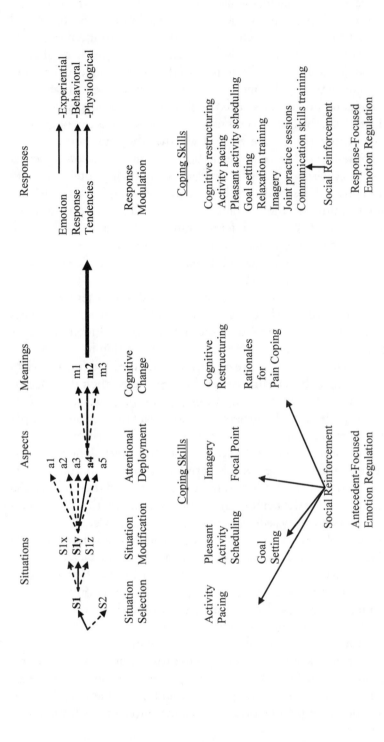

Figure 10.1. A process model framework for categorizing coping skills used in partner-assisted pain coping skills training. Adapted from "Emotion Regulation in Adulthood: Timing Is Everything," by J. Gross, 2001, *Current Directions in Psychological Science, 10,* p. 215. Copyright 2001 by Blackwell Publishing. Adapted with permission.

2001) and likely exert their effects by constructing overly negative meanings of events (e.g., "I'm having so much pain sitting today, I'll never be able to drive again"). Presenting patients and partners with rationales for pain coping skills such as the gate control theory (Melzack & Wall, 1965) can help them see pain as a more complex, multidimensional experience that is influenced by feelings, thoughts, and behaviors and reconceptualize their own abilities to exert control over pain. Cognitive restructuring is also used to teach patients and partners how to recognize overly negative appraisals of pain and to replace them with more realistic and adaptive appraisals. These more realistic appraisals can enhance positive mood and enable patients and their partners to avoid feeling depressed, guilty, and angry.

Many of the skills used in partner-assisted pain coping skills training can also be helpful in *response modulation*, that is, coping with and modifying emotions once they have occurred. When patients or their partners are overwhelmed by strong feelings of depression or fear, negative cognitions are quite prominent and cognitive restructuring of these negative thoughts can be especially helpful. At times of intense emotion, cognitive restructuring not only changes emotional responses but also enhances patients' and partners' willingness to use other learned coping skills that can be helpful in both emotion and pain regulation. Methods to alter activity patterns (e.g., activity pacing, pleasant activity scheduling, goal setting) and physiological arousal (e.g., relaxation training, imagery) can also be used to directly modulate emotions such as depression or anxiety. By engaging in joint practice sessions with learned coping skills, couples have important opportunities for learning to help each other modulate emotions brought on by pain flares or relapses in coping efforts. Communication skills training also provides an excellent means of helping patients and partners defuse pain-related emotional conflicts.

Finally, social reinforcement skills are especially important when couples are challenged with applying coping skills during emotionally demanding situations, and they are applied to coping skills used for both antecedent-focused and response-focused emotion regulation. Partner-assisted coping skills training protocols teach partners and patients how to use social reinforcement techniques to enhance the learning and maintenance of coping skills. For example, partners are often taught how to use attention and praise to foster the practice and application of learned coping skills. The resultant shift in the couple's attention from maladaptive coping efforts to more adaptive coping can increase the overall level of positive interactions and enhance mood and relationship satisfaction.

In sum, the process model of emotion regulation provides one way of conceptualizing many of the coping skills used in partner-assisted pain coping skills interventions. The categorization of coping skills described here is intended to be illustrative of how pain coping skills may be used for emotion regulation rather than to provide a definitive statement of their function in this regard. In the next section, we review the empirical studies testing the efficacy of partner-assisted coping skills training in the management of two common, painful diseases (arthritis and cancer). We also analyze the training approaches used from the perspective of the process model of emotion regulation.

EMPIRICAL FOUNDATIONS

Partner-based approaches to pain management have been evaluated in a number of studies. In this section, we consider the empirical foundations supporting the efficacy of partner-based interventions for arthritis pain and cancer pain.

Partner-Based Biopsychosocial Interventions for Arthritis Pain

The two most common forms of arthritis are osteoarthritis (OA) and rheumatoid arthritis (RA). Patients with OA and RA often experience persistent and disabling pain (Keefe et al., 2002). Further, conventional medical and surgical treatments often fail to provide adequate pain control or have side effects that limit their use (Simon et al., 2002). Finally, there is evidence that arthritis pain has a substantial impact not only on patients but also on their partners (Manne & Zautra, 1990).

Radojevic et al. (1992) were among the first to systematically evaluate a partner-assisted intervention for managing arthritis pain. In this study 65 persons diagnosed as having RA were randomly assigned to receive a psychosocial pain management intervention with family support, a psychosocial intervention alone, an education–information intervention with family support, or no treatment. All treatment was conducted in group sessions, and patients in the family support conditions attended the group sessions with a family member, usually their partner. In the psychosocial treatment with family support condition, patients were provided with a rationale for coping skills training and then trained in three pain coping skills (cognitive restructuring, imagery, and relaxation training). Their partners were trained in how to use behavioral principles (e.g., social reinforcement) to help patients acquire and maintain these skills and to avoid reinforcing maladaptive pain coping responses. The coping skills training provided to partners was based on a behavioral model (Fordyce, 1976) and was focused on teaching partners to provide social reinforcement for adaptive coping behaviors (e.g., increasing activity level) while withholding reinforcement for maladaptive coping behaviors (e.g., spending excessive time in bed). In the psychosocial treatment condition alone, the same training in pain coping skills was provided to patients, but no family members participated in the treatment sessions. In the education–information with family support condition, patients and family members attended sessions in which they were given extensive information about RA and how it is managed but no training in cognitive or behavioral pain coping skills. Treatment outcome was assessed at posttreatment and follow-up. Results showed that, when compared with the education–information with family support condition or no treatment condition, both of the psychosocial interventions produced significant reductions in joint pain at follow-up. It is interesting to note that the psychosocial intervention with family support intervention was significantly more effective than the psychosocial intervention alone in reducing joint swelling at posttreatment. Taken together, these results suggest that a partner-assisted psychosocial intervention can be effective in managing RA pain and that involving the partner may have unique benefits.

We conducted the first randomized, controlled study of a partner-assisted pain coping skills intervention for persons having OA (Keefe et al., 1996). Eighty-eight OA patients with persistent knee pain and their partners were randomly assigned to (a) partner-assisted coping skills training, (b) a conventional coping skills training condition alone, or (c) an arthritis education partner support control condition. As in the Radojevic et al. (1992) study, all treatment was conducted in group sessions, and patients in the partner conditions attended the group sessions with their partner. Patients in the partner-assisted coping skills training condition received training in a menu of cognitive and behavioral pain coping skills (relaxation, imagery, distraction techniques, activity pacing, goal setting, and cognitive restructuring), and they and their partners received training in a menu of couples skills (joint practice, communication skills, behavioral rehearsal, problem solving, and maintenance training; see Table 10.1 for a full listing of coping skills). Patients in the conventional coping skills intervention received training in the menu of cognitive and behavioral pain coping skills but no training in the couples skills. Patients and partners in the arthritis education social support control condition received lecture discussion sessions providing basic information on OA and its medical and surgical management.

Data analyses revealed a consistent pattern of outcomes across six of the seven outcome measures: Patients in the partner-assisted coping skills training had the best outcomes, those in the conventional coping skills training the next best outcomes, and those in the arthritis education social support control condition the worst outcomes. Correlational analyses were conducted to determine whether changes in marital adjustment were related to treatment outcome. For patients in the partner-assisted coping skills training condition, there was a significant relation between improvements in marital adjustment occurring over the course of treatment and improvements in psychological disability (i.e., anxiety and depression). It is interesting to note that a 12-month follow-up study also revealed that improvements in marital adjustment occurring over the initial course of treatment were related to long-term outcome (Keefe et al., 1999). Specifically, patients who showed

TABLE 10.1
Coping Skills Used in Partner-Assisted Pain Coping Skills Training

Skill	Description
Relaxation training	Achieving deep muscle relaxation by alternately tensing and slowly relaxing major muscle groups in the body
Imagery	Mentally focusing on a pleasant or distracting scene
Distraction techniques	Intentionally focusing concentration on a specific activity (e.g., counting numbers backward, viewing a picture, listening to music) to divert one's attention
Activity pacing	Alternating periods of activity and rest throughout the day to provide regular rest breaks and gradually build up activity level
Pleasant activity scheduling	Identifying potentially reinforcing activities (i.e., those that provide a sense of pleasure or mastery) and intentionally scheduling them into the day
Goal setting	Identifying, setting, and tracking attainment of a variety of meaningful short- and long-term goals
Cognitive restructuring	Identifying and challenging overly negative, maladaptive thoughts related to emotional distress and replacing these thoughts with more realistic and adaptive thoughts
Joint practice sessions	Scheduling and participating in sessions in which patient and partner practice learned coping skills together
Behavioral rehearsal	Role-playing in which patient and partner practice applying coping skills to specific challenging situations
Communication skills training	Training patient and partner in verbal and nonverbal skills to facilitate sharing of feelings and thoughts
Problem solving	Teaching patient and partner how to better identify and analyze problem situations to better develop and implement problem solutions
Social reinforcement	Training patient and partner how to use social reinforcement (e.g., attention and praise) to change patient, partner, and couple behavior patterns
Maintenance training	Teaching patient and partner how to use relapse prevention methods (e.g., identifying high-risk situations using naturally occurring prompts, developing a plan for dealing with setbacks/relapses) to maintain learned coping skills

increases in marital adjustment were much more likely to show lower levels of psychological disability, physical disability, and pain behavior at 12-month follow-up. Changes in marital adjustment were not related to long-term improvements in outcome among patients in the conventional coping skills training or education social support control condition. These findings suggest that a partner-assisted pain coping skills intervention may have promise as a method for reducing pain and psychological disability in patients suffering from OA and that changes in marital adjustment are related to the outcome of this intervention.

To date, there have been relatively few studies testing the efficacy of partner-assisted coping skills training for persons suffering from OA and RA. The studies that have been conducted, however, feature important methodological strengths including random assignment to treatment conditions, comparisons to appropriate control conditions, and use of well-validated measures. Their results suggest that these protocols are beneficial in reducing pain and emotional distress.

The coping skills training protocols used in these studies vary in terms of their comprehensiveness and emphasis on processes of emotion regulation. For example, although Radojevic et al. (1992) provided RA patients with training in a variety coping skills that could potentially be used in emotion regulation, the approach they used in training partners was much more limited. This approach, based on a behavioral model (Fordyce, 1976), was focused on teaching partners to provide social reinforcement for adaptive coping behaviors (e.g., increasing activity level) while withholding reinforcement for maladaptive coping behaviors (e.g., spending excessive time in bed.) As shown in Figure 10.1, social reinforcement can provide a strategy for enhancing patients' use of both antecedent- and response-focused emotion regulation coping strategies. However, social reinforcement fails to provide partners with direct training in many other strategies that Gross's process model (chap. 1, this volume) suggests could be useful in regulating their own emotions.

The partner-assisted coping skills protocol used in our own study of OA patients (Keefe et al., 1996), in contrast, applied Baucom and Epstein's (1990) broader cognitive–behavioral model of couples interactions to pain coping. This model maintains that to effectively treat couples one must first understand how they experience emotions, think, and behave when coping with pain and then systematically train them in couples coping skills for managing pain-related problems. In our training protocol we taught patients and their partners a full array of cognitive and behavioral coping skills (see Table 10.1). Although the protocol emphasized the utility of these skills in pain control, it also underscored the role that each of the skills could play in controlling patients' and partners' own emotional responses to pain and in addressing important dyadic processes (e.g., improving emotional exchanges between partners). Several couples skills were used to facilitate and underscore these skills as techniques for enhancing each couple's coping skills repertoire (see Table 10.1). A behavioral rehearsal method was used in which patients and partners role-played ways of coping with emotionally challenging pain-related situations and were provided reinforcement, feedback, and (if needed) guidance on alternative coping strategies. Couples also received formal training in communication skills designed to improve their communication about problem areas and successes and difficulties in applying newly learned pain coping skills. Finally, couples were instructed to schedule joint practice sessions for rehearsing learned coping skills and to use in vivo practice sessions in which they were to apply the coping skills in particularly challenging situations.

The coping strategies used in the Keefe et al. (1996) study are also noteworthy because they provide both patients and their partners with training in upward and downward emotion regulation strategies. Upward regulation strategies are those designed to regulate emotion by enhancing positive emotions (e.g., joy) and by promoting optimism, hopefulness, compassion, empathy, and caring support for the other partner's plight. Strategies such as pleasant activity scheduling or pleasant imagery are upward regulation strategies because they directly help patients and partners increase the frequency of positive emotional experiences. Rationales for coping skills training (e.g., the gate control theory; Melzack & Wall, 1965) that emphasize the role that emotion, thoughts, and behavior can play in pain also can promote understanding and optimism in both patient and partner. Joint practice sessions, behavioral rehearsal, and communication skills training all provide strategies to help couples develop and foster a more caring and empathic couples approach to pain coping. Downward regulation strategies, in contrast, are those designed to regulate emotions by decreasing or minimizing negative emotions such as depression, worry, fear, anger, or resentment of either partner. Cognitive structuring is a helpful downward regulation strategy because it decreases the frequency of negative emotional experiences.

The skills used in partner-assisted coping skills training also can be thought of as varying along a dimension that ranges from intrapersonal to interpersonal. Some interventions can be considered more intrapersonal in nature in that they likely exert their effects primarily by helping the patient or partner manage his or her own pain-related emotions (e.g., relaxation training, imagery). Other interventions (e.g., communication skills training, joint practice sessions) can be considered more interpersonal in that they are designed to assist both partners in regulating the emotions that occur during their interactions.

To date, partner-assisted pain coping skills training protocols used in OA and RA have not focused sufficiently on identifying and altering specific, negative interactional cycles such as those described by Goldman and Greenberg (chap. 11, this volume). In part, this may be due to the fact that couples in these studies have generally reported high levels of marital satisfaction. Nevertheless, persistent pain can threaten emotional connectedness and separation in ways that can lead to negative interaction patterns. For example, faced with a patient who is suffering from a flare in RA pain, a partner may experience a sense of fear and inadequacy about his or her ability to help the patient and may react by withdrawing. The patient, in turn, may become angry and escalate attempts to secure support from the partner, who may react by withdrawing even more. The end result is a maladaptive negative interaction pattern that contributes to rising emotional conflict. Techniques derived from emotion-focused couples therapy (chap. 11, this volume) could be incorporated into pain coping skills training protocols to better address such negative interactional cycles.

Partner-Based Biopsychosocial Interventions for Cancer Pain

A substantial body of descriptive research documents the impact of cancer on the patient's spouse and the patient–spouse relationship as well as on the patient. Partners of cancer patients having pain have been found to experience significant levels of psychological distress (Haddad, Pitceathly, & Maguire, 1996), and there are indications that some spouses suffer more emotional distress than the patient (Northouse, Mood, Templin, Mellon, & George, 2000). Furthermore, during cancer treatment and recovery, many cancer patients experience disruptions in their roles within their family or workplace, which then affect the partner and broader family. For example, it has been found that family functioning and social support decrease over the first year after the cancer diagnosis despite improvements in individual adjustment (Arora et al., 2001).

There is also a good deal of descriptive research documenting the importance of the spouse's support in contributing to the patient's adjustment. The bulk of research in this area focuses on the spouse's provision of social support, which is subcategorized into emotional, instrumental, and informational support (see Helgeson & Cohen, 1996, for a review). Emotional support from the spouse has been found to be particularly important in contributing to the patient's adjustment. There has been little direct attention to the spouse's role in helping the patient to manage cancer pain symptoms or side effects of cancer treatments. This role is often subsumed under the larger umbrella of caretaking tasks, which can include administering medications, communicating with health care professionals, and assisting with activities of daily living. However, the spouse, who is often the patient's primary caregiver, can play a pivotal role in helping the patient manage symptoms, particularly pain. For instance, spouses often have concerns and misconceptions regarding pain medications that can pose a barrier to the patient receiving adequate pain relief (Berry & Ward, 1995). Spouses also often attempt to use nondrug interventions such as distraction and help with positioning, to varying degrees of effectiveness. Thus, it may be advantageous to include spouses in cancer pain management interventions.

There have been very few published biopsychosocial pain management intervention studies with cancer patients that have taken a couples approach. The studies that have been conducted have tended to focus exclusively on reducing psychological distress. For example, Christensen (1983) examined the efficacy of a couple's communication training protocol for women with breast cancer and their spouses. The intervention resulted in improvements in the woman's mood and in the couple's sexual satisfaction following mastectomy. In other studies, the interventions included spouses only (Bultz,

Speca, Brasher, Geggie, & Page, 2000), were conducted separately for patients and spouses (Donnelly et al., 2000), or included spouses of only some of the patients (Heinrich & Schag, 1985). None of these interventions, however, targeted pain symptom management or included measures of cancer pain symptoms.

We recently completed a study that tested the effects of a partner-guided pain management intervention for patients having cancer pain at the end of life (Keefe, Ahles, et al., 2005). In this study, 78 patients having cancer pain who met criteria for hospice eligibility were randomly assigned to receive a biopsychosocial pain management intervention or usual care. Because patients were sick and at the end of life, the intervention was brief (three sessions) and conducted in patients' homes. The intervention, delivered by a nurse, integrated educational information about cancer pain with training in three pain coping skills (relaxation, imagery, and activity pacing). Although these skills were described as pain coping skills, it was also emphasized that they could play an important role in controlling patient and partner emotional responses and important dyadic challenges (e.g., exchanging feelings) that occurred in this end-of-life treatment context. Behavioral rehearsal and joint practice sessions were included in the training to facilitate the ability of couples to learn these coping skills. Results indicated that patients in the intervention tended to report reduced levels of pain, although this finding was not statistically significant. In addition, spouses assigned to the intervention condition showed significant improvements in their sense of self-efficacy for helping the patient control pain and self-efficacy for managing other cancer symptoms and tended to report reduced levels of caregiver strain. These findings are promising and suggest that involving partners in a pain management program at the end of life may be beneficial.

Our research team is currently conducting another partner-based study focused on symptom management in patients with early-stage lung cancer. In this study, 500 patients with early-stage lung cancer and their caregivers will be randomly assigned to receive either 14 sessions of coping skills training or 14 sessions of cancer education. The primary aim of the study is to evaluate whether coping skills training is effective in reducing symptoms of lung cancer including pain, fatigue, shortness of breath, and coughing. The caregivers, who are primarily spouses, learn the coping skills along with the patients and are taught to coach the patient in their use of these strategies.

Numerous descriptive studies have shown that cancer has a substantial impact on partners' emotional adjustment. Descriptive research also shows that social support, particularly emotional support, is associated with improvements in patients' adjustment to cancer. To date, very few studies have been conducted on partner-assisted coping skills interventions for cancer pain management.

Our recent study of cancer patients at the end of life thus represents one of the first systematic attempts to test the efficacy of partner-assisted pain coping skills training in the management of cancer pain. Because of the demands of working with patients and partners at the end of life, the protocol used in this study was briefer and less comprehensive than that used in our study of OA patients. However, it did emphasize that coping skills training could benefit not only the patient's pain but also the patient's and partner's emotional life. It is of interest that the major significant effects were on partner outcomes, including improvements in partners' self-efficacy for controlling pain, self-efficacy for controlling other cancer symptoms, and caregiver strain.

The end-of-life context is a particularly appropriate one in which to study emotion regulation skills in couples. Caring for a partner who has pain at the end of life is emotionally demanding and can challenge what Goldman and Greenberg (chap. 11, this volume) have called "couples' emotion systems." Expressing and sharing emotions in this context can be difficult. Indeed, some partners' own emotional responses to the patient's cancer (e.g. their own fear, feelings of abandonment) may be so strong as to hinder their abilities to effectively provide emotional support. Nevertheless, our own research suggests that couples in this situation are faced with the concrete task of managing the patient's pain, and that interactions around this task may provide important opportunities for emotional expression. Anecdotally, couples in our study reported that the process of learning pain coping skills did enable them to have valued conversations and interactions that they may have otherwise avoided.

Given the importance of social support and emotion regulation in cancer patients having pain, additional research is needed to explore the benefits of partner-based pain coping skills training interventions.

FUTURE RESEARCH DIRECTIONS

Although partner-based biopsychosocial interventions for managing pain are relatively new, they appear to have potential. If this potential is to be fully realized, however, additional research is needed. In particular, research on partner-based interventions could benefit immensely from a greater emphasis on emotional and interpersonal processes.

First, those developing partner-based interventions need to more carefully consider the emerging literature on pain and emotion. In a recent review we identified four topics in this area that are particularly relevant to partner-based interventions. First, there is growing evidence from longitudinal studies that interpersonal stress can influence disease-related pain conditions. Interpersonal stress appears to be particularly important for persons having RA. Zautra et al. (1998), for example, found that interpersonal stress led to changes in immune function, inflammation, and pain in persons with RA. It is interesting that another study by this group found that whereas interpersonal stress was strongly related to physiological changes and depression in persons with RA, stress of a noninterpersonal nature was not (Zautra, Burleson, Matt, Roth, & Burrows, 1994). Interpersonal stress also was significantly more likely to relate to changes in physiology and depression in persons with RA than in persons with OA. This suggests that the effects of interpersonal stress may differ in persons having different disease-related pain conditions. These findings suggest that stress management interventions focused on reducing interpersonal stress potentially may be beneficial for persons having RA. To date, however, no studies have tested the effects of a partner-assisted stress management protocol for patients with RA.

Catastrophizing, an emotionally focused response to pain, has emerged as one of the most consistent predictors of pain and disability (Sullivan et al., 2001). The term *catastrophizing* refers to an individual's tendency to focus on and exaggerate the threat value of painful stimuli and negatively evaluate one's own ability to deal with pain (Rosensteil & Keefe, 1983). Persons who catastrophize have higher levels of pain, increased pain-related disability, and higher health care use and show more pain behavior (Sullivan et al., 2001). It is noteworthy that the effects of catastrophizing are evident even after controlling for pain severity. In a recent study, we examined the social context of pain catastrophizing in patients with gastrointestinal (GI) cancer (Keefe et al., 2003). It was hypothesized that patients who were high in catastrophizing would receive more support from their caregivers but that these caregivers would also report higher levels of burden and negative responses toward the patient. Findings supported these hypotheses, suggesting that patient catastrophizing may serve to elicit support from significant others but that it does so at a cost to both the patient's and caregiver's well-being. Future intervention studies focused on modifying couples' interactions regarding the patient's methods of eliciting spouse support may be useful for reducing patient pain catastrophizing and improving individual and relationship adjustment for both patients and spouses.

Recent studies have also highlighted the important role that fear and avoidance play in the adjustment to pain. Persons who are highly fearful of pain avoid situations and activities that are associated with pain and as a result can become inactive, sedentary, and overly dependent on others, responses that can heighten the behavioral impact of a pain condition (Picavet, Vlaeyen, & Schouten, 2002). Vlaeyen and his colleagues have recently developed a graded in vivo exposure protocol designed to help patients overcome pain-related fears by exposing them to feared situations (Vlaeyen & Linton, 2000). The protocol involves development of a fear hierarchy, physician education about unrealistic fears, and sessions in which patients expose themselves in a graded fashion to progressively more difficult anxiety-provoking situations. The efficacy of this in vivo graded exposure protocol has been examined in two studies using experimental single-case designs. Both studies, conducted with patients suffering from chronic musculoskeletal pain conditions, found that exposure led to significant improvements in pain-related fear, disability, and activity level.

Pain-related fear and avoidance can be a problem not only for patients but also for their partners and significant others. Partners who are excessively worried about pain may become overly solicitous and interfere with the patient's efforts to remain engaged in activities. It is surprising that no studies have tested whether involving partners in an in vivo graded exposure protocol can reduce their anxieties about pain and improve the quality of couples' relationships.

Furthermore, there is evidence that persons with pain are more likely to experience alexithymia—that is, difficulty identifying, understanding, and communicating their emotions (Sifneos, 1980). Research has shown that persons with chronically painful diseases such as irritable bowel syndrome, rheumatoid arthritis, and chronic pain conditions score significantly higher on measures of alexithymia than do healthy controls (Lumley, Asselin, & Norman, 1997). These studies have led to interest in interventions designed to improve adjustment to pain by fostering emotional disclosure. Kelley, Lumley, and Leisen (1997) conducted a study of RA patients in which they tested the effects of an emotional disclosure intervention modeled after that developed by Pennebaker (1993). Patients assigned to this intervention were instructed to talk privately into a tape recorder about stressful experiences that they had not shared with others for 30 minutes on 4 consecutive days. Patients assigned to a control condition were asked to talk about neutral topics for the same time period. Data analyses revealed that the emotional disclosure intervention led to immediate increases in negative affect but significant improvements in affective disturbance 3 months later. Among patients in the emotional disclosure condition, those who experienced the largest initial increases in negative affect had the best outcomes in terms of improvement in joint condition at 3-month follow-up. Taken together, these findings suggest that emotional disclosure may provide a useful strategy for enhancing adjustment to RA.

Emotional disclosure, however, often occurs in an interpersonal context, and interventions that foster interpersonal emotional disclosure may be particularly helpful for persons having persistent pain. We are currently testing this possibility in several studies. The first study is designed to evaluate the efficacy of a nurse-assisted emotional disclosure intervention for RA. In this study, a nurse who is specially trained to help RA patients identify and express emotions assists patients during emotional disclosure sessions. In the second study, we are testing the effects of an intervention designed to increase the degree to which patients with GI cancer disclose their cancer-related concerns to their partners. We hypothesize that enhancing disclosure between patients and spouses may be beneficial for increasing the well-being of both patients and spouses as well as improving aspects of their relationship such as intimacy.

Patients and their partners are likely to vary in their response to partner-assisted interventions. Attachment style may be one variable that moderates responses to such interventions. Research has demonstrated that adult attachment styles can be conceptualized in terms of *avoidance* and *anxiety* (Hazan & Shaver, 1990). Securely attached people tend to be less anxious and exhibit less avoidant behavior in threatening or stressful situations (Feeney & Kirkpatrick, 1996). Securely attached individuals are also more likely to engage in support seeking, because they are confident that others will be available in times of need (Mikulincer, Florian, & Weller, 1993). Insecurely attached individuals, in contrast, tend to react with greater anxiety or avoidant behavior when confronted with stressful situations and are less likely to seek social support. This stems from their lack of trust in the availability of significant others in times of need.

Attachment styles are likely to have important implications for partner-assisted pain coping skills interventions. The experience of pain is a stressful situation that is likely to elicit emotional reactions characteristic of an individual's attachment style. Partner-assisted interventions are based on the rationale that pain is a couples issue, and on the belief that teaching couple-based skills such as communication and joint practice and training the partner in individual skills such as goal setting and maintenance are critical to the patient's success (Keefe et al., 1996). Insecure attachment can interfere with partner-assisted interventions at various levels, beginning with the rationale provided for engaging in couples skills training: that pain is not simply an individual issue, but a couples issue. To accept this rationale, insecure individuals must overcome some of the fundamental components of their attachment style, including distrust of their partner, fear of rejection, emotional distancing, and avoidance of closeness. Insecure reactions to distressing situations on the part of the patient or spouse could interfere with the ability of the couple to successfully use coping skills. Avoidant attachment has been linked with denial and suppression of emotion (Mikulincer et al., 1993) and the maintenance of emotional distance from one's partner (Brennan, Clark, & Shaver, 1998). This could hinder many components of skills training. For instance, during behavioral rehearsal, patients provide feedback concerning the assistance given by their spouse in demanding situations. Suppression and denial could interfere with the patient providing constructive feedback, and emotional distancing could hinder a spouse's ability to prompt use of cognitive coping skills.

Future studies also need to examine other patient and partner characteristics that are related to the outcome of such interventions. Are these interventions more helpful for younger versus older couples? Are couples who report high satisfaction with their relationship more responsive to these interventions than those who do not? Do the effects of these interventions differ on the basis of the racial or ethnic backgrounds of the participants?

Studies designed to answer these questions can significantly advance our understanding of the utility of partner-assisted interventions.

CLINICAL, SOCIAL, AND PUBLIC POLICY IMPLICATIONS

As noted earlier, the study of partner-assisted pain management interventions is a relatively new development. If future research continues to demonstrate that these interventions are effective, then one needs to more carefully consider their implications for clinical, social, and public policy.

At present, psychological interventions in general, and partner-assisted interventions in particular, are not widely available for patients having pain. Reimbursement for delivery of psychological services for pain management has been reduced sharply over the past decade, leading to shortages in care providers. Thus, a key clinical and public policy issue that is likely to emerge is how to increase access to partner-assisted pain management interventions. One way of dealing with this problem is to have nonpsychologists deliver these interventions. Nurses, for example, are often involved in health education efforts for persons with chronic diseases. Over the past decade, there has been heightened interest in the role that nurses can play in delivering biopsychosocial pain management interventions, particularly to persons with cancer (Dalton, Keefe, Carlson, & Youngblood, 2004). Another option is to devise partner-assisted interventions that can be delivered by less costly methods such as by telephone or the Internet. Telephone-based and Internet-based educational interventions focused on self-management have shown promise in the treatment of arthritis pain and disability, but to date no studies have adapted these formats to deliver a partner-assisted intervention. However, in our ongoing NIH-supported research we are testing the efficacy of a number of protocols that involve a combination of face-to-face and telephone partner-assisted treatment sessions.

Another important clinical issue is the early detection by health care providers of patients who might benefit from partner-assisted interventions. Biopsychosocial theory and clinical practice suggest that intervening early is more likely to be successful than intervening late. Certain couples may have strengths (e.g., high levels of intimacy, effective communication skills) that, if detected early in the course of a painful disease, may make them particularly amenable to couples-based interventions. Other couples may cope with a painful disease with problematic coping styles, such as emotional avoidance, that could be more effectively treated if they are detected early before they become entrenched. Health care providers (e.g., physicians, nurses, psychologists) who work with patients having disease-related pain need to be educated about the benefits of couples-based interventions for pain management and encouraged to identify those who are likely to respond to these treatments.

Another important public policy initiative is educating the public about the link between pain and emotion, and the impact of persistent pain on family members. All too often pain is viewed by the general public as simply a sensory event, with little recognition of the important role that emotion and the social environment play in influencing the pain experience. Efforts need to be made to inform the public about the results of recent studies on the association of disease-related pain and emotion. Along these lines, the American Pain Society has been involved in a broad array of public education initiatives as part of the congressionally mandated Decade of Pain Control and Research (see American Pain Society, n.d.). Information about the psychosocial aspects of pain is now available to the public through educational handouts, Web sites, and speakers. These and related efforts are likely to increase the public's awareness of the important role that partners can play in the management of pain.

REFERENCES

American Pain Society. (n.d.) *Decade of Pain Control and Research*. Retrieved December 3, 2004, from http://www.ampainsoc.org/decadeofpain

Arora, N. K., Gustafson, D. H., Hawkins, R. P., McTavish, F., Cella, D. F., Pingree, S., et al. (2001). Impact of surgery and chemotherapy on the quality of life of younger women with breast carcinoma. *Cancer, 92*, 1288–1298.

Baucom, D. H., & Epstein, N. (1990). *Cognitive–behavioral marital therapy*. New York: Brunner Mazel.

Berry, P. E., & Ward, S. E. (1995). Barriers to pain management in hospice: A study of family caregivers. *Hospice Journal, 10*, 19–33.

Bonica, J. J., Bentafridda, V., & Twycross, R. G. (1990). Cancer pain. In J. J. Bonica (Ed.), *The management of pain* (2nd ed., pp. 440–460). Philadelphia: Lea & Febiger.

Brennan, K. A., Clark, C. L., & Shaver, P. R. (1998). Self-report measurement of adult attachment: An integrative overview. In J. A. Simpson & W. S. Rholes (Eds.), *Attachment theory and close relationships* (pp. 46–76). New York: Guilford Press.

Bultz, B. D., Speca, M., Brasher, P. M., Geggie, P. H., & Page, S. A. (2000). A randomized controlled trial of a brief psychoeducational support group for partners of early stage breast cancer patients. *Psycho-Oncology, 9*, 303–313.

Christensen, D. N. (1983). Postmastectomy couple counseling: An outcome study of a structured treatment protocol. *Journal of Sex and Marital Therapy, 9*, 266–275.

Dalton, J. A., & Feuerstein, M. (1989). Fear, alexithymia, and cancer pain. *Pain, 38*, 159–170.

Dalton, J. A., Keefe, F. J., Carlson, J., & Youngblood, R. (2004). Tailoring cognitive–behavioral treatment for cancer pain. *Pain Management Nursing, 5*, 3–18.

Donnelly, J. M., Kornblith, A. B., Fleishman, S., Zuckerman, E., Raptis, G., Hudis, C. A., et al. (2000). A pilot study of interpersonal psychotherapy by telephone with cancer patients and their partners. *Psycho-Oncology, 9*, 44–56.

Evers, A. W. M., Kraaimaat, F. W., Geenen, R., Jacobs, J. W. G., & Bijlsma, J. W. J. (2003). Pain coping and social support as predictors of long-term functional disability and pain in early rheumatoid arthritis. *Behavior Research and Therapy, 41*, 1295–1310.

Feeney, B. C., & Kirkpatrick, L. A. (1996). Effects of adult attachment and presence of romantic partners on physiological responses to stress. *Journal of Personality and Social Psychology, 70*, 255–270.

Fordyce, W. E. (1976). *Behavioral methods for chronic pain and illness*. St. Louis, MO: Mosby, Inc.

Gross, J. J. (2001). Emotion regulation in adulthood: Timing is everything. *Current Directions in Psychological Science, 10*, 214–219.

Haddad, P., Pitceathly, C., & Maguire, P. (1996). Psychological morbidity in the partners of cancer patients. In L. Baider, C. L Cooper, & A. Kaplan De-Nour (Eds.), *Cancer and the family* (pp. 257–271). New York: Wiley.

Hazan, C., & Shaver, P. R. (1990). Love and work: An attachment-theoretical perspective. *Journal of Personality and Social Psychology, 59*, 270–280.

Heinrich, R. L., & Schag, C. C. (1985). Stress and activity management: Group treatment for cancer patients and spouses. *Journal of Consulting and Clinical Psychology, 53*, 439–446.

Helgeson, V. S., & Cohen, S. (1996). Social support and adjustment to cancer: Reconciling descriptive, correlational, and intervention research. *Health Psychology, 15*, 135–148.

Jakobsson, U. L. F., & Hallberg, I. R. (2002). Pain and quality of life among older people with rheumatoid arthritis and/or osteoarthritis: A literature review. *Journal of Clinical Nursing, 11*, 430–443.

Jensen, M. P., Romano, J. M., Turner, J. A., Good, A. B., & Wald, L. H. (1999). Patient beliefs predict patient functioning: Further support for a cognitive–behavioral model of chronic pain. *Pain, 81*, 95–104.

Keefe, F. J. (1982). Behavioral assessment and treatment of chronic pain: Current status and future directions. *Journal of Consulting and Clinical Psychology, 50*, 896–911.

Keefe, F. J., Abernathy, M., & Campbell, L. (2005). Psychological approaches to understanding and treating disease-related pain. *Annual Review of Psychology, 56*, 601–630.

Keefe, F. J., Ahles, T. A., Sutton, L., Dalton, J., Baucom, D., Pope, M. S., et al. (2005). Partner-guided cancer pain management at end-of-life: A preliminary study. *Journal of Pain and Symptom Management, 29*, 263–272.

Keefe, F. J., Caldwell, D. S., Baucom, D., Salley, A., Robinson, E., Timmons, K., et al. (1996). Spouse-assisted coping skills training in the management of osteoarthritis knee pain. *Arthritis Care and Research, 9*, 279–291.

Keefe, F. J., Caldwell, D. S., Baucom, D., Salley, A., Robinson, E., Timmons, K., et al. (1999). Spouse-assisted coping skills training in the management of knee pain in osteoarthritis: Long-term follow-up results. *Arthritis Care and Research, 12*, 101–111.

Keefe, F. J., Caldwell, D. S., Williams, D. A., Gil, K. M., Mitchell, D., Robertson, C., et al. (1990). Pain coping skills training in the management of osteoarthritic knee pain: A comparative study. *Behavior Therapy, 21*, 49–62.

Keefe, F. J., Lefebvre, J. C., Egert, J. R., Affleck, G., Sullivan, M. J., & Caldwell, D. S. (2000). The relationship of gender to pain, pain behavior, and disability in osteoarthritis patients: The role of catastrophizing. *Pain, 87*, 325–334.

Keefe, F. J., Lipkus, I., Lefebvre, J. C., Hurwitz, H., Clipp, E., Smith, J., et al. (2003). The social context of gastrointestinal cancer pain: A preliminary study examining the relation of patient pain catastrophizing to patient perceptions of social support and caregiver stress and negative responses. *Pain, 103*, 151–156.

Keefe, F. J., Rumble, M. E., Scipio, C. D., Giordano, L., & Perri, L. M. (2004). Psychological aspects of persistent pain: Current state of the science. *Journal of Pain, 5*, 195–211.

Keefe, F. J., Smith, S. J., Buffington, A. L. H., Gibson, J., Studts, J. L., & Caldwell, D. S. (2002). Recent advances and future directions in the biopsychosocial assessment and treatment of arthritis. *Journal of Consulting and Clinical Psychology, 70*, 640–655.

Kelley, J. C., Lumley, M. A., & Leisen, J. C. (1997). Health effects of emotional disclosure in rheumatoid arthritis patients. *Health Psychology, 16*, 331–340.

Lefebvre, J. C., Keefe, F. J., Affleck, G., Raezer, L. B., Starr, K., Caldwell, D. S., et al. (1999). The relationship of arthritis self-efficacy to daily pain, daily mood, and daily pain coping in rheumatoid arthritis patients. *Pain, 80*, 425–435.

Lumley, M. A., Asselin, L. A., & Norman, S. (1997). Alexithymia in chronic pain patients. *Comprehensive Psychiatry, 38*, 160–165.

Manne, S. L., & Zautra, A. J. (1990). Couples coping with chronic illness: Women with rheumatoid arthritis and their healthy husbands. *Journal of Behavioural Medicine, 13*, 327–342.

Melzack, R., & Wall, P. D. (1965, November 19). Pain mechanisms: A new theory. *Science, 150*, 971–979.

Miaskowski, C., Kragness, L., Dibble, S., & Wallhagen, M. (1997). Differences in mood states, health status, and caregiver strain between family caregivers of oncology outpatients with and without cancer-related pain. *Pain, 13*, 138–147.

Mikulincer, M., Florian, V., & Weller, A. (1993). Attachment styles, coping strategies, and posttraumatic psychological distress: The impact of the Gulf War in Israel. *Journal of Personality and Social Psychology, 64*, 817–826.

Northouse, L. L., Mood, D., Templin, T., Mellon, S., & George, T. (2000). Couples' patterns of adjustment to colon cancer. *Social Science and Medicine, 50*, 271–284.

Pennebaker, J. W. (1993). Putting stress into words: Health, linguistic, and therapeutic implications. *Behaviour Research and Therapy, 31*, 539–548.

Picavet, H. S., Vlaeyen, J. W., & Schouten, J. S. (2002). Pain catastrophizing and kinesiophobia: Predictors of chronic low back pain. *American Journal of Epidemiology, 156,* 1028–1034.

Radojevic, V., Nicassio, P. M., & Weisman, M. H. (1992). Behavioral intervention with and without family support for rheumatoid arthritis. *Behavior Therapy, 23,* 13–30.

Rosensteil, A. K., & Keefe, F. J. (1983). The use of coping strategies in chronic low back pain patients: Relationship to patient characteristics and current adjustment. *Pain, 17,* 33–44.

Sifneos, P. E. (1980). Ongoing outcome research on short-term dynamic psychotherapy. *Psychotherapy and Psychosomatics, 33,* 233–241.

Simon, L., Lipman, A. G., Allaire, S. G., Caudill-Slosberg, M., Gill, L. H., Keefe, F. J., et al. (2002). *Guideline for the management of acute and chronic pain in osteo and rheumatoid arthritis.* Glenview, IL: American Pain Society.

Sullivan, M. J. L., Thorn, B., Haythornthwaite, J., Keefe, F. J., Martin, M., Bradley, L., et al. (2001). Theoretical perspectives on the relation between catastrophizing and pain. *Journal of Clinical Pain, 17,* 52–64.

Turk, D. C., Meichenbaum, D., & Genest, M. (1983). *Pain and behavioral medicine: A cognitive–behavioral perspective.* New York, Guilford Press.

Turner, J. A., & Chapman, C. R. (1982). Psychological interventions for chronic pain: A critical review: 2. Operant conditioning, hypnosis, and biopsychosocial therapy. *Pain, 12,* 23–46.

Vlaeyen, J. W. S., & Linton, S. J. (2000). Fear-avoidance and its consequences in chronic musculoskeletal pain: A state of the art. *Pain, 85,* 317–332.

Waltz, M., Kriegel, W., & van't Pad Bosch, P. (1996). The social environment and health in rheumatoid arthritis: Marital quality predicts individual variability in pain severity. *Arthritis Care and Research, 11,* 356–374.

Zautra, A. J., Burleson, M. H., Matt, K. S., Roth, S., & Burrows, L. (1994). Interpersonal stress, depression, and disease activity in rheumatoid arthritis and osteoarthritis patients. *Health Psychology, 13,* 139–148.

Zautra, A. J., Hoffman, J. M., Matt, K. S., Yocum, D., Potter, P., Castro, L., et al. (1998). An examination of individual differences in the relationship between interpersonal stress and disease activity among women with rheumatoid arthritis. *Arthritis Care and Research, 11,* 217–229.

Zautra, A. J., & Smith, B. W. (2001). Depression and reactivity to stress in older women with rheumatoid arthritis and osteoarthritis. *Psychosomatic Medicine, 63,* 687–696.

11

PROMOTING EMOTIONAL EXPRESSION AND EMOTION REGULATION IN COUPLES

RHONDA N. GOLDMAN AND LESLIE S. GREENBERG

The last decade has seen increasing recognition of the importance of emotion regulation and emotional intelligence in the promotion of health and well-being. Although the traditional structure of the family has changed over the last century, the family remains the primary vehicle through which models for emotional expression are developed. From infancy onward, children learn a great deal about emotional expression. Present data suggest that 43% of American couples and 37% of Canadian couples who married in 1996 will divorce. Although there is controversy about the impact of divorce on children, there is little controversy over the impact of relationship distress on both children and adults. There is strong evidence that children are upset by conflict and anger expression in families, and parental conflict has been linked to a wide range of negative child outcomes (Cummings & Davies, 1994; see also chap. 8, this volume). Research has shown a link between relationship distress and clinical depression, as well as anxiety disorders such as posttraumatic stress disorder (Whisman, 1999). Research has also demonstrated the ill effects of a lack of positive relationships; for example, loneliness has been linked to heart disease and reduced immune system responsiveness (Kiecolt-Glasser & Newton, 2001). It is thus crucially important to develop therapeutic strategies to maintain and support stable, healthy relationships.

A deeper understanding of emotional connections and how they become disrupted in couples and families is of primary importance in helping to promote therapeutic change. Emotion coordinates experience and provides it with direction. In other words, emotion tells people what is important, and knowing what is important tells them what they need to do and who they are. Emotions provide access to wishes or needs, which in turn are a source of action. In other words, every feeling has a need, and every need has a direction for action (Elliott, Watson, Goldman, & Greenberg, 2003; Greenberg, 2002). It is thus essential to access emotions in couple and family therapy to understand where things are going wrong and to help partners or family members identify how to meet their own and each other's needs.

The emotion-focused couples therapy (EFCT) approach views the negative interactional cycles that couples engage in as a major source of dysfunction and thus a primary focus of therapy. Conflict stems from failures to resolve struggles for identity and security. Generally, negative interactional cycles are viewed as being driven by secondary emotions that serve to cover or obscure rapid-acting, primary adaptive emotions. Conflict then results from escalating interactions that rigidify into negative interactional cycles. The fundamental task of therapy is to identify negative cycles related to threats to security and identity and engender positive interactional cycles driven by primary, adaptive emotions.

The therapist in EFCT is viewed as an emotion coach who helps people deal more effectively with their emotions (Greenberg, 2002). The key concept in coaching people to resolve conflict in intimate relationships is helping them reveal the primary core, "softer," vulnerable emotions underlying their "harder" secondary or defensive emotions, thus facilitating de-escalation. It is important to note that although the metaphor of replacing hard emotions with softer ones is useful in evoking a picture of the change process, sometimes it can be therapeutic for the so-called harder emotion of anger to replace a softer emotion of fear or shame, especially in partners prone to withdrawal or submission. Our goal is to help people reveal the underlying and generally more vulnerable emotions of sadness, fear, or shame, or—in the case of persons who exhibit excessive withdrawal or submission—the empowering emotion of anger. However, people often find it difficult to acknowledge and share some of their more vulnerable or dreaded emotions.

This chapter discusses our view of how change in couples' emotion systems occurs through emotionally focused couples therapy (Greenberg & Johnson, 1988) and the role of emotion regulation in resolving couples' conflict. We outline the major principles of change from an EFCT perspective and discuss strategies to promote emotional change and emotion regulation within couples. We also review specific research efforts that describe the emotion regulation processes that lead to change through the EFCT process. Finally, we make recommendations for future research on the emotional change process in couples therapy and further cross-disciplinary collaboration to promote healthier emotion expression within the family system.

CONCEPTUAL AND THEORETICAL UNDERPINNINGS OF EMOTION-FOCUSED COUPLES THERAPY

In this section we outline how emotions are related to core attachment and identity concerns. In addition, we distinguish among different types of emotions and outline the principles of emotion regulation and change from the EFCT perspective.

Emotion Theory

Emotional connectedness and separation are universal factors operating in systems and are identifiable by the emotions expressed. Emotions organize both the self and interactions with others. Members in a family are highly connected to each other through this emotion system. They read each other's emotional signals with great care and this reading dominates their interactions. The amygdala, at the core of the emotional brain, has been shown to be particularly attentive and reactive to subliminal facial expressions of fear and anger, indicating how automatically and rapidly people react to facial expressions of emotion (Schupp et al., 2004). In addition, people form close bonds through emotion systems. Being close calms fears, regulates physiology, and provides security (Schore, 2003). Emotions are an important part of the glue that holds family members and marital partners together.

According to Frijda (1986), emotions are most noticeable as changes in relational action tendencies that occur in response to events relevant to personal concerns. For example, it is only in relation to a need or wish to be close that one feels insecure or afraid when one's partner is rejecting or distant. Emotions therefore emerge in relation to the social environment, arising in response to events real or imagined that are appraised as implying possibilities for gratifying or obstructing needs, goals, and desires.

People not only have emotions but also experience the need to regulate them. Too much or too little emotion can disrupt effective responding to environmental challenges. In the narrow sense, emotion regulation refers to the processes by which people influence which emotions they have, when they have them, and, most important, how they experience and express them (see also chap. 1, this volume). Cicchetti, Ackerman, and Izard (1995, p. 4) have stressed that a central component of emotion regulation is the "inter-co-ordination of the emotions and cognitive systems." In a broader sense emotion regulation also describes the ability of the cognitive system to gain information from the emotion system. Emotion regulation refers to all aspects of emotional processing, to its awareness, utilization, and transformation (Greenberg, 2002). One needs to specify what types of emotion to access, which ones to down-regulate, and which to increase.

Emotional Intimacy Within Couples: Attachment and Identity

Humans have been primed by evolution to feel pleasant feelings when close to caretakers and unpleasant feelings when unwillingly separated from them. Emotions are the infant's primary signaling system (Bowlby, 1989). They continue to be a primary form of communication into adulthood, signaling to intimate others how well they are meeting relational needs and expectations (Sroufe, 1996). Humans are highly interdependent, attachment-oriented beings. Secure attachment in adulthood, a perception that attachment figures are available, facilitates optimal functioning, promotes a sense of connectedness, and makes people more likely to seek support as a distress-regulating strategy. Alternatively, when attachment figures are felt to be unavailable, a sense of security is not attained and inadequate strategies of affect regulation such as avoidance and anxiety are sought (see chap. 4, this volume).

Basic concerns in intimate attachment relationships are proximity ("Are you there when I need you?"), availability ("Can you give me the things I need, such as affection, support, care?"), and responsiveness and receptiveness ("Can you understand me and what I need?"). Adults have developed capacities for empathy, sympathy, and motivation to be compassionate (Gilbert, 2000a). Intimate caregiving involves concerns with proximity, availability, and receptiveness. Caregivers try to intuit their partner's needs and respond to them. When the partner is receptive, the role of successful caring is achieved and is associated with positive affect. When the partner is not receptive and there is misattunement, the caregiver often responds with negative affect and behavior (Gilbert, 2000b; Johnson & Whiffen, 2003).

In addition to attachment and intimacy needs, autonomy and identity needs also are an important basis of relationships (Greenberg, 2002, in press). Emotions such as embarrassment, shame, humiliation, and pride reflect concerns about identity and social rank or status (Gilbert & McGuire, 1998). These identity-related emotions arise when one feels socially threatened. People have thus evolved to possess emotional capacities that are influenced by interpersonal experiences forming a complex affective, cognitive, motivational, and behavioral system.

When there are challenges to identity or status, the primary vulnerable emotions generally are shame at diminishment or invalidation and fear from threat to one's standing or sense of control. To avoid feeling primary shame, people often respond with anger. Here anger is a secondary protective or assertive emotional response that both regulates and obscures the vulnerable emotional response to identity threats. Therapeutically, helping partners stimulate positive affect in each other rather than fear or submission is an important way of allowing each person to maintain position and validate identity needs. In addition, helping partners learn to tolerate and regulate their own fear and shame rather than fly into a rage to regulate self-esteem is an important goal.

Hence, the focus of therapy is to identify maladaptive interactional cycles and to get underneath the positions people take in them to access primary attachment and identity-related emotions and the need-based self-organizations underlying couples' interactions. Core relational needs for attachment and identity drive the cycle. Redefining problems in terms of needs helps partners be more responsive to each other's vulnerabilities.

Types of Emotion

Not all emotions are the same; hence, therapists don't simply help clients get in touch with feelings or encourage the expression of all emotions. Rather, they distinguish among different types of emotions to guide their interventions. Therapists intervene differentially with members of the family, helping them to accept and integrate certain emotions, to acknowledge but bypass others, to express those that will enhance the relationship, and to contain and soothe, or explore and transform others. This approach to differential intervention is based on the premise that some emotional expressions are adaptive whereas others are maladaptive. For example, anger may be adaptive or maladaptive, depending on the function it serves in a given interaction. In the following paragraphs, we briefly explain our typology of emotions (Greenberg, 2002).

Primary adaptive emotions are the person's most fundamental, original reactions to a situation and are productive. These include rapid-acting emotional reactions that originate from noncortical areas of the brain, such as the amygdala (LeDoux, 1996). Those underlying attachment and identity-related emotions need to be acknowledged and communicated in intimate relationships to help resolve conflict. They include sadness in relation to loss, anger in response to violation, and fear in response to threat.

Secondary emotions are those responses that are secondary to other, more primary internal processes and may be defenses against these processes. Secondary emotions are our reactions to our own emotional responses to a stimulus rather than the responses to the situation itself. They involve more implicit and explicit processing than primary responses, are much more influenced by conscious processing, and involve the evaluation and sometimes the inhibition or distortion of primary responses. Examples include feeling angry in response to feeling hurt, feeling afraid about feeling angry, or feeling guilty about a traumatic event by attributing responsibility to oneself for the event. In couples' interactions, secondary emotions are generally the harder, relationship-damaging emotions of anger, disgust, and contempt. Secondary emotions need to be explored to get at their more primary generators. The key premise is that it is the awareness of adaptive primary emotions that promotes bonding, conflict resolution, and problem solving.

Maladaptive primary emotions involve repetitive negative feelings that resist change. In being the very first reaction one has to one's partner, these are primary emotions, but they are based on wounds and unresolved past experience rather than on adaptive responses to present circumstances. These are feelings such as a core sense of loneliness, abandonment, shame, or worthlessness, or recurrent feelings of anxious inadequacy, or the explosive anger or abusive contempt that destroys relationships. Such feelings result in conflict and leave partners feeling stuck, often hopeless, helpless, and in despair. These are the emotions we want to help clients regulate and transform.

The negative cycle that couples enter on the basis of their maladaptive responses often involves a dance that they may later refer to as moments of insanity rather than a representation of how they truly feel. In these dances both partners may shift into what they later see as "not me" states of emotion dysregulation. The problem is that these are negative states that are self-absorbing. Once one is in them, these states often self-reinforce and intensify. These "not me" states are maladaptive emotional states that need to be transformed.

A good example of this type of maladaptive state is when a husband wants to be close whereas his wife is distant. He reacts to something she has said and feels hurt and ignored. He had hoped to be close and make love. In these states his sense of longing may become physical, and he yearns for something from her from deep within his body. He feels hurt and angry and sees her as cold and rejecting. He tries to tell her what he is feeling, maybe indirectly, and gets angry because she won't listen. He describes what she is doing that is so damaging to him and interrogates her about why she does this. He feels he desperately needs her softness and begins to feel intensely powerless and then angry. He loses all contact with her and just feels the wall she has put up between them. He becomes enraged at the wall, and all he can think of is destroying it because it prevents him from getting what he so desperately wants. He sees her as cruelly withholding and wishes to destroy the barrier. He hardly recognizes her expressions, so intent is he on removing the barrier.

His wife may feel a desperate need to protect herself from destruction. She just hears his voice, sees that familiar angry expression on his face. She does not know exactly what happened but just experiences this as dangerous. She fears becoming overwhelmed by him and sees him as intrusively powerful, and she closes up, becomes rigid, and walls out any contact. She feels tremendously attacked and powerless. He just seems to keep coming at her with angry words, questions, and accusations. She does not listen; she just wants him to stop and go away. These extreme states reflect an activation of

TABLE 11.1
Primary and Secondary Emotions in Couples' Negative Interactional Cycles

Position	Primary	Secondary
Active Partner		
Attachment Pursuer	Fear of abandonment, sadness at loss	Anger, contempt
Identity Dominant	Shame at loss of face, fear of threat to position	Contempt, anger
Reactive Partner		
Attachment Withdrawer	Anxiety at abandonment, shame at inadequacy, or anger at intrusion	Defensive anger, absence of emotion or avoidance, depression or boredom
Identity Submitter	Fear of inadequacy, anger at control	Caring, placating

both partners' core maladaptive emotion states. He has entered his feeling of powerless, anxious abandonment and rages against this. She has entered her fear of intrusion and annihilation and walls off to protect herself. Both of these maladaptive states are based on past experience, in which the partners suffered emotional injuries to their sense of security and identity. These emotional states need to be confronted and transformed.

Couples' conflict results from negative interactional cycles supported by secondary or maladaptive emotional states (Greenberg, in press). Cycles of attack and defense are supported predominantly by anger and fear, whereas dominant and submissive cycles are governed by contempt and shame. Table 11.1 shows both the primary and the secondary emotions in each position. In the attachment cycle the primary emotion in response to threats to security in the pursuer is fear, but the expressed secondary emotion is anger. In the withdrawer the primary emotions are fear of inadequacy or anger, but the expressed secondary emotions are related to avoidance and involve withdrawn depression, a cold wall, or defensive rejection. By contrast, when the conflict is in the identity domain, the threat is not to connection or security but rather to identity and status. Here the dominant person's social status, sense of worth, and self-esteem are challenged. As shown in Table 11.1, when people's dominant roles or views of self are threatened, they respond with secondary or instrumental anger or contempt to protect their position in their own and in the other's eyes. In the submissive person one sees secondary placating, caretaking, or pleasing expressions, but the more primary feelings are fear and anger. Expressions of underlying shame and fear beget more empathic and compassionate responses.

This illustrates that one way to regulate emotions is by accessing more underlying emotions. Once these are accessed and revealed to the partner, the partner is more likely to respond in a more understanding way, and a positive cycle is initiated.

Principles of Emotional Change in Therapy

In this section we articulate principles for emotion regulation in EFCT. Although these principles of emotional change were derived specifically for EFCT, they are as applicable to and potentially useful for other established couple therapy approaches, particularly those that include emotional components in their treatment. For example, integrative behavioral couple therapy (IBCT; Dimidjian, Martell, & Christensen, 2002) adopts acceptance strategies that, like EFCT, involve encouraging empathic joining between the partners. Object relations couple therapy (Scharff & Bagnini, 2002) and insight-oriented couples therapy (Snyder & Schneider, 2002) involve work to move beyond defensive processes to access underlying affective processes. Cognitive–behavioral couple therapy has also come to recognize the importance of working with emotion, helping people to access and differentiate restricted emotions, and contain overwhelming emotional responses (Baucom, Epstein, & LaTaillade, 2002).

The empirically grounded principles of EFCT described in the following section (Greenberg, 2002) relate to both emotional arousal and emotion regulation in the broad sense of these terms.

The Therapeutic Relationship

First, therapists join and connect emotionally with couples and families. This is important in regulating emotion because a good working alliance with the family involving a respectful, emotion-validating therapeutic bond is a crucial element of helping people calm down. Therapists also selectively attend to primary adaptive emotions and thereby shift clients' focus of attention and begin to change their manner of processing emotion.

Emotional Awareness and Expression

The therapist helps clients to symbolize emotions in words and express them to someone. Putting emotion into words can be curative in and of itself. In couple therapy this helps partners reveal their inner worlds both to themselves and to each other in a manner that has not previously occurred. This type of emotional awareness is not just talking about feeling; it involves experiencing the feeling in awareness and having one's partner perceive it in one's face and voice. Accessing and experiencing emotions also are important in that they involve overcoming avoidance. Partners learn that by facing and acknowledging their most dreaded feelings and painful emotions and surviving they are more able to cope (Greenberg & Bolger, 2001).

There are three ways in which this principle operates within EFCT. First, helping individuals gain emotional awareness of softer, underlying attachment- and identity-oriented emotions such as fear and shame underneath their anger or contempt, and autonomy- or boundary-oriented emotions such as anger under withdrawal, is key to interactional change. In couples, secondary emotions such as angry, blaming responses tend to fuel conflict. They represent attempted solutions to the problem of not getting needs for closeness and autonomy met, but instead these solutions become the problem. These responses tend to focus on the other person and involve attack and attempts to destroy. In these states people use "you" language (i.e., "You are bad, wrong, to blame" and so forth). Expressing secondary anger that obscures hurt and vulnerability does not dissipate the anger or enhance communication but rather just tends to lead couples into further negative cycles and the therapy process in circles. Expression of the more vulnerable emotions of fear and shame allows partners to draw closer. Thus, if a partner feels secondary rage, he or she needs to learn how to calm the rage and access what is at the bottom of it. If one often gets very angry, one needs not only to control one's anger but also to learn to experience and express more vulnerable feelings beneath the anger. Usually this involves feelings of shame, powerlessness, vulnerability, helplessness, sadness, loneliness, or abandonment. Expressing underlying fear, shame, or hurt will have a very different impact on one's partner than expressing destructive rage. Hence, being aware and getting in touch with core feelings as they arise are key ways to prevent the development of destructive rage. Therapists need to help people develop the ability to soothe their own maladaptive emotional states and insecurities and also to soothe these states in their partner. One of the best antidotes to negative escalation is the ability to soothe vulnerability in the self and other.

Second, awareness of the role of emotional responses in driving interactions leads to the possibility of developing new patterns. When a couple's attention is brought to the role of their emotions in perpetuating negative cycles, they can choose to change their interactions and engender new patterns.

Third, helping couples to explicate beliefs and past experiences around emotional expression helps partners to reframe each other's emotional behavior. Awareness of past socialization around emotional expression can help partners to depersonalize negative emotional expression. Couples then have a choice about how to create new, more positive emotional interactions.

Emotion Regulation

Therapeutically, it is important to distinguish between problems of overregulation and underregulation. These two types present quite different clinical pictures and we work with them in different ways. The overregulated person is highly constricted and avoids feelings, intellectualizes, interrupts any emergent expression, or avoids situations that might evoke feeling. Within couple therapy, the overregulated person who is highly constricted and avoidant requires help in increasing emotional awareness and expression. Accentuating pleasant experience as well as accessing suppressed, unpleasant, or negative emotional experience is important. For example, a person who has become overly rational will not be able to express warmth and love and help a partner feel loved.

By contrast, partners who struggle with underregulated emotions describe emotions as overwhelming, getting the better of them, and making them feel out of control. They may explode in rage, be overwhelmed by tears, or shrink into the floor in shame. Emotions that require down-regulation in couples generally are either secondary emotions such as anger or resignation or primary maladaptive emotions such as the shame of being worthless, the anxiety of basic insecurity, or panic. Overwhelming grief or sudden anger may also need to be regulated.

Therapeutic skills useful in down-regulation with couples involve such things as helping individuals establish a working distance from feelings of hopelessness or worthlessness; increasing positive emotions such as joy, hope, or caring; reducing vulnerability to overwhelming fear, shame, and hopelessness; self-soothing, time-outs, relaxation, development of self-empathy and compassion, and self-talk. The ability to regulate breathing and the ability to observe emotions and let them come and go are important in helping to regulate many types of emotional distress. Skills useful in down-regulating escalating interactions involve such things as focusing on self rather than other, learning about and avoiding things that provoke a partner's escalation, being able to step back or see the humor in conflict situations, soothing one's partner, and soft start-ups—approaching one's partner with more vulnerable emotions—in conflict situations.

In fears of abandonment and feelings of shame, two of the most important skills for individuals to master are taking an observer's stance to get a working distance from overwhelming despair and hopelessness and developing self-soothing capacities to calm and comfort core anxieties and humiliation. Physiological soothing involves activation of the parasympathetic nervous system to regulate heart rate, breathing, and other sympathetic functions that speed up under stress. At the more deliberate behavioral and cognitive levels, promoting partners' abilities to recognize and be compassionate to their emerging painful emotional experience is the first step toward tolerating emotion and self-soothing. Soothing comes interpersonally in the form of empathic attunement to affect and through acceptance and validation by another person.

Reflection on Emotion

In addition to recognizing emotions, promoting further reflection on emotional experience allows partners to integrate their emotions into their own stories. Reflection helps to create new meaning and develop new narratives to explain experience (Greenberg & Pascual-Leone, 1997). Reflection also allows both people to reframe emotions and take a new position vis-à-vis one's partner. Thus, rather than expressing one feeling, "I can't survive. I need you," a person can say, "I need you but I see that you have needs too." In a similar way, reflecting on anger may allow one to change one's position from "I am angry. I hate you and it is all your fault that I feel so alone and abandoned" to "Yes, I do feel angry at you but it is not all your fault. I realize some of my anger belongs to my mother."

Transforming Emotion

The final and probably most fundamental change principle involves the *changing of emotion with emotion.* Change from this perspective involves focusing on each individual's maladaptive emotional response, helping partners access the maladaptive emotions at the core of their vulnerabilities, and then transforming them by accessing more attachment- and identity-related adaptive emotions. In other words, once the evaluation is made that a person's response in an interactional cycle is maladaptive and needs to be changed, the maladaptive emotion needs to be aroused and another, more adaptive feeling that will help undo or replace the maladaptive state needs to be evoked. Reason alone or insight into patterns or origins of emotion is seldom sufficient to alter the thoughts and feelings associated with these maladaptive states. In a similar way, exposure alone is not enough to change these maladaptive states. The maladaptive feeling does not simply attenuate by being felt. Rather, a new experience that will generate an alternative feeling is necessary to transform, replace, or undo it.

For example, therapists can help couples identify the negative interactional cycle in which one partner is blaming and critical and the other is silent and withdrawn. The therapist can help the first partner to identify the fear of abandonment and desire for emotional closeness that are driving the attacking behavior. It is ironic that the emotional expression serves to push the other away. By helping this partner express emotional needs and fears underlying the hostile attack, the therapist helps the withdrawn partner see vulnerability and move out of the defensive, withdrawn position into a more compassionate one. The second partner can similarly articulate the anxiety and fears of inadequacy that lie behind his or her silent, withdrawn stance. Specific methods of evoking alternate emotions have been explicated by Greenberg (2002, 2003). These include such interventions as shifting the focus of attention to subdominant emotions, accessing needs to get to other emotions, and changing interactions to evoke new emotions.

EFCT can also be helpful in addressing pathogenic beliefs within the maladaptive emotions and provide corrective emotional experiences. For example, in the case of adults who have been sexually abused as children, they may have learned to associate physical closeness with fear. Therapy can then focus on evoking the maladaptive emotional response in the one partner from the abuse situation, evoking the positive and nurturing response in the other partner, and restructuring the interaction so that the partner coming from the abuse situation can see that overtures of physical closeness do not indicate withdrawal or attack but rather indicate a move toward closeness, love, or security.

Therapist Emotional Processes

It is essential that the emotion-focused couple therapist stay attuned to the ongoing moment-by-moment emotional processes of the couple to maintain the therapeutic alliance with both partners, as well as to help partners to increase emotional awareness and regulate emotion. Therapists need to suspend their own value frameworks and be careful not to reach for closure too quickly (Rice, 1974). A high tolerance for ambiguity is demanded of the emotion-focused therapist.

Therapists bring a number of cognitive–affective capacities to their ability to be empathically attuned, the most important of these being imagination (Rogers, 1975). By actively imagining clients' experiences, therapists infer what clients feel, asking what they themselves might feel in response to the experiences clients describe. This provides the basis for empathic exploration of partners' inner experiences and allows therapists to make process distinctions between partners' expression of core emotions and other (secondary or maladaptive) emotions (Watson, Goldman, & Vanaerschot, 1997).

Such attunement requires therapists to be fully congruent, being able at a given moment to recognize their own emotional experience so that they can take note of it and use it productively. EFCT therapists therefore need to be sufficiently emotionally aware so that they do not miss important aspects of partners' emotional experience or become overwhelmed by their own emotional experience. It is thus necessary for therapists, at times, to pursue their own emotion-focused therapy or to seek supervision or consultation if they do not feel able to be fully present and empathically attuned in such a relationship.

EMPIRICAL FOUNDATIONS

The central focus of the empirical work on emotion-focused couple therapy has been to determine its efficacy for treating marital distress. Studies have examined the impact of EFCT on distressed couples as assessed by a wide range of indices including psychological and dyadic adjustment, intimacy, and target complaints about the relationship. A meta-analysis has been conducted (Johnson, Hunsley, Greenberg, & Schindler, 1999) on outcome measures (dyadic adjustment, intimacy, target complaints) reported in four randomized clinical trials in which couples were seeking treatment for their relationship distress and were assigned to either an EFCT condition, an alternative form of couples therapy, or a wait-list control group (Goldman & Greenberg, 1992; James, 1991; Johnson & Greenberg, 1985; Walker, Johnson, Masion, & Clothier, 1996). The mean weighted effect size across studies was 1.28—a large and clinically meaningful effect size for psychotherapy trials.

Beyond treating general relationship distress, Dessaulles, Johnson, and Denton (2003) compared 14 sessions of EFCT with pharmacotherapy in treating wives' major depression in 18 couples randomly assigned to treatment condition. Both interventions were equally effective in reducing depressive symptoms, although there was some evidence that women receiving EFCT made greater improvement following termination than those receiving pharmacotherapy.

In a recent study, Greenberg and colleagues (Greenberg et al., 2003) examined the effects of EFCT for 20 couples in which 1 member had an unresolved emotional injury involving his or her current partner. EFCT treatment was short term, lasting 10 to 12 sessions. At the end of treatment, couples scored significantly better than wait-list controls on all indices of change including dyadic adjustment, symptoms of individual emotional or behavioral distress, forgiveness, and empathy and acceptance toward self and partner.

In a follow-up task analysis, Greenberg et al. (2003) found that revealing the impact of the injury and expressing the hurt, pain, and anger from the emotional injury was an important first step toward resolution. Then it was important for the injurer to acknowledge and tolerate the partner's distress and to resist the desire to make the other's distress go away or to minimize it. It was essential that injurers empathized both with how deeply their partner was wounded by the injury and with how their initial empathic failure to respond to the wound constituted another injury, often as important as the initial one. It was important for the therapist at this stage to create a safe, supportive, validating environment to model empathy and to help the partners explore and communicate their corresponding roles in the unfolding of events at the time of the injury as well as before and after the injury happened. Most important was to promote empathic responsiveness in the injurer to the injured partner's wounds. Empathy is one of the great emotion regulators in that it soothes the hurt.

After recognizing and empathizing with the partner's woundedness and pain resulting from the injury, the injurer needed to make an unqualified apology by taking responsibility for the harm done. In this regard, the injurer's expression of shame for what was done, in which the action tendency is to shrink into the ground, was more important than the expression of guilt, in which the action tendency is to apologize and atone. Expressions of "I'm sorry" did not help in these situations of betrayal and eventually promoted frustration in the apologizer. Those partners who expressed shame at what they had done evoked compassion from their partners. These were the beginning steps toward establishing trust and forgiveness. Whereas shame is usually viewed as a self-destructive, problematic emotion that one wants to change in therapy, in this context it was an adaptive expression that had a positive impact on the injured partner. When injured partners saw that betrayers truly felt remorseful and that the betrayers judged themselves to have failed some standard fundamental to their identities, they were more likely to trust that the betrayers would not repeat the injury.

The therapist needed to promote the expression of remorse and regret but be careful not to shame the betrayer. The injurer needed to *feel* shame but not *be* shamed. The therapist also needed to put the injury in the context of the negative cycle that had preceded it and help identify partners' underlying vulnerabilities that were involved in the cycle. It was very important for the injured partner to acknowledge and own the need for a protective wall; both the injuring partner and therapist needed to respect the other partner's need for it. The therapist could help the betrayer to ask for, but not demand, forgiveness. Finally both partners took responsibility for their own part in the injury. The injured person then needed to express specifics of what was needed for him or her to trust again, and the injuring partner needed to receive these requests without blame.

A handful of studies have investigated the change process in EFCT. One study (Johnson & Greenberg, 1987) compared best sessions for three couples with those of three couples who did not show significant improvement. Videotapes of best sessions (chosen by the couples) were independently rated on the Experiencing scale (Klein, Mathieu, Gendlin, & Kiesler, 1969) and for affiliative and autonomous responses using the Structural Analysis of Social Behavior (Benjamin, 1974). In addition, "softenings" were identified, defined as moments when a previously critical partner expresses vulnerability and asks for comfort and connection from his or her partner. The high-change couples showed significantly higher levels of experiencing in best sessions. The blaming partner was also more likely to move to a more affiliative, less coercive position toward the other partner in this session. On average, five softening change events were found in the sessions of the successful couples, and none were found in the sessions of the low-change couples.

A second study (Alden, 1989) compared peak session events to poor session events in 16 cases of EFCT. Results revealed that in peak session events, 84% of the statements were affiliative, as opposed to 65% in the poor session events. Also, peak session events revealed a greater proportion of self-focused (rather than other-focused) positive statements. Results suggested that a greater self-focus that involved turning inward to experience one's responses to situations and acceptance of the other rather than focusing and blaming the other was important in resolving conflict.

Another study of 16 couples demonstrated that therapist-facilitated intimate, emotionally laden self-disclosure was more likely to lead to affiliative statements by the partner than randomly selected responses. That is, revealing underlying experience in an intimate manner led to a change in interaction (Greenberg, Ford, Alden, & Johnson, 1993). Finally, a recent task analysis of four EFCT sessions by Bradley and Furrow (2004) found that emotional experiencing and the disclosure of attachment-related affect and fears were the key client features of successful softening events; moreover, consistent with proposed mechanisms of change in EFCT, specific therapist interventions linked to softening events involved intensifying a couple's emotional experience and promoting intrapsychic awareness and interpersonal shifts in attachment-related interactions.

FUTURE DIRECTIONS IN RESEARCH ON EMOTION-FOCUSED COUPLES THERAPY

Further research needs to be conducted to understand the process of therapeutic change by examining the effect of EFCT on specific client emotional processes such as overcoming anger and the process of forgiving. In the forgiveness study described earlier, it appears that dealing with anger and sadness rather than avoiding it is important as an early step in approaching forgiveness. In addition, it appears that revealing shame by the wrongdoer is far more convincing to the spouse than is apology or guilt (Greenberg, Warwar, & Malcolm, 2003). The effect of dealing with underlying shame and powerlessness in dominance processes and in certain subgroups of violent men also needs to be studied.

Cross-disciplinary collaboration with developmental and clinical psychology and family process research would benefit EFCT in a number of ways. For example, research on the suitability of this treatment for different attachment styles would benefit from collaboration with those who have expertise in measuring attachment styles. Further research demonstrating the importance of attachment bonds in promoting resilience in the face of stress and flexibility in information processing (Mikulincer, Florian, & Weller, 1993) would lend additional support to the EFCT process. Family process researchers can provide a focus on the effects of emotional disconnection in families. For example, a recent study (Liddle et al., 2000) revealed the negative impacts of emotional disconnection in families and the potential for change when fears about rejection and abandonment are shared.

Additional research should be conducted to examine the effects of EFCT in engendering conflict resolution that is less damaging to children. For example, Gottman and colleagues (Gottman, 1997) hypothesized that the optimal approach to parenting involves a positive emotion-coaching philosophy. Such emotion coaching has been related to a number of positive child outcomes including the ability to self-soothe, academic achievement, and physical health (Gottman, Katz, & Hooven, 1997). Further research should link couples' styles of emotional relating developed through the EFCT process to parental emotional coaching styles.

It is clear that further research needs to be done to test the effects of EFCT with different forms of relational distress and their concomitant problems, to understand the role of individual differences in resolving emotional problems, and to delineate the specific aspects of EFCT that are effective and that prevent relapse. Perhaps most important, future research needs to be directed toward a further delineation of the specific individual and interpersonal processes that lead to emotional change as a result of EFCT.

REFERENCES

Alden, L. (1989). *A process comparison of peak and poor sessions in emotionally focused marital therapy*. Unpublished master's thesis, University of British Columbia, Vancouver, Canada.

Baucom, D. H., Epstein, N., & LaTaillade, J. J. (2002). Cognitive–behavioral couple therapy. In A. S. Gurman & N. S. Jacobson (Eds.), *Clinical handbook of couple therapy* (pp. 26–58). New York: Guilford Press.

Benjamin, L. S. (1974). Structural analysis of social behavior. *Psychological Review, 81*, 392–425.

Bowlby, J . (1989). *A secure base. Clinical applications of attachment theory*. London: Routledge.

Bradley, B., & Furrow, J. L. (2004). Toward a mini-theory of the blamer softening event: Tracking the moment-by-moment process. *Journal of Marital and Family Therapy, 30*, 1–12.

Cicchetti, D., Ackerman, B. P., & Izard, C. E. (1995). Emotions and emotion regulation in developmental psychopathology. *Development and Psychopathology, 7*, 1–10.

Cummings, E. M., & Davies, P. T. (1994). *Children and marital conflict: The impact of marital dispute and resolution*. New York: Guilford Press.

Dessaulles, A., Johnson, S. M., & Denton, W. H. (2003). Emotion-focused therapy for couples in the treatment of depression: A pilot study. *American Journal of Family Therapy, 31*, 345–353.

Dimidjian, S., Martell, C. R., & Christensen, A. R. (2002). Integrative behavioral couple therapy. In A. S. Gurman & N. S. Jacobson (Eds.), *Clinical handbook of couple therapy* (pp. 251–277). New York: Guilford Press.

Elliott, R., Watson, J., Goldman, R. N., & Greenberg, L. S. (2003). *Learning emotion-focused therapy: The process-experiential approach to change*. Washington, DC: American Psychological Association.

Frijda N. (1986). *The emotions*. Cambridge, England: Cambridge University Press.

Gilbert, P. (2000a). Social mentalities: Internal "social" conflicts and the role of inner warmth and compassion in cognitive therapy. In P. Gilbert & K. G. Bailey (Eds.), *Genes on the couch: Explorations in evolutionary psychotherapy* (pp. 118–150). Hove, England: Brenner-Routledge.

Gilbert, P. (2000b). Varieties of submissive behaviour: Their evolution and role in depression. In L. Sloman & P. Gilbert (Eds.), *Subordination and defeat: An evolutionary approach to mood disorders* (pp. 3–46). Hillsdale, NJ: Erlbaum.

Gilbert, P., & McGuire, M. (1998). Shame, social roles, and status: The psychobiological continuum from monkey to human. In P. Gilbert & B. Andrews (Eds.), *Shame: Interpersonal behavior, psychopathology, and culture* (pp. 99–125). New York: Oxford University Press.

Goldman, A., & Greenberg, L. S. (1992). Comparison of integrated systemic and emotionally focused approaches to couples therapy. *Journal of Consulting and Clinical Psychology, 60,* 962–969.

Gottman, J. M. (1997). *The heart of parenting: How to raise an emotionally intelligent child.* New York: Simon & Schuster.

Gottman, J. M., Katz, L. F., & Hooven, C. (1997). Parental meta-emotion philosophy and the emotional life of families: Theoretical models and preliminary data. *Journal of Family Psychology, 10,* 243–291.

Greenberg, L. S. (2002). *Emotion-focused therapy: Coaching clients to work through their feelings.* Washington, DC: American Psychological Association.

Greenberg, L. S. (2003). Evolutionary perspectives on emotion: Making sense of what we feel. *Journal of Cognitive Psychotherapy, 16,* 331–348.

Greenberg, L. S. (in press). Emotions in interpersonal conflict. In A. Meier & M. Rovers (Eds.), *Conflict resolution.*

Greenberg, L. S., & Bolger, E. (2001). An emotion-focused approach to the over-regulation of emotion and emotional pain. *Journal of Clinical Psychology, 57,* 197–212.

Greenberg, L. S., Ford, L., Alden, L., & Johnson, S. (1993). In-session change in emotionally focused therapy. *Journal of Consulting and Clinical Psychology, 61,* 25–38.

Greenberg, L. S., & Johnson, S. M. (1988). *Emotionally focused couples therapy.* New York: Guilford Press.

Greenberg, L. S., & Pascual-Leone, J. (1997). Emotion in the creation of personal meaning. In M. Power & C. Brewin (Eds.), *Transformation of meaning* (pp. 157–174). London: Wiley.

Greenberg, L. S., Warwar, S., & Malcolm, W. (2003, August). *Emotion-focused therapy of emotional injury; Forgiveness and letting go.* Paper presented at the annual meeting of the American Psychological Association, Toronto, Ontario, Canada.

James, P. (1991). Effects of a communication training component added to an emotionally focused couples therapy. *Journal of Marital and Family Therapy, 17,* 263–267.

Johnson, S., & Greenberg, L. S. (1985). The differential effectiveness of experiential and problem solving interventions in resolving marital conflict. *Journal of Consulting and Clinical Psychology, 53,* 175–184.

Johnson, S., & Greenberg, L. S. (1987). Relating process to outcome in marital therapy. *Journal of Marital and Family Therapy, 14,* 175–184.

Johnson, S., Hunsley, J., Greenberg, L. S., & Schindler, D. (1999). Emotionally focused couples therapy: Status and challenges. *Clinical Psychology: Science and Practice, 6,* 67–79.

Johnson, S., & Whiffen, V. (Eds.). (2003). *Attachment theory: A perspective for couple and family therapy.* New York: Guilford Press.

Kiecolt-Glasser, J. K., & Newton, T. L. (2001). Marriage and health: His and hers. *Psychological Bulletin, 127,* 472–503.

Klein, M. H., Mathieu, P. L., Gendlin, E. T., & Kiesler, D. J. (1969). *The experiencing scale: A research and training manual.* Madison: University of Wisconsin.

LeDoux, J. E. (1996). *The emotional brain.* New York: Simon & Schuster.

Liddle, H. A., Rowe, C., Diamond, C. R., Sessa, F. M., Schmidt, S., & Ettinger, D. (2000). Towards a developmental family therapy: The clinical utility of research on adolescence. *Journal of Marital and Family Therapy, 26,* 485–500.

Mikulincer, M., Florian, V., & Weller, A. (1993). Attachment styles, coping strategies, and post-traumatic psychological distress. *Journal of Personality and Social Psychology, 64,* 817–826.

Rice, L. N. (1974). The evocative function of the therapist. In D. Wexler & L. N. Rice (Eds.), *Innovations in client-centered therapy.* New York: Wiley.

Rogers, C. R. (1975). Empathic: An unappreciated way of being. *The Counseling Psychologist, 5,* 2–10.

Scharff, J. S., & Bagnini, C. (2002). Object relations couple therapy. In A. S. Gurman & N. S. Jacobson (Eds.), *Clinical handbook of couple therapy* (pp. 59–85). New York: Guilford Press.

Schore, A. N. (2003). *Affect dysregulation and disorders of the self.* New York: Norton.

Schupp, H., Ohman, A., Junghofer, M., Weike, A., Stockburger, J., & Hamm, A. (2004). The facilitated processing of threatening faces: An ERP analysis. *Emotion, 4,* 189–200.

Snyder, D. K., & Schneider, W. J. (2002). Affective reconstruction: A pluralistic, developmental approach. In A. S. Gurman & N. S. Jacobson (Eds.), *Clinical handbook of couple therapy* (3rd ed., pp. 151–179). New York: Guilford Press.

Sroufe, L. A. (1996). *Emotional development: The organization of emotional life in the early years.* New York: Cambridge University Press.

Walker, J., Johnson, S., Masion, I., & Clothier, P. (1996). An emotionally focused marital intervention for couples with chronically ill children. *Journal of Consulting and Clinical Psychology, 64,* 1029–1036.

Watson, J. C., Goldman, R. N., & Vanaerschot, G. (1997). Empathic: A postmodern way of being? In L. S. Greenberg, J. C. Watson, & G. Lietaer (Eds.), *Handbook of experiential therapy* (pp. 61–81). New York: Guilford Press.

Whisman, M. A. (1999). Marital dissatisfaction and psychiatric disorders: Results from the National Co-Morbidity Study. *Journal of Abnormal Psychology, 108,* 701–706.

12

INTERVENING WITH COUPLES AND FAMILIES TO TREAT EMOTION DYSREGULATION AND PSYCHOPATHOLOGY

ALAN E. FRUZZETTI AND KATHERINE M. IVERSON

Couple and family interactions affect individual well-being and psychopathology in a variety of ways. For example, couple and family interactions influence (a) the etiology of individual distress and psychopathology, (b) the maintenance of distress and disorder, (c) the treatment outcomes, (d) relapse versus maintenance of treatment gains, and (e) the naturalistic course of wellness or disorder (cf. Fruzzetti, 1996; Fruzzetti & Iverson, 2004b; Snyder & Whisman, 2004). In addition, individual disordered behaviors (e.g., depression, substance abuse, suicidality, borderline personality disorder) have been demonstrated to have a deleterious effect on the quality of relationship functioning, both in couples and in parent–child relationships.

However, the mechanisms through which family processes affect individual psychopathology, and through which individual psychopathology affects relationship functioning, have not been clearly established. Whisman (2001) has highlighted the importance of research aimed at understanding the specific factors that mediate the relation between psychopathology and relationship dysfunction. In this chapter we maintain that accurate disclosure of private experiences (e.g., emotions, wants, thoughts), along with validating and invalidating responses to those disclosures, mediates the relation between individual emotion regulation (and psychopathology) and relationship distress and dysfunction.

To date, research has focused less on identifying the specific family interactions that mediate the relation between individual and couple or family dysfunction, and more on the role of common relationship events or generic processes. For example, research shows that physical abuse, aggression, or domestic violence; poor communication; poor problem solving; nonegalitarian relationship functioning; low warmth; negative affect; and other relationship processes and events have significant deleterious effects on individual functioning. However, few studies have tried to explain how these factors influence individual emotion regulation and well-being. In a similar way, few attempts have been made to develop unifying models that use tested mechanisms that explain (rather than simply describe) the relation between individual disordered behavior and behavior of a partner or family member with whom the individual transacts. Moreover, given the current zeitgeist regarding adult psychopathology in particular, it is almost automatically assumed that one will look at the individual's biology to understand and treat individual psychopathology. This is evident in the popularity of antidepressants to treat depression and anxiety, despite relatively few advantages in outcomes compared with placebo (e.g., Kirsch, Moore, Scoboria, & Nicholls, 2002). In the service of improving treatment, it is important for researchers and clinicians to understand the family and social factors that influence biological factors both developmentally and cross-sectionally, and how these processes operate, including the potential impact of reciprocal causality. But it is also essential to transcend biological and other linear models of psychopathology and instead evaluate individual problems in their interpersonal or familial context (Fruzzetti & Iverson, 2004b).

Although it addresses many of the same basic questions as other chapters in this volume, the specific purposes of this chapter are (a) to develop a coherent, scientifically based model that explains how individual emotion regulation or dysregulation and partner or family member validating and invalidating responses mediate the relation between individual distress or psychopathology and couple or family dysfunction; and (b) to describe some of the specific clinical interventions with couples and families that follow logically from this model.

CONCEPTUAL, THEORETICAL, AND METHODOLOGICAL ISSUES

Although disagreement remains about the essential components of emotion regulation or dysregulation, there is some emerging convergence about what is involved. For example, Gross (1998, p. 275) suggested that emotion regulation includes a variety of specific behaviors and "processes by which individuals influence which emotions they have, when they have them, and how they experience and express these emotions." In addition, Thompson (1994) maintained that emotion regulation processes necessarily are in the service of the individual's larger, long-term goals rather than only in the service of short-term goals. We agree, and we note that emotion dysregulation often includes such a high level of experienced aversive emotional arousal that the individual may engage in problematic behaviors simply to escape from these short-term unpleasant private experiences (e.g., substance use, withdrawal, or verbal aggression). Emotion dysregulation occurs when the individual is not able to accept an emotional experience successfully and simultaneously is not able to change it effectively (Fruzzetti & Iverson, 2004b; Fruzzetti, Shenk, Mosco, & Lowry, 2003). Instead, the dysregulated person engages in behaviors that are problematic either because they exacerbate the negative arousal in the short term or because they lead to more problems later on, often interpersonally. For our purposes, emotion dysregulation is different from simply being upset or having a lot of emotional intensity or arousal, during which a person can continue to manage his or her situation or experience in ways that are compatible with both short- and long-term goals.

We will explicate a set of components of emotion regulation and dysregulation that help to clarify the role of couple and family interactions in the development of emotion regulation versus dysregulation tendencies and the development of emotion regulation skills. Although this particular model of emotion regulation is different in some respects, it is generally compatible with prominent models of emotion regulation in most ways (e.g., Eisenberg, Cumberland, & Spinrad, 1998; Gross, 1998; Gross et al., chap. 1, this volume; Linehan, 1993; Plutchik, 1994; Saarni & Crowley, 1990; Southam-Gerow & Kendall, 2002; Thompson, 1994).

Components of Emotion Dysregulation

The present model for emotion dysregulation includes three major components. Although any one component, if sufficiently problematic, could result in dysregulation, the presence of more than one component significantly increases the chance of dysregulation. These components are (a) vulnerability to negative emotion, specifically high sensitivity, high reactivity, and slow return to baseline (cf. Linehan, 1993), which together influence present-state emotional arousal; (b) deficient emotion-relevant skills or competencies that allow a person to choose situations in which he or she can act effectively; manage social interactions effectively; be aware of relevant stimuli; discriminate more relevant from less relevant stimuli; identify, label, tolerate, and express private experiences accurately; and manage arousal in ways that are consistent with long-term goals and values (cf. Fruzzetti et al., 2003);

and (c) problematic responses of others (especially partners and parents) to expressions of emotion, wants, thoughts, and goals (Fruzzetti & Fruzzetti, 2003; Fruzzetti & Iverson, 2004b; Fruzzetti, Shenk, & Hoffman, 2005). One can respond to another person's display, expression, or disclosure of an emotion, want or desire, thought, action, or other experience either by validating or invalidating that experience or behavior. When people acknowledge or legitimize a person's experience or behavior, they "accept" it as true. Validation is the communication of this acceptance and understanding, which typically moderates high emotional arousal. Alternatively, one can ignore, criticize, pathologize, or fail to legitimize a person's actual experience or behavior. Invalidation occurs when people communicate that they reject or fail to understand true or legitimate experiences or behaviors, which typically creates or exacerbates negative emotional arousal.

Next we consider each component in this model of emotion regulation and dysregulation in more detail.

1. Vulnerability to Negative Emotions

Sensitivity to Relationship Stimuli. Sensitivity refers to an individual's ability to notice a relevant stimulus and bring it into his or her awareness while not being overwhelmed with less relevant stimuli. A person is constantly affected (or not) by available stimuli occurring both in the world "outside" the person (public events) and events "inside" the person (private events and experiences). These events are happening simultaneously. Each individual's general "sensitivity" to stimuli directly contributes to his or her vulnerability to emotional reactivity and subsequent ability to regulate his or her emotions. Moderate sensitivity to a broad array of stimuli in one's internal and external environment contributes to effective self-management processes. Hypersensitive people discriminate emotionally relevant stimuli quickly and exhibit a low threshold for an emotional reaction (Linehan, 1993); alternatively, hyposensitive people may not discriminate very many emotionally relevant stimuli and have a high threshold for any emotional reaction. Thus, highly sensitive people may be more vulnerable to becoming emotionally activated. However, hyposensitive people may be unaware of important events in their world, sometimes leading to misunderstandings and missed opportunities for giving and receiving support, problem prevention or problem solving, and closeness.

Emotional Arousal or Reactivity. Attending to a stimulus usually elicits some amount of automatic emotional arousal, which typically is considered reactivity. When individuals react normatively to a stimulus or match the arousal of others, they are better able to manage their own relationship behaviors and ultimately maintain effective communication. Communication is optimized at moderate levels of arousal. When one has low reactivity, the response or lack thereof may communicate misunderstanding or a lack of caring and leave the other person feeling misunderstood or not cared for (e.g., "he is not taking me seriously") and lead to withdrawal or conflict escalation. However, an emotionally reactive person, although highly supportive and loving in many situations, may be highly negative in situations of conflict or distress.

Slow Return to Baseline. Finally, people with emotion regulation deficits often experience a slower return to emotional baseline once arousal has been activated (cf. Linehan, 1993). Furthermore, when someone's emotional reactivity is slower to return to baseline, the impact of hypersensitivity and hyperreactivity to other relationship events is multiplied. That is, events that would otherwise elicit a moderate reaction trigger dysregulated responses when the person's arousal is still high from previous reactions.

The combination of relational sensitivity, reactivity, and slow return to baseline likely perpetuate the well-known "negative escalation" and "demand and withdraw" cycles exhibited in distressed couples (Fruzzetti & Jacobson, 1990; Weiss & Heyman, 1990).

2. Deficiencies in Emotion-Relevant Skills

Poor Situation Awareness, Selection, and Management. Some parents and partners continue blithely to recapitulate problem interactions, perhaps never learning to discriminate relationally "dangerous" situations or how to negotiate them differently. This task is similar to the strategy of "situation selection" noted by Gross et al. (chap. 1, this volume) but includes additional, more relationship-specific skills to manage conflict situations.

Lack of Awareness of Emotion. Skillful behavior involves an awareness of the fact that one's own emotional arousal is rising. Dysregulated individuals are often unaware that their arousal is increasing, especially at lower levels of arousal, and may display labile emotions.

Difficulty Tolerating Primary Emotions. Many dysregulated people "escape" to anger or another emotion to avoid difficult emotions such as disappointment, hurt, guilt, or fear. To label an emotion accurately, a person must be able to tolerate that emotion until it runs its course and subsides naturally, or at least tolerate it long enough to use effective change strategies. Primary emotions are considered the authentic, normative, and accurate emotional response in a given situation, whereas secondary emotions are considered learned responses to the primary emotion (cf. Greenberg & Safran, 1989). Reactivity from secondary emotions, such as anger or defensiveness, usually functions to exacerbate misunderstanding and arousal and to retard communication and support. That is, when individuals allow a secondary emotion to guide their behavior while interacting with another person, they actually express an inaccurate view of their experience, making understanding and acceptance by the other person quite difficult. In contrast, when individuals understand their own emotional reaction ("I'm feeling defensive because my partner used an accusatory tone"), they are self-validating and will likely be more able to stop the negative escalation process in the service of relationship goals. They may also be more able to express their experience accurately and descriptively rather than blaming the other, increasing the chances of a validating response from the other person.

Ineffective Attention Control. Because narrow attention to a negatively arousing stimulus can promote dysregulation, it is more effective either to place a negative stimulus into a larger context, such that one is responding to more than just the negative stimulus, or simply to distract oneself from the arousing stimulus. In contrast, focusing excessively on a negative emotion per se, rather than titrating attention to the emotion, can further increase arousal or lead to secondary emotional responses.

Lack of Awareness of the Relation Between the Stimulus and the Emotion. If a strong negative emotion occurs and one is not able to connect that response to a relevant stimulus, one may become more aroused and more likely to inaccurately attach the emotion to a less relevant but available stimulus. This may lead to frustrated attempts to problem solve, invalidation from others, and further emotion escalation. Instead of reifying thoughts that accompany an emotional reaction, additional mindfulness skills may help one to realize that thoughts are just thoughts in a context, and that one's reaction may be different with more information or in a different context (e.g., starting with a lower baseline of arousal).

Inaccurate Labeling of Emotional Responses and Self-Validation. Inaccurate labels interfere with accurate expression and effective problem solving. It is easier to become stuck on one emotional response and therefore to engage in judging self or other, which fuels further and prolonged emotional arousal. Alternatively, accurate labeling of emotions is itself self-validating, leading to decreased arousal and reactivity and fewer judgments, thus making it easier for others to validate (Fruzzetti & Iverson, 2004b; Swann, 1997).

Dysfunctional Cognitive Responses. Judgments ("right vs. wrong" or "should vs. shouldn't") and inaccurate negative attributions are particularly common and problematic cognitive responses to both emotional stimuli and to rising emotional reactions. Both judgments and inaccurate negative attributions exacerbate negative emotional arousal, which in turn makes it easier to produce more judgments and inaccurate negative attributions. Judgments and inaccurate negative attributions may be about oneself, the other person, or the situation. Alternatively, describing emotions and the stimuli that triggered them is self-validating, helps to reduce negative arousal, and sets the stage for good communication and problem solving (Fruzzetti & Iverson, 2004b).

Inaccurate Expression. Accurate self-disclosure skills help all individuals to state their thoughts and feelings in a precise and accurate manner, without judgment or hostility. When reactivity is high or a person is feeling judgmental, it is unlikely that he or she will be able to express feelings in a manner that the other person is able to receive in a nonjudgmental way. This often results in heightened vulnerability and increased chances of invalidation by others.

Lack of General Relationship Skills or Motivation to Use Skills. Between situations of high arousal there are many opportunities for relationship enhancement and, conversely, many opportunities to create or exacerbate relationship malcontent. Building positive and intimate relationship experiences helps to reduce vulnerability, and practicing the other skills related to emotion regulation under ordinary, low-arousal conditions contributes to improved skillfulness. Alternatively, avoiding situations that are problematic, or staying stuck in negative arousal, contributes toward poorer outcomes for the relationship and for the individuals involved. Also, during any interaction, relationship skills will increase the likelihood of understanding and validation and decrease the chances of invalidation and negative emotion escalation.

3. Problematic Responses of Others

Lack of Acceptance and Validation Skills in the Partner or Family Member. Invalidating responses communicate that the other's private experiences (thoughts, feelings, or desires) are not comprehensible, legitimate, or reasonable, do not make sense, are erroneous, or are otherwise unacceptable. Invalidating responses subtly or overtly challenge the legitimacy of the other person's thoughts, wants, emotions, beliefs, values, and goals, along with their disclosure. Because people typically define and value themselves according to their thoughts, feelings, wants, and behaviors, invalidation functionally conveys rejection and disregard for the other person's self-repertoire. Furthermore, when a person feels invalidated, arousal goes up and the probability of subsequent accurate, vulnerable self-disclosure decreases. In contrast, there are specific acceptance and validation skills that promote de-escalation of arousal, attention to the partner or other person, and effective communication. Skills that are more "accepting" in nature involve acknowledging or otherwise validating reactions and other behaviors.

Lack of Change or Problem Management Skills in the Partner or Family Member. There are also many relationship skills that focus on change and promote de-escalation of arousal, attention to the partner or other person, and effective communication. More "change-oriented" skills include proactively targeting behavior for change, staying inclusive and nonblaming ("our problem" vs. "your problem"), defining problems descriptively, actually solving problems, or simply managing disagreements in ways that are effective.

Linking Psychopathology and Emotion Dysregulation to Family Interactions

Problems in emotion regulation always occur in a context, and that context is likely to be interpersonal (see chap. 1, this volume). Distressed relationships typically demonstrate both dysfunctional couple or parent–child processes and individual emotion regulation deficits, at least in the context of their relationship problems. An individual may be perfectly capable of effective emotion regulation and communication in some relationships; however, his or her partner or parent may provide particular stimulus properties that elicit dysregulated responses. Couple and family therapists experience the unique challenge of managing each person's emotional reactivity toward the other, as well as treating each family member's own level of individual distress (Fruzzetti & Fruzzetti, 2003; Fruzzetti & Iverson, 2004a; Snyder & Whisman, 2004).

A transactional (reciprocal) model that highlights individual dysregulation, inaccurate expression, and invalidation provides one set of links between individual psychopathology and couple or family interactions (cf. Fruzzetti, Shenk, & Hoffman, 2005). Specifically, this model suggests that partner and family behaviors that are invalidating may create, maintain, or exacerbate emotion reactivity and dysregulation and that this heightened arousal makes inaccurate expression more likely, which in turn makes invalidation more likely. Left unchecked, this reciprocal process is self-maintaining and contributes to increased negative interactions, decreased positive interactions, increased individual distress, and diminished relationship satisfaction. Over time, this pattern may further deteriorate into many of the problematic behaviors we see in distressed and reactive couples and families. From an intervention standpoint, targeting an increase in the use of emotion regulation skills, as well as a reduction of invalidating behaviors and increased validating behaviors, follows logically from this model.

EMPIRICAL FOUNDATIONS: KNOWN AND UNKNOWN

Despite burgeoning knowledge at the interface of family interaction and psychopathology, most models of psychopathology are individual models, and most treatments focus on the individual. It is important to highlight both what the evidence tells us in support of efforts to build more useful theories and interventions and what the limitations are in the knowledge base.

Established Empirical Support: What We Know

The rationale for treating individual distress or psychopathology with couple and family treatments stems from a substantial amount of research in which relationship factors have been shown to be relevant to individual psychopathology, and vice versa, in a number of different ways (e.g., Snyder & Whisman, 2004). For example, people with affective disorders, anxiety disorders, substance abuse problems, and co-occurring disorders are more likely to report relationship dissatisfaction (Goering, Lin, Campbell, Boyle, & Offord, 1996; Whisman, 1999; Whisman & Uebelacker, 2003). Furthermore, couple and family treatments have been shown to be very effective in treating many forms of both psychological and medical disorders (Campbell, 2003; Gupta, Coyne, & Beach, 2003; Kelly & Fals-Stewart, 2002; Snyder & Whisman, 2004).

Although the specific mechanisms responsible for the relation between individual emotion dysregulation or psychopathology and family interactions are still unclear, there are many studies that demonstrate the effects of family responses on emotional arousal. For example, Swann (1997) has shown that social failure to "verify" or validate individual experiences (including cognitive "self-constructs") leads to affective arousal and dysregulation in general. Recent work in our lab has found similar effects when evaluating the immediate impact of increasing validating and decreasing invalidating responses by male partners: Female partners reported decreased negative affect and increased positive affect, and demonstrated increased self-disclosure (Sayrs & Fruzzetti, 2005). In a sample of severely and chronically distressed individuals, validating partner responses at Time 1 predicted stability or improvement (vs. relapse or deterioration) at Time 2, 3 months later (Thorp & Fruzzetti, 2005).

We have also found evidence that validating and invalidating partner behaviors mediate individual distress and relationship satisfaction. In a sample of 22 couples participating in a six-session couples group focusing on decreasing invalidating and increasing validating responses, increased validating or decreased invalidating responses pre- to posttreatment predicted decreased levels of individual and relationship distress posttreatment in a moderately distressed sample (Fruzzetti & Mosco, 2005).

In addition, treatments specifically targeting emotion regulation, such as dialectical behavior therapy (DBT; Fruzzetti, 2002; Linehan, 1993), have demonstrated consistently positive outcomes with adolescents and adults who are severely distressed, self-injurious, or suicidal or have been diagnosed with substance abuse or eating disorders (e.g., Linehan, Armstrong, Suarez, Allmon, & Heard, 1991; Rathus & Miller, 2002; Verheul et al., 2003). DBT is a cognitive–behavioral approach originally developed to treat the severe emotion dysregulation of borderline personality disorder (BPD; Linehan, 1993). The biosocial or transactional theory underlying DBT (Fruzzetti et al., 2005; Linehan, 1993) suggests that BPD is a disorder of emotion dysregulation that results from emotionally vulnerable individuals transacting with an invalidating social and family environment. DBT includes multiple components to help clients learn the developmental tasks related to emotion regulation (Linehan, 1993; Miller, Wyman, Huppert, Glassman, & Rathus, 2000): (a) mindfulness (to facilitate attention control, decrease cognitive dysregulation, and increase self-awareness and self-management); (b) interpersonal effectiveness (to help reduce chaos and invalidation in one's social environment); (c) emotion regulation (to reduce emotional vulnerability, reactivity, and misery and to facilitate emotion modulation); and (d) distress tolerance (to interrupt negative emotion escalation, endure difficult situations without engaging in dysfunctional behavior, and to "accept" things in life that are unchangeable).

Lacking Empirical Support: What We Do Not Know

It is clear that there are many things about emotion regulation and its relation to social and family interaction that we do not know. Perhaps most important, psychologists lack agreed-on parameters defining emotion regulation and dysregulation, as well as reliable and valid measurement tools to unify research in this area. Although some aspects or specific components of emotion regulation are beginning to be measured well (e.g., chap. 2, this volume), to date there is no reliable and valid omnibus measure of emotion regulation, nor agreement about what components are crucial and how to measure them.

In addition, although there is some evidence that validating and invalidating responses affect emotional responses in both community and clinical samples, and that validating responses predict better outcomes in clinical samples, we do not know whether (a) validating responses have a salutary effect (immediate or long term) for persons with many forms of psychopathology or are only important for specific disorders (e.g., depression, borderline personality disorders); (b) the lack of validating responses or presence of invalidating responses is important in the development of emotion dysregulation problems; or (c) altering invalidating processes is comparatively more useful in helping to regulate others' emotions than targeting other family processes for improvement (e.g., expression of positive affect, or constructive problem solving).

Furthermore, we do not have enough basic science that describes the psychophysiological mechanisms mediating the relation between validating responses and diminished emotional arousal or explains how emotion dysregulation per se is related to simple emotional arousal. Nor do we know the long-term impact of validating versus invalidating processes. For example, the relation may be linear (more validating responses are always better for emotion regulation) or curvilinear (too much validation leads to reliance on external regulation; too little leaves the individual both without self-regulation skills and in a stressful family environment). Of course, there are myriad other unknowns, but these in particular are central to understanding whether and how family interventions can help reregulate family members who are chronically dysregulated emotionally.

CLINICAL IMPLICATIONS

Dialectical behavior therapy with couples and families (Fruzzetti & Fruzzetti, 2003; Fruzzetti & Iverson, 2004a; Fruzzetti et al., 2005) is a treatment approach that directly targets reduction of emotion dysregulation in the context of couple and familial distress in an effort to reduce both individual and family distress. That is, individual emotion management skills are used to facilitate healthier couple and family interactions, and partner and parent skills are used in family interactions to facilitate individual emotion regulation. Engaging individuals and families on both sides of this reciprocal transaction fosters improvements in both individual well-being and relationship quality.

One relevant set of skills has been adapted for couples and families from the original DBT treatment for borderline personality disorder (Linehan, 1993). These skills are designed to reduce emotional dysregulation that contributes to both individual and relationship distress and interpersonal conflict, and also interferes with closeness with others. The second set of skills includes relationship skills to decrease couple and family distress and enhance intimacy between partners (e.g., Fruzzetti & Fruzzetti, 2003; Hoffman & Fruzzetti, 2005). There is a specific emphasis on skill acquisition to allow each partner to manage his or her own relationship behaviors while also managing the relationship. These intervention strategies are designed to follow a hierarchy of intervention targets, to balance acceptance skills with change skills, and to occur in a context of ongoing functional assessment. Moreover, once the basic skills are learned, they are used to solve long-standing problems in couple and family interaction. For purposes of this chapter, we highlight specific individual and relationship skills vis-à-vis emotion regulation. Other strategies and treatment procedures may be found in Fruzzetti and Fruzzetti (2003).

Mindfulness

Mindfulness skills are essential to effective emotion regulation and family interactions. These skills, which facilitate awareness, acceptance, and full participation in the present moment, are adapted largely from Linehan's (1993) work. Specifically, individual mindfulness skills increase self-awareness, including emotional awareness and experiencing, awareness of long-term goals, and self-management skills. During mindfulness training, partners learn both what to do when trying to be mindful and how to engage in these behaviors in the service of their individual and relationship goals. Mindfulness training functions in part as discrimination training for internal and external events that may affect both sensitivity and reactivity. By learning to observe both internal and external stimuli and then to describe these stimuli, a person may either increase or decrease sensitivity. Furthermore, attention to problematic or arousing stimuli may be titrated, which may decrease reactivity. Moreover, mindful description reduces inaccurate attributions and judgments that exacerbate sensitivity and reactivity. Partners and family members learn how to become aware of sensory experiences through noticing or observing and then how to describe them without judgment. For example, one person may practice describing another person's clothing, facial expression, or posture in a descriptive and nonjudgmental manner. Family members then learn how to discriminate thoughts from feelings, with an emphasis placed on accurately labeling emotions.

Learning how to engage in an interaction without judgments, or how to let go of judgments quickly, is an essential part of how to engage mindfully. Family members are encouraged to recognize judgments and let go of evaluations such as good or bad, right or wrong, and should or shouldn't. The therapist first blocks and points out the ineffectiveness of such judgments and models truly descriptive language. Meanwhile, family members are encouraged to put their energy into one thing at a time, keeping in mind both short-term and longer-term goals. Clients learn how to discriminate thoughts and feelings and sort through this difficult process: "What am I trying to do right now? What is my true goal? And how am I going to achieve my goal?" By focusing on observation and description as opposed to quickly reacting and judging, parents or partners reduce sensitivity, negative reactivity, and conflict escalation and may also enjoy time together more by noticing things other than what the other person is doing wrong. Being able to enjoy being together facilitates a kind of "relationship activation," which allows reactivity to abate further among all participants (Fruzzetti & Fruzzetti, 2003).

It is important to note that engaging in an interaction mindfully does not mean giving up emotional reactions. Quite the contrary, mindful engagement means noticing and titrating current reactions in the service of longer-term goals and includes experiencing emotion and self-validation. For example, engaging mindfully includes awareness of such thoughts as "This is the person I love," which puts problematic behavior in a meaningful and constructive context. Using mindfulness skills, partners can share feelings and thoughts, including negative ones, rather than letting them build up by attempting to avoid conflict. Mindfulness sets the stage for emotion management and accurate expression (discussed in the following section) because the ability to accept one's own experiences is required before one can understand and accept another person's feelings or behaviors.

Identifying and Labeling Emotions Accurately

Mindfulness of one's private experiences is essential for the development of effective emotion regulation skills. To regulate emotions, partners must learn how to identify and accurately label their actual emotions. First, for them to manage their emotions effectively, they must learn to recognize when emotional arousal and reactivity are increasing. Then, they can learn to identify the proximal stimulus, antecedents, or "triggers" for an emotional reaction. Emotions may be triggered by an event (e.g., partner or adolescent child came home from work late), by an interpretation of an event ("She came home late because she does not care about me"), or thoughts ("I'm a bad partner or parent"), memories, or other private events. Reactions may also be influenced by high vulnerability or high baseline arousal. This heightened arousal baseline might be the result of nonrelationship factors (e.g., tough day at work, a lot of traffic) or may be related to the relationship (e.g., unresolved conflict or recent quick negative escalation in a similar situation). It is important that parents and partners learn to notice thoughts and interpretations about an event and remember that interpretations are not facts. Furthermore, it may be useful to point out when negative, and especially inaccurate or unbalanced, attributions or interpretations bias interactions and encourage description instead. Depending on the situation, emphasis may be placed on identifying bodily responses that accompany different emotional reactions to help identify the accurate emotions, or on taking a "third-party" observing perspective. This skill can be enhanced by videotaping problematic conversations and reviewing them in a different context (Fruzzetti & Fruzzetti, 2003).

Identifying and Managing Action Urges

It is also important for each partner to identify his and her own problematic action urges when identifying emotions and to tolerate those urges while engaging in more skillful alternatives. Do certain situations and emotions elicit urges to engage in ineffective strategies: that is, to attack, demand, withdraw, or hide from the other? Often, specific action urges are a learned response to specific difficult emotions. For example, a person may have learned to demand attention when feeling sad or to avoid contact with his or her partner when feeling ashamed. In other words, both partners have likely learned behaviors that further reinforce emotional distress. Partners must therefore learn to be aware of interpretations, triggers, and behaviors associated with emotions to accurately identify and label emotions. Slowing down and becoming aware of the costs (e.g., further corrosion of the relationship, exacerbated sensitivity and reactivity), as well as the benefits (e.g., immediate relief or escape from a challenging and painful situation), may facilitate effective alternatives (e.g., accurate expression, validation).

Sorting Out Primary and Secondary Emotional Responses

It is important for clients to learn to discriminate between primary and secondary emotional responses, and to pay attention to and soothe their primary emotions while ignoring or letting go of secondary reactions. For example, if individuals get stuck on a secondary emotion, they are both actively invalidating their own primary emotions (e.g., attending to anger while failing to validate fear, hurt, or love) and making it difficult for a partner or family member to identify and validate their primary emotion. This requires considerable practice and skill at description through mindfulness. Partners typically respond to secondary emotions with defensiveness and escalation, whereas they are more likely to respond to primary emotions with validation (Fruzzetti et al., 2003). Of course, becoming aware of primary emotions and processing them in a healthy way requires the ability to tolerate painful emotions.

Tolerating Painful Emotions: Balance and Self-Validation

To experience and accurately label an emotion, a person must be able to tolerate the emotion until it naturally dissipates or until he or she can use effective change strategies. There are a number of strategies and skills that may facilitate this. First, being able to titrate attention away from the stimulus for the emotion and away from the emotion itself is essential. Extended focus on the negative stimulus (e.g., "she's late again . . . she's late again . . . she's late again. . . .") increases arousal without any benefit. Conversely, distracting attention away from the negative stimulus and the emotion provides more balance and more opportunity to identify the primary emotion, an action that in turn is self-validating and paradoxically enhances tolerance (e.g., "she's late . . . I'll work on starting dinner . . . this looks good"; arousal starts to diminish, which then allows "I'm worried" or "I don't think she knows how much I worry—we'll have to talk about her letting me know when she's going to be late").

It may also be useful to counterbalance experiencing a negative emotion with stimuli that elicit different, more positive, emotional experiences. For example, reading a love note or looking at a picture from a recent holiday might "recontextualize" a problem by reminding one partner that the other loves him or her in an experiential way. This might make current frustration or disappointment easier to tolerate without jumping to a secondary emotional response (e.g., anger), which would elicit judgments and likely lead to negative escalation.

It is also important to learn how to validate one's own emotions, thoughts, desires, and goals directly. People who are emotionally dysregulated tend to invalidate their own emotions, which leads to increased reactivity and dysregulation (Fruzzetti et al., 2003). Although accurately labeling emotions is self-validating by explicitly acknowledging the emotional response, legitimizing that experience may be even more validating, and consequently more soothing. For example, if individuals are able to recognize that they are feeling sad, as well as to understand the triggers, they may be able to self-soothe in some way. By recognizing their triggers, they are implicitly saying: "I feel sad, I am willing to experience this emotion and it makes sense that I feel this way." However, if they were to identify the sadness but tell themselves either overtly or covertly, "I should not be sad, I have nothing to feel sad about, I need to just get over it," then they would be self-invalidating and therefore punishing their primary emotional response, making self-soothing and validation from others less likely. Dysregulated people often criticize and pathologize their own experiences (e.g., "I'm stupid" or "I'm wrong" or "I shouldn't feel or want that"), so this kind of self-invalidation is not only painful itself but is compounded by making invalidation from others more likely.

Self-invalidation makes it more difficult to stay with the primary emotion. If the partner previously discussed began to say, "She should be home" rather than "I miss her; I wish she were home," anger would become more likely, and this would invalidate his disappointment and sadness, resulting in increased negative arousal. One important function of mindfulness is for partners and other loved ones to accept and experience their own emotions, which enables them to reduce arousal and keep attention partially focused on the other person as well, facilitating communication and understanding as the transaction continues.

Relationship Mindfulness

Like individual mindfulness skills, relationship mindfulness skills promote awareness and understanding, but in this case the focus is on the partner or family member and the larger relationship goals. Of course, to practice mindfulness of one's partner or family member, one must integrate mindfulness of one's own experience with mindfulness of the other and the larger relationship context.

Once family members have learned to manage their own emotional arousal or reactivity in difficult interactions, it is possible to participate in the relationship mindfully, which includes both listening mindfully and speaking mindfully. Mindfulness and relationship mindfulness decrease reactivity, negative escalation, criticality, and invalidating responses. Mindfulness of the other person sets the stage for understanding and is the most basic type of validation, involving attention, active listening, and noticing without judgments. In general, mindfulness of a partner, child, or other family member involves noticing the other's behavior (e.g., facial expressions, reactivity, verbal descriptions), describing his or her behavior, describing the connection between his or her behavior and one's own reactions, listening, and participating in the transaction.

Accurate Expression

Accurate expression and self-disclosure have two key components: accurately discriminating among one's thoughts, feelings, and goals privately and then accurately expressing these private events to one's partner or family member. Mindfulness is used to help parents and partners become aware of their own private emotions, wants, or thoughts. Accurate expression involves using mindfulness, discerning one's own goal in a particular situation, and expressing emotions, desires, and so on in a nonjudgmental and descriptive manner. Goals may include (a) sorting out one's feelings, (b) communicating a desire or opinion, (c) changing the other person's behavior, (d) supporting the other person, and (e) repairing a situation or misstep. Depending on the goal, different types of expression would be required. Thus, emotion regulation is enhanced by high awareness of one's own wants, goals, opinions, and emotions and an ability to convey these descriptively without judgment. Accurate self-expression necessarily is easier to hear because it is descriptive rather than accusatory or blaming, requesting rather than demanding, and communicates openness to understanding rather than rigidity or self-righteousness. This not only helps keep the person in the expressing or describing role more regulated, it helps keep the other person more regulated and makes validation much more likely; by contrast, blame, demands, and self-righteousness are likely to trigger escalation in the other person.

Validation Skills

Validation is important because it communicates understanding and acceptance (Fruzzetti & Iverson, 2004b). Thus, validation can transform potential aversive conflict into understanding in the present and help to reduce sensitivity and reactivity in the future. Although it may be unusual to consider the response of others as central to one's own emotion regulation or dysregulation, social or interactional situations provide the most common context for emotion regulation and dysregulation.

Validation skills include learning how to find what parts of the other person's expression are valid, figuring out the ways in which they are valid, and then communicating understanding of those valid parts. Partner validation functions to decrease negative emotional arousal and increase positive emotional arousal (Fruzzetti & Mosco, 2005; Swann, 1997). When someone's negative emotion is escalating, a partner or parent can use validation skills to help bring arousal back down to help the other stay regulated or to reregulate. Any public or private behavior of another person can be legitimized, understood, or acknowledged in some way. Partners and family members can learn to validate emotions, thoughts, behaviors, wants, beliefs, opinions, and values. There are at least eight different ways to validate: (a) mindful listening; (b) reflecting and acknowledging the other's experience; (c) clarifying and summarizing the other's experience; (d) putting problem behavior in a larger, more balanced context; (e) normalizing emotional reactions and experiences; (f) expressing equality and respect, treating the other as an equal; (g) reciprocating or matching vulnerability; and (h) responding with effective and compassionate action (Fruzzetti & Iverson, 2004a). Any of these behaviors is likely to have a salutary effect on the other person's emotional arousal and regulation and consequently on the relationship.

FUTURE DIRECTIONS IN RESEARCH

The research agenda regarding couple and family interventions for emotion dysregulation is large and should include the following, which are germane to the model presented in this chapter in particular, but also to the understanding of emotion regulation more generally: (a) evaluate couple and family treatment effects of validation for specific populations (e.g., depression, substance abuse) to determine whether emotion regulation patterns vary by individual diagnosis or by dysfunctional couple or family processes, whether mechanisms vary across combinations of individual and family distress; and whether targeting validation is more useful than other interventions; (b) develop agreed-on measures of emotion regulation and dysregulation (at least at a component level); (c) evaluate the psychophysiological impact of validating and invalidating responses naturalistically and longitudinally, testing for links to emotional arousal and dysregulation; (d) evaluate further the specificity of self-disclosure and validating response reciprocity across disorders and in heterogeneous distressed families; and (e) evaluate the role of validating and invalidating responses in the development of emotion dysregulation and psychopathology longitudinally.

By integrating our understanding of at least some versions of psychopathology into their social and family context, psychologists contextualize disorders and make them more amenable to broad intervention approaches. If we better understand the relations among emotion regulation, psychopathology, and family interactions, we can engage in primary and secondary prevention efforts and develop more effective treatments. Further research will be necessary to evaluate hypotheses regarding the specific mechanisms by which family processes influence individual and relationship dysfunction or well-being. However, an emerging body of evidence already demonstrates clearly the importance of couple and family interactions in individual emotion regulation and dysregulation.

REFERENCES

Campbell, T. L. (2003). The effectiveness of family interventions for physical disorders. *Journal of Marital and Family Therapy, 29*, 263–281.

Eisenberg, N., Cumberland, A., & Spinrad, T. L. (1998). Parental socialization of emotion. *Psychological Inquiry, 9*, 241–273.

Fruzzetti, A. E. (1996). Causes and consequences: Individual distress in the context of couple interactions. *Journal of Consulting and Clinical Psychology, 64*, 1192–1201.

Fruzzetti, A. E. (2002). Dialectical behavior therapy for borderline personality and related disorders. In T. Patterson (Ed.), *Comprehensive handbook of psychotherapy* (pp. 215–240). New York: Wiley.

Fruzzetti, A. E., & Fruzzetti, A. R. (2003). Partners with borderline personality disorder: Dialectical behavior therapy with couples. In D. K. Snyder & M. A. Whisman (Eds.), *Treating difficult couples: Managing emotional, behavioral, and health problems in couple therapy* (pp. 235–260). New York: Guilford Press.

Fruzzetti, A. E., & Iverson, K. M. (2004a). Couples dialectical behavior therapy: An approach to both individual and relational distress. *Couples Research and Therapy, 10,* 8–13.

Fruzzetti, A. E., & Iverson, K. M. (2004b). Mindfulness, acceptance, validation, and "individual" psychopathology in couples. In S. C. Hayes, V. M. Follette, & M. M. Linehan (Eds.), *Mindfulness and acceptance: Expanding the cognitive–behavioral tradition* (pp. 168–208). New York: Guilford Press.

Fruzzetti, A. E., & Jacobson, N. S. (1990). Toward a behavioral conceptualization of adult intimacy: Implications for marital therapy. In E. Blechman (Ed.), *Emotions and the family: For better or for worse* (pp. 117–135). Hillsdale, NJ: Erlbaum.

Fruzzetti, A. E., & Mosco, E. (2005). *Dialectical behavior therapy adapted for couples and families: A pilot group intervention for couples.* Manuscript submitted for publication.

Fruzzetti, A. E., Shenk, C., & Hoffman, P. D. (2005). Family interaction and the development of borderline personality disorder: A transactional model. *Development and Psychopathology, 17,* 1007–1030.

Fruzzetti, A. E., Shenk, C., Mosco, E., & Lowry, K. (2003). Emotion regulation. In W. T. O'Donohue, J. E. Fisher, & S. C. Hayes (Eds.), *Cognitive behavior therapy: Applying empirically supported techniques in your practice* (pp. 152–159). New York: Wiley.

Goering, P. N., Lin, P., Campbell, D., Boyle, M. H., & Offord, D. R. (1996). Psychiatric disability in Ontario. *Canadian Journal of Psychiatry, 41,* 564–571.

Greenberg, L. S., & Safran, J. D. (1989). Emotion in psychotherapy. *American Psychologist, 44,* 19–29.

Gross, J. J. (1998). The emerging field of emotion regulation: An integrative review. *Review of General Psychology, 2,* 271–299.

Gupta, M., Coyne, J. C., & Beach, S. R. H. (2003). Couples treatment for major depression: Critique of the literature and suggestions for some different directions. *Journal of Family Therapy, 25,* 317–346.

Hoffman, P. D., & Fruzzetti, A. E. (2005). Family interventions. In M. C. Zanarini (Ed.), *Borderline personality disorder.* New York: Marcel Dekker.

Kelly, M. L., & Fals-Stewart, W. (2002). Couples- versus individual-based therapy for alcohol and drug abuse: Effects on children's psychosocial functioning. *Journal of Consulting and Clinical Psychology, 70,* 417–427.

Kirsch, I., Moore, T. J., Scoboria, A., & Nicholls, S. S. (2002). The emperor's new drugs: An analysis of antidepressant medication data submitted to the U.S. Food and Drug Administration. *Prevention and Treatment, 5,* Article 23. Retrieved December 22, 2005, from http://www.journals.apa.org/prevention/volume5/pre0050023a.html

Linehan, M. M. (1993). *Cognitive–behavioral treatment of borderline personality disorder.* New York: Guilford Press.

Linehan, M. M., Armstrong, H. E., Suarez, A., Allmon, D., & Heard, H. (1991). Cognitive–behavioral treatment of chronically suicidal borderline patients. *Archives of General Psychiatry, 48,* 1060–1064.

Miller, A. L., Wyman, S. E., Huppert, J. D., Glassman, S. L., & Rathus, J. H. (2000). Analysis of behavioral skills utilized by adolescents receiving dialectical behavior therapy. *Cognitive and Behavioral Practice, 7,* 183–187.

Plutchik, R. (1994). *The psychology and biology of emotion.* New York: HarperCollins.

Rathus, J. H., & Miller, A. L. (2002). DBT adapted for suicidal adolescents. *Suicide and Life-Threatening Behavior, 32,* 146–157.

Saarni, C., & Crowley, M. (1990). The development of emotion regulation: Effects on emotional state and expression. In E. A. Blechman (Ed.), *Emotions and the family: For better or for worse* (pp. 53–73). Hillsdale, NJ: Erlbaum.

Sayrs, J. H. R., & Fruzzetti, A. E. (2005). *Partner invalidating responses in couples: Impact on affect and self behaviors.* Unpublished manuscript.

Snyder, D. K., & Whisman, M. A. (2004). Treating distressed couples with coexisting mental and physical disorders: Directions for clinical training and practice. *Journal of Marital and Family Therapy, 30,* 1–12.

Southam-Gerow, M. A., & Kendall, P. C. (2002). Emotion regulation and understanding: Implications for child psychopathology and therapy. *Clinical Psychology Review, 22,* 189–222.

Swann, W. (1997). The trouble with change. *Psychological Science, 8,* 177–180.

Thompson, R. A. (1994). Emotion regulation: A theme in search of definition. *Monographs of the Society for Research in Child Development, 59*(2–3, Serial No. 204), 24–52.

Thorp, S. R., & Fruzzetti, A. E. (2005). *Validating and invalidating partner behaviors as predictors of course of illness in a severe and chronic sample.* Manuscript submitted for publication.

Verheul, R., van den Bosch, L. M. C., Koeter, M. W. J., de Ridder, M. A. J., Stijen, T., & van den Brink, W. (2003). Dialectical behaviour therapy for women with borderline personality disorder: 12-month, randomised clinical trial in the Netherlands. *British Journal of Psychiatry, 182,* 135–140.

Weiss, R. L., & Heyman, R. E. (1990). Observation of marital interaction. In F. D. Fincham & T. N. Bradbury (Eds.), *The psychology of marriage* (pp. 87–117). New York: Guilford Press.

Whisman, M. A. (1999). Marital dissatisfaction and psychiatric disorders: Results from the National Comorbidity Survey. *Journal of Abnormal Psychology, 108,* 701–706.

Whisman, M. A. (2001). The association between depression and marital dissatisfaction. In S. R. H. Beach (Ed.), *Marital and family processes in depression: A scientific foundation for clinical practice* (pp. 3–24). Washington, DC: American Psychological Association.

Whisman, M. A., & Uebelacker, L. A. (2003). Comorbidity of relationship distress and mental and physical health problems. In D. K. Snyder & M. A. Whisman (Eds.), *Treating difficult couples: Helping clients with coexisting mental and relationship disorders* (pp. 3–26). New York: Guilford Press.

13

WHO TOOK MY HOT SAUCE? REGULATING EMOTION IN THE CONTEXT OF FAMILY ROUTINES AND RITUALS

BARBARA H. FIESE

By their very nature, families are emotional systems. The family, as a group, is charged with calibrating emotional expression such that family norms are established, and what is acceptable in one family may be undesired in another. When children venture out from their homes, they are often surprised by how emotions are regulated differently in their friends' homes. Statements like "But John's mom lets him make animal sounds at the dinner table" reflect how expectations for affective expressions are part and parcel of repeated family interactions. Many of the chapters in this book highlight the ways in which emotion is regulated in a social context. Whether between parents and children (chap. 6, this volume), in response to marital conflict (chap. 8, this volume), or in social moments of everyday life (chap. 1, this volume), emotion is cast as affecting and being affected by the interpersonal state of affairs.

Preparation of this chapter was supported, in part, by a grant from the National Institute of Mental Health, 2R01MH051771.

The focus of this chapter is on whole-family processes that promote emotion regulation across members as well as regulation processes that promote family process. Rather than consider how particular emotions are regulated in the family context or how the family may socialize emotional expression (Kennedy-Moore & Watson, 1999), this chapter addresses how families, in their organized collective behaviors, create emotional connections through their repetitive routines and rituals. Following the outline of the other chapters in this volume, this chapter examines the theoretical and methodological issues associated with the study of family routines and rituals. Then, following a brief overview of current empirical knowledge, I address the clinical implications of this work, with specific guidelines for clinicians and educators. I conclude with implications for public policy and attention to bolstering family strengths and emotion regulation in challenging societal times. Throughout the chapter, I use mealtimes as the context for portrayals of family emotion regulation.

A nagging problem in family research is how to capture group process as a whole. Certainly, the roots of family studies are based on the assumption that the whole is greater than the sum of its parts. Something happens when family members come together as a group that is not necessarily predicted by features of any one individual. This belief is widely held by clinicians, yet difficult to view with a scientific lens. The bulk of what we know about individual outcomes arises from direct observations of dyadic interactions and individuals' self-reports. Indeed, the chapters in this volume represent the cutting edge of research documenting how attachment and parent–child interaction patterns foster competence (Eisenberg et al., 2003; Mikulincer, Shaver, & Pereg, 2003; Parke et al., 2002). The work of Cummings and colleagues adds to this discussion through their documentation of how the marital dyad may affect parent–child relationships and child affect regulation (Cummings, Davies, & Campbell, 2000). How might a consideration of the family as a group contribute to an understanding of emotion regulation in families? Typically we consider emotions as residing within the individual and their regulation as subject to how one individual interacts with another— such as parent to child, peer to peer, and husband to wife. The framework proposed in this chapter focuses on repetitive group interactions and interpretations of these events that form a family identity. Unique family identities may, in turn, be one of the factors that calibrate how emotion is regulated in this social context. Thus, the first problem to be addressed is how to ascertain whole-family process. Family routines and rituals afford such an examination.

From the outset, it is important to recognize that family routines and rituals are not necessarily the best or most parsimonious way to access family emotion regulation. What I am proposing is that family routines and rituals make sense to families, they afford the possibility of examining both how families act and what they believe, and they may be used systematically in therapeutic interventions. In this regard, the practice of family routines and the meaning ascribed to family rituals provide access to how the family is organized as a group and how group and individual processes transact with each other (Sameroff & Fiese, 2000).

CONCEPTUAL, THEORETICAL, AND METHODOLOGICAL ISSUES

The study of family routines such as mealtime and the beliefs associated with family traditions such as religious observances may seem out of sync with the postmodern family. Putnam (2000) presented evidence taken from national polls conducted from the late 1970s to the late 1990s that suggests families spend fewer mealtimes together, attend fewer religious services together, and spend less time "just sitting and talking" together in the late 1990s than they did in the 1970s. Whereas these statistics are often used as evidence of the demise of the American family (Popenoe, 1993), they do not tell the whole story of family life. It may be accurate that families spend less time overall together as group. However, recent polls suggest that families with children under age 18 eat dinner together always or frequently (77% of the time; Wolcott, 2001). These polled estimates are consistent with direct observations of families in their homes (Fiering & Lewis, 1987; Landesman, Jaccard, & Gunderson, 1991; Martini, 1996). These gatherings are not necessarily elaborate, as most meals last between 18 and 20 minutes. Thus, if a family gathers at the table four times a week they are spending time together that is roughly equivalent to one 90-minute television show.

In a recent epidemiological study of over 4,000 adolescents, frequency of family mealtimes was found to be associated with a host of adolescent health outcomes (Eisenberg, Olson, Neumark-Sztainer, Story, & Bearinger, 2004). Approximately 65% of the respondents reported that their family ate together three or more times per week. Greater frequency of family meals was associated with less cigarette, alcohol, and marijuana use and fewer depressive symptoms. Thus, the empirical data are contrary to popularly perceived notions that families do not spend time together and that the family meal is a tradition of the past.

Defining Family Routines and Rituals

The majority of researchers active in the study of family routines and rituals agree that operationally defining routines and rituals is a challenge, at best (Boyce, Jensen, James, & Peacock, 1983; van der Hart, 1983; Wolin & Bennett, 1984). There are several sources for this challenge. First, it is likely that every family and every family member has an individual definition of what constitutes a routine or ritual. Indeed, it is this personalized and individualized aspect of family organization that may provide special meaning to group activities and gatherings. Second, rituals are highly symbolic in nature. They are dense with physical, patterned, and affective symbols. Thus, they are not always detectable by the outsider and often only recognized by those inside the family. Take, for example, a family who participated in one of our studies. The family was videotaped during a mealtime and subsequently interviewed while watching the videotape of their gathering. The family was instructed to stop the videotape whenever they noted something fairly typical or something out of the ordinary. One family held a rather lengthy discussion about peanut butter and jelly sandwiches. The conversation revolved around who liked jelly on the sandwich and who did not. To the researcher interviewing the family, this appeared to be a very tedious exchange. However, the father stopped the tape and remarked that they had this conversation several times a week. As it turned out, having jelly (or not) on one's sandwich was not just an indication of food preference but identified personality types and relationships within and outside the family. The father and older daughter preferred jelly on their sandwich, whereas the mother and younger daughter did not. The "jellied pair" were known as the cutups in the family and could be relied on to tell a good joke. The other pair, however, were the organizers in the family and could be counted on to get things done. Not only had the family catalogued preferences within the family, they could also identify neighborhood members by their jelly preferences. This example serves to illustrate how even relatively mundane comments may hold significant meaning when repeated over time in routine settings.

Family rituals involve not only the directly observable practices but also the personal, subjective, and interior held meanings associated with the routine events. Rather than consider these two dimensions incompatible with each other, it is possible to distinguish between the routines of daily living and rituals in family life.

Routines and rituals can be contrasted along the dimensions of communication, commitment, and continuity (Fiese et al., 2002). Routines typically involve instrumental communication such that information is conveyed that this is "what needs to be done." The language of routines is direct, implies action, and often includes designation of roles. Routines involve momentary time commitment. Once the act is completed, there is little afterthought and daily life flows on uninterrupted. Routines are repeated over time, with little alteration, and can be directly observed by outsiders.

Rituals, however, involve symbolic communication and signify that this is "who we are as a group." The language of rituals is multilayered such that what may appear as the outsider as a mundane phrase may be dense with meaning for family members, as in the case of the peanut butter and jelly family. The affective commitment to rituals provides feelings of belongingness and felt rightness to the activity. When routines are disrupted, it is a hassle. Someone forgets to stop at the grocery store after work, so there is no milk for

TABLE 13.1
Definitions of Routines and Rituals

Characteristic	Routines of daily living	Rituals in family life
Communication	Instrumental "This is what needs to be done."	Symbolic "This is who we are."
Commitment	Perfunctory and momentary Little conscious thought given after the act.	Enduring and affective "This is right." The experience may be repeated in memory.
Continuity	Directly observable and detectable by outsiders Behavior is repeated over time.	Meaning extends across generations and is interpreted by insiders "This is what we look forward to and who we will continue to be across generations."

Note. Reprinted from "A Review of 50 Years of Research in Naturally Occurring Family Routines and Rituals: Cause for Celebration?," by B. H. Fiese, T. Tomcho, M. Douglas, K. Josephs, S. Poltrock, and T. Baker, 2002, *Journal of Family Psychology, 16*, p. 382. Copyright 2002 by the American Psychological Association.

breakfast cereal. When rituals are disrupted, there is a threat to group cohesion. Failure to attend an important family event such as a wedding often indicates a shift in family alliances and definitions of who is in or out of the family. The distinguishing features of routines and rituals are presented in Table 13.1.

Conceptual Challenges

In many ways, there is nothing new about considering directly observable behavior and beliefs as central elements in understanding child development and adjustment. Whether referred to as *family style and worldview* (Minuchin, 1988), *parenting practices and styles* (Darling & Steinberg, 1993), or the *practicing and representing family* (Reiss, 1989), these theoretical models share the perspective that family life is organized around repetitive practices and beliefs that extend across generations and are altered with time. I have found Reiss's distinction between the practicing and representing family a useful one and one that is pertinent to this discussion. Family practices are directly observable and repeated over time and shift in response to developmental changes of the family. Family representations, on the other hand, are indirectly assessed through the interpretive process of the family and may guide behavior, particularly in response to a stressor. Ultimately, family practices and representations affect one another through a series of transactions over time. Reiss's model may be used as a heuristic to direct our attention to how to go about studying emotion regulation in families. The model calls for looking directly at how families interact as well as how they interpret or represent family relationships. To date, the model has not generated clear-cut predictions and may be seen more accurately as a guide for asking questions rather than a fully formulated theory. The transactional nature of representations and behavior is gaining some empirical support in the attachment literature (e.g., Carlson, Sroufe, & Egeland, 2004). Thus, the constructs presented in this chapter should be considered as part of an organizational framework in which emotion regulation is part of a transactional process whereby repeated experiences in the family inform representations that in turn guide behavior.

Families create rules about the expression of emotion when gathered together as a group. These rules may be expressed directly, as in the case of expectations for manners. Over time, the rules become internalized and there is little need to verbally reprimand an emotional display, as a slight raise of the eyebrow or emphatic use of a person's name may be sufficient to regulate affect. The research described in this chapter is mainly correlational and descriptive. We are not yet at the point where it is possible to offer convincing evidence that certain routines or rituals are causally linked to variability in emotion regulation. It is possible, however, to consider the interplay between family practices and representations such that convergences from various studies suggest future directions in using more rigorous research designs. I return to this point when I consider the empirical evidence to date.

Pertinent to the discussion of family regulation is how emotions are expressed and interpreted during repetitive gatherings. Contrasting how emotions are directly observed with how emotional experiences are interpreted allows us to consider how routines and rituals may provide an organizational framework and, ultimately, suggest avenues of intervention. Let us first turn to empirical evidence that suggests that predictable routines and meaningful rituals are associated with the health and well-being of individuals and that disruptions in routines may portend poor affect regulation.

Affect Regulation at the Dinner Table

In a previously published report, my colleague and I (Fiese & Marjinsky, 1999) examined how the directly observed behavior at the dinner table corresponded to representations of family of origin and current family relationships in a storytelling task. The overall aim of the study was to consider how directly observed affect in a group setting was related to how parents represented family relationships in their narratives. Generally, we found that positive affect at the dinner table was positively related to how parents depicted the trustworthiness of relationships in their current family and their family of origin. The reverse held true for negative affect portrayed at the dinner table. Families who talk about relationships in a positive and rewarding way also tend to interact in positive and supportive ways when gathered together. On the one hand, this makes intuitive sense and may just indicate that positive family features are consistent across different measures (i.e., observational and narrative). On the other hand, we can speculate on the transactional nature of family practices and representations in regulating affect.

Parents who depict relationships as rewarding carry a working template of expectations that can be validated through routine interactions. Repeated interactions that are affectively positive serve to reinforce representations of relationships as sources of reward and encourage sustained positive interaction. We have not been able to confirm the directional nature of this process in our cross-sectional studies. It is clear that longitudinal and intervention research needs to be conducted before direction of effects can be identified. In addition to examining the transactional process over time, it will be important to consider other variables that may be moderating the effects. For example, maternal depression may affect how routines are carried out and the regulation of affect during family gatherings (Dickstein, St. Andre, Sameroff, Seifer, & Schiller, 1999).

In an effort to tease apart the role of affect in the narratives and regulation of behavior, we examined the degree to which the affect expressed during the storytelling task matched the overall theme of the story. We reasoned that telling a family story not only reveals thematic content but is also potentially an emotionally evocative task, as parents use affect to highlight different aspects of the story. We found that for some parents there is a mismatch between content and affect. For example, a story of rejecting or harmful relationships may be marked by nervous laughter and poorly modulated affect. For mothers, we found that when there was a mismatch between affect and story content there was a greater risk for their children to develop behavior problems. We speculated that when children are repeatedly exposed to an affective model that is marked by poor regulation, they have difficulty managing their own behavior. It is also possible that a child with poorly modulated behavior also presents a greater challenge to parents in regulating their own affect.

Children are exposed to emotion and affect in a variety of family settings, and there appears to be cross-situational consistency in the expression of affect and representation of relationships. In the context of dinnertime, parents typically negotiate a variety of demands in a relatively short period of time. This includes expectations for manners and good behavior (Gleason, Perlmann, & Greif, 1984) as well as regulation of negative affect. For some families, the collective gathering is marked by negative affect and expectations that relationships will be unrewarding and a source of irritation. For other families, the collective gathering is marked by a sense of predictable order and expectations that relationships will be personally fulfilling. The following two stories told about mealtimes serve to illustrate.

> **Story 1:** I remember my stepmother and father arguing, and we were eating corn on the cob. They were fighting at the table, and we ate corn on the cob, and we had butter smeared all over our faces, and grandpa was smoking a cigarette at the table. And grandma got mad at him because they were fighting, and she picked up an ashtray and threw it at him, and ashes stuck to his whole face because there was butter all over it. Not the greatest story, but that's the truth.

Story 2: We talk about current events, geography, school activities, their sports activities. Occasionally we get to some of the most sensitive issues. We might get halfway through dinner and somebody tells a joke, and everybody is cracking up, and all of a sudden you get into a heavy conversation. Somebody was just waiting for the right time, and you could tell this was safe now and it's OK to bring this up now. And so we'll then sort of change the tone and kinda go with what the person needs to talk about at that point in time. And sometimes if we start laughing, it just kinda carries through and milk comes out of everybody's noses.

In the first instance, gathering around the table evokes strong and negative affect. It was acceptable, although not necessarily desirable, to allow intense feelings to escalate to the point of potential physical harm. In stark contrast is the second story, in which dinner is a time for telling jokes but also a safe place where personal concerns can be aired with the expectation that the individual will be heard and, perhaps, his or her problem solved.

Children may be particularly sensitive to disruptions experienced during routine gatherings. On the one hand, the predictability of routines provides a sense of order and markers for what is considered expectable behavior. Family rules of conduct may be repeatedly reinforced during a typical mealtime (Gleason et al., 1984). Thus, the directly observable and predictable aspects of family routines provide behavioral guideposts and regulate the expression of emotion. The symbolic aspects of the ritual gathering, on the other hand, may provide a sense of belonging and emotional security. As mentioned in the second story, the meal was seen as a safe gathering where sensitive topics could be discussed. Over time, the repeated practice of regular routines evolves into a ritual that suggests connections and bonds built on positive emotions and feelings of belonging to a group. The repetitive routine practices serve as the substance of the representations that constitute a ritual. Oftentimes, these representations are marked by strong emotions and are dense in meaning. One way to determine whether a routine has turned into a ritual is to consider whether it is anticipated and would be missed if it didn't happen, and whether elements are replayed in memory. My colleagues and I are only just beginning to explore these distinctions in empirical studies, paying particular attention to how emotion is a key element of rituals and how the affective aspect of family life may serve to protect individuals from risk conditions. Let us first examine how children depict routines and then consider how rituals may promote mental and physical health.

My colleagues and I have examined how children respond to disruptions in family mealtimes through the use of a storytelling procedure (Fiese, Wamboldt, Howell, & Spagnola, 2003). Children, age 5 to 12, were presented with a picture of a relatively well-organized kitchen (e.g., places are set at the table, the counter is clear of clutter, and the chairs are arranged around the table) and asked to tell a story about a family at dinner in this kitchen. After the story is told, they are presented with a second picture that depicts the kitchen in disarray (e.g., trash is overflowing in the garbage, a chair is turned over, the plants are dead in the windowsill). They are again prompted to tell a story about a family in this kitchen. Responses to the organized kitchen scene are overall more affectively positive, relationships are seen as more rewarding, and routines more clearly identified. In contrast, children's responses to the disorganized kitchen were more likely to include negative affect, aggressive behavior, and lack of order. The degree to which children saw relationships as rewarding in the organized scene was significantly related to overall family functioning and negatively related to parent report of child behavior problems. The following examples, drawn from the same 8-year-old boy, serve to illustrate.

> **Organized Kitchen Scene:** First of all, the brother sits there, the sister sits there, and the mother sits there, and the father sits there. And, they make sure the kids have washed their hands. And then they all sit down and wait for everybody to get to the table and they just sort of start eating and talking about their day.
>
> **Disorganized Kitchen Scene:** Well this family nobody cares if they wash their hands or not, they just start scarfing down dinner. The brother's talking about how he wants this video game, and the sister's talking about how she wants these dolls, and the father's talking about how many times other states have lost the Super Bowl, and the mother is talking about how many dishes are in the sink and complaining, and they're all talking at the same time, so it doesn't make any sense.

These examples illustrate how perceptions of order are associated with predictability of relationships, and that once the order is disrupted there is a greater likelihood of negative affect and disappointment, and relationships don't make any sense. These qualitative distinctions have been supported in larger quantitative studies examining how routines and rituals may protect individuals from stressors associated with being raised in alcoholic households (Bennett, Wolin, & Reiss, 1988; Fiese, 1993; Wolin, Bennett, Noonan, & Teitlebaum, 1980), reduce the effects of chronic pain on daily activities (Bush & Pargament, 1997), and protect children from mental health problems under conditions of a chronic illness (Markson & Fiese, 2000). A consistent finding in these studies has been the distinguishing roles of routines and rituals in promoting mental and physical health. For example, in the Bush and Pargament study of couples in which one member was experiencing chronic pain, it was the affective meaning of family rituals that was most closely associated with partners' satisfaction with family life and the routine factor that was most closely associated with patients' satisfaction with family life and pain-specific adjustment. For individuals experiencing a painful condition, the predictability of routines was associated with fewer pain symptoms, perhaps suggesting a more organized and less stressful environment. For spouses involved in the care of the pain patient, the affective meaning associated with family rituals may have provided a sense of family identity that extended beyond the daily care of the patient.

The predictability of routines and amount of perceived burden linked to routines associated with disease management in the case of a chronic illness suggests that there is a direct link between routines and emotions. When parents report that carrying out a routine is a burden, they are more likely to report a poorer quality of life overall, and their children are more likely to report emotional distress connected to their physical condition (Fiese, Wamboldt, & Anbar, 2005). Specifically, we have found that when daily health-related routines are seen as a chore, then parents also feel overwhelmed and experience more disruptions in their daily life, and their children are more emotionally affected by their illness. It is also plausible that when one is emotionally distressed, it is more taxing to implement regular routines.

To better understand the relative contribution of routines and rituals to emotional distress and affect regulation in the family, it appears that intervention and longitudinal designs are warranted. Using more rigorous methodologies does not come without challenges, however. For example, intervention trials would need to take into account the individualized nature of routines and the representational nature of rituals. Thus, merely prescribing routines without attending to their emotional significance may not be particularly effective. As outlined in the section on clinical implications, an accurate assessment of family rituals may suggest tailored rather than uniform interventions. We also know very little about the ebb and flow of family rituals. Using daily recording techniques such as ecological momentary assessment (e.g., Smyth & Stone, 2003) may shed light on whether changes in routines precede or follow alterations in mood and emotions.

Taken together, these examples serve to illustrate several points about whole-family process and emotion regulation. First, emotions expressed during routine collective gatherings are calibrated to reflect what is acceptable behavior within a given family. For some families, these repetitive interactions are marked by open expression of affect within an expectedly secure environment. For other families, negative affect is allowed to escalate to the point that individual members may feel threatened, and there are few guides for acceptable behavior. Second, over time these repetitive group interactions form the basis of internalized representations of family identity. Repetitive interaction patterns are dense with symbolic meaning that may only make sense to the family. Shorthand communication may develop such that a phrase innocuous to the outsider signifies meaningful exchanges within the family. Third, when faced with stressors, families are often challenged to reorganize their routines and may confront a need to redefine their rituals. I now turn to how the reorganization of routines and redefinition of rituals can be useful to clinicians and educators.

CLINICAL IMPLICATIONS

Routines and rituals are readily accessible to clinicians. Not only may they provide a vehicle for behavior change, they may also aid the clinician in understanding the context of emotion regulation within a specific family. The clinical implications of understanding emotion regulation in the context of family routines and rituals are multifold. They can provide guides for assessment and a framework for family typologies and can be used as a form of intervention. I address each aspect in turn.

Assessment of Family Routines and Rituals

There are several avenues for assessing the relative presence and strength of family rituals. Several questionnaires exist that include a description of the frequency with which particular routines are practiced (Boyce et al., 1983) and the presence of family celebrations (McCubbin, Thompson, & McCubbin, 1996). My colleague and I have developed the Family Ritual Questionnaire (Fiese & Kline, 1993), which distinguishes between routine practices and ritual meaning across seven different settings (dinnertime, weekends, vacations, annual celebrations, special celebrations, religious holidays, cultural events). These questionnaires have been used primarily for the empirical study of routines and rituals in nonclinical samples. Recently, my colleagues and I have developed a subscale that measures disease management routines that can be used with populations with a chronic health condition (Fiese et al., 2005). Interviews are more likely to be used in a clinical setting. Several interviews have been developed that focus on family routines and rituals. Wolin and colleagues have developed the Family Ritual Interview (Wolin, Bennett, & Jacobs, 2003), whose original application was in the study of alcoholic families. The interview attends to level of ritualization, the role of family heritage effects on current family practices, purposefulness in creating rituals, adaptability, and maintenance of rituals. Interviews are coded along the lines of high, medium, and low for each dimension. Kubicek has developed the Caretaking Routines Interview (Kubicek, 2002), which focuses specifically on routines created to care for young children. Weisner and colleagues have developed the Ecocultural Family Interview, aimed at understanding how families organize the daily routine activities of children (Weisner, 2002). Field workers provide summaries of the family's activities as well as scoring items in response to particular domains of family routines such as support from kin, role of the father in child care, and availability of resources. My colleagues and I have gained valuable insights from the work of our peers and have incorporated several aspects of these interviews into our own work on family routines and rituals evident in the care and adjustment of families who have a child with a chronic illness. For illustrative purposes, we describe portions of the interview we use in our research protocol that can be adapted for clinical purposes, with attention to how problematic family emotion regulation may disrupt routines or how deliberately planned routines may aid in regulating emotions under stressful conditions.

As part of the Asthma Impact Interview (Wamboldt & O'Connor, 1997), families are asked to tell the story of how the illness has affected their lives and to "walk us through a typical day" with their family. One of the features of this interview is the ability to identify whether families deliberately plan around routine care or whether they respond in a way that is chaotic and disorganized. We have found that families who create plans and routines together are more likely to have children with fewer disease symptoms and better quality of life than families who respond chaotically and rarely make deliberate plans (Fiese et al., 2005; Fiese & Wamboldt, 2003). Two examples serve to illustrate.

> **Family partnership:** At first we could kind of like deal with it, I was kind of up already on things to do as far as taking carpets out of his room, changing curtains, things like that to keep him from coughing, watching for stuff that might be triggering it. The worst part came when he started having seizures from the medication. That was the worst. That was the worst because we weren't sure, and even the doctors were a little bit worried, like what are we going to do? That was really hard for us, really hard, just really so depressing, and I thought, wow, then I guess the only thing we could do next was to try and eliminate everything that was causing it. So we did; he didn't have any carpet in his room. We wet-mopped the room all the time, we just changed a lot of stuff like that.
>
> The family listens more when they hear stuff about asthma. They see brochures and they're more aware of what asthma does and you know, like his brother will say something like "Frank has asthma. We should watch this. Or listen to this." They're talking about asthma. Uh, I think it has made everybody just a little bit more aware of stuff like that. We got information. We picked up a lot of stuff, like at the pharmacy they have the tapes on how to use your inhalers and stuff like that, and the kids will pick them up. His brothers and sisters will pick things up. We just kind of watch out for him.
>
> **Reactive style:** Well we more or less suspected that she had asthma for a while. And I guess you know I noticed more that she complained about feeling tight in her chest or whatever, and she was doing some wheezing, um, but I come from a family where my mother was a hypochondriac, and I know from my own experience kids do tend to, when they don't want to go to school or something, make up things about why they don't want to go, so I just chose to ignore a lot of it. One night she was upset about something. I think we had an argument or something, and she was crying. It was late at night, it was about 10 o'clock at night, and I was very angry with her, and she was complaining about this tightness in her chest, and she needed to get to the doctor, and of course I just thought it was a way to get my attention, and I was ignoring her, but she kept insisting, so as angry as I was I loaded her in the middle of the night, we went to the emergency room.
>
> I think about it and I worry because it's been so mild, and it was mild, and I was hoping she would grow out of it um, and I hope, I worry about

her not using her medications properly, and I hope that it won't cause her to have an asthma attack.

In the first example, the entire family has rallied around the management of the child's condition. There are clear plans executed on a daily basis, and routine trips to the pharmacist are watchful reminders about daily care. In contrast, the second example is marked by intense negative affect and distrust of the child's condition. No plans are evident, and emergency care is sought after a series of escalating negative exchanges. Worry and anxiety prevent deliberate planning and organized routines. It should not be surprising to the reader that the first family scored relatively high on self-report measures of family routines, whereas the second family scored relatively low. Lest the reader be left with the impression that an examination of the relative presence or absence of routines is yet another way to categorize families into "good" or "bad," let us now consider different typologies of family practices that may be useful to clinicians and provide another window into family emotion regulation.

Family Ritual Typologies

Family therapists have provided several typologies for the practice of rituals as well as types of rituals useful for therapeutic interventions. Roberts's (2003) typology is particularly suitable for our discussion. She listed six ways in which families practice rituals in their daily lives: underritualized, rigidly ritualized, skewed ritualization, hollow rituals, interrupted rituals, and flexible or adaptive rituals. Families may fall into one or more categories, and typologies may change given different stressors or during transitions such as marriage and divorce. Returning to the earlier distinction made between routines and rituals, one can identify four typologies that vary in their combination of predictable observable routines and meaningful symbolic rituals.

In this schema, it is possible to identify four subtypes that vary in their combination of predictable routines and meaningful rituals. (See Figure 13.1.) Although these subtypes make clinical and intuitive sense, researchers are only just beginning to empirically examine the relative presence and correlates of these groupings. For illustrative purposes, I provide examples drawn from our mealtime observations that highlight how emotion is regulated in these four subtypes.

Chaotic: Who Took My Hot Sauce?

In this mealtime example, there are four children and one mother present at the table. The father is standing to the side of the table while the others eat. The meal begins with the father yelling to the children, "Just eat and shut up." As the children begin to joke with each other, the father follows with the comment "Next person to talk doesn't get to go to the store." After battling over food, the children ask if there is any hot sauce. The father responds that there is just a little bit left and leaves the room. A few minutes

Routines

	Low	High
Low	Chaotic	Rigid and Hollow
High	Flexible and Variable	Enriched

Rituals

Figure 13.1. Four-fold typology of family rituals.

later he returns and asks, "Who took my hot sauce?" When he finds the bottle almost empty, he grabs the bottle from the child, remarks, "You animal," and leaves the room again. As the meal ends, the children start to clear the table, and the father yells from the other room to tell one child to get down from the table.

In this example, there is no predictable order to the meal and exchanges are marked by either strong negative affect or an attempt to control positive emotional expression. Movement in and out of the kitchen and failure to engage in sustained communication suggests that daily life overall is fairly chaotic and little planning is involved. Indeed, this family's response to the Family Ritual Questionnaire endorsed dinnertime as "no big deal" and revealed that "little planning" is involved.

Rigid and Hollow: Eat Your Salad!

In this type of family ritual, there is a strong emphasis on order and routine, with an absence of emotional connection. One family, in particular, comes to mind. The meal begins with the table already set and the father distributing the plates to each of his two children and his wife. Before he sits down, the children begin to eat the bread. He grabs the bread from the daughter, scolds her for not eating her salad first, and says that she cannot have anymore bread until she eats the rest of her food. The father's harsh exchanges continue throughout the meal. At the end of the meal, the father and mother tell the children that the governor has decided to cancel summer vacation and that they will be going to school throughout the summer months. In a family accustomed to joking and sarcasm, this might have been an emotionally positive exchange. However, in this family, where controlling and

282   BARBARA H. FIESE

negative affect predominates, the children are dumbstruck and not allowed in on the joke.

Whereas chaotic families may have escalation of negative affect, families who are more rigid in their routine practices may be more controlling and attempt to dampen the expression of affect, either positive or negative.

Flexible and Variable: Cheetos in the Mashed Potatoes?

In this example there are four children between the ages of 5 and 22. The oldest child is home from college. The meal begins with an extended period of people making their way to the table, children getting up and down, and the mother distributing dishes from the kitchen. There are multiple conversations going on, but there is not a sense of chaos as much as a continuous flow of engagement. Early in the meal the youngest child says, "Daddy, I love you" and his father responds, "I love you too." This is followed by a conversation with the oldest son on conducting site surveys, interrupted by the middle son showing off his muscles, and then a conversation between the youngest son and mother as he puts his Cheetos into the mashed potatoes. The affect is relatively well modulated—there are no extremes in terms of either sustained laughter and joking or squelching of negative affect. Rather there is a stream of shifting conversations that allows everyone to participate on their own level and in their own way.

Enriched: Crazy Aunt Jessy

In this family of four, the meal is fairly well ordered. Dishes are passed in a set order, there are expectations for good manners (son is asked to excuse himself to blow his nose), and dessert is not shared until everyone at the table has finished his or her meal. A thread throughout the conversation is "What makes someone weird?" Discussions ensue about whether a particular classmate is "weird" and then whether the son and daughter are "weird." This is all done with kindhearted joking and positive affect. The son makes a remark about Aunt Jessy and how she would probably do something weird at the dinner table while they were being taped. The mother jumps in to talk about Crazy Aunt Jessy and some of her antics. The conversation ends, however, with "Well, she really is a good person and we love her." In this scenario, the children are allowed to explore the symbolic meaning of what it means to possess particular characteristics that may be shared across family members. Clinicians will surely note that in this safe environment the children have the opportunity to explore their fears and anxieties without concern about retribution or being told to be quiet. By pulling in the example of the aunt, there is an enriched tone to the conversation as extended family members may be illustrative of the larger family identity.

Emotions may be overregulated and controlled as part of the routine, as in the "salad" family, or they may be the subject of exploration, as in "Crazy Aunt Jessy's" family. It is clear that more empirical research is needed with clinical samples to determine whether these typologies provide a reliable and valid way to examine different styles of routine and ritual practices across families.

CLINICAL DECISION MAKING

In earlier reports, the potential for routines and rituals to aid in clinical decision making has been proposed (Fiese & Wamboldt, 2001; Sameroff & Fiese, 2000). Expanding on Sameroff and Fiese's (2000) three *R*'s of intervention, Fiese and Wamboldt proposed that routine interventions may take one of four forms: remediation, redefinition, reeducation, or realignment. All of these interventions are based on the assumption that when a family faces a stressor there is a potential for routines to be disrupted. Steinglass has proposed that the first sign of family distress is a disruption in its routines (Steinglass, Bennett, Wolin, & Reiss, 1987). To illustrate, I consider how the diagnosis of a chronic illness may affect family functioning and, in particular, how emotion regulation may be affected when routines are altered or disrupted. The diagnosis of a chronic illness often calls for a change in daily routines such that alterations in diet, taking medications, and reducing emotional stressors are often part of medical prescriptions (Fisher & Weihs, 2000). I focus on how the management of a pediatric chronic illness, asthma, may disrupt routines and affect emotional regulation in the family. These disruptions are not unique to pediatric asthma, and readers may want to consider conditions pertinent to their own experiences.

The first step is to determine whether the family's routines have been disrupted since the diagnosis of the illness. If the routines have been disrupted and the family previously practiced meaningful rituals, then it is important to *redefine* the newly created routines so that they fit within the family's notion of meaningful rituals. For example, previously established bedtime storytelling may have been replaced with a focus on taking medications. The child may experience a sense of loss of the ritual and have difficulty soothing him or herself to sleep. In this instance, it would be important to redefine activities such that the previously existing routine (bedtime storytelling) and the new routine demand (taking nighttime medications) can coexist without affective disruption.

If routines have not been disrupted, then it is possible to use preexisting routines as a way to *remediate* the situation. For example, if the child regularly and reliably brushes his or her teeth every morning and evening, then the medicine may be placed next to the child's toothbrush. This does not cause an alteration in the routine as much as it builds on a preexisting routine that can be easily altered with little affective disruption.

If there is an absence of routines, then two strategies should be considered. The clinician needs to first determine whether the family is knowl-

edgeable about the importance of routines and whether there are any historical examples they can draw from. The "chaotic" type of family mentioned
previously is often one that has had little experience with routines in its
families of origin. In these instances, it is important to assist the family in
creating new routines that have the potential to turn into meaningful rituals,
a form of reeducation. Because there have been few historical examples to
draw from, it is important to carefully evaluate the family's tolerance for
implementing family-level change. It may be prudent to begin with a routine
that is time limited and relatively easy to implement. For example, creating
a bedtime routine that is tied to a particular time of the evening may be
easier to implement than creating a mealtime routine for the entire family.
Focusing on routine interventions where there is little previous experience is
important when considering the potential for routines and rituals to be emotionally provocative as well as soothing. This brings us to the fourth form of
intervention: realignment.

For some families, routines are disrupted because there is conflict among
family members about the importance of specific routines. My colleagues
and I have noted that families who have undergone a divorce sometimes
hold disparate views about the importance of their child taking daily-
prescribed medications. In these cases, routines may exist in one household
but not in the other. The child is caught between two sets of expectations,
and often conflict ensues. In this instance, it is important to realign the
parents in the service of a common goal. By reducing conflict over the
importance of the routine, parents may protect the child from the potentially harmful effects of marital disagreements (see chap. 8, this volume). A
decision tree outlining the four types of routine interventions is presented in
Figure 13.2.

POLICY IMPLICATIONS

There is no question that families encounter multiple demands on their
time— extended work hours, after-school activities, and lengthy homework
assignments can all disrupt family routines. In this chapter I argue that when
routines are disrupted there is an emotional cost to the family as a whole. It is
essential that policy makers attend to the complexity of family life as well as
aid in promoting healthy practices. Flexible work hours, schools setting aside
a "no homework night" every week, "no TV" nights, and "family game night"
are all examples of opportunities to create meaningful rituals. Inexpensive
and simple interventions such as providing guidelines for structuring mealtime in a positive way for families on welfare, having schoolchildren talk
about their unique family traditions, and encouraging teenagers to spend three
nights a week at home with their families may have far-reaching effects. Recall that rituals need not be elaborate or time consuming. Societal institu-

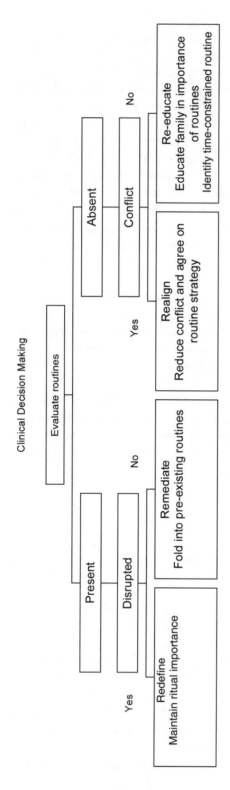

Figure 13.2. Clinical decision making.

tions, however, should be receptive to their importance and aid families in setting aside these important times.

Family routines and rituals have multifaceted connections to emotion regulation. On the one hand, rituals by their very nature are emotional gatherings, sometimes evoking sentimentality and also potentially evoking negatively charged interactions in which emotions are constrained or allowed to escalate out of control. On the other hand, rituals and routines may be used as an emotion regulation strategy. Expectations for conduct and norms for affective expression are implicit in the practice of daily routines such as mealtime gatherings, and they reinforce family values and identity. This dual nature of routines and rituals may complicate our understanding of emotion regulation as it moves beyond the identification of specific emotions and individual regulation and force us to attend to the organizing nature of family systems. Future efforts may inform how the group's regulation of emotion transacts with feelings experienced by the individual. As researchers look to the future, it is relevant to consider Evan Imber-Black's closing statement in the second edition of *Rituals in Families and Family Therapy* (2003):

> The shape of tomorrow's rituals will, no doubt, look somewhat like today's and be somewhat different. That there will be rituals—to tell us who we are to each other, to help us heal, to express our beliefs, to hold dear what is most human—of that there is no doubt. (p. 419)

Families will continue to regulate emotion as a group, and rituals will continue to promote emotion regulation, whether through peanut butter and jelly sandwiches, eating your salad first, or having enough hot sauce—the processes will no doubt remain the same.

REFERENCES

Bennett, L. A., Wolin, S. J., & Reiss, D. (1988). Deliberate family process: A strategy for protecting children of alcoholics. *British Journal of Addiction, 26,* 821–829.

Boyce, W. T., Jensen, E. W., James, S. A., & Peacock, J. L. (1983). The Family Routines Inventory: Theoretical origins. *Social Science and Medicine, 17,* 193–200.

Bush, E. G., & Pargament, K. I. (1997). Family coping with chronic pain. *Families, Systems, & Health, 15,* 147–160.

Carlson, E. A., Sroufe, L. A., & Egeland, B. (2004). The construction of experience: A longitudinal study of representation and behavior. *Child Development, 75,* 66–83.

Cummings, E. M., Davies, P. T., & Campbell, S. B. (2000). *Developmental psychopathology and family process.* New York: Guilford Press.

Darling, M., & Steinberg, L. (1993). Parenting style as context: An integrative model. *Psychological Bulletin, 113,* 487–496.

Dickstein, S., St. Andre, M., Sameroff, A. J., Seifer, R., & Schiller, M. (1999). Maternal depression, family functioning, and child outcomes: A narrative assessment. In B. H. Fiese, A. J. Sameroff, H. D. Grotevant, F. S. Wamboldt, S. Dickstein, & D. Fravel (Eds.), The stories that families tell: Narrative coherence, narrative interaction, and relationship beliefs. *Monographs of the Society for Research in Child Development, 64*(2, Serial No. 257), 84–104.

Eisenberg, M. E., Olson, R. E., Neumark-Sztainer, D., Story, M., & Bearinger, L. H. (2004). Correlations between family meals and psychosocial well-being among adolescents. *Archives of Pediatric and Adolescent Medicine, 158,* 792–796.

Eisenberg, N., Zhou, Q., Losoya, S. H., Fabes, R. A., Shepard, S. A., Murphy, B. C., et al. (2003). The relations of parenting, effortful control, and ego control to children's emotional expressivity. *Child Development, 74,* 875–895.

Fiering, C., & Lewis, M. (1987). The ecology of some middle class families at dinner. *International Journal of Behavioral Development, 10,* 377–390.

Fiese, B. H. (1993). Family rituals in alcoholic and nonalcoholic households: Relation to adolescent health symptomatology and problematic drinking. *Family Relations, 42,* 187–192.

Fiese, B. H., & Kline, C. A. (1993). Development of the Family Ritual Questionnaire: Initial reliability and validation studies. *Journal of Family Psychology, 6,* 1–10.

Fiese, B. H., & Marjinsky, K. A. T. (1999). Dinnertime stories: Connecting relationship beliefs and child behavior. In B. H. Fiese, A. J. Sameroff, H. D. Grotevant, F. S. Wamboldt, S. Dickstein, & D. Fravel (Eds.), The stories that families tell: Narrative coherence, narrative interaction, and relationship beliefs. *Monographs of the Society for Research in Child Development, 64*(2, Serial No. 257), 52–684.

Fiese, B. H., Tomcho, T., Douglas, M., Josephs, K., Poltrock, S., & Baker, T. (2002). Fifty years of research on naturally occurring rituals: Cause for celebration? *Journal of Family Psychology, 16,* 381–390.

Fiese, B. H., & Wamboldt, F. S. (2001). Family routines, rituals, and asthma management: A proposal for family-based strategies to increase treatment adherence. *Families, Systems, & Health, 18,* 405–418.

Fiese, B. H., & Wamboldt, F. S. (2003). Tales of pediatric asthma management: Family-based strategies related to medical adherence and health care utilization. *Journal of Pediatrics, 143,* 457–462.

Fiese, B. H., Wamboldt, F. S., & Anbar, R. D. (2005). Family asthma management routines: Connections to medical adherence and quality of life. *Journal of Pediatrics, 146,* 171–176.

Fiese, B. H., Wamboldt, F. S., Howell, K. J., & Spagnola, M. (2003, April). *Scarfing down dinner: Connecting children's perceptions of family dynamics with child behavior through the stories that they tell.* Paper presented at the biennial meeting of the Society for Research in Child Development, Tampa, FL.

Fisher, L., & Weihs, K. L. (2000). Can addressing family relationships improve outcomes in chronic disease? *The Journal of Family Practice, 49,* 561–566.

Gleason, J. B., Perlmann, R. Y., & Greif, E. B. (1984). What's the magic word: Learning language through politeness routines. *Discourse Processes, 7,* 493–502.

Imber-Black, E. (2003). Afterword. In E. Imber-Black, J. Roberts, & R. A. Whiting (Eds.), *Rituals in families and family therapy* (2nd ed., p. 419). New York: Norton.

Kennedy-Moore, E., & Watson, J. (1999). *Expressing emotion: Myths, realities, and therapeutic strategies.* New York: Guilford Press.

Kubicek, L. F. (2002). Fresh perspectives on young children and family routines. *Zero to Three, 22,* 4–9.

Landesman, S., Jaccard, J., & Gunderson, V. (1991). The family environment: The combined influence of family behavior, goals, strategies, resources, and individual experiences. In M. Lewis & S. Feinman (Eds.), *Social influences and socialization in infancy* (pp. 63–96). New York: Plenum Press.

Markson, S., & Fiese, B. H. (2000). Family rituals as a protective factor against anxiety for children with asthma. *Journal of Pediatric Psychology, 25*(7), 471–479.

Martini, M. (1996). "What's new?" at the dinner table: Family dynamics during mealtimes in two cultural groups in Hawaii. *Early Development and Parenting, 5,* 23–34.

McCubbin, H., Thompson, A., & McCubbin, A. (1996). *Family assessment.* Madison: University of Wisconsin Press.

Mikulincer, M., Shaver, P., & Pereg, D. (2003). Attachment theory and affect regulation: The dynamics, development, and cognitive consequences of attachment-related strategies. *Motivation and Emotion, 27,* 77–102.

Minuchin, P. (1988). Relationships within the family: A systems perspective on development. In R. A. Hinde & J. Stevenson-Hinde (Eds.), *Relationships within families* (pp. 7–26). Oxford, England: Clarendon Press.

Parke, R. D., Simpkins, S. D., McDowell, D. J., Kim, M., Killian, C., Dennis, J., et al. (2002). Relative contributions of families and peers to children's social development. In P. K. Smith & C. H. Hart (Eds.), *Handbook of childhood social development* (pp. 156–177). Malden, MA: Blackwell.

Popenoe, D. (1993). American family decline 1960–1990: A review and appraisal. *Journal of Marriage and the Family, 55,* 527–542.

Putnam, R. D. (2000). *Bowling alone: The collapse and revival of American community.* New York: Simon & Schuster.

Reiss, D. (1989). The practicing and representing family. In A. J. Sameroff & R. Emde (Eds.), *Relationship disturbances in early childhood* (pp. 191–220). New York: Basic Books.

Roberts, J. (2003). Setting the frame: Definition, functions, and typology of rituals. In E. Imber-Black, J. Roberts, & R. Whiting (Eds.), *Rituals in families and family therapy* (Rev. ed., pp. 3–48). New York: Norton.

Sameroff, A. J., & Fiese, B. H. (2000). Transactional regulation: The developmental ecology of early intervention. In S. J. Meisels & J. P. Shonkoff (Eds.), *Early intervention: A handbook of theory, practice, and analysis* (pp. 3–19). New York: Cambridge University Press.

Smyth, J. M., & Stone, A. A. (2003). Ecological momentary assessment research in behavioral medicine. *Journal of Happiness Studies, 4*, 35–52.

Steinglass, P., Bennett, L. A., Wolin, S. J., & Reiss, D. (1987). *The alcoholic family.* New York: Basic Books.

van der Hart, O. (1983). *Rituals in psychotherapy: Transitions and continuity.* New York: Irvington Publishers.

Wamboldt, F. S., & O'Connor, S. (1997). *Asthma impact interview.* Denver, CO: National Jewish Medical Research Center.

Weisner, T. S. (2002). Ecocultural understanding of children's developmental pathways. *Human Development, 45*, 275–281.

Wolcott, J. (2001, September 5). Reports of demise of family dinner are greatly exaggerated; some 63% of American families eat dinner together often or always. *Christian Scientist Monitor,* p. 15.

Wolin, S. J., & Bennett, L. A. (1984). Family rituals. *Family Process, 23*, 401–420.

Wolin, S. J., Bennett, L. A., & Jacobs, J. S. (2003). Assessing family rituals in alcoholic families. In E. Imber-Black, J. Roberts, & R. A. Whiting (Eds.), *Rituals in families and family therapy* (Rev. ed., pp. 253–279). New York: Norton.

Wolin, S. J., Bennett, L. A., Noonan, D. L., & Teitlebaum, M. A. (1980). Disrupted family rituals: A factor in generational transmission of alcoholism. *Journal of Studies on Alcohol, 41*, 199–214.

IV

INTEGRATION

14

FAMILY EMOTION REGULATION PROCESSES: IMPLICATIONS FOR RESEARCH AND INTERVENTION

DOUGLAS K. SNYDER, JAN N. HUGHES, AND JEFFRY A. SIMPSON

Research on emotion regulation in couples and families has the potential to advance not only basic science regarding family and relationship processes but also applications related to promoting individual and family well-being, preventing disruptions to emotional or physical health, and intervening with couples and families in distress. For basic and applied research on emotion regulation to progress, investigators will need to address both conceptual and theoretical issues and methodological concerns, including measurement and data-analytic strategies and the translational challenges of extending basic research findings into effective interventions.

CONCEPTUAL AND THEORETICAL ISSUES

Investigators should articulate both their general conceptualization of emotion regulation and specific components targeted by their research. Research on emotion regulation will best proceed when investigators articulate the nomological net (Cronbach & Meehl, 1955) that defines their broadband view of emotion regulation as well as their focus on specific components of emotion regulation processes. Specifically, emotion regulation needs to be differentiated from related constructs of emotional intelligence or understanding, emotional expressiveness or suppression, affect or mood regulation, affective reactivity, temperament, effortful versus reactive control, emotion decoding, coping, interpersonal problem solving, and social competence.

How should emotion regulation be conceptualized within a broader theory of emotions? Grewal, Brackett, and Salovey (chap. 2, this volume), for example, define emotion "management" as one of four core components of emotional intelligence that involve abilities to access, accurately label, and modify feelings in oneself and others. From this perspective, the management of feelings is distinguished from related abilities to perceive and understand emotions and to use emotions to facilitate thought and language. Others (see, e.g., chap. 1) regard emotion regulation as multifaceted, consisting of diverse cognitive and behavioral responses that include attentional and interpretive processes both prior to and following emotion arousal.

Common throughout most conceptualizations of emotion regulation is the premise that, at its most fundamental level, emotion regulation involves strategies that individuals (alone or in concert with significant others) use to influence the content, subjective experience, and expression of emotions. Investigators may vary in the extent to which they emphasize conscious or automatic mechanisms of emotion regulation, their intrapersonal versus interpersonal components, strategies deployed before versus after emotion arousal, and efforts to increase versus decrease emotional experience and expression. To date, research on emotion regulation has emphasized primarily the down-regulation of negative affect (e.g., anger) from an intrapersonal perspective. Complementary emphases on the enhancement of positive emotions (e.g., empathy and intimacy) from an interpersonal perspective are equally critical to understanding emotion regulation processes in couples and families.

Investigation of emotion regulation should attend to both conscious and nonconscious regulatory responses. An important conceptual issue that receives insufficient attention in the emotion regulation literature is the distinction between emotion regulation and initial emotion arousal processes. In general, the field of emotion regulation has largely ignored the processes of emotional arousal or initial emotional reactivity, focusing on "the intra- and extraorganismic factors by which emotional arousal is redirected, controlled, modulated, and modified to enable an individual to function adaptively in emotionally arousing situations" (see chap. 6, this volume, pp. 124–125). Emotional arousal processes would include Gross et al.'s (chap. 1) antecedent-focused, largely conscious strategies deployed prior to confronting an emotionally arousing situation, as well as nonconscious processes that temper arousal intensity (Fitzsimons & Bargh, 2004). Internal working models and other knowledge structures that operate outside awareness (see chaps. 4 and

8) as well as biological processes that govern the intensity of affective arousal are examples of nonconscious emotion regulatory processes. Mikulincer et al.'s experimental studies (chap. 4) suggest the potential value of activating secure attachment representations, which normally operate outside conscious awareness, as a means of coping with intense threats to one's security. In general, sensitive and responsive parenting may affect children's emotion regulation and social competence indirectly through its effects on children's social goal orientation, felt security, and other mental structures that operate largely outside conscious awareness (Heidgerken, Hughes, Cavell, & Willson, 2004).

Investigations of emotion regulation should attend to biological and genetic processes. Many of the processes subsumed under the term "emotion regulation" have their basis in temperament—that is, "constitutionally based individual differences in emotional, motor, and attentional reactivity and self regulation" (Rothbart & Bates, 1998, p. 109). This conceptualization emphasizes the biological bases of temperament, influenced by genetic inheritance but shaped by maturation and experience. Among the individual-difference variables that have a strong basis in temperament are activity level, impulsivity, mood, emotional reactivity, fearfulness, affective intensity, aggression, and many other characteristics associated with emotion regulation. Despite the broad consensus that temperament plays a significant role in emotion regulation, insufficient research has examined how temperament-based individual differences interact with the environment in a reciprocal causal process that accounts for observed differences in emotion arousal and regulation. Such research holds the promise of early intervention with approaches tailored to an individual's biological constitution. In addition, the role of temperament in emotion regulation indicates that the playing field is not level for all individuals when it comes to controlling impulses and modulating emotional expression.

Investigations of emotion regulation should attend to both intrapersonal and interpersonal processes. Emotion regulation never occurs in a vacuum and most often proceeds in an interpersonal context. Hence, emotion regulation processes will best be understood when the study of intrapersonal processes is complemented by research explicating how intrapersonal regulation operates in concert with situational facets (including interpersonal exchanges) to generate positive or negative outcomes. The situational context may be relatively focused (e.g., couple or family based) or broad (e.g., social contextual stressors of poverty or war). In a similar way, emotion regulation should be viewed as involving individuals' efforts to regulate not only their own emotions but also the emotions of significant others. Such efforts may entail strategies to provoke or increase affect in the other (e.g., empathy) or to minimize or contain the other's affect (e.g., hostility or anguish).

For example, in treating persons struggling with physical pain, Keefe, Porter, and Labban (chap. 10, this volume) note that some interventions emphasize intrapersonal mechanisms by helping the patient manage his or her own pain-related emotions (e.g., through relaxation training or imagery), whereas other interventions (e.g., communication skills training) emphasize interpersonal mechanisms to help partners regulate difficult emotions that occur during their interactions.

Research should examine both individual and situational moderators of emotion regulation. Obvious candidates for investigation include individual differences in gender, age, and ethnicity. For example, women may be more aware of emotional processes in intimate relationships and be more willing and able to regulate them. Among children and adolescents, developmental differences in emotion regulation are immense, even though research by Gross and colleagues (Gross et al., 1997; John & Gross, 2004) suggests that a trajectory across age toward increasingly healthy emotion regulation is also observed among adults. Moreover, the specific content of both positive and negative emotions (glee vs. relief, anger vs. sorrow) is likely to influence emotion regulation strategies across both antecedent (e.g., attentional) and consequent (e.g., expressive) phases.

Separate from individual differences are situational features likely to influence the experience and expression of emotions. Intimate relationships between spouses or between parents and children, for example, may enhance both the intensity of emotions and the likelihood of their expression. Even within intimate dyads, emotion regulation processes should vary as a function of their privacy (e.g., managing conflict with a spouse or child at home versus in public) and the degree of emotional security experienced in the moment (e.g., expressions of vulnerability or tenderness during times of closeness vs. conflict).

Interventions promoting well-being or targeting dysfunction may be enhanced by components that extend beyond intrapersonal strategies to build on situational contexts that are most conducive to effective emotion regulation. For example, Mikulincer, Shaver, and Horesh (chap. 4, this volume) cite experimental evidence suggesting that environmental "priming" of secure attachment representations helps individuals remain focused, organized, and balanced in the face of traumatic events.

Both conceptual and empirical advances in understanding emotion regulation processes in families will be enhanced when these processes are contextualized within broader theories of individual and interpersonal functioning. Placing emotion regulation processes within a broader theoretical framework should expand the potential for formulating testable hypotheses linking emotion processes to a broader spectrum of individual and interpersonal mechanisms that promote or impede emotion regulation. Attachment theory provides one such framework particularly relevant to families by emphasizing interpersonal experiences as a source of individual differences in emotion activation and regulation (see Rholes & Simpson, 2004). Basic research from social psychological perspectives (e.g., see chap. 4, this volume) and more clinical perspectives (e.g., chap. 11) emphasizes the importance of security-based strategies, which may result in either emotional hyperactivation, the suppression of emotions, or emotional deactivation. Both attachment theory and other interpersonal formulations of emotion activation and arousal could profit by integrating basic research from the cognitive and physiological approaches, which emphasize intrapersonal mechanisms of emotion regulation identified in laboratory research. Theories may also be enhanced by incorporating new biopsychosocial perspectives that extend beyond attachment phenomena to include broader components of psychological and social functioning (e.g., work described in chap. 10).

Advances in understanding emotion regulation are more likely to occur through collaborations among investigators trained in different theoretical and methodological traditions. Social psychological perspectives on emotion regulation in community samples, for instance, may benefit from clinical approaches to conceptualizing individual or relational emotion dysfunction. In a similar way, family system approaches to emotion regulation might benefit from conceptual and methodological enhancements associated with developmental and behavioral genetics perspectives.

METHODOLOGICAL ISSUES

Emotion regulation processes are best studied using multiple methods that target diverse components across behavioral, experiential, and physiological domains. As with many domains in psychology, individual differences in emotion regulation have typically been explored using single-measurement strategies, most often self-report. Although subjective aspects of emotional experience require self-report methods, both the susceptibility of self-reports to various response biases (Messick, 1991) and the importance of other cognitive and behavioral components of emotion regulation argue for the use of multimodal measurement strategies across diverse domains. For example, the research described by Pietromonaco, Feldman Barrett, and Powers (chap. 3, this volume) indicates that more anxiously attached individuals evince less affective reactivity when assessed with self-report measures than with hormonal measures. Hence, multiple strategies that tap into different emotion response systems are essential—including physiological measures of arousal, laboratory and field-relevant measures of emotion attention, and observational strategies for coding emotions in interpersonal interactions.

Related to multiple approaches to measuring emotion regulation are considerations about including multiple respondents. On the one hand, multiple informants increase the opportunity to distinguish construct-relevant variance from measurement method or source variance—a particular concern when one relies exclusively on self-reports of conceptually distinct constructs from the same individual. On the other hand, previous research on measures of emotional and behavioral functioning in children and adolescents has shown considerable divergence across informants (e.g., mothers, fathers, teachers, or peers). Parents' reports of their children's functioning may be biased by their own psychological characteristics (e.g., maternal depression; Najman et al., 2001). In a similar way, partner reports of emotion regulation (or dysregulation) in couples often have poor interrater reliability (Moffitt et al., 1997). Finally, issues of criterion contamination arise when measures of emotion regulation and related constructs obtained from the same informant (e.g., teachers) are used to assess both independent and dependent variables (e.g., emotion regulation and social competence in children). Future research may benefit from using data-analytic strategies in which relevant constructs are treated as latent variables, which are assessed by multiple measurement techniques that vary in terms of modality and type of informant.

Emotion regulation should be studied using diverse paradigms that vary in evocative stimuli, response options, and social-interpersonal contexts. Both the content of emotion regulation processes and their precursors and consequents are likely to vary across diverse contexts. For example, the spontaneous or reflexive processes that occur automatically in response to "everyday events" may differ dramatically from those that involve deliberate, effortful regulation in response to atypical, laboratory-based stressors or critical relationship incidents marked by conflict or emotional distress.

The chapters in this volume showcase several diverse paradigms that could facilitate a more robust theory of emotion regulation, independent of specific paradigms or experimental contexts. Exemplars of such diversity include (a) studies of spontaneous emotion regulation processes in daily living (chap. 1, this volume) versus in response to the trauma of war (chap. 4); (b) a focus on emotion regulation processes driven by the distress of one person (e.g., chap. 10, on dyadic responses to physical illness) versus emotion regulation processes in relationships in which the individual is a member (e.g., the couple-based research described in chap.11; the focus on parent–child interactions described in chap. 7) or a proximal observer (e.g., the work summarized in chap. 8 regarding children's response to marital conflict); and (c) studies of emotion regulation within a broader family or social context as it relates to social competence (e.g., the work described in chap. 6), aggression (chap. 5), or risk-taking behaviors (chap. 9). The paradigms also vary in their focus on vivid demonstrations of emotion dysregulation in couples and families (e.g., the research described in chap. 12) as opposed to emotion regulation in the everyday life of healthy families at the system level (e.g., chap. 13).

Extensions of emotion regulation research across new or expanded paradigms are also likely to benefit from consideration of diverse situational and temporal contexts. Emotion regulation processes observed in attachment-relevant contexts may not necessarily generalize to emotion processes observed in nonrelational threatening or arousing contexts. For example, spouses' abilities to access and disclose vulnerable emotions such as disappointment or hurt, and partners' abilities to respond empathically, might vary depending on whether the source of those feelings lies within or outside the relationship (Gee, Scott, Castellani, & Cordova, 2002). In a similar manner, emotion regulation processes witnessed in intimate dyads during a hurtful or distressing exchange may differ considerably from emotion regulation processes that occur hours or days afterward. That is, efforts to restore emotional equilibrium through various relationship-repair strategies can be viewed from either a proximal perspective (i.e., emotion regulation processes in the moment) or a distal perspective that regards interpersonal sequences as reflecting emotion regulation processes that unfold across several days. The evolution of emotion regulation processes at both the individual and the interpersonal level argues for the importance of longitudinal designs, especially those that can delineate reciprocal relations among parenting, children's emotion regulation, and children's social functioning (see chaps. 6 and 7, this volume).

Comprehensive understanding of emotion regulation processes is likely to evolve from aggregate findings based in diverse sampling strategies. Because emotion regulation processes typically occur in interpersonal or broader social contexts, robust theories of emotion regulation will require experimental paradigms that treat individuals, intimate dyads, entire families, and broader social groups as the units of analysis. For example, work by Pietromonaco and colleagues (chap. 3, this volume) demonstrates that emotion regulation may be governed not only by the attachment style of the individual but also by the style of his or her romantic partner. Fiese's work (chap. 13) regarding the emotion-regulating function of rituals requires sampling at the family system level, where such rituals are expressed.

In a similar way, theories of emotion regulation in couples and families must account not only for emotional processes in college- or community-based samples but also for emotion regulation (or dysregulation) processes that occur in clinically distressed couples and families. To date, most of the basic research on emotion regulation processes in intimate dyads has focused on young, unmarried couples who may not be representative of more established married couples in terms of commitment, history of relationship trauma, or other situational factors that may contribute to or compromise relationship resilience. Findings regarding strategies for up-regulating positive emotions in nondistressed populations may facilitate intervention and prevention efforts in clinical settings, just as research on down-regulation of potentially destructive or harmful emotions with clinical samples may facilitate interventions with community samples of couples or families struggling with normative challenges of daily living.

Also, virtually nothing is known about emotion regulation processes in older adults, for whom the expression or regulation of affect may be limited by cognitive impairments related to aging. Neither is much known about the role of culture in how families regulate emotions, or how spouses from diverse cultural backgrounds regulate emotions within their marriages.

Research should examine emotion regulation not only as an outcome of individual and interpersonal processes but also as a mediator of these processes. Emotions are both regulated and regulating at intrapersonal as well as interpersonal levels. For example, individual differences in emotion regulation processes have been linked to posttraumatic symptoms following exposure to intense or prolonged social stressors (chap. 4, this volume), interpersonal aggression in children (chap. 5), and risk-taking behaviors in adolescents (chap. 9).

Valiente and Eisenberg (chap. 6, this volume) note that, in addition to having direct effects on their emotional well-being, children's emotion regulation processes can also mediate or moderate the relations between emotion-related parenting practices and children's social behavior and social competence. Research described by Parke and colleagues (chap. 7) and by Cummings and Keller (chap. 8), for instance, highlights how emotion regulation processes mediate linkages between marital conflict and children's social competence, possibly through internalized representations of social exchange that reduce the threshold for perceiving threat and promote either inappropriate social withdrawal or peer aggression. Fruzzetti and Iverson (chap. 12) extend this conceptualization by positing dysfunctional partner or family behaviors such as invalidation, which appears to mediate the relation between individual emotion regulation and psychopathology.

Several lines of research suggest that emotion regulation processes may also interact with other individual or interpersonal factors en route to influencing personal and social well-being. For example, family interactions that promote emotion regulation abilities may be particularly critical in children and adolescents who are biologically predisposed to greater emotional reactivity. Parke and colleagues (chap. 7, this volume) argue that to disentangle genetic contributions from socialization influences on the development of emotion regulation skills require genetically sensitive designs in which two or more siblings in the same family are assessed on the same regulatory processes. Moreover, differences in how each parent manages emotion regulation issues with each child in a family need to be assessed.

APPLICATION ISSUES

Basic research findings from studies of emotion regulation should be used to develop programs that promote emotional well-being across the life span. A recurrent theme in the chapters of this volume is that emotional and social well-being in children may be enhanced by fostering emotionally healthy family contexts. Eisenberg, Spinrad, and Cumberland (1998), for example, have identified four ways in which parents socialize emotions in their children: (a) through parents' direct reactions to children's emotions, (b) through parents' discussion of emotions, (c) through parents' expression of emotions, and (d) through parents' selection and modification of emotionally relevant situations. Research with adults by Gross and colleagues (chap. 1, this volume) indicates that parents may promote health in their children by serving as emotion coaches and promoting such emotion regulation strategies as cognitive reappraisal. Research by Parke and colleagues (chap. 7) indicates that parents who are more intrusive or controlling may actually compromise their children's emotion regulation abilities by providing them with fewer opportunities to "try out" different emotional responses.

Programs promoting greater emotional well-being in children by using parents as emotion coaches require providing skills to parents in a form and at a time when parents are most amenable to learning such skills. Examples may include group instruction for couples who are transitioning to parenthood and more individualized instruction to parents of children who are struggling with emotional or physical disabilities. It is clear that some parents may remain ill equipped to serve as emotion coaches, either because of their own deficits or because of persistent marital conflict. In such cases, alternative modalities for promoting emotion regulation skills might include church- or school-based interventions that draw on relationships with healthy adult mentors or parent surrogates (e.g., Meehan, Hughes, & Cavell, 2003).

Research by Gross and colleagues (chap. 1, this volume) on emotion regulation in everyday life exemplifies the manner in which basic findings may be generalized to education and prevention programs with couples and families. Their finding that cognitive reappraisal is more effective than suppression in regulating affect in negative-emotion-eliciting contexts could be easily integrated within couple and family prevention programs that target dysfunctional attributions as principal sources of relationship distress. Research by Fiese (chap. 13) on family rituals as emotion-regulating devices similarly suggests the potential benefits of promoting such family patterns as a prophylactic means of fostering more intimate connections and greater emotional security.

Interventions targeting emotion regulation processes in distressed couples and families should integrate individual and interpersonal mechanisms and should specify guidelines for selecting, sequencing, and pacing treatment components. The research with distressed couples and families described in this volume affirms the need to target both individual and interpersonal processes, whether intervening with couples who are experiencing relationship distress (chap. 11, this volume), physical illness (chap. 10), or more severe psychopathology (chap. 12). Intrapersonal mechanisms critical to emotion regulation include promoting adaptive emotional awareness and expression, particularly relating to the "softer" or more vulnerable emotions of fear, hurt, disappointment, and shame (see also Jacobson & Christensen, 1996; Johnson & Whiffen,

2003). Interpersonal processes essential to emotion regulation at the couple or family level involve disrupting maladaptive recursive cycles of escalating negative affect and, in their place, promoting partners' empathic responsiveness. As Fruzzetti and Iverson note, the precise individual and interpersonal mechanisms that facilitate rather than disrupt emotion regulation in couples and families warrant further study. For example, basic research is needed to explicate the psychophysiological mechanisms mediating the relation between validating responses and diminished emotional arousal. In a similar way, additional research comparing alternative intervention strategies is needed to determine whether altering invalidating processes is more useful in regulating spouses' or family members' emotions than is targeting other processes, such as the expression of positive affect or constructive problem solving.

Just as critical as the content of treatment are the sequencing and pacing of interventions. The treatment of couples or families characterized by frequent or intense emotion dysregulation, for example, may require alternating attention between individual members to promote emotion regulation abilities that emphasize intrapersonal mechanisms and then targeting relationship processes to promote members' adaptation to each other's changes and collaboration in mutually supportive exchanges (Snyder & Whisman, 2003). Deciding which mechanisms to target (e.g., disrupting negative emotions or promoting positive ones) at which level (e.g., individual versus interpersonal) at any given point in treatment requires an explicit organizational model that integrates multiple facets of family system emotion functioning.

Existing couple- and family-based treatments will be enhanced by incorporating basic research on emotion regulation processes. Couple- and family-based interventions vary considerably in their attention to emotion and emotion regulation processes. One means of enhancing existing therapies is by complementing behavioral and cognitive treatments with interventions that are specifically grounded in emotion regulation research. For example, Pietromonaco and colleagues (chap. 3, this volume) note that changing emotional reactivity to relationship threats is likely to be difficult because emotional associations are resistant to extinction and counterconditioning. As a consequence, such reactivity may be more readily modified by promoting accurate identification or alternative interpretations of threatening events. Research described by Goldman and Greenberg (chap. 11) similarly offers the potential to extend emotion-focused couple interventions to treatment with couples recovering from specific relationship trauma such as emotional or physical abuse. Research by Fiese (chap. 13) suggests the incremental benefit of promoting family routines and rituals for those whose established patterns have previously been deficient or are challenged by current situational stressors.

Not only may emotion-based strategies complement existing treatments, they might contribute to new approaches for intervening with couples or families in which emotion regulation processes constitute a core feature of specific disorders. Keefe and colleagues (chap. 10, this volume), for example, note that physical pain is too often viewed as merely a sensory event, with little recognition of the important role that emotion or the social environment plays in affecting the perception of pain. Similarly, couple-based emotion regulation interventions might have significant therapeutic effects on individual disorders in which emotional arousal plays a central role—such as affective disorders, appetitive disorders such as alcohol or substance abuse, disorders of sexual desire and arousal, physical aggression, or other impulse-control disorders. As noted by Fruzzetti and Iverson (chap. 12), additional research explicating the relations among emotion regulation, psychopathology, and family interactions should facilitate both primary and secondary prevention efforts and the design of more effective treatments for specific populations.

As may be expected in an emerging field, clinical researchers diverge to some degree in their recommended interpersonal emotion regulation strategies. Divergence on how to respond to a partner's expressed negative emotions is an example of such apparent inconsistencies. Consistent with cognitive theory, Keefe et al. (chap. 10, this volume) suggest that partners of people with chronic pain should use cognitive restructuring with them so they can learn "how to recognize overly negative appraisals of pain and replace them with more realistic and adaptive appraisals" (p. 213). Alternatively, Goldman and Greenberg (chap. 11), using an emotion-focused couple therapy approach, advocate an empathic, validating response to a partner's expression of pain. Such inconsistencies in clinical applications will be resolved only through well-designed clinical research studies.

Findings from both basic and applied research should influence public policy in a manner that protects and strengthens families. Throughout this volume, one recurring theme has been an emphasis on the importance of emotional connections and a sense of community as vital sources of emotional security and adaptive emotion regulation. At the family level, emotional connections can be promoted through the universal delivery of primary prevention programs that promote emotion regulation in couples and families—for example, through state-based initiatives funded in part through marriage license fees, or by mandatory participation in interventions that target collaborative parenting of children and adolescents to reduce the negative consequences of divorce. In addition to reducing the deleterious impact of couple distress, families may be protected and strengthened by corporate policies in the work setting that are designed to promote family connections—for example, by encouraging flexible work schedules or aggregating personal leave on a voluntary basis to be allocated to employees during times of family crisis. At the community level, emotion regulation in families might be facilitated by recognizing families at risk and extending an explicit structure to provide greater support. Exemplars of such community-based interventions can be found in support programs for families in the armed services in which one family member has been deployed abroad or faces challenges reintegrating into the family following exposure to combat.

Widespread delivery of interventions targeting emotion regulation processes is not likely to occur without corporate or public policy initiatives that facilitate the availability of such programs by increasing the number of qualified providers. Keefe and colleagues (chap. 10, this volume) address these issues in their discussion of partner-assisted pain management interventions. They accentuate the importance of (a) more efficient identification of couples who potentially could benefit from targeted interventions by educating health care providers about available treatment programs, (b) expanding the array of allied professionals who could deliver such interventions, and (c) extending the modality of interventions to group formats or to reduced-cost methods such as telephone- or Internet-based consultation.

CONCLUSIONS

As noted in our introduction to this book, individuals' ability to effectively regulate their emotions—especially in interpersonal contexts that involve potentially caustic exchanges—plays a pivotal role in keeping individuals and their significant relationships functioning well. Considerable research is still needed to clarify the basic individual and interpersonal emotion regulation processes in couples and families that make up the core pathways to dysfunction or to emotional and physical health. Understanding these processes requires identifying both the major precursors and the major consequences of emotion regulation across affective, cognitive, and behavioral domains at both the individual and the interpersonal level. No single research paradigm—whether defined in terms of theoretical context, measurement or sampling techniques, or data-analytic strategy—will yield a comprehensive theory of emotion regulation in families. Ultimately, both basic and applied research on family emotion regulation processes must contribute to interventions that promote individual and interpersonal well-being; prevent emotional and physical disorders; and effectively treat dysfunction at the individual, dyadic, and family levels.

REFERENCES

Cronbach, L., & Meehl, P. (1955). Construct validity in psychological tests. *Psychological Bulletin, 52,* 281–302.

Eisenberg, N., Spinrad, T. L., & Cumberland, A. J. (1998). Socialization of emotion: Reply to commentaries. *Psychological Inquiry, 9,* 317–333.

Fitzsimons, G. M., & Bargh, J. A. (2004). Automatic self-regulation. In R. F. Baumeister & K. D. Vohs (Eds.), *Handbook of self-regulation: Research, theory, and applications* (pp. 151–170). New York: Guilford Press.

Gee, C. B., Scott, R. L., Castellani, A. M., & Cordova, J. V. (2002). Predicting 2-year marital satisfaction from partners' discussion of their marriage checkup. *Journal of Marital and Family Therapy, 28,* 399–407.

Gross, J. J., Carstensen, L. L., Pasupathi, M., Tsai, J., Gottestam, K., & Hsu, A. Y. C. (1997). Emotion and aging: Experience, expression, and control. *Psychology and Aging, 12,* 590–599.

Heidgerken, A. D., Hughes, J. N., Cavell, T. A., & Willson, V. L. (2004). Direct and indirect effects of parenting and children's goals on child aggression. *Journal of Clinical Child and Adolescent Psychology, 33,* 684–693.

Jacobson, N. S., & Christensen, A. (1996). *Integrative couple therapy: Promoting acceptance and change.* New York: Norton.

John, O. P., & Gross, J. J. (2004). Healthy and unhealthy emotion regulation: Personality processes, individual differences, and lifespan development. *Journal of Personality, 72,* 1301–1334.

Johnson, S. M., & Whiffen, V. E. (2003). *Attachment processes in couple and family therapy.* New York: Guilford Press.

Meehan, B. T., Hughes, J. N., & Cavell, T. A. (2003). Teacher–student relationships as compensatory resources for aggressive children. *Child Development, 74,* 1145–1157.

Messick, S. (1991). Psychology and methodology of response styles. In R. E. Snow & D. E. Wiley (Eds.), *Improving inquiry in social science: A volume in honor of Lee J. Cronbach* (pp. 161–200). Hillsdale, NJ: Erlbaum.

Moffitt, T. E., Caspi, A., Krueger, R. F., Magdol, L., Margolin, G., Silva, P. A., & Sydney, R. (1997). Do partners agree about abuse in their relationship? A psychometric evaluation of interpartner agreement. *Psychological Assessment, 9,* 47–56.

Najman, J. M., Williams, G. M., Nikles, J., Spence, S., Bor, W., O'Callaghan, M., et al. (2001). Bias influencing maternal reports of child behaviour and emotional state. *Social Psychiatry and Psychiatric Epidemiology, 36,* 186–194.

Rholes, W. S., & Simpson, J. A. (2004). *Adult attachment: Theory, research, and clinical implications.* New York: Guilford Press.

Rothbart, M. K., & Bates, J. E. (1998). Temperament. In W. Damon & N. Eisenberg (Eds.), *Handbook of child psychology: Vol. 3. Social, emotional, and personality development* (pp. 105–176). New York: Wiley.

Snyder, D. K., & Whisman, M. A. (2003). Understanding psychopathology and couple dysfunction: Implications for clinical practice, training, and research. In D. K. Snyder & M. A. Whisman (Eds.), *Treating difficult couples: Helping clients with coexisting mental and relationship disorders* (pp. 419–438). New York: Guilford Press.

AUTHOR INDEX

Numbers in italics refer to listings in the references.

Gray, J. A., 127, *141*, 186, 189, *201*
Green, C., 98
Greenberg, L. S., 70, *72*, 232, 234, 235, 237,
    238, 240, 241, 242, 243, 244, 245,
    246, *247*, *248*, 253, 266
Greenberg, M., 110, *120*
Greenberg, M. T., 50, *52*, 138, *141*
Greenwald, M., 21, 35
Greenwood, D., 63, 64, *73*
Greenwood, G., 43, *52*
Greif, E. B., 275, *289*
Grelling, B. Z., 97
Grewal, D., 44, 47, *52*, *53*
Grich, J., 63, *73*
Gross, J. J., 13, 14, 15, 16, 17, 18, 22, 25, 29,
    30, 31, 32, *33*, *34*, 35, 41, 42, 43,
    49, *52*, 125, 126, *141*, 150, 159, *160*,
    181, 211, 212, 227, 251, 266, 296,
    305
Grossman, 106
Grotevant, H. D., 288
Grusec, J. E., 129, *141*
Grych, J. H., 163, 164, 174, *181*
Gunderson, V., 271, *289*
Gunlicks, M., 64, 66, *73*
Gunnar, M. R., 177, *181*
Gupta, M., 257, *266*
Gupta, R., 188, *202*
Gurman, A. S., *246*, *248*
Gustafson, D. H., 226
Guthrie, I. V., 129, *140*

Haddad, P., 219, *227*
Haggerty, D. J., 55
Halberstadt, A. G., 132, *139*, 148, *160*
Hall, L. E., 55
Hallberg, I. R., 207, *227*
Hamelin, M., 64, *71*
Hamm, A., 21, *35*, 248
Hannish, L., *160*
Hansen, W. B., *203*
Hardy, D. F., 132, *141*
Harlan, E. T., 129, *141*
Harless, D. W., 184, *201*
Harnish, J., 106, *119*
Harold, G. T., 164, 167, 180, *181*
Harrington, H., *200*
Harris, P. L., *120*, *162*
Harrist, A. W., 144, 145, *160*
Hart, C. H., *162*
Hart, J., 177, *181*

Harter, S., 104, *120*
Hartrup, W. W., *162*
Hawkins, J. D., 50, *52*
Hawkins, R. P., *226*
Hayes, S. C., 266, *266*
Haythornthwaite, J., *229*
Hazan, C., 57, 59, 59n, 60, 62, *72*, 80, 81,
    82, 99, 224, *227*
Heard, H., 257, *267*
Heffner, K. L., 168, *181*
Heidgerken, A. D., 295, *305*
Heindel, S., 169, *181*
Heinrich, R. L., 220, *227*
Helgeson, V. S., 219, *227*
Helson, R., 31, *34*
Henrich, C. C., 49, *51*
Henry, B., 191, *200*
Hesse, E., 86, 98
Hetherington, E. M., *162*
Heyman, R. E., 253, *267*
Hibbs, E. D., *201*
Higgins, E. T., 55, *73*, *200*
Hill, C., *201*
Hinde, R. A., *289*
Hinshaw, S. P., 198, *201*
Hirschberger, G., 94, 98
Ho, K., 3, 185, *202*
Hoffman, J. M., 129, *141*, 229
Hoffman, M., 104, 109, 110, 111, *120*
Hoffman, P. D., 252, 256, 259
Hoffman, R., 115, *119*
Holmes, B., 64, *73*
Holt, R., 148, *160*
Hooven, C., 32, *34*, 130, *140*, 151, *160*, 245,
    247
Horesh, N., 87, 98
Horowitz, L. M., 60, 62, 71, 83, 84, 98
Horvath, P., 190, *201*
Howell, K. J., 276, *288*
Hoyle, R. H., 188, 190, *201*
Hsee, C. K., 38, *53*, 185, *202*
Hsu, A. Y. C., *34*, *305*
Hubbard, J. A., 148, *160*
Hudis, C. A., *227*
Huffman, L. C., 124, 138, *141*
Hughes, J. N., 295, 301, *305*
Hunsley, J., 242, *248*
Huppert, J. D., 257, *267*
Hurwitz, H., *228*
Hussong, A. M., 188, 190, *201*

Iavnieli, D., 63, *72*

Wolin, S. J., 271, 277, 279, 284, *287*, *290*
Wood, P. K., 193, *200*
Wootton, J., 113, 114, *120*, *121*
Wyer, M. M., 17, *33*
Wyman, S. E., 257, *267*

Yaeger, A., 187–188, *203*
Yazdani, N., 198, *203*
Yocum, D., *229*
Young, K., 38, *55*
Youngblood, R., 225, *226*

Zahn-Wexler, C., 175, *179*
Zautra, A. J., 209, 214, 221, 222, *228*, *229*
Zeitlin, S. B., 186, *203*
Zelko, F., 103, *119*
Zhou, Q., 132, 133, 135, *140*, *142*, *288*
Zins, J. E., *52*, *54*
Zuckerman, E., *227*
Zuckerman, M., 189, 190, 197, *201*, *203*

SUBJECT INDEX

and public policy, 303–304
and relationship mindfulness, 263
therapeutic relationship with, 238
unrepresentative samples of, 299
whole process of, 270
See also Parenting
"Familycentric" affect cues, 148
Family correlates, of emotional regulation, 151–152
Family Ritual Interview, 279
Family Ritual Questionnaire, 279, 282
Family routines and rituals, 270–271
    and affect regulation at dinner table, 274–278
    benefits of, 271, 301, 302
    and clinical decision making, 284–285, 286
    clinical implications of, 278–279
        assessment, 279–281
        family ritual typologies, 281–284
    conceptual challenges to, 273–274
    defining of, 271–273
    and emotion regulation, 274, 278, 287
    and chronic illness, 284
    policy implications of, 285, 287
Family therapy, complex of relationships in, 256
Fear
    in attachment cycle, 237
    in couples' conflict, 239
    extent of control of, 26, 27
    in pain adjustment, 222–223
Fearful-avoidant prototype, 60–61, 62
Felt security, 57, 59, 78, 94, 111
Flexible and variable routine/ritual type, 283
Friendship, and managing emotions, 46
Frustration-aggression-anger theories and model, 106, 108, 116

Gate control theory, 213
Genetic contributions to emotional regulation, 158
    research needed on, 295, 300
Gleeful taunting, 105
Goal setting, as coping skill, 216
Group interactions, repetitive, in family identity, 270
Guilt
    in couples therapy, 245
    extent of control of, 26, 27
    and shame, 243

Gulf War (1991), reactions to Scud attacks in, 85

"Happy victimization," 7, 102–104
    and adolescents' emotion attributions, 106–108
    and emotion dysregulation, 108–110
        and attachment-empathy-relation, 110–112
        and parental contribution, 114–116, 118
        and parenting-empathy-aggression relation, 112–114
    future research on and policy implications of, 116–118
    observational studies on, 104–105
    questions on, 102
    and reactive vs. proactive aggression, 105–106
Health, and emotion regulation in everyday life, 30–31
Hierarchical linear modeling (HLM), 88–90
HOME Scale, 156
Hostile attributional bias, 106, 113
Hostility
    and risk-taking behavior, 197
    See also Anger
Hyperactivating strategies, 79, 80
    of anxious or anxious-ambivalent, 60, 94
    and emotional or adjustment problems, 81–82
    in PTSD, 84
Hypothalamic-pituitary-adrenal (HPA) axis, and physiological responses to stress, 66, 67

Identity, as relationship need, 234, 235, 237
Illness, chronic
    and family functioning, 277–278, 284
    in asthma cases, 280
    See also Pain from disease
Imagery, as coping skill, 216
Imagination, of therapist, 242
Impulsivity, 190–191, 192, 194, 197
Inaccurate expression and labeling, 254
Individual differences
    in adult attachment style, 59–61
        and mental health, 81
    in emotion regulation
        research on, 297
        and strategies, 296

and emotional understanding, 148
and emotion encoding or decoding,
147–148
and children's social functioning, 127
and effortful vs. reactive control, 127
emotion-coaching philosophy in, 32,
245, 301
ERSBs in, 127–129
and children's effortful control, 129–
135
and children's social functioning,
136
fathers as well as mothers in, 146–147,
151–152, 159
See also Family
Parenting Dimensions Inventory (PDI), 115,
116
Partner-assisted pain management
for arthritis, 214–218
on biopsychosocial model, 210
for cancer, 219–221
clinical, social and policy implications
of, 225–226
coping skills in, 209–214, 216
emotion regulation in, 210–214
for arthritis, 217–218
in end-of-life context, 221
and family rituals, 277
future research directions for, 221–225
increased number of providers needed
for, 225, 304
and negative interactional cycles, 218–
219
Partners. *See* Couples
Pathogenic beliefs, EFCT as addressing, 241–
242
PATHS (Promoting Alternative THinking
Strategies), 49–50
PDI (Parenting Dimensions Inventory), 115,
116
Peer competence of children, 143
and display rules, 152–153
and emotional regulation, 154–155
and managing emotions, 46
and marital conflict, 154–155
and parental relationship qualities, 144–
145
assumptions in study of, 145–147
and emotional expressiveness, 148–
149
and emotional understanding,
148

and emotion encoding or decoding,
147–148
See also Social competence
Perceiving of emotions, 39, 40, 147
Perspectives
biopsychosocial, 297
proximal vs. distal, 299
Physiological reactivity and regulation, and
attachment (adult), 66–68
Physiological soothing, 240
Planning, around routines for illness, 280
Pleasant activity scheduling, as coping skill,
216
Positive emotions, extent of regulation of,
25, 26, 27
Posttraumatic growth, 95
Posttraumatic stress disorder (PTSD), 83
and attachment, 83–85
empirical findings on, 85–94
implications of and future directions
for, 94–97
and PTSD Inventory, 92
and relationship distress, 231
Preoccupied prototype, 60, 62, 171, 172,
176–177. *See also* Anxious-ambiva-
lent prototype
Prevention programs, 33, 301, 303
Pride, extent of regulation of, 25, 26, 27, 28
Primary adaptive emotions, 235
Primary emotional responses, 261–262
Primary emotions, difficulty in tolerating,
253–254
Primary maladaptive emotions, 236–237
Prisoners of war, and attachment-PTSD as-
sociation, 85–86
Proactive aggression happiness, 107–108
Problematic responses of others, 255
Problem solving, as coping skill, 216
Process model of emotion regulation, 15–17
Prosocial tendencies, and attachment, 81,
96–97
Psychological defenses, 14, 15
Psychopathology
and children's emotion regulation, 101
and couples or families, 255–256
and empirical foundations, 256–258
and relationship dysfunction, 249–250
PTSD. *See* Posttraumatic stress disorder
PTSD Inventory, 92

Reactive control, 6, 126
Realignment, as intervention, 284, 285, 286

and rituals, 276
    See also Family routines and rituals
Rumination, as strategy, 42

Sadness, extent of control of, 26, 27
Schools
    and emotional intelligence, 49–50
    See also Education and prevention programs
Seattle Social Development Project, 50
Secondary attachment strategies, 78
Secondary emotional responses, 261–262
Secondary emotions, 235–236, 253
    couples' conflict from, 239, 240
Secure prototype, 60, 62, 171, 171–172, 176
Security, as relationship need, 237
Security-based strategies of affect regulation, 79–80
Self-blame, and marital discord, 174
Self-control, lack of (impulsivity), 190–191, 192, 194, 197
Self-disclosure, 263, 265
    in couples therapy, 244–245
Self-disclosure skills, 254
Self-regulation, of children
    importance of, 124
    See also Emotion regulation in children
Self-reported measures of affect, 67
Self-reported patterns of affective reactivity and regulation, 65
Self-Report Emotional Intelligence Test, 44
Self-report methods, 43, 45, 297
Self-validation, 262–263
    in accurate labeling of emotions, 254
SEM (structural equation modeling), 131, 194
Semistructured interview, 19–22
    limitations of, 23
Sensitivity to relationship stimuli, 252, 259
Sensitization hypothesis, 169–170
Sex (male/female), and emotion regulation, 25–28
Shame, 234
    in couples' conflict, 237, 239, 243–244, 245
    extent of control of, 26, 27
SIP (social information processing) model of children's adjustment and competence, 106, 118
Situation awareness, selection, and management, 253
Situation modification, 16, 17

Situation modification skills, 211
Situation selection, 15–17, 211
Social cognitive skills, 145
Social competence
    and attention regulation, 155–157
    and children's emotion regulation, 101
    research on, 157–158
    See also Peer competence of children
Social context. *See* Contexts, social
Social Decision Making and Social Problem Solving program, 50
Social Development Project, University of California, Riverside (UCR), 144, 151, 152, 154, 156
Social information processing (SIP) model of children's adjustment and competence, 106, 118
Social interaction, and emotional intelligence, 45–47
Socialization, of emotion (ERSBs), 127–129
    and children's effortful control, 129–135
Social learning theory, and harmfulness of marital discord, 173
Social reasoning, and reactive aggression, 117
Social reinforcement, as coping skill, 216
Social skills in childhood, 143
Socioeconomic status (SES), and behavior problems, 110
"Softening," 244, 245
"Softer" emotions, 232
Soothing, physiological, 240
Stability, and emotive regulation in everyday life, 31–32
Status, as relationship need, 234, 237
Stimulus-emotion relation, lack of awareness of, 254
Stoic philosophers, 38
Story Stem Battery, MacArthur (MSSB), 115
Strange Situation, 60
Stress
    and disease/related pain, 221–222
    and parents' influence on children, 130
    physiological responses to, 66
Stroop color-naming task, 91–92, 93, 94
Structural equation modeling (SEM), 131, 194
Suppression, expressive. *See* Expressive suppression
Surgency, 191
Surprise, extent of control of, 26, 27